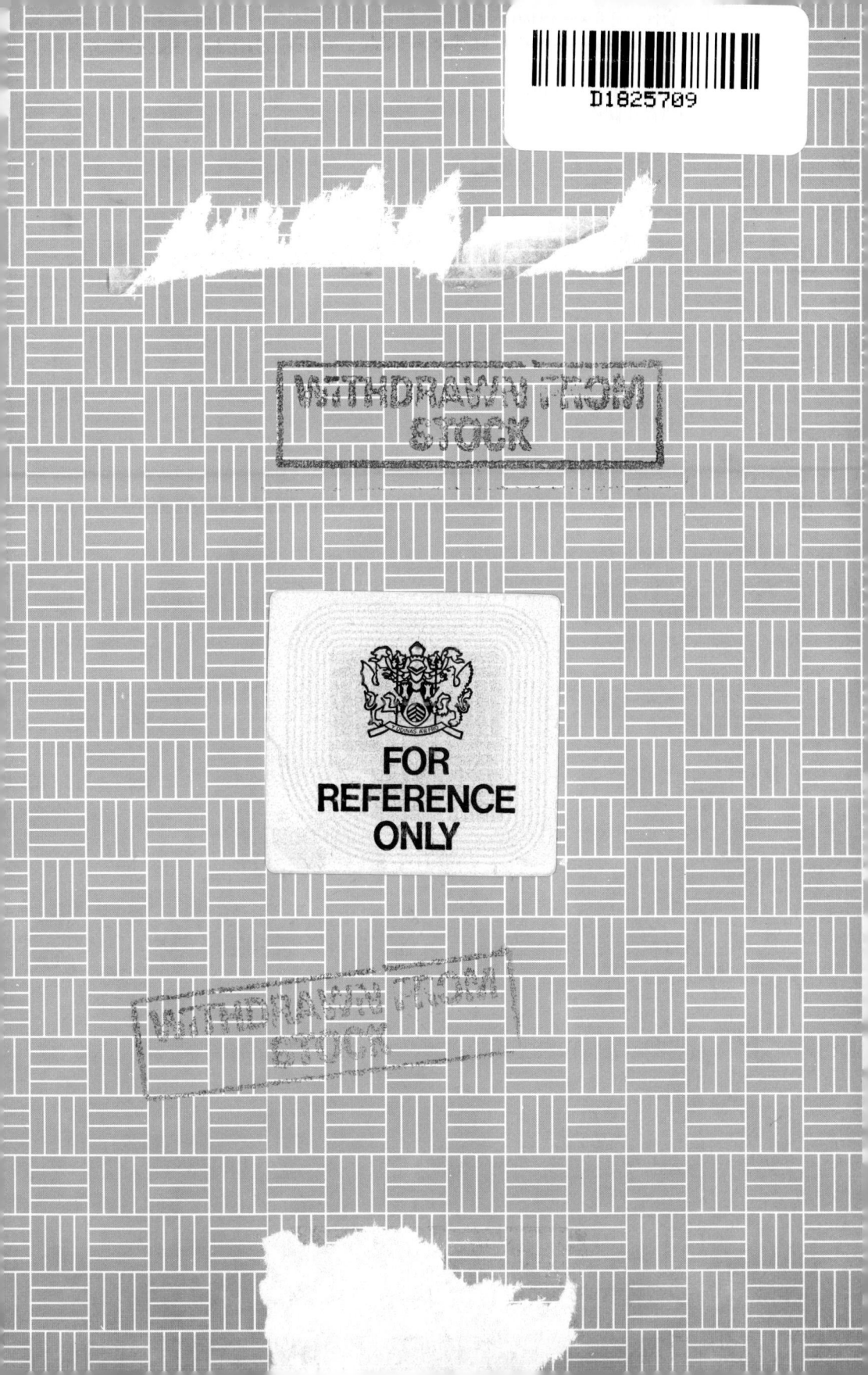

Directory of Language Training and Services for Business

Directory of Language Training and Services for Business

A Guide to Resources in Further and Higher Education

Colin Mellors
David Pollitt
Andrew Radtke
University of Bradford, UK

London

First published in 1993
by Routledge
11 New Fetter Lane, London EC4P 4EE

Printed in Great Britain by TJ Press (Padstow) Ltd., Cornwall

British Library Cataloguing in Publication Data
A catalogue record for this book is available from the British Library.

ISBN 0-415-09998-6

CONTENTS

ACKNOWLEDGEMENTS

The research for this *Directory* was conducted under the auspices of the PICKUP Europe initiative, funded by the former Department of Education and Science. The authors gratefully acknowledge the support of the Department of Education and Science and its successor, the Department for Education. The initiative led to the establishment of the PICKUP Europe Unit in 1990, comprising a consortium of the University of Bradford, South Bank Polytechnic and Leeds Polytechnic (now South Bank University and Leeds Metropolitan University). The unit, based at South Bank, aimed to help further and higher education to meet training needs resulting from developments in Europe, notably the creation of the single European market. Two related research projects have been published by the unit – *Trade Associations and Professional Bodies: Facing the Single Market* (1991) and *Training for Europe: Single Market Expertise in Further and Higher Education* (1992).

Any volume such as this requires the help of many people in its preparation, not least all those who responded, often at short notice, to requests for information about the foreign language training and facilities available at their institution. In addition, the editors would like to thank Alan Moys (Centre for Information on Language Teaching and Research), Professor John Green and Reg Hindley (University of Bradford), Paul Bangs (South Bank University), Jonathan Smith (Association of Language-Export Centres) and Shân Millie (Routledge). Thanks are also due to Brenda Pollitt, for imposing order on a mass of papers, and to Patricia Wilson, for cheerfully and efficiently processing the large quantity of information gathered. Any errors and omissions, of course, are solely the responsibility of the authors.

GUIDE FOR USERS

THE NEED FOR FOREIGN LANGUAGE TRAINING

In December 1990, the European Commission published the results of a sixteen-nation survey which affirmed English to be the dominant language of international business.[1] The results are hardly surprising: many technical and business terms are English. English is the global language of the computer and is even challenging French as the language of international diplomacy. It is quite feasible to get by in daily life throughout most of the world while speaking and understanding only English. Easier travel means that many more people now visit other countries, but this has not generally brought about any noticeable improvement in awareness of foreign languages and culture. The fact that so many other nationals can speak *our* language has done little to disturb our natural complacency and insularity.

At the same time, however, changing patterns of trade have made clear that such complacency is misplaced. Since the 1970s, there has been a steady decline in British trade with the English-speaking countries in North America and the Common-wealth, and a corresponding increase in trade with non-English-speaking continental Europe. Approximately 60 per cent of British trade is now with the other eleven countries of the European Community – a percentage that is likely to increase with the completion of the single market. The entry into force of the single European market on 1 January 1993 gave British business access to a 'domestic' market of more than 320 million people – 82 per cent of whom do not speak English as their mother tongue.

This has important implications for the skills that are demanded of the labour force, and means that there is a growing need for personnel at all levels of British industry and commerce who are able to operate effectively across different languages and cultures. Moreover, freedom of movement of people, which is an important principle of the single market, and consequent European Community directives on the mutual recognition of qualifications, are likely to stimulate cross-European recruitment and place at a premium workers who can offer competence in several languages as well as their professional qualifications. Nevertheless, while business people from other European countries are often fluent in English, the converse is less common. A recent study of UK directors, for example, revealed that 84 per cent speak no foreign language. Even among companies that are heavily reliant upon overseas

1

trade, there is a massive deficiency of senior staff who are able to operate in a foreign language.[2] The report concludes: 'Unless British boards take rapid steps to acquire international skills and experience, UK Ltd is in danger of becoming a foreign subsidiary. . . . This alarm bell must be heeded in the boardrooms of Britain.'

Such results mirror those of numerous other studies in pointing out how unprepared most British businesses are for the opportunities and threats brought about by the removal of trade barriers in Europe. It is all too common to believe that competence in foreign languages matters only if (i) the company is an active exporter and (ii) the personnel concerned are employed in marketing positions. Both are false assumptions. On the positive side, businesses in other Community member states may increasingly seek to buy British products and services in areas where there has previously been a relatively small export opportunity. On the negative side, however, British firms will find themselves competing increasingly with European firms in what was hitherto the domestic market place. Although it may be generally true that importance of foreign language competence increases in relation to the status of personnel, it is not only senior staff who need to be able to work in a foreign language. The most obvious examples are telephonists and receptionists. Even so, a survey of major London companies revealed that few switchboard operators possessed even the most basic skills necessary to cope with calls made in a foreign language.[3] In some cases, they could not recognise the language in which the call was being made, while in others they were unable to deal with a call confidently, often using colloquialisms or switchboard 'dialect' which can leave even the most fluent of non-native English speakers at a loss.

These findings, which are replicated in numerous other surveys, underline the high price in lost business that can be the direct result when companies fail to train staff adequately in foreign languages. To put it simply, companies involved in exporting must be able to sell in the language of their customers. At the very least, it is obviously essential that trade literature and correspondence is in a language that the customer can understand. Not all foreign business people can speak English, and even those who do may not always want to – hence the adage, 'I sell in the language of the customer but buy in my own language'. As one senior UK chief executive, himself a language graduate, has observed, 'If you are serious about business abroad, you must be serious about foreign language skills. . . . I would go so far as to say that it is a case of "no language, no business".'[4]

Not all firms, of course, have neglected the place of foreign language skills in their recruitment and staff development policies. This is especially true of the major multinationals. Rowntree, now part of Nestlé, issued its annual report in English, Dutch, German, French, Italian and Xhosa. The message is getting across to others. A recent survey of almost 2,000 British firms by the Institute of Manpower Studies suggested that many British companies do recognise that lack of language skills is harming business.[5] All the companies surveyed which had some level of export/ import activity identified unmet needs in respect of the language of their most important business contacts. Nearly a quarter observed that their failure to be able to work in a particular language created an insurmountable barrier to trading with that country.

The extent to which foreign language competence is perceived to be important, and the kinds of skill sought, vary according to position in the organisation. In the Institute of Manpower survey, managers ranked highest (cited by 58 per cent of companies with foreign trade links), followed by sales and marketing personnel (49 per cent), professional and technical staff (46 per cent), secretaries, receptionists and telephonists (40 per cent). These broad figures, however, conceal different perceptions about the level and quality of language competence needed. Sales staff, for example, were seen to need high levels of fluency in all forms of communication (including, in some instances, knowledge of technical vocabulary) whilst secretaries and telephonists were regarded as first points of contact where basic speaking and listening skills could often suffice. However, such distinctions are becoming less pronounced as the greater use of electronic communications, especially telephones and fax machines, bring staff at all levels closer to their foreign counterparts.

What, then, are the key language skills that business people need? In general, they are those skills that enable staff to undertake their daily work or to 'survive' whilst travelling abroad or coping with social occasions, i.e. the ability to 'do business' via the telephone, letters and faxes, and in face-to-face meetings. The more technical tasks – translation, drafting reports, taking dictation and conducting detailed business negotiations – demand higher-level skills and are properly the preserve of the professional linguist. One survey of 1,500 companies produced the following order of language skills used by employees: reading letters/faxes (58 per cent), travelling abroad (53 per cent), using the telephone (45 per cent), writing short letters/memos (39 per cent), social conversation (37 per cent), reading technical/sales literature (35 per cent), writing trade documents (26 per cent), listening to talks (10 per cent), giving speeches (9 per cent).[6]

Which are the languages most in demand? In 1929, the French Academy announced confidently that there were precisely 2,796 languages in the world. Others subsequently put the figure much higher, at around 5,000. It is impossible to be exact because there is no agreed definition of a distinct language. Pronunciation, the use of local phrases or colloquialisms, and grammatical construction all make the distinction between a 'language' and a 'dialect' difficult to draw. One suggestion is simply that 'a dialect is a language that has failed'.

Whatever the total number, most business needs focus on the languages spoken in the main trading nations of the world. The survey of 1,500 companies mentioned above produced the following listing: French (required by 64 per cent of the firms surveyed), German (58 per cent), Spanish (23 per cent), Italian (19 per cent), Arabic (6.5 per cent), Japanese and Dutch (both 4.5 per cent), Russian (4 per cent) and Chinese (2.5 per cent). These are, of course, aggregate figures and ignore variations by region (there are often close links between specific regions, for example the North East of England with Scandanavia) and industrial sector, and trends in the demand for certain languages (notably the growing importance of Spanish, Japanese and Arabic). More recently, following the major political and economic changes in central and eastern Europe, there has been considerable increase in demand for these hitherto 'minority' languages by businesses anxious to exploit the commercial opportunities afforded by the opening of new markets.

3

ABOUT THE DIRECTORY

The *Directory* contains details on language training and related services in 435 institutions covering seventy languages, organised in a way that is intended to help businesses and other readers to find quickly a source that will help them to meet their language needs.

Information was gathered through a questionnaire sent to all further and higher education institutions in England, Scotland, Wales and Northern Ireland, and twenty-seven Language-Export (LX) Centres. The latter were originally jointly sponsored by the Department of Education and Science and the Training Agency, and comprised a consortium of colleges and partners from local industry. Many LX Centres are still based in further and higher education, although some have become private companies. Like many other further and higher education institutions, LX Centres provide language consultancy, training needs analyses, language audits, language training for specific purposes, cultural briefings, interpreting, translation, materials production and advice and support for exporters. Apart from these Centres, private sector providers of language training are not included in this *Directory*.

The information was collected during the summer and autumn of 1992 and, therefore, represents language training for business available in institutions at the start of the 1992–3 academic year.

USING THE GUIDE

The *Directory* is divided into three sections:

- language index
- main directory
- index of institutions by county

Language index

The language index allows rapid search for institutions offering training or other services in the required language. (If readers are unsure which language is spoken in any particular country, they should consult the table of world languages which is at the end of this introduction.) The more common languages appear alphabetically, in individual columns; the more unusual languages are listed by name in the final column. By searching vertically through the index, the reader will quickly be able to identify which of the 435 providers included in the *Directory* offer the required language.

Seventy world languages feature in the guide but, for the reasons discussed above, dialects are generally omitted. Thus, for example, Mandarin and Cantonese are included under the single entry 'Chinese', since they are essentially different dialects of the same language. Catalan, however, is listed as a language in its own right, since it differs significantly from Castilian Spanish. Gaelic is included to refer to Scottish Gaelic, which is a different language from Irish. Training in English as a foreign language is not included. In each case, the first spelling of a language in the *Oxford English Dictionary* is used.

Main directory

Having identified the institutions that offer the required language, the reader should turn to the main directory to discover the precise range of training and other services available. Entries are listed alphabetically, and each is organised according to a standard format:

- contact details
- language training available
- other language services (i.e. translation and interpreting)
- facilities that may be used/hired
- other information

Most of the information in the entries will be readily understood, but it is appropriate to give a few words of explanation about how the material is organised, and to define how terms have been used in the three main sections: *language training, language services* and *language facilities*.

Language training

For each entry, all of the languages for which training is offered are listed, including the type(s) of training available, the method(s) of delivery used, and any specialisms.

Type of training covers the location of the training (at clients' premises or at the institution offering the training), whether the training is in groups or on a one-to-one basis, and whether training can be tailored to the specific needs of clients. In selecting a provider, users of the guide should give careful thought to the type of training that is most appropriate to their needs. Group training is obviously more economic than one-to-one teaching, but its success depends upon members of the group beginning at roughly the same level of foreign language ability. They should also have similar aptitudes to advance in their studies if some are not to be demotivated. Also, it is preferable if their needs coincide. It is not hard to imagine, for example, that a person wanting language skills to use as a telephonist will quickly lose interest in a class made up predominantly of lawyers, if the teaching method focuses primarily on the needs of the latter group.

Method of delivery looks at how training is provided – intensive, non-intensive, open or flexible. In practice, rigorous definitions of 'intensive' and 'non-intensive' training do not exist and each respondent was given the opportunity to describe these terms within the context of practices at their own institution. From these responses, it is clear that perceptions about what constitutes 'intensive' training vary considerably. For example, a course of two hours per week over a ten-week period was described as 'intensive' by one institution, but would be regarded as 'non-intensive' by most others. On average, intensive courses tend to involve more than five hours of weekly class contact over a number of weeks, while non-intensive courses involve between one and three hours a week of class contact over a period of months or years. Intensive courses are perhaps most useful for helping beginners to make rapid progress, or enabling someone with knowledge of a language to acquire extra skills quickly. Non-intensive courses, by contrast, may be more useful for maintaining and building language skills.

'Open learning' is best seen as a supplement to tutored sessions since motivation, when working entirely alone, can be difficult to maintain. Books, audio tapes and other materials can be a useful supplement when developing listening and reading skills and allow the learner to determine the pace of learning. However, by itself, open learning cannot offer the same level of support as extensive interaction with fluent speakers.

Institutions were also given the opportunity to indicate language training *specialisms*, i.e. training using specialist vocabularies, taught in the context of the sector concerned. Such specialisms include, among many others, business, hotel and catering, financial, and legal. The benefits to the learner, who has language needs that relate to a specific business sector, of studying in an institution that offers such specialisms may, of course, extend beyond access to specialist language training. Often the language specialism has developed out of, and complements, more general expertise within the institution in that particular sector. In the *Directory*, where specialisms relate to an individual language, they are included in brackets after the language. Where the specialisms refer to all the languages offered at a given institution, they are listed near the end of the section. Reference to a specialism does not, of course, imply that training is available only in the areas specified.

Language services

This section gives details of translating and interpreting services offered by the institution. Translating can be 'into' or 'out of' English (or both), while interpreting can be simultaneous or consecutive. Once again, specialisms are indicated where appropriate, but the listing of specialisms does not indicate that translating or interpreting services are available only in the areas specified.

Language facilities

The third section indicates the facilities and materials available at the institution. These include: language laboratories by size (fewer than 10 places, 10–25 places and more than 25 places) and also whether these are fixed or portable; conference interpreting facilities by size (fewer than 10 places, 10–25 places, 26–100 places and more than 100 places); self-teaching language equipment and materials (e.g. computer-assisted language learning facilities, audio-visual aids such as satellite television or stocks of audio and videocassettes).

Other information

The final section describes briefly any additional foreign language training, services or facilities on offer. This includes whether the institution has experience of undertaking language training needs analyses. Any company that has decided to introduce foreign language training must first decide the exact nature of the training that is required. The key issues are: 'Who needs training?' and 'What skills do they require?' Needs analyses of language training ensure that any language training is properly focused and thus saves time, effort and money.

Index of institutions by county

In order to help clients to find providers in their region, an index of all of the institutions appearing in the *Directory*, listed by county, is given at the end of the guide. By using this index, in combination with the *language index*, the reader will quickly be able to identify appropriate language training providers who are close at hand.

ENSURING QUALITY

The number of business language training providers has increased rapidly in recent years. In the public sector, this has frequently taken the form of established institutions setting up new language training programmes and facilities specifically aimed at the business market rather than full-time students. In delivering their language training, both public and private sectors often rely heavily on native speakers of the foreign language. These can usually offer a greater variety of expression and more authentic accent than English speakers, but they may not be part of a co-ordinated staff development programme and may miss out on formal induction procedures.[7] Businesses seeking language training for employees with no foreign language skills may prefer to opt for native English-speaking tutors, since English speakers will have more insight into the problems of English learners. The main aim should always be to find teachers who are skilled in teaching a foreign language to adults.

Businesses should also be cautious of descriptions of courses, methods, learning materials or equipment which suggest that *rapid* results can be achieved with little effort. Learning a foreign language properly will take months and years rather than hours and weeks. Descriptions such as 'survival level' and 'manager level' can be misleading if they are taken to imply a guaranteed outcome after a limited number of hours. Account has to be taken of, for example, an individual's entry level, aptitude, learning style and motivation. The London Chamber of Commerce has calculated that some 600 hours of trainer contact time are needed to reach a useful 'operational' level.

When selecting language training, therefore, suitability and quality should be important considerations. The growth of language provision specifically for non-linguists has prompted a demand for common standards for measuring achievement.

Both employers and students stand to benefit from widely recognised standards that can be clearly understood.

The Languages Lead Body – a working party established in 1990 with representatives from key employers, professional associations and experts in the language field – intends to publish a set of national standards for languages, designed specifically for the work place. These standards will cover professional users, such as interpreters and translators, as well as those such as managers, sales staff, engineers, and telephonists, who may need some degree of language ability in performing their job. The national standards will help employers to identify what level of skills is required to do jobs effectively, and to allow for the recognition of earlier work experience and current language ability. They will also mean that providers of language training will be able to tailor language courses to suit employer needs and, at completion of the course, to give an assessment that can lead to a National or Scottish Vocational Qualification. Employers will then be able to set out in job specifications the NVQ or SVQ level required, and be confident that the person who has such a qualification will have the necessary language ability.[8] Similarly, the Royal Society of Arts (RSA) examinations board is developing a Certificate in Business Language Competence, including five levels – basic, survival, threshold, operational and advanced. The Association of Language-Export Centres is closely involved in these initiatives, and is working towards a complete quality system, along the lines of BS5750, the recognised British standard for quality assurance.

How, then, can the customer of language training make some preliminary assessment of the quality of the large number of language providers? One simple check-list has been produced by the chairperson of the Association of Language-Export Centres.[9]

(a) *Method:* Do the providers use a modern, communicative approach which emphasises practical use of the language throughout the training?

(b) *Materials:* What is the nature of the course materials used? Are they published ones, their own or, preferably, a combination of the most suitable materials for the clients' needs? It should readily be apparent, even to non-specialists, whether they are well-presented, user-friendly and relevant to the business sector concerned.

(c) *Media:* What use is made of additional media such as audio, video and satellite television to support training programmes? This is important to reinforce training and to add variety and interest.

(d) *Professionalism:* What teaching experience and qualifications are possessed by language trainers? Perhaps the most important criteria are that they are effective teachers, fluent in the language, preferably with a formal qualification (degree or equivalent) in modern languages, an additional teaching qualification, and experience of training business people. No language trainer can be effective without appropriate training and experience, whether native speaker or not.

(e) *Training needs analyses:* As noted earlier, the most effective training will be that which is geared to specific needs. Before needs can be met, of course, they have to be identified, and professional providers will examine training needs in detail and design a programme. Many will make a written proposal giving details of timing, aims, materials, evaluation procedures and costs.

(f) *Language audit:* In the case of large organisations with some residual foreign language capability, clients may wish providers to undertake an audit and evaluation of these residual skills.

(g) *Quality assurance:* Quality is rapidly becoming an important aspect of educational provision at all levels. Essentially, it means ensuring that the provision is 'fit for its intended purpose'. Training needs analyses and language audits are wasted if they are not complemented by appropriate mechanisms designed to ensure quality. This is especially important in the field of language training where so much teaching is often sub-contracted to hourly paid staff. Clients, therefore, should consider enquiring about how institutions evaluate a trainer's performance, assess the progress of trainees and obtain customer feedback.

(h) *Track record:* Whilst being experienced in the field and well known are not by themselves guarantees of quality, clients should be conscious of the need to check the track record of providers. In the private sector, in particular, there is a rapid turnover of providers promising speedy results. It is reasonable to ask if providers are part of a reputable training organisation or members of a professional body. Local chambers of commerce, the regional Department of Trade and Industry office, or Euro Info Centres may be sources of advice in identifying the best trainers.

(i) *Training outcomes:* What standards are used to evaluate the effectiveness of language training, for instance recognised qualifications such as RSA, Institute of Linguists, or London Chamber of Commerce?

(j) *Competence:* Often this may be assessed by the overall impression given by an organisation in terms of how quickly it responds to enquiries, whether it has a professional and business-like approach, and its sensitivity to clients' needs.

This check-list is not exhaustive and it would be impractical for individual clients to seek detailed answers to every question raised above before choosing a training provider. They should, however, be conscious of all of the issues when making a choice and perhaps look for more detailed information where this is not readily available in promotional literature or when making personal contact. Finally, of course, where companies are buying training for a group of staff, the monitoring of foreign language training should be regularly and jointly conducted by the company training manager and training organisation, to judge how well objectives are being achieved and solve any problems that may have arisen.

COSTS

The issue of training quality obviously needs to be considered alongside training costs. Entries do not contain details about charges for training, translating and interpreting services, partly because the information would quickly become out-of-date, but mainly because charges are often related to size of groups, the extent to which training is tailored to client needs, and the level of technical speciality involved.

As a guide, however, the following range of scales was indicated by respondents:

Training: £25 to £60 an hour.

Translations: £30 to £125 per thousand words (average of approximately £65). Charges generally vary according to: the language involved, whether the text involves technical or specialised vocabulary, and whether translations are required into or out of English. Generally, translations involving French, Spanish, Italian and German are cheaper than those for other languages. One institution has four price bands. French, Spanish and Italian are cheapest, followed by German, Dutch, Danish, Norwegian, Swedish and Portuguese. A third group of languages consists of Bulgarian, Russian, Romanian, Polish and Czech, while the most expensive translations cover Arabic, Greek, Hungarian, Turkish, Chinese and Japanese.

Interpreting: £15 to £80 per hour. Again, the language involved and amount of technical or specialised vocabulary also affect prices, and the same guidelines as for translation apply.

NOTES

1 E. van Hest and M. Oud-de Glas, *A Survey of Techniques Used in the Diagnosis and Analysis of Foreign Language Needs in Trade and Industry*, LINGUA, Brussels, 1990, p. 19.
2 Michael Brandon, *The 1992 Board of Directors Study, United Kingdom*, Korn/Ferry International, London, 1992.
3 *LINGUA News*, No. 5, Summer 1992.
4 Peter Blackburn, 'Languages in a Multinational Business', in S. Hagen (ed.), *Languages in British Business*, Newcastle upon Tyne Polytechnic Products, Newcastle upon Tyne, 1988, p. 151.
5 Hilary Metcalf, *Foreign Language Needs of Business*, Institute of Manpower Studies Report No. 215, Brighton, 1991.
6 Hagen *op. cit.*, Table 6.
7 Gwynneth Rigby and Robert G. Burgess, *Language Teaching in Higher Education: A Discussion Document*, Centre for Educational Development, Appraisal and Research, University of Warwick, Coventry, 1992.
8 *Languages Lead Body News*, Issue No. 2, August 1992.
9 J. Smith, *The Financial Times*, 28 September 1991.

WORLD LANGUAGES

The following list indicates the languages and dialects spoken in individual countries and territories. In general, the languages are listed in order of popularity. In the case of the former Soviet Union, only the official language is shown for each component state.

Afghanistan:	Pushtu, Afghan Persian (Dari), Turkic languages (primarily Uzbek and Turkmen), 30 minor languages (primarily Balochi and Pashai)
Albania:	Albanian, Greek
Algeria:	Arabic, French, Berber dialects
American Samoa:	Samoan, English (most people are bilingual)
Andorra:	Catalan, French, Spanish
Angola:	Portuguese, various Bantu dialects
Anguilla:	English
Antigua and Barbuda:	English
Armenia:	Armenian
Argentina:	Spanish, English, Italian, German, French
Aruba:	Dutch, Papiamento (a Spanish, Portuguese, Dutch, English dialect), English, Spanish
Australia:	English, native languages
Austria:	German
Azerbaijan:	Azerbaijani
Bahamas:	English, Creole
Bahrain:	Arabic, English, Farsi, Urdu
Bangladesh:	Bangla; English is also widely used
Barbados:	English
Belgium:	Flemish (Dutch), French, German
Belize:	English, Spanish, Maya, Garifuna (Carib)
Benin:	French; Fon and Yoruba are the most common vernaculars in south; at least six major tribal languages in north
Bermuda:	English
Bhutan:	Bhotes speak various Tibetan dialects (most widely spoken is Dzongkha); Nepalese speak various Nepalese dialects

11

Bolivia:	Spanish, Quechua, Aymara
Botswana:	English, Setswana
Brazil:	Portuguese, Spanish, English, French
British Virgin Islands:	English
Brunei:	Malay, English, Chinese
Bulgaria:	Bulgarian
Burkina:	French, Sudanic tribal languages
Burma:	Burmese
Burundi:	Kirundi, French, Swahili
Byelorussia:	Byelorussian
Cambodia:	Khmer, French
Cameroon:	English, French, 24 major African language groups
Canada:	English, French
Cape Verde:	Portuguese, Crioulo (a blend of Portuguese and West African words)
Cayman Islands:	English
Central African Republic:	French, Sangho, Arabic, Hunsa, Swahili
Chad:	French, Arabic, Sara and Sango (south), more than 100 other different languages and dialects
Chechen:	Russian
Chile:	Spanish
China:	Standard Chinese (Putonghua) or Mandarin (Beijing dialect); also Yue (Cantonese), Wu (Shanghainese), Minbei (Fuzhou), Minnan (Hokkien-Taiwanese), Xiang, Gan, Hakka dialects
Christmas Island:	English
Cocos (Keeling) Islands:	English
Colombia:	Spanish
Comoros:	Shaafi Islam (a Swahili dialect), Malagasy, French
Congo:	French, various African languages (notably Lingala and Kikongo)
Cook Islands:	English
Costa Rica:	Spanish, English
Cuba:	Spanish
Cyprus:	Greek, Turkish, English
Czechoslovakia:	Czech, Slovak, Hungarian
Denmark:	Danish, Faroese, Greenlandic (an Eskimo dialect)
Djibouti:	French, Arabic, Somali, Afar
Dominica:	English, French patois
Dominican Republic:	Spanish
Ecuador:	Spanish, Indian languages (notably Quechua)
Egypt:	Arabic, English, French
El Salvador:	Spanish, Nahua
Equatorial Guinea:	Spanish, pidgin English, Fang, Bubi, Ibo
Estonia:	Estonian
Ethiopia:	Amharic, Tigrinya, Orominga, Guaraginga, Somali, Arabic, English
Falkland Islands:	English
Faroe Islands:	Faroese, Danish
Fiji:	English, Fijian, Hindustani

Finland:	Finnish, Swedish
France:	French, some regional dialects (Provençal, Breton, Alsatian, Corsican, Catalan, Basque, Flemish)
French Guiana:	French
French Polynesia:	French, Tahitian
Gabon:	French, Fang, Myene, Bateke, Bapounou/Eschira, Bandjabi
Gambia, the:	English, Mandinka, Wolof, Fula, other indigenous vernaculars
Gaza Strip:	Arabic, Hebrew (Israeli settlers), English is widely understood
Georgia:	Georgian
Germany:	German
Ghana:	English, various African languages (Akan, Moshi-Dagomba, Ewe, Ga)
Gibraltar:	English, Spanish; also Italian, Portuguese, and Russian
Greece:	Greek, English, French
Greenland:	Eskimo dialects (Greenlandic), Danish
Grenada:	English, some French patois
Guadeloupe:	French, Creole patois
Guam:	English, Chamorro (most are bilingual), Japanese
Guatemala:	Spanish, 18 Indian dialects (including Quiche, Cakchiquel, Kekchi)
Guernsey:	English, French
Guinea-Bissau:	Portuguese, Criolo, various African languages
Guinea:	French, various tribal languages
Guyana:	English, Amerindian dialects
Haiti:	French; Creole is universally understood
Honduras:	Spanish, Indian dialects
Hong Kong:	Chinese (Cantonese), English
Hungary:	Hungarian
Iceland:	Icelandic
India:	Hindi, English,14 other official languages – Bengali, Telugu, Marathi, Tamil, Urdu, Gujarati, Malayalam, Kannada, Oriya, Punjabi, Assamese, Kashmiri, Sindhi, and Sanskrit; 24 other major languages (Hindi is the national language; English is major business language)
Indonesia:	Bahasa Indonesia (modified form of Malay), English, Dutch, Javanese
Iran:	Farsi, Turkic and Turkic dialects, Kurdish, Luri, Baloch, Arabic, Turkish
Iraq:	Arabic, Kurdish (official in Kurdish regions), Assyrian, Armenian
Ireland:	English, Irish (Gaelic)
Israel:	Hebrew, Arabic (official for Arab minority), English
Italy:	Italian, also German (parts of Trentino-Alto Adige region), French (Valle d'Aosta region), Slovene (Trieste-Gorizia area)
Ivory Coast:	French (official), over 60 native dialects; Dioula most widely spoken
Jamaica:	English, Creole
Japan:	Japanese

Jersey:	English, French
Jordan:	Arabic; English is also widely used as a business language
Kazakhstan:	Kazakh
Kenya:	English, Swahili
Kirghizia:	Kirghiz
Kiribati:	English (official), Kiribatese
Korea, North:	Korean
Korea, South:	Korean
Kuwait:	Arabic; English is also widely used
Laos:	Lao, French, English
Latvia:	Latvian
Lebanon:	Arabic, French, Armenian, English
Lesotho:	Sesotho (southern Sotho), English, also Zulu and Xhosa
Liberia:	English, more than 20 local languages
Libya:	Arabic; Italian and English are also widely understood
Liechtenstein:	German
Lithuania:	Lithuanian
Luxembourg:	Luxembourgish, German, French; English is widely understood
Macao:	Portuguese; Cantonese is main business language
Madagascar:	French, Malagasy
Malawi:	English, Chichewa
Malaysia:	Peninsular Malaysia – Malay, English, Chinese dialects, Tamil; Sabah – English, Malay, various tribal dialects, Mandarin and Hakka dialects predominate among Chinese; Sarawak – English, Malay, Mandarin, numerous tribal languages
Maldives:	Divehi; English is widely used in business
Mali:	French, Bambara, various African languages
Malta:	Maltese, English
Man, Isle of:	English, Manx Gaelic
Marshall Islands:	English, Marshallese dialects, Japanese
Martinique:	French, Creole patois
Mauritania:	Hasaniya Arabic (national), French, Toucouleur, Fula, Sarakole, Wolof
Mauritius:	English, Creole, French, Hindi, Urdu, Hakka, Bojpoori
Mayotte:	Mahorian (a Swahili dialect), French
Mexico:	Spanish
Micronesia, Federated States of:	English, Trukese, Pohnpeian, Yapese, Kosrean
Moldavia:	Romanian
Monaco:	French, English, Italian, Monegasque
Mongolia:	Khalkha Mongol, Turkic, Russian, Chinese
Montserrat:	English
Morocco:	Arabic, several Berber dialects; French is language of business
Mozambique:	Portuguese
Namibia:	English; Afrikaans is common language of most of population
Nauru:	Nauruan; English is widely used for business

Nepal:	Nepali, 20 other languages
Netherlands Antilles:	Dutch, Papiamento; English is widely spoken; Spanish
Netherlands:	Dutch
New Caledonia:	French, 28 Melanesian-Polynesian dialects
New Zealand:	English, Maori
Nicaragua:	Spanish, English
Niger:	French, Hausa, Djerma
Nigeria:	English, Hausa, Yoruba, Ibo, Fulani
Niue:	Polynesian tongue closely related to Tongan and Samoan, English
Norfolk Island:	English
Northern Mariana Islands:	English, Chamorro, Carolinian
Norway:	Norwegian, small Lapp- and Finnish-speaking minorities
Oman:	Arabic, English, Balochi, Urdu, Indian dialects
Pacific Islands:	Palauan; English is widely used; Trukese (south western islands)
Pakistan:	Urdu, English, Punjabi, Sindhi, Pushtu, Urdu, Balochi
Panama:	Spanish, English,
Papua New Guinea:	715 indigenous languages; pidgin English widespread and English by a small proportion; Motu (Papua region)
Paraguay:	Spanish, Guarani
Peru:	Spanish, Quechua, Aymara
Philippines:	Philipino, English
Pitcairn Islands:	English
Poland:	Polish
Portugal:	Portuguese
Puerto Rico:	Spanish; English is widely understood
Qatar:	Arabic; English is widely understood
Reunion:	French; Creole is widely used
Romania:	Romanian, Hungarian, German
Russia:	Russian
Rwanda:	Kinyarwanda, French; Kiswahili is used in business
Saint Helena:	English
Saint Kitts and Nevis:	English
Saint Lucia:	English, French patois
Saint Pierre and Miquelon:	French
Saint Vincent and the Grenadines:	English, some French patois
San Marino:	Italian
São Tomé and Príncipe:	Portuguese
Saudi Arabia:	Arabic
Senegal:	French, Wolof, Pulaar, Diola, Mandingo
Seychelles:	English, French, Creole
Sierra Leone:	English, Mende, Temne
Singapore:	Chinese, Malay, Tamil, and English
Solomon Islands:	120 indigenous languages; Melanesian pidgin is lingua franca; English (limited usage)
Somalia:	Somali, Arabic, Italian, English

South Africa:	Afrikaans, English, many vernacular languages, including Zulu, Xhosa, North and South Sotho, Tswana
Spain:	Spanish, Catalan, Galician, Basque
Sri Lanka:	Sinhalese, Tamil; English is commonly used in business
Sudan:	Arabic, Nubian, Ta Bedawie, diverse dialects of Nilotic, Nilo-Hamitic and Sudanic languages, English
Surinam:	Dutch; English is widely spoken; Sranan Tongo, Hindi Surinam Hindustani (a variant of Bhoqpuri), Javanese
Svalbard:	Russian, Norwegian
Swaziland:	English is mainly used in business; siSwati
Sweden:	Swedish; small Lapp- and Finnish-speaking minorities
Switzerland:	German, French, Italian, Romansch
Syria:	Arabic, Kurdish, Armenian, Aramaic, Circassian; French is widely understood
Taiwan:	Mandarin Chinese; Taiwanese and Hakka dialects are also used
Tajikistan:	Tajik
Tanzania:	Swahili, English (main business language)
Tatar:	Russian
Thailand:	Thai; English is the secondary language of the elite; ethnic and regional dialects
Togo:	French (main business language), Ewe, Mina, Dagomba, Kabye
Tokelau:	Tokelauan, English
Tonga:	Tongan, English
Trinidad and Tobago:	English, Hindi, French, Spanish
Tunisia:	Arabic, French
Turkey:	Turkish, Kurdish, Arabic
Turkmenistan:	Turkmen
Turks and Caicos Islands:	English
Tuvalu:	Tuvaluan, English
Uganda:	English, Luganda and Swahili, other Bantu, Nilotic languages
Ukraine:	Ukrainian
United Arab Emirates:	Arabic; Farsi and English are widely used; Hindi, Urdu
United Kingdom:	English, Welsh, Scottish Gaelic
United States:	English; Spanish-speaking minority
Uruguay:	Spanish
Uzbekistan:	Uzbek
Vanuatu:	English, French, pidgin (known as Bislama or Bichelama)
Vatican City:	Italian, Latin
Venezuela:	Spanish, Indian dialects (remote interior)
Vietnam:	Vietnamese, French, Chinese, English, Khmer, tribal languages (Mon-Khmer and Malayo-Polynesian)
Virgin Islands:	English, Spanish, Creole
Wallis and Futuna:	French, Wallisian
West Bank:	Arabic, Hebrew (Israeli settlers); English is widely understood
Western Sahara:	Hassaniya Arabic, Moroccan Arabic
Western Samoa:	Samoan (Polynesian), English

16

Yemen:	Arabic
Yugoslavia:	Serbo-Croat, Slovene, Macedonian, Albanian, Hungarian
Zaïre:	French, Lingala, Swahili, Kingwana, Kikongo, Tshiluba
Zambia:	English, about 70 indigenous languages
Zimbabwe:	English, Shona, Sindebele

LANGUAGE INDEX

The Language index is intended to allow rapid search for institutions offering training or other services in the required language. It is possible to search laterally to assess the language coverage of an institution, or to search vertically to assess the availability of the given language across the spread of the 435 providers covered in the *Directory*. The more common languages appear alphabetically, in individual columns; the more unusual languages are listed individually by name in the final column.

Institution	Arabic	Bengali	Bulgarian	Catalan	Chinese	Czech	Danish	Dutch	Farsi	Finnish	French	German	Greek	Gujarati	Hebrew	Hindi	Hungarian	Italian
University of Aberdeen	•						•	•			•	•	•					•
Aberdeen College of FE											•	•						•
Abingdon College											•	•						
Accrington and Rossendale College											•	•						•
Afan College											•	•						•
Airedale and Wharfedale College											•	•	•	•				•
Amersham and Wycombe College											•	•						•
Anglia Polytechnic University											•	•						•
Angus College of FE	•										•	•						
Anniesland College											•	•						•
Armagh College of FE											•	•						•
Arnold and Carlton College of FE																		
Aston University								•			•	•				•	•	•
Ayr College											•							
Ballymena College											•	•						
Banff and Buchan College of FE											•	•						
University College Wales, Bangor											•	•						
Barking College of Technology											•	•	•					•
Barnet College					•						•	•	•			•		•
Barnfield College	•							•			•	•						•
Barnsley College											•	•						•
Barry College								•			•	•	•					•
Basildon College							•	•	•	•	•	•					•	•
Basingstoke College of Technology	•				•						•	•	•					•
City of Bath College											•	•						•
Bath College of Higher Education					•													
Bedford College of HE											•	•						•
Belfast Institute of FHE	•							•			•	•						•
Bell College of Technology											•	•						•
Beverley College								•			•	•						•
Bicton College	•				•						•	•						•
Bilston Community College	•				•	•		•			•	•	•	•		•		•
Birkbeck College					•						•	•						•
University of Birmingham	•	•				•		•			•	•	•					•
Bishop Burton College											•	•						•
Blackburn College	•										•	•	•	•				•
Blackpool and the Fylde College								•			•	•	•					•
Bolton Institute of HE											•	•						•
Bolton Metropolitan College											•	•						
Borders College								•			•	•						•
Boston College							•	•		•	•	•	•					•

20

Japanese	Korean	Malay	Norwegian	Polish	Portuguese	Punjabi	Romanian	Russian	Serbo-Croat	Spanish	Swedish	Turkish	Urdu	Welsh	Other languages
•			•					•		•	•				
										•					
					•						•				
										•					
•					•			•		•	•			•	
•					•			•		•			•		
										•					
•								•		•					
			•					•							
										•					
										•					
•					•			•		•					
										•					
										•					
								•							
					•			•		•					
•					•			•		•		•			
•					•					•	•				
								•		•					
								•		•					
			•				•	•		•			•		
•					•			•		•					
										•					
•															
								•		•					
•							•	•		•					Irish
				•				•		•					
•				•				•		•					
•								•		•	•				
•					•	•		•	•	•	•		•		Irish
•					•			•		•					
•				•	•	•		•	•	•	•		•		
								•							
					•			•		•			•		
					•			•		•					
								•		•					
										•					
					•			•		•					
				•	•			•		•	•				Indonesian

21

Institution	Arabic	Bengali	Bulgarian	Catalan	Chinese	Czech	Danish	Dutch	Farsi	Finnish	French	German	Greek	Gujarati	Hebrew	Hindi	Hungarian	Italian
Bournemouth University											•	•						
Bournville College of FE	•	•	•	•	•						•	•	•	•		•		•
Bracknell College								•			•	•	•					•
University of Bradford	•	•			•		•	•	•		•	•	•		•	•	•	•
Bradford and Ilkley College	•										•	•						•
Brasshouse Centre	•			•	•	•	•	•			•	•	•		•		•	•
Bridgend College of Technology								•			•	•	•					•
Bridgwater College											•	•						•
University of Brighton																		
Brighton College of Technology					•						•	•						•
Brinsbury College											•	•						•
University of Bristol		•			•		•				•	•	•					
British Institute in Paris											•							
Bromley College of Technology								•			•	•						•
Brooklyn College											•	•						
Brooksby College												•						
Broxtowe College	•										•	•					•	•
Brunel College of Technology											•	•						•
Brunel University											•	•						
University of Buckingham											•	•						•
Buckinghamshire College of HE											•	•						•
Bury Metropolitan College											•	•						
C4 Language Services	•										•	•						•
Calderdale College					•	•	•	•			•	•	•				•	•
Cambridge Regional College											•	•						•
Cambuslang College											•	•						•
Cannock Chase Technical College	•										•	•						•
Canterbury Christ Church College																		
Cardiff Institute of HE											•	•						•
Cardiff Tertiary College			•					•			•	•						•
Cardonald College		•			•						•	•					•	•
Carlisle College	•										•	•						•
Castlereagh College of FE											•	•						
Central College of Commerce					•						•	•						•
University of Central England											•	•						
University of Central Lancashire																		
Charles Keene College																		
Chelmsford College of FE	•							•			•	•						•
Cheltenham & Gloucester College											•	•	•					•
Chester College							•	•			•	•						•
Chippenham Technical College					•						•	•	•				•	•

22

Japanese	Korean	Malay	Norwegian	Polish	Portuguese	Punjabi	Romanian	Russian	Serbo-Croat	Spanish	Swedish	Turkish	Urdu	Welsh	Other languages
										•					
•	•			•	•	•	•	•		•			•		Irish
•								•		•					
			•		•	•		•		•	•	•	•		
•								•		•					
•			•	•	•		•	•	•	•	•	•			Irish, Ukrainian
•			•					•		•					
										•	•				
								•		•					
•	•		•		•			•	•	•	•				
										•					
•								•		•					
				•				•		•					
										•	•				
								•							
•										•					
										•					
										•					
•								•		•		•			
•				•	•			•		•	•				
•								•		•					
•								•		•					
•								•		•					
										•					
•					•			•		•					
				•				•		•					
								•		•					
										•					
•								•		•					
										•					
•								•		•	•				
•								•		•					
•				•	•			•		•					
•					•			•		•		•			

Institution	Arabic	Bengali	Bulgarian	Catalan	Chinese	Czech	Danish	Dutch	Farsi	Finnish	French	German	Greek	Gujarati	Hebrew	Hindi	Hungarian	Italian
City and East London College											•	•						•
City College (Norwich)							•				•	•						•
City University					•						•	•	•					•
Clarendon College	•						•				•	•	•			•		•
Clydebank College											•	•				•		•
Colchester Institute							•				•	•						•
Coleg Pencraig											•	•						
Coleraine Technical College											•	•						
Collingham, Brown & Brown	•				•		•	•	•	•	•	•						•
Coventry University											•	•						•
Cranfield Institute of Technology											•	•						
Crawley College of Technology	•										•	•						•
Cricklade College											•	•						•
Crosskeys College											•	•					•	•
Croydon College											•	•						•
Cumbernauld College											•	•						•
Darlington College of Technology	•					•	•	•			•	•	•			•		•
Daventry Tertiary College											•	•						•
De Montfort University								•			•	•						•
Derby College (Mackworth)											•	•						•
Derby College (Wilmorton)											•	•						
Derwentside College							•				•	•			•			•
Dewsbury College							•				•	•	•	•				•
Doncaster College											•	•						•
Dorset Business School											•	•						•
Dudley College of Technology							•				•	•						•
University of Dundee	•										•	•				•		•
Dundee College of FE											•	•						•
Dundee Institute of Technology											•	•						
Dungannon College of FE											•	•						
Dunstable College											•	•						•
University of Durham						•	•	•		•	•	•					•	•
Univ of East Anglia LX Centre							•			•	•	•						•
East Birmingham College								•			•	•						
East Devon College							•				•	•						•
University of East London											•	•						•
East Midlands LX Centre	•		•		•	•	•	•		•	•	•	•				•	•
East Surrey College	•										•	•	•					•
East Warwickshire College											•	•						•
East Yorkshire College											•	•						
Eastleigh College											•	•						•

24

Japanese	Korean	Malay	Norwegian	Polish	Portuguese	Punjabi	Romanian	Russian	Serbo-Croat	Spanish	Swedish	Turkish	Urdu	Welsh	Other languages
								•		•					
•								•		•					
•								•		•					Latin
•			•	•	•			•	•	•	•				
•								•		•			•		Gaelic (Scottish)
•				•				•		•	•		•		
•														•	
										•					
•		•	•	•	•			•	•	•	•			•	
								•		•					
								•		•					
•					•			•		•			•		
										•					
•										•					
					•					•					
										•					
•			•	•	•			•	•	•		•			Afrikaans, Swahili, Zulu
								•		•					
					•					•					
•						•		•		•			•		
										•					
										•					
•					•			•		•			•		
										•					
										•					
					•			•		•					
•								•		•			•		
								•		•					
								•		•					
										•					
			•							•					
•			•		•			•	•	•	•				Albanian
•			•					•		•	•				Faroese, Greenlandic
										•		•			
•					•			•		•	•				
								•		•					
•			•	•	•		•	•		•	•				Albanian
•					•			•		•		•			
•										•					
										•					
				•				•		•					

Institution	Arabic	Bengali	Bulgarian	Catalan	Chinese	Czech	Danish	Dutch	Farsi	Finnish	French	German	Greek	Gujarati	Hebrew	Hindi	Hungarian	Italian
Easton College											•	•						
Edge Hill College of HE											•	•						•
University of Edinburgh	•				•			•			•	•						•
Elmwood Business Training											•	•						
Enfield College											•	•						•
Erith College											•	•						•
University of Essex																		
Euro-Com Languages for Business						•		•			•	•						•
University of Exeter	•				•	•		•			•	•	•					•
Exeter College											•	•						•
Falkirk College of Technology								•			•	•						•
Farnborough Coll of Technology								•			•	•						•
Fife College of Technology								•			•	•						•
Filton College											•	•						•
French Institute											•							
Frome Community College											•	•						•
Furness College											•	•						•
Gateshead College											•	•	•					•
University of Glamorgan											•	•						•
University of Glasgow							•	•			•	•						•
Glasgow Coll of Food Technology											•	•						•
Glasgow Coll of Nautical Studies											•	•						
Glasgow Caledonian University											•	•						•
Glenrothes College LX Centre							•	•			•	•						•
Gloucestershire Coll of Arts Tech					•			•			•	•						•
Gorseinon College											•	•						•
Great Yarmouth College of FE	•							•			•	•	•					•
Greenhill College	•				•			•			•	•	•	•		•		•
University of Greenwich											•	•						•
Grimsby Coll of Tech &Arts											•	•						•
Guildford College of Technology											•	•						
Gwynedd Technical College	•				•	•		•		•	•	•	•					•
Hackney College	•	•			•						•	•		•		•		•
Hall Green College	•									•	•	•		•				•
Halton College of FE											•	•						•
Hammersmith &West London Coll											•	•						
Handsworth College											•	•				•		
Harlow College											•	•						•
Harper Adams Agricultural Coll											•							
Harrogate Coll of Arts & Tech											•	•						•
Hartlepool College of FE								•			•	•						

Japanese	Korean	Malay	Norwegian	Polish	Portuguese	Punjabi	Romanian	Russian	Serbo-Croat	Spanish	Swedish	Turkish	Urdu	Welsh	Other languages
										•					
•					•			•		•					
								•		•					
•								•		•					
										•					
								•							
•								•		•					Maltese
•					•			•		•					
								•		•					
								•		•			•		
•					•			•		•					
								•		•					
										•					
										•					
•								•		•					
•					•			•		•	•				
					•					•				•	
•						•		•		•					
•										•					
										•					
								•		•					
								•		•					
				•				•		•					
•					•			•		•		•			Estonian
								•		•				•	
					•			•		•					
					•			•		•			•		
										•					
								•		•					
										•					
•					•			•		•				•	
•			•			•		•		•		•	•		Amharic, Hausa, Ibo, Somali, Swahili, Tigrean, Vietnamese, Yoruba
•							•			•			•		Pushtu
					•					•	•				
										•					
						•				•			•		Vietnamese
•								•		•					
										•					
					•			•		•					
								•							

Institution	Arabic	Bengali	Bulgarian	Catalan	Chinese	Czech	Danish	Dutch	Farsi	Finnish	French	German	Greek	Gujarati	Hebrew	Hindi	Hungarian	Italian
Hastings Coll of Arts and Tech	•							•			•	•						•
Havering College of FHE	•										•	•						•
Hendon College of FE	•										•	•	•	•			•	•
Henley College	•				•						•	•						•
Henley College (Coventry)											•	•						
Herefordshire College of Tech											•	•						•
Heriot-Watt University						•	•			•	•	•					•	•
Hertford Reg. Coll (Broxbourne)											•	•						•
Hertford Reg. Coll (Ware)								•			•	•	•					•
University of Hertfordshire											•	•	•					•
High Peak College											•	•	•					•
Hopwood Hall College											•	•						•
Hounslow Borough College								•			•	•						•
University of Huddersfield	•				•		•	•		•	•	•	•					•
Huddersfield Technical College	•										•	•	•					•
University of Hull	•						•	•			•	•	•					•
Hull College of Further Education											•	•						•
Huntingdonshire College					•			•			•	•	•					•
IBEX (Epsom)			•								•	•	•					•
IBEX (Winchester)								•			•	•						•
International House											•	•						•
Inverness College of FHE								•			•	•					•	•
Isle College								•			•	•						•
Isle of Man College of FE											•	•						•
James Watt College											•	•						
University of Keele					•						•	•						
Keighley College											•	•						•
Kendal College											•	•						•
University of Kent at Canterbury	•										•	•	•					•
Kilmarnock College											•	•						•
King Alfred's College								•			•	•						•
King's College (London)											•	•	•					•
Kingston College of FE											•	•						•
Kingston Language-Export Centre					•						•	•						•
Kingston University																		
Kirby College	•					•		•			•	•	•					•
Kitson College		•									•	•		•				•
Knowsley Community College											•	•						
Knuston Hall Adult Residential					•						•	•						•
Lancashire & Cumbria LX Centre					•			•		•	•	•						•
Lancashire College	•	•			•		•	•	•	•	•	•	•	•			•	•

Japanese	Korean	Malay	Norwegian	Polish	Portuguese	Punjabi	Romanian	Russian	Serbo-Croat	Spanish	Swedish	Turkish	Urdu	Welsh	Other languages
								•		•					
•					•			•		•		•			
•								•		•			•		
								•		•					
										•					
		•		•				•		•	•				
•								•		•					
•					•			•		•				•	
•					•			•		•					
								•		•					
								•		•			•		
•			•	•				•	•	•					
•			•	•	•			•		•	•				
•					•			•		•					
•		•	•		•			•		•	•				Thai
										•	•				
•								•		•					
•			•	•				•		•	•				
•			•	•				•		•					
•										•					
•				•				•		•					Gaelic (Scottish)
•								•		•					
										•					
										•					
•								•		•					
•					•			•		•			•		
										•					
•					•			•		•	•	•			
										•					
•				•	•			•		•					
•					•			•		•					
										•					
•								•		•					
•		•			•			•		•	•				
				•	•			•		•			•		
										•					
					•			•		•					
•			•	•	•			•		•	•				
•			•	•	•	•	•	•		•	•	•	•		Swahili, Thai

Institution	Arabic	Bengali	Bulgarian	Catalan	Chinese	Czech	Danish	Dutch	Farsi	Finnish	French	German	Greek	Gujarati	Hebrew	Hindi	Hungarian	Italian
Adult College (Lancaster)											•	•						•
Lancaster and Morecambe College											•	•						•
Langley College											•	•						•
Lauder College						•					•	•						•
University of Leeds	•		•		•	•					•				•			
Leeds Metropolitan University	•	•	•		•	•	•	•		•	•	•	•	•		•		•
Leek College of Further Education											•	•	•					
Leicester South Fields College											•	•		•				•
Leigh College											•	•						•
Lews Castle College											•							
Limavady College of FE											•	•						
Lincolnshire College of Ag.											•							
Lincolnshire College of Art											•	•						•
University of Liverpool																		
City of Liverpool Community Coll	•				•			•			•	•	•					•
Liverpool Institute of HE											•	•						
Liverpool John Moores University					•	•		•		•	•	•						•
Llandrillo Technical College					•						•	•	•					•
Llysfasi College											•	•						•
London Guildhall University											•	•						•
University College London							•	•		•	•	•						•
Univ of London (C&E Europe Off)		•			•					•							•	
Univ of London (Cont Educ)	•				•						•	•						•
London LX											•	•						•
Longlands College of FE							•				•	•						•
Loughborough College		•		•			•	•			•	•	•	•		•		•
Loughborough University																		
Lowestoft College							•				•	•						•
Loxley College											•	•						•
LSU College of Higher Education											•	•						•
Lurgan College of FE											•	•						•
Lydbury English Centre											•	•						•
Macclesfield College								•			•	•						•
Magherafelt College of FE											•	•						
Managed Learning											•	•						•
University of Manchester	•									•	•	•	•		•			•
Manchester Business School	•				•		•	•			•	•						•
Manchester Coll of Arts and Tech	•				•			•			•	•						•
UMIST											•	•						
Manchester LX Centre							•	•			•	•						•
Matthew Boulton College											•	•			•			•

30

Japanese	Korean	Malay	Norwegian	Polish	Portuguese	Punjabi	Romanian	Russian	Serbo-Croat	Spanish	Swedish	Turkish	Urdu	Welsh	Other languages
								•		•					
								•		•					
								•		•					
•			•	•	•					•					
•					•			•		•					Mongolian, Ukrainian
•	•	•	•	•	•	•	•	•	•	•	•	•	•	•	Afrikaans, Icelandic, Indonesian, Irish, Thai, Ukrainian, Vietnamese
								•		•					
								•		•					
								•							Gaelic (Scottish)
										•					
										•					
										•					
•					•			•		•	•				
										•					
•								•		•	•				
•								•		•				•	
										•				•	
										•					
•			•					•		•	•				
				•			•	•	•						Albanian, Estonian, Slovak, Ukrainian
•					•			•		•					
								•		•					
										•		•			
			•		•	•		•		•	•				
								•		•					
										•					
								•		•					
					•					•					
										•		•			
•					•			•		•					
										•					
•	•							•		•					
•								•		•		•			Aramaic, Armenian, Azeri, Kazakh, Kurdish, Tajik, Uighur, Uzbek, Yiddish
•	•				•		•	•	•	•	•	•			
•					•			•		•			•		
•										•					
•					•			•		•					
								•		•			•		

Institution	Arabic	Bengali	Bulgarian	Catalan	Chinese	Czech	Danish	Dutch	Farsi	Finnish	French	German	Greek	Gujarati	Hebrew	Hindi	Hungarian	Italian
Merseyside Language-Export Cen	•				•	•		•			•	•	•				•	•
Merthyr Tydfil Technical College								•			•	•						•
Mid-Cheshire College of FE					•			•			•	•						•
Mid-Cornwall College											•	•						•
Mid-Kent College of HFE								•		•	•	•	•				•	•
Mid-Warwickshire College of FE											•	•					•	•
Middlesex University	•										•	•	•					•
Milton Keynes College	•										•	•	•					•
Milton Keynes Language Centre	•								•	•	•	•						•
Monkwearmouth College					•		•	•			•	•	•					
Moray College of FE											•	•						•
Motherwell College											•	•						
Nailsea & Clevedon Adult Ed											•	•						•
Napier University	•				•	•		•			•	•	•					•
Neath College											•	•						•
Nelson and Colne College											•	•						•
New College											•	•						•
New College (Durham)	•					•	•				•	•	•					•
Newark and Sherwood College						•					•	•			•			•
Newbury College											•	•						•
Newcastle College	•				•						•	•				•		
Newcastle College of FE											•	•						
University of Newcastle upon Tyne					•						•	•						•
Newcastle-under-Lyme College											•	•						•
Newport College		•						•			•	•						•
Norfolk College of Arts and Tech								•			•	•						•
North Antrim College of FE											•	•						
North Cheshire College			•								•	•						•
North Devon College											•	•						
North East Export Associates			•		•	•	•	•			•	•	•					•
North East Worcestershire College											•	•						•
North Glasgow College			•								•	•						•
North Hertfordshire College	•	•			•			•			•	•	•	•		•		•
North Lindsey College	•	•									•	•	•					•
University of North London						•	•				•	•						•
North Trafford College	•				•		•	•			•	•	•		•		•	•
North Tyneside College	•										•	•	•					•
North Warwickshire College											•	•						•
North West Kent College of Tech	•										•	•						•
College of North West London		•									•	•	•	•		•		
Northampton College of FE											•	•						•

32

Japanese	Korean	Malay	Norwegian	Polish	Portuguese	Punjabi	Romanian	Russian	Serbo-Croat	Spanish	Swedish	Turkish	Urdu	Welsh	Other languages
•				•	•			•		•					
•										•					
•					•			•		•		•			
										•					
•					•			•		•					
•					•			•		•					
•					•			•		•		•			
										•					
•					•			•		•	•				
•		•								•					
										•					
										•					
										•					
•			•	•				•		•					
										•				•	Irish
						•				•		•			
•										•					
•										•	•				
•			•					•		•					Slovak
•								•		•					
								•		•			•		Swahili
										•					
•	•							•		•					
•					•			•		•					
•					•			•		•	•		•	•	Somali
								•		•					
										•					
•					•			•		•					
								•		•					
•		•	•	•	•		•	•	•	•	•				Slovak
•								•		•					
•								•		•					
•					•	•		•		•			•		Tamil
•						•		•		•			•		
										•					
•			•		•			•		•				•	
			•							•					
										•					
•					•			•		•					
						•				•			•		
										•					

33

Institution	Arabic	Bengali	Bulgarian	Catalan	Chinese	Czech	Danish	Dutch	Farsi	Finnish	French	German	Greek	Gujarati	Hebrew	Hindi	Hungarian	Italian
Northern Ireland Hotel & Catering											•							
Northumberland Coll Arts & Tech											•	•						•
Univ of Northumbria at Newcastle																		
Norton College											•	•	•					•
Norton Radstock College											•	•						•
University of Nottingham					•			•			•	•						•
Nottingham Trent University	•		•		•	•		•		•	•	•	•			•	•	•
Oaklands College (Oaklands)	•										•	•						•
Oaklands College (St Albans)											•	•						•
Oldham College		•									•	•						•
University of Oxford											•	•	•					•
Oxford Brookes University	•						•	•			•	•	•					•
Oxford College of FE	•				•		•	•			•	•	•					•
University of Paisley											•	•						•
Park Lane College					•			•			•	•	•					•
Parkwood College											•	•						
Parson Cross College											•	•						
Pembrokeshire College											•	•						•
People's Coll of Tertiary Education											•	•						•
Perth College of Further Education											•	•						
College of FE (Plymouth)						•		•			•	•						•
University of Plymouth											•	•						•
Pontypool and Usk College											•	•						
Pontypridd Technical College											•	•						•
Portadown College											•	•						
University of Portsmouth	•						•	•			•	•						
Preston College	•							•			•	•	•	•				•
Queen's College (Glasgow)											•	•						
Queen's University of Belfast	•							•			•	•	•				•	•
University of Reading											•	•						•
Reading Adult College	•							•			•	•	•			•		•
Redbridge College of FE											•	•						•
Reid Kerr College											•	•						•
Rhondda College											•	•						•
Richmond Adult & Com Coll	•							•			•	•						•
Richmond upon Thames College											•	•						•
Univ Coll of Ripon & York St John											•	•						•
Robert Gordon University											•	•						
Rockingham College	•		•	•	•	•	•	•	•		•	•	•					•
Rotherham College of Arts & Tech											•	•						•
Royal Agricultural College											•	•						•

34

Japanese	Korean	Malay	Norwegian	Polish	Portuguese	Punjabi	Romanian	Russian	Serbo-Croat	Spanish	Swedish	Turkish	Urdu	Welsh	Other languages
•										•					
				•	•					•					
										•					
							•	•		•					
•					•			•		•					
•			•	•	•			•	•	•	•	•	•		Afrikaans, Kiribatese, Icelandic, Slovak, Swahili
•										•					
•								•		•					
										•		•			
					•			•		•					
•		•			•			•		•					
•				•	•			•		•	•		•		
•					•			•		•					
•				•	•	•		•		•			•		
						•				•			•		
								•		•					
										•			•		
					•			•		•					
										•					
										•					
•								•		•				•	
										•					
•					•			•		•					
•					•			•		•		•	•		
•				•	•			•		•	•				Irish
•								•		•	•				
•					•	•		•		•			•		Thai
								•		•					
										•					
										•					
•					•			•		•	•				
								•		•					
			•							•	•				
•				•	•		•	•	•	•		•			Afrikaans, Maltese, Slovak, Swahili, Ukrainian
								•		•	•				
•								•		•					

35

Institution	Arabic	Bengali	Bulgarian	Catalan	Chinese	Czech	Danish	Dutch	Farsi	Finnish	French	German	Greek	Gujarati	Hebrew	Hindi	Hungarian	Italian
Royal Forest of Dean College											●	●						●
Royal Holloway											●	●						●
Runshaw College								●			●	●	●					●
Ruskin College											●	●						
Rycotewood College											●	●						
S. Martin's College							●	●			●	●	●					●
University College Salford	●										●	●						●
University of Salford	●				●			●			●	●	●					●
Salford College of FE	●										●	●						●
Salisbury College	●						●	●			●	●	●					●
Sandwell College of FHE	●	●			●	●					●	●		●		●		●
School of Oriental & African Stud	●				●													
Scottish College of Textiles											●	●						●
University of Sheffield					●						●	●						●
Sheffield Hallam University	●				●	●	●	●	●		●	●	●				●	●
Shipley College	●	●									●	●						●
Shrewsbury College of Art & Tech	●				●			●			●	●	●					●
Solihull College of Technology								●			●	●	●					●
Somerset College of Arts and Tech											●	●						●
Soundwell College											●	●						●
South Bank University					●						●	●						●
South Bristol College											●	●						●
South Cheshire College LX Centre	●				●			●			●	●					●	●
South Devon College	●										●	●						●
South Downs College	●				●			●			●	●	●					●
South East Derbyshire College											●	●						●
South East Essex Coll Art & Tech	●									●	●	●						●
South Kent College							●	●			●	●	●					●
South Thames College																		
South Trafford College of FE											●	●	●					●
South Tyneside College											●	●						●
South Wales LX Centre											●	●						●
University of Southampton				●							●	●					●	●
Southampton Institute of HE			●				●				●	●						●
Southampton Technical College											●	●						●
Southgate College											●	●	●					●
Southwark College		●			●						●	●						●
University of St Andrews	●				●		●	●			●	●	●				●	●
College of St Mark and St John	●							●			●	●						●
Stafford College											●	●						●
Staffordshire LX Centre											●	●						●

Japanese	Korean	Malay	Norwegian	Polish	Portuguese	Punjabi	Romanian	Russian	Serbo-Croat	Spanish	Swedish	Turkish	Urdu	Welsh	Other languages
								•		•					
•										•					
•								•		•		•			
								•		•					
•					•			•		•					
					•					•					
•	•				•		•	•		•	•	•			
								•		•					
•					•			•		•					
•			•			•	•	•		•			•		Ukrainian
•	•											•			Indonesian, Swahili, Thai
										•					
•	•	•								•					
•			•	•	•		•	•		•	•	•			
•								•		•		•			
•				•	•			•		•	•			•	
•			•							•					
										•					
										•					
•					•			•		•					
								•		•			•		
•			•		•			•		•					
•										•					
•			•		•			•		•	•	•			
								•		•					
•							•	•		•	•	•			
					•			•	•	•	•				
•					•			•		•					
								•		•					
•								•		•					
•					•			•		•					
								•		•					
										•					
										•					
										•					
•			•	•	•					•		•			
•										•					
								•		•					
•								•		•					

Institution	Arabic	Bengali	Bulgarian	Catalan	Chinese	Czech	Danish	Dutch	Farsi	Finnish	French	German	Greek	Gujarati	Hebrew	Hindi	Hungarian	Italian
Staffordshire University																		
Stevenson College of FE											•	•						•
University of Stirling											•	•						•
Stockport College of FHE	•				•		•	•			•	•	•					•
Stockton-Billingham Tech Coll											•	•	•					•
Stoke-on-Trent College								•			•	•	•					•
Stradbroke College											•	•						•
Stratford-upon-Avon College								•			•	•						•
University of Strathclyde											•	•						•
Stroud College of FE											•	•						•
Suffolk College	•				•		•	•		•	•	•	•				•	•
University of Sunderland											•	•						•
University of Surrey											•	•						
Sussex and Kent LX Centre	•				•						•	•	•				•	•
Sutton Coldfield College of FE	•			•				•			•	•						•
Sutton College of Liberal Arts					•			•			•	•	•					•
University College of Swansea																		
Swansea College	•										•	•	•					•
Swansea Institute of HE											•	•						•
Swindon College								•			•	•						•
Tameside College of Technology											•	•						•
Tamworth College											•	•						•
University of Teesside								•			•	•	•					•
Telford College							•				•	•						•
Telford College of Arts and Tech							•				•	•						•
Thames Valley Univ LX Centre											•	•						•
The City Lit	•				•	•		•	•		•	•	•		•		•	•
Thomas Danby College											•	•		•				•
Thurrock Technical College	•				•						•	•					•	•
Thurso Technical College											•	•						•
Tresham Institute of FHE						•	•	•			•	•	•					•
Trinity and All Saints College											•	•						
Trinity College											•	•						
Trowbridge College											•	•						•
University of Ulster at Jordanstown	•				•		•	•			•	•					•	•
Uxbridge College											•	•						•
Wakefield College											•	•						•
Walford College of Agriculture											•	•						
Walsall College of Technology							•	•			•	•	•					•
Waltham Forest College											•	•						•
University of Warwick	•				•	•	•	•			•	•	•					•

Japanese	Korean	Malay	Norwegian	Polish	Portuguese	Punjabi	Romanian	Russian	Serbo-Croat	Spanish	Swedish	Turkish	Urdu	Welsh	Other languages
•										•					
•										•					
•			•		•			•		•					
•										•					
•					•			•		•		•	•		
•								•		•			•		
								•		•					
								•		•					
•				•				•		•					
•			•	•	•			•		•	•				
•								•		•					
								•		•	•				
•					•				•	•					
•					•			•		•					Ukrainian
•					•			•		•					
•					•			•		•				•	
•										•				•	
								•		•					
										•					
•								•		•					
•								•		•	•				
•					•			•		•					
										•				•	
•								•		•					
•				•	•			•		•				•	Gaelic (Scottish), Latin
										•		•			
•				•	•	•		•		•	•				
										•					
•					•			•		•					
										•					
								•		•				•	
										•					
•				•	•			•		•	•	•			Indonesian
								•		•					
•								•		•					
										•					
•								•		•					
										•					
•			•	•	•	•		•		•	•	•		•	

39

Institution	Arabic	Bengali	Bulgarian	Catalan	Chinese	Czech	Danish	Dutch	Farsi	Finnish	French	German	Greek	Gujarati	Hebrew	Hindi	Hungarian	Italian
Warwickshire Coll for Agriculture											•							
Wearside College								•			•	•						•
West Cheshire College											•	•						•
West Cumbria College											•	•						
West Hertfordshire College								•			•	•	•					•
West Kent College	•		•		•			•			•	•	•					•
University of the West of England	•							•			•	•						•
West Suffolk College											•	•						•
West Sussex Institute of HE																		
City of Westminster College											•	•						•
University of Westminster	•	•	•		•	•	•	•		•	•	•	•	•	•	•	•	•
Westminster College											•	•						•
Weymouth College											•	•						•
Wigan College of Technology											•	•						•
Wigston College of FE								•			•	•						•
Univ of Wolverhampton LX Centre								•			•	•						•
Woolwich College		•			•						•	•		•		•		•
Worcester College of Technology											•	•						
Worcestershire Coll of Agriculture											•	•						•
Worth Consulting											•	•						•
Wulfrun College											•	•						•
Yeovil College								•			•	•						•
University of York	•						•	•			•	•	•					•
York College of FHE							•	•			•	•					•	•
Yorkshire Coast College of FHE	•							•			•	•	•					•

Japanese	Korean	Malay	Norwegian	Polish	Portuguese	Punjabi	Romanian	Russian	Serbo-Croat	Spanish	Swedish	Turkish	Urdu	Welsh	Other languages
			•					•		•					
•								•		•					
								•		•					
•				•	•			•		•	•	•			
•								•		•					
•				•	•			•		•	•				
•								•		•					
					•										
•	•	•	•	•	•	•	•	•	•	•	•	•	•		Indonesian, Slovene, Swahili, Thai
•								•		•					
•								•		•					
					•			•		•					
					•			•		•					
•								•		•					
•						•		•		•			•		
•										•					
										•					
					•					•					
			•	•		•		•		•					
								•		•					
•			•	•	•			•		•	•	•			Thai
•					•			•		•	•				
					•			•		•					

THE DIRECTORY

1   University of Aberdeen

Language Centre
Regent Walk
Aberdeen   Telephone   (0224) 272536
AB9 2UB   Fax   (0224) 276730

Contact   Mrs C. Burgess, Language Services Co-ordinator

TRAINING

Arabic   *Type:* client-based; institution-based; group; one-to-one; bespoke
              Method: intensive; non-intensive; open or flexible
Danish   *Type:* client-based; institution-based; group; one-to-one; bespoke
              Method: intensive; non-intensive; open or flexible
Dutch   *Type:* client-based; institution-based; group; one-to-one; bespoke
              Method: intensive; non-intensive; open or flexible
French   *Type:* client-based; institution-based; group; one-to-one; bespoke
              (specialism: oil industry)
              Method: intensive; non-intensive; open or flexible
German   *Type:* client-based; institution-based; group; one-to-one; bespoke
              Method: intensive; non-intensive; open or flexible
Greek   *Type:* client-based; institution-based; group; one-to-one; bespoke
              Method: intensive; non-intensive; open or flexible
Italian   *Type:* client-based; institution-based; group; one-to-one; bespoke
              Method: intensive; non-intensive; open or flexible
Japanese   *Type:* client-based; institution-based; group; one-to-one; bespoke
              Method: intensive; non-intensive; open or flexible
Russian   *Type:* client-based; institution-based; group; one-to-one; bespoke
              (specialism: oil industry)
              Method: intensive; non-intensive; open or flexible
Spanish   *Type:* client-based; institution-based; group; one-to-one; bespoke
              (specialism: oil industry)
              Method: intensive; non-intensive; open or flexible
Other   Additional languages can be offered, with notice

SERVICES
Translating
Arabic   into and out of English
Danish   into and out of English
Dutch   into and out of English
French   into and out of English
German   into and out of English
Italian   into and out of English
Japanese   out of English
Norwegian   into and out of English
Russian   into and out of English

Spanish	into and out of English
Swedish	into English
Interpreting	
Arabic	simultaneous
Danish	simultaneous
Dutch	simultaneous
French	simultaneous
German	simultaneous
Italian	simultaneous
Japanese	simultaneous
Norwegian	simultaneous
Russian	simultaneous
Spanish	simultaneous
Swedish	simultaneous

FACILITIES

Language labs:	under 10 places - 2 fixed; 10–25 places - 4 fixed; over 25 places - 1 fixed
Equipment and materials:	satellite television; videocassettes

NOTES
• has experience of undertaking language training needs analyses for employers
• offers translating services in various other languages

2   Aberdeen College of Further Education

Gallowgate
Aberdeen   Telephone   (0224) 640366
AB9 1DN   Fax   (0224) 647178

Contact   Mrs J. Martin, Head of Communication, Language and Media
                            Studies

TRAINING
French   *Type:* client-based; institution-based; group; one-to-one; bespoke
              Method: intensive; non-intensive
German   *Type:* client-based; institution-based; group; one-to-one; bespoke
              Method: intensive; non-intensive
Italian   *Type:* client-based; institution-based; group; one-to-one; bespoke
              Method: intensive; non-intensive
Spanish   *Type:* client-based; institution-based; group; one-to-one; bespoke
              Method: intensive; non-intensive

SERVICES
Translating
French   into English
German   into English
Italian   into English
Spanish   into English
Interpreting
French   simultaneous; consecutive
German   simultaneous; consecutive
Italian   simultaneous; consecutive
Spanish   simultaneous; consecutive

FACILITIES
Language labs: 10–25 places - 3 fixed

NOTES
• has experience of undertaking language training needs analyses for employers

3   Abingdon College

Northcourt Road
Abingdon   Telephone   (0235) 555585
OX14 1NN   Fax   (0235) 553168

Contact   Mr M. Bloom, Lecturer in Modern Languages

TRAINING
French   *Type:* client-based; institution-based; group; one-to-one; bespoke
               Method: intensive; non-intensive; open or flexible
German   *Type:* client-based; group
               Method: intensive; non-intensive; open or flexible
Portuguese   *Type:* client-based; institution-based; group; one-to-one; bespoke
               Method: non-intensive
Swedish   *Type:* client-based; institution-based; group; one-to-one; bespoke
               Method: non-intensive

FACILITIES
Language labs: under 10 places - 1 fixed; 10–25 places - 1 fixed

NOTES
• has experience of undertaking language training needs analyses for employers

4   Accrington and Rossendale College

Sandy Lane
Accrington   Telephone   (0254) 393521
BB5 2AW   Fax   (0254) 301236

Contact   Mr D. Tyas, Head of General Education and Science Division

TRAINING

French	*Type:* institution-based; group
	Method: non-intensive
German	*Type:* institution-based; group
	Method: non-intensive
Italian	*Type:* institution-based; group
	Method: non-intensive
Spanish	*Type:* institution-based; group
	Method: non-intensive
Other	Additional languages can be offered, with notice

SERVICES

Translating

French	into and out of English
German	into and out of English
Italian	into and out of English
Spanish	into and out of English

FACILITIES

Language labs: 10–25 places - 1 fixed, 1 portable

5   Afan College

Margam
Port Talbot   Telephone   (0639) 882107
SA13 2AL   Fax   (0639) 886163

Contact   Mrs G. Suff, European Officer

TRAINING
French   *Type:* client-based; institution-based; group; one-to-one; bespoke
                 Method: intensive; non-intensive; open or flexible
German   *Type:* client-based; institution-based; group; one-to-one; bespoke
                 Method: intensive; non-intensive; open or flexible
Italian   *Type:* client-based; institution-based; group; one-to-one; bespoke
                 Method: intensive; non-intensive
Japanese   *Type:* institution-based
                 Method: non-intensive
Spanish   *Type:* client-based; institution-based; group; one-to-one; bespoke
                 Method: intensive; non-intensive
Welsh   *Type:* client-based; institution-based; group; one-to-one; bespoke
                 Method: intensive; non-intensive; open or flexible
Other   Portuguese, Swedish and Russian can be offered, with notice

SERVICES
Translating
French   into and out of English
German   into and out of English (specialism: engineering)
Italian   into and out of English
Spanish   into and out of English
Welsh   into and out of English

FACILITIES
Language labs: 10–25 places - 1 portable; over 25 places - 1 fixed

NOTES
• has experience of undertaking language training needs analyses for employers

6   Airedale and Wharfedale College

Calverley Lane
Leeds   Telephone   (0532) 591139
LS18 4RQ   Fax   (0532) 591138

Contact   Ms S. Heleine, Industrial Development Unit Deputy Manager

TRAINING

French	*Type:* client-based; group; bespoke (specialisms: information technology; vehicle recovery and breakdown)
	Method: intensive; non-intensive; open or flexible
German	*Type:* client-based; group; bespoke (specialism: accountancy)
	Method: intensive; non-intensive; open or flexible
Greek	*Type:* client-based; institution-based
	Method: intensive; non-intensive
Italian	*Type:* client-based; institution-based
	Method: intensive; non-intensive; open or flexible
Japanese	*Type:* client-based; institution-based
	Method: intensive; non-intensive
Portuguese	*Type:* client-based; institution-based
	Method: intensive; non-intensive
Russian	*Type:* client-based; institution-based
	Method: intensive; non-intensive
Spanish	*Type:* client-based; group; one-to-one; bespoke (specialisms: media; accountancy)
	Method: intensive; non-intensive; open or flexible
Other	Urdu and Gujarati can be offered, with notice

SERVICES

Translating
French   into and out of English
German   into and out of English
Spanish   into and out of English
Interpreting
French   simultaneous; consecutive
German   simultaneous; consecutive
Spanish   simultaneous; consecutive

FACILITIES

Language labs: 10–25 places - 1 portable
Equipment and
   materials: audio and videocassettes; computer-assisted language learning

NOTES
• has experience of undertaking language training needs analyses for employers

7   Amersham and Wycombe College

Amersham Business Centre
Oxford Road
High Wycombe   Telephone   (0494) 462607
HP11 2EG   Fax   (0494) 473766

Contact   Mrs M. Heidemann, Business Language Development Officer

TRAINING
French   *Type:* client-based; institution-based; group; one-to-one; bespoke
                     Method: intensive; non-intensive; open or flexible
German   *Type:* client-based; institution-based; group; one-to-one; bespoke
                     Method: intensive; non-intensive; open or flexible
Italian   *Type:* client-based; institution-based; group; one-to-one; bespoke
                     Method: intensive; non-intensive; open or flexible
Spanish   *Type:* client-based; institution-based; group; one-to-one; bespoke
                     Method: intensive; non-intensive; open or flexible

SERVICES
Translating
French   into and out of English
German   into and out of English
Spanish   into English
Interpreting
French   simultaneous; consecutive
German   simultaneous; consecutive

FACILITIES
Language labs: 10–25 places - 1 fixed
Interpreting
 facilities: 10–25 places - 1 fixed

NOTES
• has experience of undertaking language training needs analyses for employers

8   Anglia Polytechnic University

East Road
Cambridge   Telephone   (0223) 63271
CB1 1PT   Fax   (0223) 352973

Contact   Mr R. Bruce-Wilson, Head of Anglia Language Training Services

TRAINING
French   *Type:* client-based; institution-based; group; one-to-one; bespoke
                   (specialism: construction industry site safety)
German   *Type:* client-based; institution-based; group; one-to-one; bespoke
Italian   *Type:* client-based; institution-based; group; one-to-one; bespoke
                   (specialisms: air cabin crew; legal)
Japanese   *Type:* client-based; institution-based; group; one-to-one
Russian   *Type:* client-based; institution-based; group; one-to-one; bespoke
Spanish   *Type:* client-based; institution-based; group; one-to-one; bespoke

9   Angus College of Further Education

Keptie Road
Arbroath   Telephone   (0241) 72056
DD11 3EA   Fax   (0241) 76169

Contact   Mr W. Forbes, Head of Communication and Language

TRAINING

French	*Type:* client-based; institution-based
	Method: non-intensive
German	*Type:* client-based; institution-based
	Method: non-intensive
Norwegian	*Type:* one-to-one
	Method: open or flexible
Russian	*Type:* one-to-one
	Method: open or flexible
Other	Arabic can be offered, with notice

FACILITIES

Language labs: 10–25 places - 1 portable
Equipment and
  materials: computer-assisted learning in basic French; audio-visual materials in German and French

10   Anniesland College

Hatfield Drive
Glasgow   Telephone   041-357 3969
G12 0YE   Fax   041-337 2201

Contact   Mr H. Walker, Principal

TRAINING

French	*Type:* client-based; institution-based; group; bespoke
	Method: intensive; non-intensive; open or flexible
German	*Type:* client-based; institution-based; group; bespoke
	Method: intensive; non-intensive; open or flexible
Italian	*Type:* client-based; institution-based; group; bespoke
	Method: intensive; non-intensive; open or flexible
Spanish	*Type:* client-based; institution-based; group; bespoke
	Method: intensive; non-intensive; open or flexible
Specialism	tourism
Other	Additional languages can be offered, with notice

FACILITIES

Language labs: 10–25 places - 1 fixed
Equipment and
  materials: interactive video

NOTES
• has experience of undertaking language training needs analyses for employers
• has experience of providing training for front of house staff in large, city centre hotels

11 Armagh College of Further Education

Lonsdale Street
Armagh   Telephone   (0861) 522205
BT61 7HN   Fax   (0861) 526011

Contact   Mr A. Smith, Director of Language Centre

TRAINING
French   *Type:* client-based; institution-based; group; one-to-one; bespoke
                    Method: intensive; non-intensive; open or flexible
German   *Type:* institution-based; group; one-to-one
                    Method: intensive; non-intensive; open or flexible
Italian   *Type:* institution-based; group; one-to-one
                    Method: intensive; non-intensive; open or flexible
Spanish   *Type:* institution-based; group; one-to-one
                    Method: non-intensive; open or flexible

SERVICES
Translating
French   into and out of English
German   into English
Italian   into English
Spanish   into English
Interpreting
French   simultaneous

FACILITIES
Language labs: 10–25 places - 1 fixed
Equipment and
  materials: electronic dictionary; group audio; television; interactive video;
                    audio and videocassettes

NOTES
• has experience of undertaking language training needs analyses for employers

12   Arnold and Carlton College of Further Education

Digby Avenue
Mapperley
Nottingham   Telephone   (0602) 876503
NG3 6DR   Fax   (0602) 871489

Contact   Ms J. Bradley, Section Head, Languages and Secretarial

FACILITIES
Language labs: 10–25 places - 1 fixed

NOTES
• has experience of undertaking language training needs analyses for employers

13   Aston University

International Communication for Business
Aston Triangle

Birmingham	Telephone	021-359 3611
B4 7ET	Fax	021-359 6153

Contact   Miss J. E. Ramsden, Business Administrator

TRAINING

French	*Type:* client-based; institution-based; group; one-to-one; bespoke (specialism: business) *Method:* intensive; non-intensive; open or flexible
German	*Type:* client-based; institution-based; group; one-to-one; bespoke (specialism: engineering) *Method:* intensive; non-intensive; open or flexible
Italian	*Type:* client-based; institution-based; group; one-to-one; bespoke (specialism: telephone skills) *Method:* intensive; non-intensive
Japanese	*Type:* client-based; institution-based; group; one-to-one; bespoke
Russian	*Type:* client-based; institution-based; group; one-to-one; bespoke
Spanish	*Type:* client-based; institution-based; group; one-to-one; bespoke (specialism: business) *Method:* intensive; non-intensive; open or flexible
Other	Hungarian, Dutch and Portuguese can be offered, with notice

SERVICES
Translating

French	into and out of English
German	into and out of English
Spanish	into and out of English

Interpreting

French	simultaneous; consecutive
German	simultaneous; consecutive

FACILITIES

Language labs:	over 25 places - 1 fixed
Equipment and materials:	computer-assisted language learning; audio and videocassettes

NOTES
• has experience of undertaking language training needs analyses for employers
• arranges consultancy for companies and recruiting of linguists
• has its own computer-assisted language learning courses in French and German

14   Ayr College

Dam Park
Ayr   Telephone   (0292) 265184
KA8 0EU   Fax   (0292) 263889

Contact   Mrs I. Thomson, PICKUP Director

French can be offered, with notice

FACILITIES
Language labs: under 10 places - 1 portable

15   Ballymena College

Trostan Avenue
Ballymena   Telephone (0266) 652871
BT43 7BN   Fax   (0266) 659245

Contact   Dr M. Todd, Head of Liberal Studies Department

TRAINING

French   *Type:* institution-based; group
     Method: intensive; non-intensive; open or flexible
German   *Type:* institution-based; group
     Method: intensive; non-intensive; open or flexible
Spanish   *Type:* institution-based
     Method: non-intensive

FACILITIES

Language labs: 10–25 places - 1 fixed
Equipment and
 materials: audio and videocassettes; computer-assisted language learning

NOTES

• has experience of undertaking language training needs analyses for employers

16 Banff and Buchan College of Further Education

Henderson Road
Fraserburgh   Telephone   (0346) 25777
AB43 5GA   Fax   (0346) 25370

Contact   Mr G. Scott, Co-ordinator, Department of Business Studies

TRAINING

French   *Type:* institution-based
                 Method: non-intensive
Spanish   *Type:* institution-based
                 Method: non-intensive
Other   German can be offered, with notice

17 University College of Wales, Bangor

College Road
Bangor   Telephone   (0248) 351151
LL55 2DG   Fax   (0248) 370451

Contact   Dr A. Ritchie, Lecturer, School of Modern Languages

TRAINING
French   *Type:* client-based; institution-based; group; one-to-one
Russian   *Type:* client-based; institution-based

SERVICES
Translating
French   into and out of English
German   into and out of English
Russian   into and out of English

FACILITIES
Language labs: 10–25 places - 2 fixed

NOTES
• offers translating services in non-technical and semi-technical French, German and
  Russian

18   Barking College of Technology

Dagenham Road
Romford   Telephone   081-599 3977
RM7 0XU   Fax   081-598 2406

Contact   Mr W. Lobley, Head of Business and Management Studies

TRAINING

French   *Type:* client-based; institution-based; group; one-to-one; bespoke
                       Method: intensive; non-intensive; open or flexible
German   *Type:* client-based; group; one-to-one; bespoke
                       Method: intensive; non-intensive; open or flexible
Spanish   *Type:* client-based; institution-based; group; one-to-one; bespoke
                       Method: intensive; non-intensive; open or flexible
Specialisms   legal; police; manufacturing; management; transport; tourism;
                       customer care; public administration
Other   Italian, Greek, Russian and Portuguese can be offered, with notice

FACILITIES

Equipment and
  materials: French, German and Spanish audio and videocassettes; French and
                       German computer-assisted learning software

NOTES
• has experience of undertaking language training needs analyses for employers
• is prepared to deliver courses outside its locality, or residential courses, if required

19   Barnet College

Wood Street
Barnet   Telephone   081-440 6321
EN5 4AZ   Fax   081-441 5236

Contact   Ms A. Wilding, Lecturer in Modern Languages

TRAINING
Chinese   *Type:* institution-based; group
                 Method: non-intensive
French   *Type:* client-based; institution-based; group; one-to-one; bespoke
                 Method: non-intensive; open or flexible
German   *Type:* client-based; institution-based; group; one-to-one; bespoke
                 Method: non-intensive; open or flexible
Greek   *Type:* institution-based; group
                 Method: non-intensive
Hindi   *Type:* institution-based; group
                 Method: non-intensive
Italian   *Type:* client-based; institution-based; group; one-to-one; bespoke
                 Method: non-intensive; open or flexible
Japanese   *Type:* institution-based; group
                 Method: non-intensive; open or flexible
Portuguese   *Type:* institution-based; group
                 Method: non-intensive
Russian   *Type:* institution-based; group
                 Method: non-intensive; open or flexible
Spanish   *Type:* client-based; institution-based; group; one-to-one; bespoke
                 Method: non-intensive; open or flexible
Turkish   *Type:* one-to-one
                 Method: non-intensive; open or flexible

SERVICES
Translating
French   into English
German   into English

FACILITIES
Language labs: 10–25 places - 2 fixed
Equipment and
  materials: computer-assisted language learning; audio and videocassettes

NOTES
• has experience of undertaking language training needs analyses for employers

20   Barnfield College

Barnfield Business Training Services
Rotheram Avenue

Luton	Telephone	(0582) 484141
LU1 5PP	Fax	(0582) 484141

Contact   Mr M. Miller, General Manager

TRAINING

Dutch	*Type:* client-based; institution-based; group; one-to-one; bespoke
French	*Type:* client-based; institution-based; group; one-to-one; bespoke
	Method: intensive; non-intensive; open or flexible
German	*Type:* client-based; institution-based; group; one-to-one; bespoke (specialisms: financial; commercial; medical; engineering)
	Method: intensive; non-intensive; open or flexible
Italian	*Type:* client-based; institution-based; group; one-to-one; bespoke (specialisms: commercial; exporting)
	Method: intensive; non-intensive; open or flexible
Japanese	*Type:* client-based; institution-based; group; one-to-one; bespoke
	Method: intensive; non-intensive; open or flexible
Portuguese	*Type:* client-based; institution-based; group; one-to-one
Spanish	*Type:* client-based; institution-based; group; one-to-one; bespoke
	Method: intensive; non-intensive; open or flexible
Swedish	*Type:* client-based; institution-based; group; one-to-one; bespoke
Other	Arabic can be offered, with notice

SERVICES
Translating

French	into and out of English
German	into and out of English
Italian	into and out of English
Spanish	out of English
Specialism	commercial

FACILITIES

Equipment and materials:	computer-assisted language learning

NOTES
• has experience of undertaking language training needs analyses for employers

21   Barnsley College

Church Street
Barnsley   Telephone   (0226) 730191
S70 2AX   Fax   (0226) 298514

Contact   Mr D. Staniforth, Programme Manager, Modern Languages

TRAINING

French	*Type:* client-based; institution-based; group; one-to-one; bespoke
	Method: intensive; non-intensive; open or flexible
German	*Type:* client-based; institution-based; group; one-to-one; bespoke
	Method: intensive; non-intensive; open or flexible
Italian	*Type:* institution-based
	Method: non-intensive
Russian	*Type:* client-based; institution-based; group; one-to-one; bespoke
	Method: intensive; non-intensive; open or flexible
Spanish	*Type:* client-based; institution-based; group; one-to-one; bespoke
	Method: intensive; non-intensive; open or flexible

FACILITIES

Equipment and
  materials: language workshop with facilities for independent study

22   Barry College

Colcot Road
Barry   Telephone   (0446) 743519
CF6 8YJ   Fax   (0446) 732667

Contact   Mr H. Scarratt, Dean of Faculty of General Education

TRAINING
French   *Type:* client-based; institution-based; group
                       Method: intensive; non-intensive
German   *Type:* client-based; institution-based; group
                       Method: intensive; non-intensive
Specialism   business
Other   Dutch, Italian, Spanish and Greek can be offered, with notice

SERVICES
Translating
French   into and out of English
German   into and out of English
Greek   into and out of English
Italian   into and out of English
Russian   into and out of English
Spanish   into and out of English
Interpreting
French   consecutive
German   consecutive
Italian   consecutive
Russian   consecutive
Spanish   consecutive

FACILITIES
Language labs: 10–25 places - 1 fixed
Equipment and
  materials: audio and videocassettes

NOTES
• has experience of undertaking language training needs analyses for employers

23 Basildon College

Nethermayne
Basildon   Telephone   (0268) 532015
SS16 5NN   Fax   (0268) 522139

Contact   Mrs C. Stylianou, Head of Communications and Languages

TRAINING

French   *Type:* client-based; institution-based; group; one-to-one; bespoke
                Method: intensive; non-intensive; open or flexible

German   *Type:* client-based; institution-based; group; one-to-one; bespoke
                Method: intensive; non-intensive; open or flexible

Italian   *Type:* client-based; institution-based; group; one-to-one; bespoke
                Method: intensive; non-intensive; open or flexible

Russian   *Type:* client-based

Spanish   *Type:* client-based; institution-based; group; one-to-one; bespoke
                Method: intensive; non-intensive; open or flexible

Other   Finnish, Dutch, Farsi, Urdu, Norwegian, Romanian, Hungarian and
                Danish can be offered, with notice

SERVICES

Translating

Danish   into and out of English
Dutch   into and out of English
Farsi   into and out of English
Finnish   into and out of English
French   into and out of English
German   into and out of English
Hungarian   into and out of English
Italian   into and out of English
Norwegian   into and out of English
Romanian   into and out of English
Russian   into and out of English
Spanish   into and out of English
Urdu   into and out of English

FACILITIES

Language labs: 10–25 places - 1 fixed
Equipment and
   materials: computer-assisted language learning

NOTES

• has experience of undertaking language training needs analyses for employers

24   Basingstoke College of Technology

Worting Road
Basingstoke   Telephone   (0256) 54141
RG21 1TN   Fax   (0256) 810007

Contact   Mrs A. Paton, Senior Lecturer in Languages

TRAINING
Arabic   *Type:* institution-based; group
                  Method: non-intensive
Chinese   *Type:* institution-based; group
                  Method: non-intensive
French   *Type:* client-based; institution-based; group; one-to-one; bespoke
                  Method: intensive; non-intensive
German   *Type:* client-based; institution-based; group; one-to-one; bespoke
                  Method: intensive; non-intensive
Greek   *Type:* institution-based; group
                  Method: non-intensive
Italian   *Type:* client-based; institution-based; group; one-to-one; bespoke
                  Method: intensive; non-intensive
Japanese   *Type:* institution-based; group
                  Method: non-intensive
Portuguese   *Type:* client-based; institution-based; group; one-to-one
                  Method: intensive; non-intensive
Russian   *Type:* institution-based; group
                  Method: intensive; non-intensive
Spanish   *Type:* client-based; institution-based; group; one-to-one; bespoke
                  Method: intensive; non-intensive
Specialisms   legal; marketing; technical; business; computers; financial
Other   Additional languages can be offered, with notice

SERVICES
Interpreting
French   consecutive
German   consecutive
Italian   consecutive
Spanish   consecutive

FACILITIES
Language labs: 10–25 places - 1 fixed

NOTES
• has experience of undertaking language training needs analyses for employers
• offers culture briefing seminars

25   City of Bath College

Avon Street
Bath   Telephone   (0225) 312191
BA1 1UP   Fax   (0225) 444213

Contact   Ms H. Norris-Evans, Deputy Head of Languages School

TRAINING
French   *Type:* client-based; institution-based; group; one-to-one; bespoke
                        Method: non-intensive; open or flexible
German   *Type:* client-based; institution-based; group; one-to-one; bespoke
                        Method: non-intensive; open or flexible
Italian   *Type:* client-based; institution-based; group; one-to-one; bespoke
                        Method: non-intensive; open or flexible
Spanish   *Type:* client-based; institution-based; group; one-to-one; bespoke
                        Method: non-intensive; open or flexible

FACILITIES
Language labs: 10–25 places - 1 fixed
Equipment and
  materials: audio and videocassettes

NOTES
• has experience of undertaking language training needs analyses for employers

26 Bath College of Higher Education

Newton Park
Bath   Telephone   (0225) 873701
BA2 9BN   Fax   (0225) 874123

Contact   Mr M. Jenkins, Manager, Japanese Business Unit

TRAINING

Chinese   *Type:* client-based; institution-based; group; one-to-one; bespoke
                  Method: intensive; non-intensive
Japanese   *Type:* client-based; institution-based; group; one-to-one; bespoke
                  (specialism: tourism)
                  Method: intensive; non-intensive; open or flexible

SERVICES
Translating
Japanese   into and out of English
Interpreting
Japanese   consecutive

NOTES
- has experience of undertaking language training needs analyses for employers
- has produced open learning products on 'Doing Business with the Japanese' and 'Teach Yourself Business Japanese'
- operates the Bath Business Japanese Programme, a one year intensive language and business course, supported by the DTI

27   Bedford College of Higher Education

Cauldwell Street
Bedford   Telephone   (0234) 345151
MK43 7PY   Fax   (0234) 342674

Contact   Mrs C. Kenyon, Curriculum Manager, Business and Computing

TRAINING

French   *Type:* client-based; institution-based; group; one-to-one
           Method: intensive; non-intensive; open or flexible
German   *Type:* client-based; institution-based; group; one-to-one; bespoke
           (specialisms: technical; engineering)
           Method: intensive; non-intensive; open or flexible
Italian   *Type:* client-based; institution-based; group; one-to-one
           Method: non-intensive; open or flexible
Russian   *Type:* client-based; institution-based; group; one-to-one
           Method: non-intensive
Spanish   *Type:* client-based; institution-based; group; one-to-one
           Method: non-intensive; open or flexible
Other   Additional languages can be offered, with notice

SERVICES
Translating
French   into and out of English
German   into and out of English
Spanish   into and out of English
Interpreting
French   consecutive
German   consecutive

FACILITIES
Language labs: 10–25 places - 1 fixed

NOTES
• has experience of undertaking language training needs analyses for employers

28   Belfast Institute of Further and Higher Education

Park House
Great Victoria Street
Belfast   Telephone   (0232) 325312
BT2 7AG   Fax   (0232) 311557

Contact   Miss C. Delargy, Language Co-ordinator

TRAINING
Dutch   *Type:* client-based; institution-based; group; bespoke
                Method: non-intensive
French   *Type:* client-based; institution-based; group; one-to-one; bespoke
                (specialisms: secretarial; financial; business; scientific; beauty
                therapy; hairdressing; tourism)
                Method: intensive; non-intensive; open or flexible
German   *Type:* client-based; institution-based; group; bespoke (specialisms:
                secretarial; beauty therapy; hairdressing; tourism)
                Method: non-intensive; open or flexible
Irish   *Type:* client-based; institution-based
                Method: non-intensive
Italian   *Type:* client-based; institution-based; group; bespoke (specialism:
                ceramics)
                Method: intensive; non-intensive
Japanese   *Type:* client-based; institution-based; group
                Method: non-intensive
Romanian   *Type:* client-based; institution-based; group
                Method: non-intensive
Russian   *Type:* client-based; institution-based; group
                Method: non-intensive
Spanish   *Type:* client-based; institution-based; group; bespoke (specialisms:
                secretarial; beauty therapy; hairdressing; tourism)
                Method: non-intensive
Other   Arabic can be offered, with notice

SERVICES
Translating
French   into and out of English
German   into and out of English
Italian   into and out of English
Japanese   into and out of English
Russian   into and out of English
Spanish   into and out of English
Specialism   business

Interpreting

Dutch	consecutive
French	consecutive
German	consecutive
Japanese	consecutive
Russian	consecutive
Spanish	simultaneous

FACILITIES

Language labs:	10–25 places - 1 fixed
Equipment and materials:	interactive video; audiocassettes

NOTES
• has experience of undertaking language training needs analyses for employers

29   Bell College of Technology

Almada Street
Hamilton   Telephone   (0698) 283100
ML3 0JB   Fax   (0698) 282131

Contact   Mr T. Lamont, Industrial Liaison Officer

TRAINING
French   *Type:* client-based; institution-based; group; one-to-one
                  Method: intensive; non-intensive
German   *Type:* client-based; institution-based; group; one-to-one
                  Method: intensive; non-intensive
Italian   *Type:* client-based; institution-based; group; one-to-one; bespoke
                  Method: intensive; non-intensive
Spanish   *Type:* client-based; institution-based; group; one-to-one; bespoke
                  Method: intensive; non-intensive

SERVICES
Translating
French   into English
German   into and out of English
Italian   into English
Polish   into and out of English
Russian   into English
Spanish   into English
Interpreting
French   consecutive
German   consecutive
Italian   consecutive
Spanish   consecutive

FACILITIES
Language labs: 10–25 places - 1 fixed

NOTES
• has experience of undertaking language training needs analyses for employers

30   Beverley College

Beverley Consultancy and Training Services
Gallows Lane
Beverley   Telephone   (0482) 863748
HU17 7DT   Fax   (0482) 866784

Contact   Ms S. Beneiche, Director of Training Services

TRAINING
Dutch   *Type:* client-based; institution-based; group; one-to-one; bespoke
French   *Type:* client-based; institution-based; group; one-to-one; bespoke
             Method: intensive; non-intensive; open or flexible
German   *Type:* client-based; institution-based; group; one-to-one; bespoke
             Method: intensive; non-intensive; open or flexible
Italian   *Type:* client-based; institution-based; group; one-to-one; bespoke
             Method: intensive; non-intensive; open or flexible
Japanese   *Type:* client-based; institution-based; group; one-to-one; bespoke
             Method: intensive; non-intensive
Polish   *Type:* institution-based
Russian   *Type:* client-based; institution-based; group; one-to-one; bespoke
             Method: intensive; non-intensive
Spanish   *Type:* client-based; institution-based; group; one-to-one; bespoke
             Method: intensive; non-intensive; open or flexible

SERVICES
Translating
French   into and out of English
German   into and out of English
Italian   into and out of English
Japanese   into and out of English
Russian   into and out of English
Spanish   into and out of English
Interpreting
French   simultaneous; consecutive
German   simultaneous; consecutive
Italian   simultaneous; consecutive
Japanese   simultaneous; consecutive
Russian   simultaneous; consecutive
Spanish   simultaneous; consecutive

FACILITIES
Equipment and
  materials: audiocassettes

NOTES
• has experience of undertaking language training needs analyses for employers

31   Bicton College

Accent International
East Budleigh   Telephone   (0395) 67789
EX9 7BY   Fax   (0395) 68195

Contact   Mr M. Waistell, Director

TRAINING
French   *Type:* client-based; institution-based; group; one-to-one; bespoke
                (specialism: business)
                Method: intensive; non-intensive
German   *Type:* client-based; institution-based; group; one-to-one; bespoke
                (specialisms: business; financial)
                Method: intensive; non-intensive
Italian   *Type:* institution-based; group; one-to-one; bespoke (specialisms:
                business; financial)
                Method: intensive; non-intensive
Spanish   *Type:* institution-based; group; one-to-one; bespoke (specialisms:
                business; financial)
                Method: intensive; non-intensive

SERVICES
Translating
Arabic   into and out of English
Chinese   into and out of English
French   into and out of English (specialism: business)
German   into and out of English (specialism: business)
Italian   into and out of English
Japanese   into and out of English
Russian   into and out of English
Spanish   into and out of English
Swedish   into and out of English
Interpreting
French   simultaneous; consecutive

FACILITIES
Language labs: under 10 places - 1 portable
Equipment and
  materials: audio and videocassettes; computer-assisted language learning

NOTES
• has experience of undertaking language training needs analyses for employers
• also has centres in Italy, Spain and France

32   Bilston Community College

Westfield Road
Bilston
Wolverhampton   Telephone   (0902) 353877
WV14 6ER   Fax   (0902) 401897

Contact   Mr M. Arthur, Senior Lecturer

TRAINING

Arabic   *Type:* client-based; institution-based; group; one-to-one
                    Method: intensive; non-intensive; open or flexible
Chinese   *Type:* client-based; institution-based; group; one-to-one
                    Method: intensive; non-intensive; open or flexible
Czech   *Type:* client-based; institution-based; group; one-to-one
                    Method: intensive; non-intensive; open or flexible
Dutch   *Type:* client-based; institution-based; group; one-to-one
                    Method: intensive; non-intensive; open or flexible
French   *Type:* client-based; institution-based; group; one-to-one
                    Method: intensive; non-intensive; open or flexible
German   *Type:* client-based; institution-based; group; one-to-one
                    Method: intensive; non-intensive; open or flexible
Greek   *Type:* client-based; institution-based; group; one-to-one
                    Method: intensive; non-intensive; open or flexible
Gujarati   *Type:* client-based; institution-based; group; one-to-one
                    Method: intensive; non-intensive; open or flexible
Hindi   *Type:* client-based; institution-based; group; one-to-one
                    Method: intensive; non-intensive; open or flexible
Irish   *Type:* client-based; institution-based; group; one-to-one
                    Method: intensive; non-intensive; open or flexible
Italian   *Type:* client-based; institution-based; group; one-to-one
                    Method: intensive; non-intensive; open or flexible
Japanese   *Type:* client-based; institution-based; group; one-to-one
                    Method: intensive; non-intensive; open or flexible
Portuguese   *Type:* client-based; institution-based; group; one-to-one
                    Method: intensive; non-intensive; open or flexible
Punjabi   *Type:* client-based; institution-based; group; one-to-one
                    Method: intensive; non-intensive; open or flexible
Russian   *Type:* client-based; institution-based; group; one-to-one
                    Method: intensive; non-intensive; open or flexible
Serbo-Croat   *Type:* client-based; institution-based; group; one-to-one
                    Method: intensive; non-intensive; open or flexible
Spanish   *Type:* client-based; institution-based; group; one-to-one
                    Method: intensive; non-intensive; open or flexible
Swedish   *Type:* client-based; institution-based; group; one-to-one
                    Method: intensive; non-intensive; open or flexible

Urdu	*Type:* client-based; institution-based; group; one-to-one
	Method: intensive; non-intensive; open or flexible
Other	Additional languages can be offered, with notice

SERVICES
Translating
Arabic	into and out of English
Chinese	into and out of English
Czech	into and out of English
Dutch	into and out of English
French	into and out of English
German	into and out of English
Greek	into and out of English
Gujarati	into and out of English
Hindi	into and out of English
Irish	into and out of English
Italian	into and out of English
Japanese	into and out of English
Portuguese	into and out of English
Punjabi	into and out of English
Russian	into and out of English
Serbo-Croat	into and out of English
Spanish	into and out of English
Swedish	into and out of English
Urdu	into and out of English

Interpreting
Arabic	simultaneous; consecutive
Chinese	simultaneous; consecutive
Czech	simultaneous; consecutive
Dutch	simultaneous; consecutive
French	simultaneous; consecutive
German	simultaneous; consecutive
Greek	simultaneous; consecutive
Gujarati	simultaneous; consecutive
Hindi	simultaneous; consecutive
Irish	simultaneous; consecutive
Italian	simultaneous; consecutive
Japanese	simultaneous; consecutive
Portuguese	simultaneous; consecutive
Punjabi	simultaneous; consecutive
Russian	simultaneous; consecutive
Serbo-Croat	simultaneous; consecutive
Spanish	simultaneous; consecutive
Swedish	simultaneous; consecutive
Urdu	simultaneous; consecutive

FACILITIES

Language labs:	under 10 places - 1 portable; 10–25 places - 3 fixed
Interpreting facilities:	10–25 places - 1 fixed
Equipment and materials:	various open learning materials; multi-lingual word processing facilities

NOTES

• has experience of undertaking language training needs analyses for employers

33   Birkbeck College

University of London
43 Gordon Square
London   Telephone   071-631 6135
WC1H 0PD   Fax   071-631 6270

Contact   Mrs J. Schrafnagl, Director, Language Centre

TRAINING

French   *Type:* client-based; institution-based; group; one-to-one; bespoke
                (specialism: business)
                Method: open or flexible
German   *Type:* client-based; institution-based; group; one-to-one; bespoke
                (specialisms: business; scientific; technical)
                Method: intensive; non-intensive; open or flexible
Japanese   *Type:* client-based; institution-based; group; one-to-one
                Method: open or flexible
Spanish   *Type:* client-based; institution-based; group; one-to-one; bespoke
                (specialism: business)
                Method: open or flexible
Other   Italian, Chinese, Russian and Portuguese can be offered, with notice

FACILITIES

Language labs: under 10 places - 1 fixed, 1 portable; 10–25 places - 1 fixed
Interpreting
  facilities: under 10 places - 1 fixed
Equipment and
  materials: computer-assisted language learning software on personal computers
                 in a range of European languages; satellite television; video; CD-
                 ROM

NOTES

- has experience of undertaking language training needs analyses for employers
- cultural briefing seminars are provided on Germany, Austria, Switzerland, France, Spain and Latin America
- French, German and Spanish translating and interpreting services (business and scientific specialisms) will be offered from 1993-94

34   University of Birmingham

Modern Languages Unit
Edgbaston
Birmingham   Telephone   021-414 3324
B15 2TT   Fax   021-414 5966

Contact   Mr J. Klapper, Modern Languages Unit Director

TRAINING
Czech   *Type:* client-based; institution-based; group; one-to-one
Dutch   *Type:* client-based; institution-based; group; one-to-one
French   *Type:* client-based; institution-based; group; one-to-one
German   *Type:* client-based; institution-based; group; one-to-one
            Method: intensive; non-intensive
Greek   *Type:* client-based; institution-based; group; one-to-one
Italian   *Type:* client-based; institution-based; group; one-to-one
            Method: non-intensive
Japanese   *Type:* client-based; institution-based; group; one-to-one
            Method: non-intensive
Portuguese *Type:* client-based; institution-based; group; one-to-one
Russian   *Type:* client-based; institution-based; group; one-to-one
Spanish   *Type:* client-based; institution-based; group; one-to-one
            Method: intensive; non-intensive
Other   Arabic can be offered, with notice

SERVICES
Translating
Arabic   out of English
Bengali   out of English
Czech   out of English
Dutch   into and out of English
French   into and out of English
German   into and out of English
Italian   into and out of English
Japanese   out of English
Polish   out of English
Portuguese   into English
Punjabi   out of English
Russian   into and out of English
Serbo-Croat   out of English
Spanish   into and out of English
Swedish   into English
Urdu   out of English

Interpreting

Arabic	consecutive
Bengali	consecutive
Czech	consecutive
Dutch	consecutive
French	consecutive
German	consecutive
Italian	consecutive
Japanese	consecutive
Polish	consecutive
Portuguese	consecutive
Punjabi	consecutive
Russian	consecutive
Serbo-Croat	consecutive
Spanish	consecutive
Swedish	consecutive
Urdu	consecutive

FACILITIES

Language labs:	10–25 places - 5 fixed
Equipment and materials:	audio and videocassettes; computer-assisted language learning

NOTES

• has experience of undertaking language training needs analyses for employers

35   Bishop Burton College

Bishop Burton
Beverley   Telephone   (0964) 550481
HU17 8QG   Fax   (0964) 551190

Contact   Mrs H. McIntyre, Business Training Liaison Officer

TRAINING

French   *Type:* client-based; institution-based; group; one-to-one (specialism: agriculture)
                Method: intensive; non-intensive
German   *Type:* client-based; institution-based; group; one-to-one
                Method: non-intensive
Italian   *Type:* client-based; institution-based; group; one-to-one (specialism: tourism)
                Method: non-intensive
Russian   *Type:* client-based; one-to-one (specialism: agriculture)
                Method: non-intensive

SERVICES

Translating
French   into English
Russian   into English
Specialism   agriculture
Interpreting
French   consecutive
Russian   consecutive
Specialism   agriculture

FACILITIES

Language labs: 10–25 places - 1 fixed
Equipment and
  materials: audio and videocassettes

NOTES
• has experience of undertaking language training needs analyses for employers

36   Blackburn College

Feilden Street
Blackburn   Telephone   (0254) 55144
BB2 1LH   Fax   (0254) 682700

Contact   Mrs L. Noon, Co-ordinator for Business Languages

TRAINING
Arabic   *Type:* institution-based; group
French   *Type:* client-based; group; one-to-one; bespoke
                    Method: intensive; non-intensive; open or flexible
German   *Type:* client-based; group; one-to-one; bespoke
                    Method: intensive; non-intensive; open or flexible
Greek   *Type:* institution-based; group
Gujarati   *Type:* institution-based; group
Italian   *Type:* client-based; institution-based; group; one-to-one
                    Method: intensive; non-intensive
Russian   *Type:* client-based; institution-based; group; one-to-one
Spanish   *Type:* client-based; one-to-one
                    Method: intensive; non-intensive; open or flexible
Urdu   *Type:* institution-based; group
Other   Portuguese can be offered, with notice

SERVICES
Translating
Arabic   into and out of English
French   into and out of English
German   into and out of English
Greek   into English
Gujarati   into and out of English
Italian   out of English
Russian   out of English
Spanish   into and out of English
Urdu   into and out of English
Interpreting
Arabic   consecutive
French   consecutive
German   consecutive
Gujarati   consecutive
Spanish   consecutive
Urdu   consecutive

FACILITIES

Language labs: 10–25 places - 1 fixed
Interpreting
  facilities: over 100 places - 1 fixed
Equipment and
  materials: satellite television; audio and videocassettes; computer-assisted language learning

NOTES
• has experience of undertaking language training needs analyses for employers

37 Blackpool and the Fylde College

Ashfield Road
Bispham
Blackpool   Telephone   (0253) 52352
FY2 0HB   Fax   (0253) 56127

Contact   Ms M. McDermott, Acting Head of Business Studies

TRAINING

Dutch   *Type:* institution-based; group
             Method: non-intensive; open or flexible
French   *Type:* client-based; institution-based; group; bespoke (specialism:
             executive assistants)
             Method: non-intensive; open or flexible
German   *Type:* client-based; institution-based; group; bespoke (specialism:
             executive assistants)
             Method: non-intensive; open or flexible
Greek   *Type:* institution-based; group
             Method: non-intensive; open or flexible
Italian   *Type:* institution-based; group
             Method: non-intensive; open or flexible
Portuguese   *Type:* institution-based; group
             Method: non-intensive; open or flexible
Russian   *Type:* institution-based; group
             Method: non-intensive; open or flexible
Spanish   *Type:* institution-based; group
             Method: non-intensive; open or flexible

FACILITIES

Language labs: 10–25 places - 1 fixed, 2 portable
Equipment and
  materials: audio and videocassettes; satellite television

NOTES

• has experience of undertaking language training needs analyses for employers

38   Bolton Institute of Higher Education

Deane Road
Bolton   Telephone   (0204) 28851
BL3 5AB   Fax   (0204) 399074

Contact   Ms K. Rosslyn, Language Network Co-ordinator

TRAINING
French   *Type:* client-based; institution-based; group; one-to-one; bespoke
                Method: intensive; non-intensive; open or flexible
German   *Type:* client-based; institution-based; group; one-to-one
                Method: intensive; non-intensive; open or flexible
Italian   *Type:* institution-based
                Method: intensive; non-intensive; open or flexible
Spanish   *Type:* client-based; institution-based; group
                Method: intensive; non-intensive
Other   Russian can be offered, with notice

SERVICES
Translating
French   into and out of English
German   into and out of English
Italian   into and out of English
Spanish   into and out of English

FACILITIES
Equipment and
  materials: computer-assisted language learning

NOTES
• has experience of undertaking language training needs analyses for employers
• all language audits are free of charge

39   Bolton Metropolitan College

Manchester Road
Bolton
BL2 1ER

Telephone	(0204) 31411
Fax	(0204) 380774

Contact   Mr M. Lane, Lecturer in Charge of Modern Languages

TRAINING

French   *Type:* client-based; institution-based; group; one-to-one
              Method: intensive; non-intensive; open or flexible

German   *Type:* client-based; institution-based; group; one-to-one
              Method: intensive; non-intensive; open or flexible

Spanish   *Type:* client-based; institution-based; group; one-to-one
              Method: intensive; non-intensive

FACILITIES

Language labs: under 10 places - 1 portable; 10–25 places - 1 fixed
Equipment and
   materials: interactive video

40 Borders College

Thorniedean
Melrose Road
Galashiels   Telephone   (0896) 57755
TD1 2AF   Fax   (0896) 58179

Contact   Ms F. Chevalier, PICKUP Language Unit Co-ordinator

TRAINING

Dutch   *Type:* institution-based; group; one-to-one
French   *Type:* client-based; institution-based; group; one-to-one; bespoke
             (specialism: business)
             Method: intensive; non-intensive; open or flexible
German   *Type:* client-based; institution-based; group; one-to-one; bespoke
             (specialism: business)
             Method: intensive; non-intensive; open or flexible
Italian   *Type:* client-based; institution-based; group; one-to-one; bespoke
             (specialism: business)
             Method: intensive; non-intensive; open or flexible
Portuguese   *Type:* institution-based; group; one-to-one
Russian   *Type:* client-based; institution-based; one-to-one
             Method: intensive
Spanish   *Type:* client-based; institution-based; group; one-to-one
             Method: intensive; non-intensive; open or flexible
Other   Japanese for business, from Stirling University, can be offered, with
             notice

SERVICES

Translating
French   into and out of English (specialism: business)
German   into and out of English (specialism: business)
Italian   into and out of English (specialisms: business; economics)
Spanish   into and out of English (specialism: business)
Interpreting
French   consecutive
German   consecutive
Italian   consecutive

FACILITIES

Language labs: under 10 places - 3 portable, 2 fixed
Equipment and
  materials: self study books and audiocassette packs, in French, German, Italian
                 and Spanish; some video packs

NOTES

• training in Russian is for beginners only

41   Boston College

Rowley Road
Boston   Telephone   (0205) 365701
PE21 6JF   Fax   (0205) 310847

Contact   Dr J. F. Glazier, Commercial Unit Manager

TRAINING
Dutch	*Type:* institution-based; group
Finnish	*Type:* institution-based; group
French	*Type:* client-based; institution-based; group; one-to-one; bespoke
	Method: intensive
German	*Type:* client-based; institution-based; group; one-to-one; bespoke
	(specialism: commercial)
	Method: intensive
Greek	*Type:* institution-based; one-to-one; bespoke
Indonesian	*Type:* client-based; institution-based; group; one-to-one; bespoke
Italian	*Type:* client-based; institution-based; group; one-to-one; bespoke
Polish	*Type:* institution-based; group
Portuguese	*Type:* client-based; institution-based; group; one-to-one; bespoke
Russian	*Type:* institution-based; group
Spanish	*Type:* client-based; institution-based; group; one-to-one; bespoke
	(specialism: Royal Air Force engineering)
	Method: intensive
Swedish	*Type:* institution-based; group

SERVICES
Translating
Danish	into English
Dutch	into and out of English
Finnish	into and out of English
French	into and out of English
German	into and out of English
Greek	into and out of English
Indonesian	into English
Italian	into and out of English
Polish	into and out of English
Portuguese	into and out of English
Russian	into and out of English
Spanish	into and out of English
Swedish	into and out of English

Interpreting
Danish	consecutive
Dutch	consecutive
Finnish	consecutive

French	consecutive
German	consecutive
Greek	consecutive
Indonesian	consecutive
Italian	consecutive
Polish	consecutive
Portuguese	consecutive
Russian	consecutive
Spanish	consecutive
Swedish	consecutive

FACILITIES
Language labs: under 10 places - 1 fixed, 2 portable

NOTES
• has experience of undertaking language training needs analyses for employers

42   Bournemouth University

Language Unit
Talbot Campus
Fernbarrow   Telephone   (0202) 595525
BH12 5BB   Fax   (0202) 515707

Contact   Mrs H. Lewis, Head of Language Unit

TRAINING
French   *Type:* institution-based; group
                   Method: non-intensive; open or flexible
German   *Type:* institution-based; group
                   Method: non-intensive; open or flexible
Spanish   *Type:* institution-based; group
                   Method: non-intensive; open or flexible
Specialism   business

FACILITIES
Language labs: over 25 places - 1 fixed
Equipment and
   materials: computer-assisted language learning; satellite television; audio and
                   videocassettes

43   Bournville College of Further Education

Bristol Road South
Northfield
Birmingham   Telephone   021-411 1414
B31 2AS   Fax   021-411 2231

Contact   Mr G. Preece, Head of Section, Foreign Languages

TRAINING

Arabic   *Type:* institution-based
                Method: intensive; non-intensive; open or flexible
Bengali   *Type:* client-based; institution-based; group; one-to-one; bespoke
Bulgarian   *Type:* client-based; institution-based; group; one-to-one; bespoke
Catalan   *Type:* client-based; institution-based; group; one-to-one; bespoke
Chinese   *Type:* group
French   *Type:* client-based; institution-based; group; one-to-one; bespoke
                Method: intensive; non-intensive; open or flexible
German   *Type:* client-based; institution-based; group; one-to-one; bespoke
                Method: intensive; non-intensive; open or flexible
Greek   *Type:* institution-based
Gujarati   *Type:* client-based; institution-based; group; one-to-one; bespoke
Hindi   *Type:* institution-based; group
                Method: intensive; non-intensive; open or flexible
Irish   *Type:* institution-based
Italian   *Type:* client-based; institution-based; group; one-to-one; bespoke
                Method: intensive; non-intensive; open or flexible
Japanese   *Type:* client-based; institution-based; one-to-one
                Method: intensive; non-intensive; open or flexible
Korean   *Type:* client-based; institution-based; group; one-to-one; bespoke
Polish   *Type:* client-based; institution-based; group; one-to-one; bespoke
Portuguese   *Type:* client-based; institution-based; group; one-to-one; bespoke
                Method: intensive; non-intensive
Punjabi   *Type:* institution-based
Romanian   *Type:* institution-based
Russian   *Type:* client-based; institution-based; group; one-to-one; bespoke
                Method: intensive; non-intensive; open or flexible
Spanish   *Type:* client-based; institution-based; group; one-to-one; bespoke
                Method: intensive; non-intensive; open or flexible
Urdu   *Type:* institution-based; group; one-to-one
                Method: intensive; non-intensive; open or flexible
Specialisms   commercial; personnel; scientific; industrial; legal

SERVICES
Translating

Arabic	into and out of English
Chinese	into and out of English
French	into and out of English
German	into and out of English
Italian	into and out of English
Japanese	into and out of English
Portuguese	into and out of English
Russian	into and out of English
Spanish	into and out of English

Interpreting

Arabic	simultaneous; consecutive
Chinese	simultaneous; consecutive
French	simultaneous; consecutive
German	simultaneous; consecutive
Hindi	simultaneous; consecutive
Italian	simultaneous; consecutive
Japanese	simultaneous; consecutive
Russian	simultaneous; consecutive
Spanish	simultaneous; consecutive
Urdu	simultaneous; consecutive

FACILITIES

Language labs:	10–25 places - 1 fixed
Equipment and materials:	audio and videocassettes; computer-assisted language learning

NOTES
• has experience of undertaking language training needs analyses for employers

44   Bracknell College

Church Road
Bracknell   Telephone   (0344) 420411
RG12 1DJ   Fax   (0344) 860720

Contact   Mrs J. Davies, Programme Manager

TRAINING
French   *Type:* client-based; institution-based; group; one-to-one; bespoke
                   (specialism: meteorological)
                   Method: non-intensive
German   *Type:* client-based; institution-based; group; one-to-one; bespoke
                   (specialism: computers)
                   Method: non-intensive
Italian   *Type:* client-based; institution-based; group; one-to-one; bespoke
                   Method: non-intensive
Japanese   *Type:* client-based; institution-based; group; one-to-one; bespoke
                   (specialism: computers)
                   Method: non-intensive
Russian   *Type:* client-based; institution-based; group; one-to-one; bespoke
                   Method: non-intensive
Spanish   *Type:* client-based; institution-based; group; one-to-one; bespoke
                   Method: non-intensive
Other   Dutch and Greek can be offered, with notice

SERVICES
Translating
French   into and out of English
German   into English
Italian   into English
Japanese   into and out of English
Russian   into and out of English
Spanish   into and out of English

FACILITIES
Language labs: 10–25 places - 1 fixed

NOTES
• has experience of undertaking language training needs analyses for employers

45   University of Bradford

Language Unit
Department of Modern Languages
Bradford   Telephone   (0274) 384578
BD7 1DP   Fax   (0274) 305340

Contact   Mr E. L. G. Harding, Director, Language Unit

TRAINING

Arabic   *Type:* institution-based; bespoke
                Method: open or flexible
Chinese   *Type:* institution-based; bespoke
                Method: open or flexible
Danish   *Type:* institution-based; bespoke
                Method: open or flexible
Dutch   *Type:* institution-based; group; bespoke
                Method: open or flexible
Farsi   *Type:* institution-based; bespoke
                Method: open or flexible
French   *Type:* institution-based; group; bespoke
                Method: open or flexible
German   *Type:* institution-based; group; bespoke
                Method: open or flexible
Greek   *Type:* institution-based; group; bespoke
                Method: open or flexible
Hebrew   *Type:* institution-based; bespoke
                Method: open or flexible
Hindi   *Type:* institution-based; bespoke
                Method: open or flexible
Hungarian   *Type:* institution-based; bespoke
                Method: open or flexible
Italian   *Type:* institution-based; bespoke
                Method: open or flexible
Norwegian   *Type:* institution-based; bespoke
                Method: open or flexible
Portuguese   *Type:* institution-based; bespoke
                Method: open or flexible
Punjabi   *Type:* institution-based; bespoke
                Method: open or flexible
Russian   *Type:* institution-based; group; bespoke
                Method: open or flexible
Spanish   *Type:* institution-based; group; bespoke
                Method: open or flexible
Swedish   *Type:* institution-based; bespoke
                Method: open or flexible

Turkish	*Type:* institution-based; bespoke
	Method: open or flexible
Urdu	*Type:* institution-based; bespoke
	Method: open or flexible
Other	Additional languages can be offered, with notice

SERVICES
Translating
Arabic	into and out of English
Bengali	into and out of English
French	into and out of English
German	into and out of English
Hindi	into and out of English
Italian	into and out of English
Portuguese	into and out of English
Punjabi	into and out of English
Russian	into and out of English
Spanish	into and out of English
Swedish	into and out of English
Urdu	into and out of English

Interpreting
Arabic	simultaneous; consccutivc
Bengali	simultaneous; consecutive
French	simultaneous; consecutive
German	simultaneous; consecutive
Hindi	simultaneous; consecutive
Italian	simultaneous; consecutive
Portuguese	simultaneous; consecutive
Punjabi	simultaneous; consecutive
Russian	simultaneous; consecutive
Spanish	simultaneous; consecutive
Swedish	simultaneous; consecutive
Urdu	simultaneous; consecutive

FACILITIES
Language labs:	10–25 places - 4 fixed
Interpreting facilities:	10–25 places - 2 fixed
Equipment and materials:	satellite television; audio and videocassettes; computer-assisted language learning

46   Bradford and Ilkley Community College

Great Horton Road
Bradford   Telephone   (0274) 753294
BD7 1AY   Fax   (0274) 753173

Contact   Mr G. Dewison, Senior Lecturer in Charge of Modern Languages

TRAINING

French   *Type:* client-based; institution-based; group; one-to-one; bespoke
                Method: non-intensive; open or flexible
German   *Type:* client-based; institution-based; group; one-to-one; bespoke
                Method: non-intensive; open or flexible
Italian   *Type:* client-based; institution-based; group; one-to-one; bespoke
                Method: non-intensive; open or flexible
Russian   *Type:* client-based; institution-based; group; one-to-one; bespoke
                Method: non-intensive; open or flexible
Spanish   *Type:* client-based; institution-based; group; one-to-one; bespoke
                Method: non-intensive; open or flexible
Other   Japanese and Arabic can be offered, with notice

FACILITIES

Language labs: 10–25 places - 5 fixed
Equipment and
  materials: audio and videocassettes

NOTES
• has experience of undertaking language training needs analyses for employers

47   Brasshouse Centre

50 Sheepcote Street
Birmingham   Telephone   021-643 0114
B16 8AJ   Fax   021-633 4782

Contact   Mrs N. Knight, Head of Brasshouse Languages Services

TRAINING

Arabic   *Type:* client-based; institution-based; group; one-to-one; bespoke
             Method: intensive; non-intensive; open or flexible
Catalan   *Type:* client-based; institution-based; group; one-to-one; bespoke
             Method: intensive; non-intensive; open or flexible
Chinese   *Type:* client-based; institution-based; one-to-one
             Method: intensive; non-intensive; open or flexible
Czech   *Type:* client-based; institution-based; group; one-to-one; bespoke
             Method: intensive; non-intensive; open or flexible
Danish   *Type:* institution-based; one-to-one
             Method: intensive; non-intensive; open or flexible
Dutch   *Type:* client-based; institution-based; group; one-to-one; bespoke
             Method: intensive; non-intensive; open or flexible
French   *Type:* client-based; institution-based; group; one-to-one; bespoke
             Method: intensive; non-intensive; open or flexible
German   *Type:* client-based; institution-based; group; one-to-one; bespoke
             Method: intensive; non-intensive; open or flexible
Greek   *Type:* institution-based; one-to-one
             Method: intensive; non-intensive; open or flexible
Hebrew   *Type:* client-based; institution-based; group; one-to-one; bespoke
             Method: intensive; non-intensive; open or flexible
Hungarian   *Type:* institution-based; one-to-one
             Method: intensive; non-intensive; open or flexible
Irish   *Type:* client-based; institution-based; group; one-to-one; bespoke
             Method: intensive; non-intensive; open or flexible
Italian   *Type:* client-based; institution-based; group; one-to-one; bespoke
             Method: intensive; non-intensive; open or flexible
Japanese   *Type:* client-based; institution-based; group; one-to-one; bespoke
             Method: intensive; non-intensive; open or flexible
Polish   *Type:* client-based; institution-based; group; one-to-one; bespoke
             Method: intensive; non-intensive; open or flexible
Portuguese   *Type:* institution-based; one-to-one
             Method: intensive; non-intensive; open or flexible
Romanian   *Type:* institution-based; group; one-to-one
             Method: intensive; non-intensive; open or flexible
Russian   *Type:* client-based; institution-based; group; one-to-one; bespoke
             Method: intensive; non-intensive; open or flexible

Spanish	*Type:* client-based; institution-based; group; one-to-one; bespoke
	Method: intensive; non-intensive; open or flexible
Swedish	*Type:* client-based; institution-based; one-to-one
	Method: intensive; non-intensive; open or flexible
Turkish	*Type:* client-based; institution-based; group; one-to-one; bespoke
	Method: intensive; non-intensive; open or flexible
Specialisms	legal; financial; computers; environment; architecture; banking
Other	Ukrainian, Serbo-Croat and Norwegian can be offered, with notice

SERVICES
Translating

Arabic	into and out of English
Catalan	into and out of English
Chinese	into and out of English
Czech	into and out of English
Danish	into and out of English
Dutch	into and out of English
French	into and out of English
German	into and out of English
Greek	into and out of English
Hebrew	into and out of English
Hungarian	into and out of English
Irish	into and out of English
Italian	into and out of English
Japanese	into and out of English
Polish	into and out of English
Portuguese	into and out of English
Romanian	into and out of English
Russian	into and out of English
Spanish	into and out of English
Swedish	into and out of English
Turkish	into and out of English
Specialisms	law; insurance; financial; medical; scientific; technical; patents; arts; media; commercial

Interpreting

Arabic	simultaneous; consecutive
Catalan	simultaneous; consecutive
Chinese	simultaneous; consecutive
Czech	simultaneous; consecutive
Danish	simultaneous; consecutive
Dutch	simultaneous; consecutive
French	simultaneous; consecutive
German	simultaneous; consecutive
Greek	simultaneous; consecutive
Hebrew	simultaneous; consecutive
Hungarian	simultaneous; consecutive

Irish	simultaneous; consecutive
Italian	simultaneous; consecutive
Japanese	simultaneous; consecutive
Polish	simultaneous; consecutive
Portuguese	simultaneous; consecutive
Romanian	simultaneous; consecutive
Russian	simultaneous; consecutive
Spanish	simultaneous; consecutive
Swedish	simultaneous; consecutive
Turkish	simultaneous; consecutive
Specialisms	legal; insurance; financial; medical; scientific; technical; patents; arts; media; commercial

FACILITIES

Language labs:	10–25 places - 1 portable
Equipment and materials:	audio and videocassettes

NOTES

- has experience of undertaking language training needs analyses for employers
- organises language weekends, Saturday schools and residential courses abroad

48   Bridgend College of Technology

Cowbridge Road
Bridgend   Telephone   (0656) 766588
CF31 3DF   Fax   (0656) 663912

Contact   Mr A. Beynon, Head of Business Centre

TRAINING

Dutch   *Type:* client-based; institution-based; one-to-one
French   *Type:* client-based; institution-based; one-to-one; bespoke
                  (specialisms: engineering; industrial)
                  Method: intensive; non-intensive; open or flexible
German   *Type:* client-based; institution-based; one-to-one; bespoke
                  (specialisms: local government; engineering)
                  Method: intensive; non-intensive; open or flexible
Greek   *Type:* client-based; institution-based; one-to-one
                  Method: intensive; non-intensive; open or flexible
Italian   *Type:* client-based; institution-based; one-to-one
                  Method: intensive
Japanese   *Type:* client-based; institution-based; one-to-one (specialism:
                  industrial)
                  Method: intensive
Norwegian   *Type:* client-based
                  Method: intensive; non-intensive; open or flexible
Russian   *Type:* client-based; institution-based; one-to-one
                  Method: intensive
Spanish   *Type:* client-based; institution-based; one-to-one
                  Method: intensive; non-intensive

FACILITIES

Language labs: 10–25 places - 2 fixed, 1 portable
Equipment and
  materials: satellite television; audio and videocassettes

103

49   Bridgwater College

Bath Road
Bridgwater   Telephone   (0278) 455464
TA6 4PZ   Fax   (0278) 444363

Contact   Mr J. Baglow, Senior Lecturer

TRAINING

French   *Type:* client-based; institution-based; group; one-to-one; bespoke
             Method: intensive; non-intensive

German   *Type:* client-based; institution-based; group; one-to-one; bespoke
             Method: intensive; non-intensive

Italian   *Type:* client-based; institution-based; group; one-to-one; bespoke

Spanish   *Type:* client-based; institution-based; group; one-to-one; bespoke
             Method: intensive; non-intensive

SERVICES

Translating
French   into and out of English
German   into and out of English
Italian   into and out of English
Spanish   into and out of English

Interpreting
French   simultaneous; consecutive
German   simultaneous; consecutive
Spanish   simultaneous; consecutive

FACILITIES

Language labs: 10–25 places - 2 fixed

NOTES

• has experience of undertaking language training needs analyses for employers

50   University of Brighton

Falmer

| Brighton | Telephone | (0273) 643339 |
| BN1 9PH | Fax | (0273) 690710 |

Contact   Ms R. Damian, Business Language Courses

NOTES
• see entry for Sussex and Kent Language-Export Centre

51 Brighton College of Technology

Pelham Street
Brighton   Telephone   (0273) 667788
BN1 4FA   Fax   (0273) 667703

Contact   Mr B. P. Moody, Head of School of Humanities

TRAINING

Chinese	*Type:* group
French	*Type:* institution-based; one-to-one
	Method: intensive; non-intensive; open or flexible
German	*Type:* institution-based
	Method: intensive; non-intensive
Italian	*Type:* institution-based
	Method: non-intensive
Spanish	*Type:* institution-based
	Method: non-intensive
Swedish	*Type:* group
	Method: non-intensive

FACILITIES

Language labs: under 10 places - 1 fixed; 10–25 places - 1 fixed
Equipment and
  materials: audio and videocassettes; satellite television; computer-assisted
                   language learning

NOTES
• offers Arabic and Dutch language training as part of its adult education programme

52   Brinsbury College

North Heath
Pulborough   Telephone   (0798) 873832
RH20 1DL   Fax   (0798) 875222

Contact   Mr A. Scott, Brinsbury Training Services Manager

TRAINING
French   *Type:* institution-based; bespoke
                Method: intensive
German   *Type:* institution-based; bespoke
                Method: intensive
Italian   *Type:* institution-based; bespoke
                Method: intensive
Russian   *Type:* institution-based; bespoke
                Method: intensive
Spanish   *Type:* institution-based; bespoke
                Method: intensive
Specialism   land-based industries

SERVICES
Translating
French   into and out of English
German   into and out of English
Italian   into and out of English
Russian   into and out of English
Spanish   into and out of English
Specialism   land-based industries
Interpreting
French   simultaneous; consecutive
German   simultaneous; consecutive
Italian   simultaneous; consecutive
Russian   simultaneous; consecutive
Spanish   simultaneous; consecutive
Specialism   land-based industries

FACILITIES
Equipment and
  materials: audio and videocassettes

53   University of Bristol

Department for Continuing Education
Queen's Road

Bristol	Telephone	(0272) 288183
BS8 1HR	Fax	(0272) 254975

Contact   Mr G. Windsor, Staff Tutor in Modern Languages

TRAINING

French
: *Type:* client-based; institution-based; group; one-to-one (specialism: business)
Method: intensive; non-intensive

German
: *Type:* client-based; institution-based; group; one-to-one (specialism: business)
Method: intensive; non-intensive

Italian
: *Type:* client-based; institution-based; group; one-to-one
Method: intensive; non-intensive

Japanese
: *Type:* client-based; institution-based; group; one-to-one

Korean
: *Type:* client-based; one-to-one (specialism: commercial)

Portuguese
: *Type:* institution-based; one-to-one (specialism: legal)

Russian
: *Type:* client-based; institution-based; group; one-to-one (specialism: politics)
Method: intensive; non-intensive

Spanish
: *Type:* client-based; institution-based; group; one-to-one
Method: intensive; non-intensive

Other
: Greek, Bulgarian, Chinese, Danish, Norwegian, Serbo-Croat and Swedish can be offered, with notice

FACILITIES

Language labs: 10–25 places - 2 fixed
Equipment and
  materials: audio and videocassettes; computer-assisted language learning

NOTES
- has experience of undertaking language training needs analyses for employers
- had for one year, full time, a member of staff to develop a programme of computer-assisted language learning materials

54   British Institute in Paris

11 rue de Constantine
75340 Paris CEDEX 07   Telephone   010 33 1 45 55 71 99
France   Fax   010 33 1 45 50 31 55

Contact   Dr E. Williamson, Head of French Department

TRAINING
French

Type: institution-based; group; one-to-one; bespoke (specialisms: legal; property; insurance; banking; social legislation; transport; communications)
Method: intensive (preparation in Britain followed by intensive course in Paris with possible back-up training in Britain or by correspondence)

SERVICES
Translating
French   into and out of English (specialisms: financial; legal)
Interpreting
French   consecutive (specialisms: financial; legal)

FACILITIES
Language labs: 10–25 places - 2 fixed
Equipment and
  materials: audiocassettes; computer-assisted language learning

NOTES
• has experience of undertaking language training needs analyses for employers

55   Bromley College of Technology

Rookery Lane
Bromley   Telephone   081-462 6331
BR2 8HE   Fax   081-462 7780

Contact   Mrs M. Miller, Deputy Head of Department - Secretarial, Language
                    and Communication Studies

TRAINING
French   *Type:* client-based; institution-based; group; one-to-one; bespoke
                    Method: intensive; non-intensive; open or flexible
German   *Type:* client-based; institution-based; group; one-to-one
                    Method: open or flexible
Italian   *Type:* client-based; institution-based; group; one-to-one
                    Method: open or flexible
Spanish   *Type:* client-based; institution-based; group; one-to-one
                    Method: non-intensive
Other   Dutch can be offered, with notice

FACILITIES
Language labs: over 25 places - 1 fixed
Equipment and
  materials: computer-assisted language learning

NOTES
• has experience of undertaking language training needs analyses for employers

\

56   Brooklyn College

Aldridge Road
Great Barr
Birmingham   Telephone   021-360 3543
B44 8NE   Fax   021-325 0828

Contact   Ms S. Akehurst, Section Leader, Languages and Communications

TRAINING
French   *Type:* client-based; institution-based; group; one-to-one; bespoke
                    Method: non-intensive; open or flexible
German   *Type:* client-based; institution-based; group; one-to-one; bespoke
                    Method: non-intensive; open or flexible
Japanese   *Type:* client-based; group
                    Method: non-intensive
Russian   *Type:* client-based; institution-based; group; one-to-one
Spanish   *Type:* client-based; institution-based; group; one-to-one; bespoke
                    Method: non-intensive; open or flexible

SERVICES
Translating
French   into and out of English
German   into and out of English
Japanese   into English

FACILITIES
Language labs: under 10 places - 2 portable

57   Brooksby College

Brooksby
Melton Mowbray   Telephone   (0664) 434291
LE14 2LJ   Fax   (0664) 434572

Contact   Miss C. Ahern, Lecturer in Business Studies

TRAINING
German   *Type:* institution-based; group
                        Method: non-intensive

FACILITIES
Language labs: under 10 places - 1 portable
Equipment and
  materials: audiocassettes; computer-assisted language learning

58   Broxtowe College

High Road Training and Consultancy
Beeston
Nottingham   Telephone   (0602) 224774
NG9 4AH   Fax   (0602) 257658

Contact   Operations Manager

TRAINING

Arabic   *Type:* client-based; institution-based; group; one-to-one; bespoke
                 Method: intensive
French   *Type:* client-based; institution-based; group; one-to-one; bespoke
                 Method: non-intensive
German   *Type:* client-based; institution-based; group; one-to-one; bespoke
                 Method: non-intensive
Hungarian   *Type:* client-based; institution-based; group; one-to-one; bespoke
                 Method: non-intensive
Italian   *Type:* client-based; institution-based; group; one-to-one; bespoke
                 Method: non-intensive
Polish   *Type:* client-based; institution-based; group; one-to-one; bespoke
                 Method: non-intensive
Russian   *Type:* client-based; institution-based; group; one-to-one; bespoke
                 Method: non-intensive
Spanish   *Type:* client-based; institution-based; group; one-to-one; bespoke
                 Method: non-intensive

FACILITIES
Language labs: 10–25 places - 1 fixed

NOTES
- has experience of undertaking language training needs analyses for employers
- although most of the institution's work is carried out in-company, it runs weekly after-work German and French sessions, which are suitable for beginners and improvers, as 'Telelang' equipment is available, as well as a tutor

59   Brunel College of Technology

Ashley Down
Bristol   Telephone   (0272) 241241
BS7 9BU   Fax   (0272) 249134

Contact   Mr D. Hughes, Senior Lecturer in Languages

TRAINING
French   *Type:* client-based; institution-based; group; one-to-one; bespoke
                Method: intensive; non-intensive
German   *Type:* client-based; institution-based; group; one-to-one; bespoke
                Method: intensive; non-intensive
Italian   *Type:* client-based; institution-based; group; one-to-one; bespoke
                Method: intensive; non-intensive
Spanish   *Type:* client-based; institution-based; group; one-to-one; bespoke
                Method: intensive; non-intensive
Other   Swedish can be offered, with notice

SERVICES
Translating
French   into and out of English
German   into and out of English
Interpreting
French   simultaneous; consecutive
German   simultaneous; consecutive

FACILITIES
Language labs: 10–25 places - 1 fixed
Equipment and
  materials: computer-assisted language learning

NOTES
• has experience of undertaking language training needs analyses for employers

60   Brunel University

Uxbridge	Telephone	(0895) 274000
UB8 3PH	Fax	(0895) 258728

Contact   Mrs U. McNab, Director of Language Centre

TRAINING

French
: *Type:* client-based; institution-based; group; one-to-one; bespoke (specialisms: engineering; scientific)
Method: intensive; non-intensive

German
: *Type:* client-based; institution-based; group; one-to-one; bespoke (specialisms: engineering; scientific)
Method: intensive; non-intensive

Russian
: *Type:* client-based; group; one-to-one; bespoke

FACILITIES
Language labs: 10–25 places - 2 fixed

NOTES
- has experience of undertaking language training needs analyses for employers
- offers a short, summer course in technical and business French

61   University of Buckingham

Hunter Street
Buckingham
MK18 1EG

Telephone   (0280) 814080
Fax   (0280) 822245

Contact   Mr D. Hunniford, Language and European Centre Director

TRAINING

French	*Type:* institution-based; group (specialisms: legal; business)
	Method: intensive; non-intensive
German	*Type:* institution-based; group (specialisms: legal; business)
	Method: intensive; non-intensive
Italian	*Type:* institution-based; group
Japanese	*Type:* institution-based; group
	Method: intensive; non-intensive
Spanish	*Type:* institution-based; group (specialisms: legal; business)
	Method: intensive; non-intensive

SERVICES
Translating

French	into and out of English (specialisms: legal; business)
German	into and out of English (specialism: business)
Italian	into and out of English
Japanese	into English
Spanish	into and out of English (specialism: business)

Interpreting

French	consecutive (specialisms: legal; business)
German	consecutive (specialism: business)
Japanese	consecutive
Spanish	consecutive

FACILITIES

Language labs:	10–25 places - 2 fixed
Interpreting facilities:	10–25 places - 1 fixed
Equipment and materials:	audiocassettes; computer-assisted language learning

62   Buckinghamshire College of Higher Education

Queen Alexandra Road
High Wycombe   Telephone   (0494) 522141
HP11 2JZ   Fax   (0494) 524392

Contact   Mrs J. Burnham, PICKUP Manager

TRAINING
French   *Type:* client-based; institution-based; group; one-to-one; bespoke
                    (specialisms: technical; computers)
                    Method: intensive; non-intensive; open or flexible
German   *Type:* client-based; institution-based; group; one-to-one; bespoke
                    (specialism: forestry)
                    Method: intensive; non-intensive; open or flexible
Italian   *Type:* client-based; institution-based; group; one-to-one; bespoke
                    Method: intensive; non-intensive
Spanish   *Type:* client-based; institution-based; group; one-to-one; bespoke
                    (specialism: management)
                    Method: intensive; non-intensive

FACILITIES
Language labs: 10–25 places - 1 fixed

NOTES
• has experience of undertaking language training needs analyses for employers

63   Bury Metropolitan College

Market Street
Bury   Telephone   061-763 1505
BL9 0BG   Fax   061-763 2228

Contact   Mrs L. Chatburn, Language Trainer

TRAINING
French   *Type:* client-based; institution-based; group; one-to-one
                Method: intensive; non-intensive; open or flexible
German   *Type:* client-based; institution-based; group; one-to-one
                Method: intensive; non-intensive; open or flexible
Spanish   *Type:* client-based; institution-based; group; one-to-one
                Method: intensive; non-intensive; open or flexible

SERVICES
Interpreting
French   consecutive
German   consecutive
Spanish   consecutive

FACILITIES
Language labs: over 25 places - 1 fixed

NOTES
• has experience of undertaking language training needs analyses for employers

64   C4 Language Services

North Holmes Road
Canterbury   Telephone   (0227) 767700
CT1 1QU   Fax   (0227) 470442

Contact   Mr A. Perkins, Principal Lecturer

TRAINING

French   *Type:* client-based; institution-based; group; one-to-one; bespoke
               Method: intensive; non-intensive; open or flexible
German   *Type:* client-based; institution-based; group; one-to-one; bespoke
               Method: intensive; non-intensive
Italian   *Type:* client-based; institution-based; group; one-to-one
               Method: intensive; non-intensive
Japanese   *Type:* client-based; institution-based; group; one-to-one
               Method: intensive; non-intensive
Russian   *Type:* client-based; institution-based; group; one-to-one
               Method: intensive; non-intensive
Spanish   *Type:* client-based; institution-based; group; one-to-one; bespoke
               Method: intensive; non-intensive
Specialisms   tourism; business; transport; chemical patents; legal
Other   Arabic and Turkish can be offered, with notice

SERVICES

Translating
French   into and out of English
German   into and out of English
Italian   into and out of English
Japanese   into and out of English
Russian   into and out of English
Spanish   into and out of English
Interpreting
French   consecutive
German   consecutive
Italian   consecutive
Japanese   consecutive
Russian   consecutive
Spanish   consecutive

FACILITIES

Language labs: under 10 places - 1 portable; 10–25 places - 1 fixed
Equipment and
   materials: audio and videocassettes; satellite television; computer-assisted
                 language learning

NOTES
- has experience of undertaking language training needs analyses for employers
- offers translation and interpreting services in most languages

65   Calderdale College

Calderdale Business Language Centre
Dean Clough Industrial Park
| Halifax | Telephone | (0422) 345631 |
| HX3 5AX | Fax | (0422) 350430 |

Contact   Ms A. Scrine, Business Language Centre Manager

TRAINING

French
: *Type:* client-based; institution-based; group; one-to-one; bespoke (specialism: legal)
Method: intensive; non-intensive

German
: *Type:* client-based; institution-based; group; one-to-one; bespoke (specialisms: financial; legal)
Method: intensive; non-intensive

Greek
: *Type:* client-based; institution-based; group; one-to-one; bespoke
Method: intensive; non-intensive

Hungarian
: *Type:* client-based; institution-based; group; one-to-one
Method: intensive; non-intensive

Italian
: *Type:* client-based; institution-based; group; one-to-one; bespoke
Method: intensive; non-intensive

Portuguese
: *Type:* client-based; institution-based; group; one-to-one; bespoke
Method: intensive; non-intensive

Russian
: *Type:* client-based; institution-based; group; one-to-one; bespoke
Method: intensive; non-intensive

Spanish
: *Type:* client-based; institution-based; group; one-to-one; bespoke (specialism: financial)
Method: intensive; non-intensive

Other
: Japanese, Chinese, Polish and Dutch can be offered, with notice

SERVICES
Translating
Czech	into and out of English
Danish	into and out of English
Dutch	into and out of English
French	into and out of English
German	into and out of English
Hungarian	into and out of English
Italian	into and out of English
Portuguese	into and out of English
Russian	into and out of English
Spanish	into and out of English
Swedish	into and out of English
Specialisms	technical; engineering; computers

Interpreting

Czech	consecutive
Danish	consecutive
Dutch	consecutive
French	simultaneous; consecutive
German	simultaneous; consecutive
Hungarian	consecutive
Italian	consecutive
Portuguese	consecutive
Russian	consecutive
Spanish	simultaneous; consecutive
Swedish	consecutive

FACILITIES

Language labs: under 10 places - 1 fixed

Equipment and
  materials: computer-assisted language learning; satellite television; audio and videocassettes

NOTES

• has experience of undertaking language training needs analyses for employers

66   Cambridge Regional College

Newmarket Road
Cambridge   Telephone   (0223) 277171
CB5 8EG   Fax   (0223) 277706

Contact   Mr P. Lett, Marketing Manager

TRAINING
French   *Type:* client-based; institution-based; group; one-to-one
                   Method: non-intensive
German   *Type:* client-based; institution-based; group; one-to-one
                   Method: non-intensive
Italian   *Type:* client-based; institution-based; group; one-to-one
Japanese   *Type:* client-based; group; one-to-one
Russian   *Type:* client-based; institution-based; group; one-to-one
Spanish   *Type:* client-based; institution-based; group; one-to-one
                   Method: non-intensive
Other   Scandinavian languages can be offered, with notice

FACILITIES
Language labs: 10–25 places - 1 fixed, 2 portable

NOTES
• has experience of undertaking language training needs analyses for employers

67   Cambuslang College

Village Centre
86-88 Main Street
East Kilbride   Telephone   (03552) 43018
G74 4JY   Fax   (03552) 31044

Contact   Mrs L. Melly, Head of Business Studies

TRAINING
French   *Type:* client-based; institution-based; bespoke (specialism: business)
                       Method: non-intensive
German   *Type:* client-based; institution-based; bespoke
                       Method: non-intensive
Other   Japanese, Spanish and Italian can be offered, with notice

SERVICES
Translating
French   into English
German   into English

NOTES
• has experience of undertaking language training needs analyses for employers

68   Cannock Chase Technical College

Progress Centre
Cannock
WS11 3JA

Telephone	(0543) 462200
Fax	(0543) 505714

Contact   Mr M. Ben L'Amri, Lecturer in Modern Languages

TRAINING

Arabic	*Type:* client-based; institution-based; group
	Method: intensive; non-intensive; open or flexible
French	*Type:* client-based; institution-based; group
	Method: intensive; non-intensive; open or flexible
German	*Type:* client-based; institution-based; group
	Method: intensive; non-intensive; open or flexible
Italian	*Type:* client-based; institution-based; group
	Method: intensive; non-intensive; open or flexible
Spanish	*Type:* client-based; institution-based; group
	Method: intensive; non-intensive; open or flexible
Other	Japanese and Russian can be offered, with notice

SERVICES
Translating

Arabic	into and out of English
French	into and out of English (specialism: technical)
German	into and out of English
Italian	into and out of English
Spanish	into and out of English

Interpreting

Arabic	simultaneous; consecutive
French	simultaneous; consecutive
German	simultaneous; consecutive
Italian	simultaneous; consecutive
Spanish	simultaneous; consecutive

FACILITIES

Language labs:	10–25 places - 1 fixed
Interpreting facilities:	10–25 places - 1 fixed

NOTES
• courses for telephonists, lorry drivers, coach drivers and the police are planned

69 Canterbury Christ Church College of Higher Education

North Holmes Road
Canterbury   Telephone   (0227) 767700
CT1 1QU   Fax   (0227) 470442

Contact   Mr A. Perkins, Principal Lecturer

NOTES
• see entry for C4 Language Services

70   Cardiff Institute of Higher Education

Colchester Avenue
Cardiff   Telephone   (0222) 551111
CF3 7XR   Fax   (0222) 480367

Contact   Mrs N. Catani, Lecturer in French

TRAINING
French   *Type:* client-based; institution-based; group; one-to-one; bespoke
                    Method: non-intensive
German   *Type:* client-based; institution-based; group; one-to-one; bespoke
                    Method: non-intensive
Spanish   *Type:* client-based; institution-based; group; one-to-one; bespoke
                    Method: non-intensive
Specialism   business
Other   Italian can be offered, with notice

SERVICES
Translating
French   into and out of English
German   into and out of English
Italian   into and out of English
Spanish   into and out of English
Interpreting
French   simultaneous; consecutive
German   simultaneous; consecutive
Spanish   simultaneous; consecutive

FACILITIES
Language labs: 10–25 places - 1 fixed
Equipment and
  materials: audio and videocassettes

NOTES
• has experience of undertaking language training needs analyses for employers

71 Cardiff Tertiary College

Trowbridge Road
Cardiff   Telephone   (0222) 794226
CF3 8XZ   Fax   (0222) 797041

Contact   Mrs M. Kane, Section Leader in Languages

TRAINING

Catalan	*Type:* client-based; institution-based; group; one-to-one; bespoke
Dutch	*Type:* client-based; institution-based; group; one-to-one; bespoke
French	*Type:* client-based; institution-based; group; one-to-one; bespoke (specialisms: engineering; geology) *Method:* intensive; open or flexible
German	*Type:* client-based; institution-based; group; one-to-one; bespoke (specialism: engineering) *Method:* intensive; open or flexible
Italian	*Type:* client-based; institution-based; group *Method:* intensive; open or flexible
Japanese	*Type:* client-based; institution-based; group; one-to-one; bespoke
Portuguese	*Type:* client-based; institution-based; group; one-to-one; bespoke
Spanish	*Type:* client-based; institution-based; group; one-to-one; bespoke *Method:* intensive; open or flexible
Other	Russian can be offered, with notice

FACILITIES

Language labs: over 25 places - 1 fixed
Equipment and
  materials: satellite television; audiocassettes

NOTES
• has experience of undertaking language training needs analyses for employers

72   Cardonald College

690 Mosspark Drive
Glasgow   Telephone   041-883 6151
G52 3AY   Fax   041-883 1315

Contact   Mr K. Bradley, International Adviser

TRAINING
Czech   *Type:* client-based; institution-based; group; one-to-one; bespoke
               Method: non-intensive
French   *Type:* client-based; institution-based; group; one-to-one; bespoke
               Method: intensive; non-intensive
German   *Type:* client-based; institution-based; group; one-to-one; bespoke
               Method: intensive; non-intensive
Hungarian   *Type:* client-based; institution-based; group; one-to-one; bespoke
               Method: non-intensive
Italian   *Type:* client-based; institution-based; group; one-to-one; bespoke
               Method: intensive; non-intensive
Polish   *Type:* client-based; institution-based; group; one-to-one; bespoke
               Method: non-intensive
Russian   *Type:* client-based; institution-based; group; one-to-one; bespoke
               Method: intensive; non-intensive
Spanish   *Type:* client-based; institution-based; group; one-to-one; bespoke
               Method: intensive; non-intensive

SERVICES
Translating
Bulgarian   into and out of English
Czech   into and out of English
French   into and out of English
German   into and out of English
Hungarian   into and out of English
Italian   into and out of English
Polish   into and out of English
Russian   into and out of English
Spanish   into and out of English
Interpreting
Czech   consecutive
French   consecutive
German   consecutive
Hungarian   consecutive
Italian   consecutive
Polish   consecutive
Russian   consecutive
Spanish   consecutive

FACILITIES
Language labs: 10–25 places - 1 fixed, 1 portable

NOTES
• has experience of undertaking language training needs analyses for employers

73   Carlisle College

Victoria Place
Carlisle   Telephone   (0228) 24464
CA1 1HS   Fax   (0228) 514677

Contact   Mr J. Morgan, Co-ordinator for Languages and Europe

TRAINING
Arabic   *Type:* client-based; institution-based; group; one-to-one
            Method: non-intensive
French   *Type:* client-based; institution-based; group; one-to-one; bespoke
            Method: intensive; non-intensive
German   *Type:* client-based; institution-based; group; one-to-one; bespoke
            Method: intensive; non-intensive
Italian   *Type:* client-based; institution-based; group; one-to-one
            Method: non-intensive
Russian   *Type:* client-based; institution-based
            Method: non-intensive
Spanish   *Type:* client-based; institution-based; group; one-to-one; bespoke
            Method: intensive; non-intensive
Other   Additional languages can be offered, with notice

FACILITIES
Language labs: under 10 places - 1 portable

NOTES
• has experience of undertaking language training needs analyses for employers

74　Castlereagh College of Further Education

Montgomery Road
Belfast   Telephone   (0232) 797144
BT6 9JD   Fax   (0232) 401820

Contact   Mrs T. Cleary, Lecturer in Modern Languages

TRAINING
French   *Type:* institution-based; group; one-to-one
                Method: non-intensive; open or flexible
German   *Type:* institution-based; group; one-to-one
Spanish   *Type:* institution-based; group; one-to-one

FACILITIES
Equipment and
　materials: interactive video

NOTES
• has experience of undertaking language training needs analyses for employers

75   Central College of Commerce

300 Cathedral Street
Glasgow   Telephone   041-552 3941
G1 2TA   Fax   041-553 2368

Contact   Mrs M. A. McKillop, Senior Lecturer in Modern Languages

TRAINING
Chinese   *Type:* client-based; institution-based; group; one-to-one; bespoke
French   *Type:* client-based; institution-based; group; one-to-one; bespoke
                    (specialisms: business; hotel trade)
                    Method: intensive; non-intensive
German   *Type:* client-based; institution-based; group; one-to-one; bespoke
                    (specialisms: business; hotel trade)
                    Method: intensive; non-intensive
Japanese   *Type:* client-based; institution-based; group; one-to-one; bespoke
                    Method: intensive; non-intensive
Spanish   *Type:* client-based; institution-based; group; one-to-one; bespoke
                    Method: intensive; non-intensive
Other   Italian and Russian can be offered, with notice

FACILITIES
Equipment and
  materials: audiocassettes

NOTES
- has experience of undertaking language training needs analyses for employers
- offers 'survival' courses, one week intensive courses to the hotel industry and one to one advanced courses for business people needing negotiating skills, all in French and German

76 University of Central England in Birmingham

Perry Barr
Birmingham
B42 2SU

Telephone   021-331 5000
Fax   021-331 6543

Contact   Mr M. Gomez-Sanchez, Senior Lecturer

TRAINING

French	*Type:* institution-based; group
	Method: non-intensive; open or flexible
German	*Type:* institution-based; group
	Method: non-intensive; open or flexible
Spanish	*Type:* institution-based; group
	Method: non-intensive; open or flexible

FACILITIES

Language labs: 10–25 places - 3 fixed
Equipment and
  materials: audio and videocassettes; satellite television

77   University of Central Lancashire

Preston   Telephone   (0772) 893132
PR1 2TQ   Fax   (0772) 892900

Contact   Mrs J. Davies, Language-Export Centre Manager

NOTES
• see entry for Lancashire and Cumbria Language-Export Centre

78   Charles Keene College

Painter Street
Leicester   Telephone   (0533) 516037
LE1 3NA   Fax   (0533) 620592

Contact   Mr T. Gutteridge, Director of Operations

NOTES
• see entry for East Midlands Language-Export Centre

79   Chelmsford College of Further Education

Moulsham Street
Chelmsford   Telephone   (0245) 265611
CM2 0JQ   Fax   (0245) 266908

Contact   Mrs A. Whalley, Language Co-ordinator

TRAINING
French   *Type:* client-based; institution-based; group; one-to-one (specialism: telephone skills)
                    Method: intensive; non-intensive; open or flexible
German   *Type:* client-based; institution-based; group; one-to-one (specialism: telephone skills)
                    Method: non-intensive; open or flexible
Italian   *Type:* client-based; institution-based; group; one-to-one
                    Method: non-intensive; open or flexible
Spanish   *Type:* client-based; institution-based; group
                    Method: non-intensive; open or flexible
Swedish   *Type:* client-based; institution-based; group; one-to-one
Other   Dutch, Arabic and Russian can be offered, with notice

SERVICES
Translating
French   into and out of English
German   into and out of English
Italian   into and out of English
Japanese   into and out of English
Russian   into and out of English
Spanish   into and out of English
Swedish   into and out of English

FACILITIES
Language labs: 10–25 places - 1 fixed
Equipment and
  materials: audio and videocassettes; satellite television

NOTES
• has experience of undertaking language training needs analyses for employers

80 Cheltenham and Gloucester College of Higher Education

The Park
Cheltenham
GL50 2QF

Telephone   (0242) 532700
Fax   (0242) 532810

Contact   Mr S. Rodgers, Senior Lecturer in Languages

TRAINING

French
Type: client-based; institution-based; group; one-to-one; bespoke
Method: intensive; non-intensive

German
Type: client-based; institution-based; group; one-to-one; bespoke
Method: intensive; non-intensive

Greek
Type: client-based; institution-based; group; one-to-one; bespoke
Method: intensive; non-intensive

Italian
Type: client-based; institution-based; group; one-to-one; bespoke
Method: intensive; non-intensive

Japanese
Type: client-based; institution-based; group; one-to-one; bespoke
Method: intensive; non-intensive

Russian
Type: client-based; institution-based; group; one-to-one; bespoke
Method: intensive; non-intensive

Spanish
Type: client-based; institution-based; group; one-to-one; bespoke
Method: intensive; non-intensive

Other
Additional languages can be offered, with notice

SERVICES

Translating

French   into and out of English
German   into and out of English
Greek   into and out of English
Italian   into and out of English
Japanese   into and out of English
Russian   into and out of English
Spanish   into and out of English

FACILITIES

Language labs: under 10 places - 2 fixed; 10–25 places - 2 fixed
Equipment and
  materials: audio and videocassettes; computer-assisted language learning

NOTES

• has experience of undertaking language training needs analyses for employers

81   Chester College

Cheyney Road
Chester   Telephone   (0244) 375444
CH1 4BJ   Fax   (0244) 373379

Contact   Ms M. Best, Head of Languages

TRAINING

French   *Type:* client-based; institution-based; group; one-to-one; bespoke
              Method: intensive; non-intensive; open or flexible
German   *Type:* client-based; institution-based; group; one-to-one; bespoke
              Method: intensive; non-intensive; open or flexible
Italian   *Type:* client-based; institution-based; group; one-to-one; bespoke
              Method: non-intensive; open or flexible
Japanese   *Type:* client-based; institution-based; group; one-to-one; bespoke
              Method: non-intensive; open or flexible
Russian   *Type:* client-based; institution-based; group; one-to-one; bespoke
Spanish   *Type:* client-based; institution-based; group; one-to-one; bespoke
              Method: non-intensive; open or flexible
Other   Dutch and Portuguese can be offered, with notice

SERVICES
Translating
Danish   into and out of English
French   into and out of English
German   into and out of English
Italian   into and out of English
Japanese   into and out of English
Polish   into and out of English
Portuguese   into and out of English
Russian   into and out of English
Spanish   into and out of English
Interpreting
French   simultaneous; consecutive
German   simultaneous; consecutive
Italian   simultaneous; consecutive
Japanese   simultaneous; consecutive

FACILITIES
Language labs: 10–25 places - 1 fixed
Equipment and
   materials: computer-assisted language learning; telephone learning packs

NOTES
• has residential conference facilities

82   Chippenham Technical College

Cocklebury Road
Chippenham   Telephone   (0249) 444501
SN15 3QD   Fax   (0249) 653772

Contact   Mr K. Williams, Head of Languages Section

TRAINING

Chinese   *Type:* client-based; group
            Method: non-intensive
French   *Type:* client-based; institution-based; group; one-to-one
            Method: intensive; non-intensive; open or flexible
German   *Type:* institution-based; group; one-to-one
            Method: intensive; non-intensive; open or flexible
Greek   *Type:* client-based; institution-based; group; one-to-one
            Method: open or flexible
Italian   *Type:* institution-based; one-to-one
            Method: intensive; non-intensive; open or flexible
Japanese   *Type:* client-based; institution-based; group; one-to-one
            Method: non-intensive
Portuguese *Type:* client-based; institution-based; group; one-to-one
            Method: non-intensive; open or flexible
Russian   *Type:* institution-based; group; one-to-one
            Method: non-intensive
Spanish   *Type:* institution-based; group; one-to-one
            Method: intensive; non-intensive; open or flexible

SERVICES
Translating
Chinese   into English
French   into English
German   into English
Greek   into English
Hungarian   into English
Italian   into English
Japanese   into English
Portuguese   into English
Russian   into English
Spanish   into English
Turkish   into English

FACILITIES

Language labs: 10–25 places - 1 fixed, 1 portable

Equipment and
  materials: computer-assisted language learning; audio and videocassettes;
satellite television

NOTES

• has experience of undertaking language training needs analyses for employers

83   City and East London College

Bunhill Row
London   Telephone   071-638 4171
EC1Y 8LQ   Fax   071-588 9024

Contact   Mr R. Oultram, Enterprise Manager

TRAINING

French   *Type:* client-based; institution-based; group; one-to-one; bespoke
                  (specialisms: banking; transport)
                  Method: intensive; non-intensive
German   *Type:* client-based; institution-based; group; one-to-one; bespoke
                  Method: intensive; non-intensive
Italian   *Type:* client-based; institution-based; group; one-to-one; bespoke
                  Method: intensive; non-intensive
Russian   *Type:* client-based; institution-based; group; one-to-one; bespoke
                  Method: intensive; non-intensive
Spanish   *Type:* client-based; institution-based; group; one-to-one; bespoke
                  Method: intensive; non-intensive
Other   Additional languages can be offered, with notice

SERVICES
Translating
French   into English
German   into English
Italian   into English
Russian   into English
Spanish   into English

FACILITIES
Language labs: 10–25 places - 1 fixed
Equipment and
  materials: audio and videocassettes; computer-assisted language learning

NOTES
• has experience of undertaking language training needs analyses for employers
• has undertaken a language needs analysis for the new British Rail international
  terminal at Waterloo Station, London

84   City College (Norwich)

Ivory House
All Saints Green
Norwich   Telephone   (0603) 767922
NR1 3NB   Fax   (0603) 760910

Contact   Ms K. Maier, Manager, City College Enterprises

TRAINING

French   *Type:* client-based; institution-based; group; one-to-one; bespoke
               Method: intensive; non-intensive; open or flexible
German   *Type:* client-based; institution-based; group; one-to-one; bespoke
               Method: intensive; non-intensive; open or flexible
Italian   *Type:* institution-based; group
               Method: intensive; non-intensive; open or flexible
Japanese   *Type:* client-based; institution-based; group; one-to-one; bespoke
               Method: intensive; non-intensive
Russian   *Type:* client-based; institution-based; group; one-to-one; bespoke
               Method: intensive; non-intensive
Spanish   *Type:* institution-based; group
               Method: intensive; non-intensive; open or flexible
Other   Dutch can be offered, with notice

SERVICES

Translating
French   into and out of English
German   into and out of English
Italian   into and out of English
Japanese   into and out of English
Russian   into and out of English
Spanish   into and out of English
Interpreting
French   simultaneous; consecutive
German   simultaneous; consecutive
Italian   simultaneous; consecutive
Spanish   simultaneous; consecutive

FACILITIES

Language labs: 10–25 places - 1 fixed
Interpreting
  facilities: under 10 places - 1 fixed
Equipment and
  materials: computer-assisted language learning; language packs

NOTES
• has experience of undertaking language training needs analyses for employers

85   City University

Northampton Square
London   Telephone   071-477 8265
EC1V 0HB   Fax   071-477 8575

Contact   Mr T. J. Connell, Director of Language Studies

TRAINING

Danish   *Type:* institution-based; one-to-one; bespoke
                Method: intensive; non-intensive
French   *Type:* client-based; institution-based; one-to-one; bespoke
                Method: intensive; non-intensive; open or flexible
German   *Type:* institution-based; client-based; one-to-one; bespoke
                Method: intensive; non-intensive; open or flexible
Greek   *Type:* institution-based; client-based; one-to-one; bespoke
                Method: intensive; non-intensive; open or flexible
Italian   *Type:* institution-based; client-based; one-to-one; bespoke
                Method: intensive; non-intensive; open or flexible
Japanese   *Type:* institution-based; client-based; one-to-one; bespoke
                Method: intensive; non-intensive; open or flexible
Russian   *Type:* institution-based
                Method: intensive; non-intensive
Spanish   *Type:* institution-based; client-based; one-to-one; bespoke
                Method: intensive; non-intensive; open or flexible
Specialisms   business; engineering; media; property valuation; optometry;
                banking; financial
Other   Additional languages can be offered, with notice

SERVICES

Translating
Danish   into and out of English
French   into and out of English
German   into and out of English
Greek   into and out of English
Italian   into and out of English
Japanese   into and out of English
Latin   into English
Russian   into and out of English
Spanish   into and out of English
Specialisms   business; engineering

FACILITIES

Equipment and
  materials: computer-assisted language learning; audio and videocassettes;
                satellite television

NOTES
- has experience of undertaking language training needs analyses for employers
- has distance learning schemes in French, German and Spanish, and is preparing a scheme in Japanese

86   Clarendon College

The Language Centre
4 Hamilton Road
Nottingham   Telephone   (0602) 691198
NG5 1AU   Fax   (0602) 857040

Contact   Mrs B. Partridge, Telelang Co-ordinator

TRAINING

Arabic   *Type:* client-based; institution-based; group; one-to-one; bespoke
                Method: intensive; non-intensive
Danish   *Type:* institution-based; one-to-one; bespoke
French   *Type:* client-based; institution-based; group; one-to-one; bespoke
                Method: intensive; non-intensive
German   *Type:* client-based; institution-based; group; one-to-one; bespoke
                Method: intensive; non-intensive
Greek   *Type:* institution-based; group; one-to-one; bespoke
Hindi   *Type:* institution-based; group; one-to-one; bespoke
Italian   *Type:* client-based; institution-based; group; one-to-one; bespoke
                Method: intensive; non-intensive
Japanese   *Type:* client-based; institution-based; group; one-to-one; bespoke
                Method: intensive; non-intensive
Polish   *Type:* client-based; institution-based; group; one-to-one; bespoke
                Method: intensive; non-intensive
Portuguese   *Type:* client-based; institution-based; group; one-to-one; bespoke
Punjabi   *Type:* institution-based; group; one-to-one; bespoke
Russian   *Type:* client-based; institution-based; group; one-to-one; bespoke
                Method: intensive; non-intensive
Serbo-Croat   *Type:* client-based; institution-based; group; one-to-one; bespoke
                Method: intensive; non-intensive
Spanish   *Type:* client-based; institution-based; group; one-to-one; bespoke
                Method: intensive; non-intensive
Swedish   *Type:* client-based; institution-based; group; one-to-one; bespoke
                Method: intensive; non-intensive

FACILITIES

Language labs: under 10 places - 3 portable
Equipment and
  materials: portable video; audiocassettes; satellite television

NOTES
• has experience of undertaking language training needs analyses for employers

87 Clydebank College

Kilbowie Road
Clydebank   Telephone   041-952 7771
G81 2AA   Fax   041-951 1574

Contact   Mr G. Wells, Senior Lecturer in Languages

TRAINING

French
Type: client-based; institution-based
Method: intensive; non-intensive

Gaelic (Scottish)
Type: client-based; institution-based
Method: non-intensive

German
Type: client-based; institution-based
Method: non-intensive

Hindi
Type: client-based; institution-based
Method: non-intensive

Italian
Type: client-based; institution-based
Method: non-intensive

Japanese
Type: client-based; institution-based
Method: non-intensive

Russian
Type: client-based; institution-based

Spanish
Type: client-based; institution-based
Method: non-intensive

Urdu
Type: client-based; institution-based
Method: non-intensive; open or flexible

FACILITIES

Language labs: under 10 places - 1 fixed; 10–25 places - 1 fixed

NOTES

• has experience of undertaking language training needs analyses for employers

88   Colchester Institute

Sheepen Road
Colchester   Telephone   (0206) 763666
CO3 3LL   Fax   (0206) 763041

Contact   Ms J. Sexton, Business Development Manager, Professional
Training Centre

TRAINING

Dutch	*Type:* client-based; institution-based; group; one-to-one; bespoke
French	*Type:* client-based; institution-based; one-to-one; bespoke
	Method: intensive; non-intensive; open or flexible
German	*Type:* client-based; institution-based; group; one-to-one
	Method: intensive; non-intensive; open or flexible
Italian	*Type:* institution-based
	Method: non-intensive; open or flexible
Spanish	*Type:* client-based; institution-based; one-to-one
	Method: intensive; non-intensive; open or flexible
Specialisms	health and safety; quality management
Other	Portuguese, Swedish and Urdu can be offered, with notice

SERVICES

Translating

Dutch	into and out of English
French	into and out of English
German	into and out of English
Italian	into and out of English
Japanese	into and out of English
Portuguese	into and out of English
Spanish	into and out of English
Swedish	into and out of English
Urdu	into and out of English

Interpreting

Dutch	simultaneous; consecutive
French	simultaneous; consecutive
German	consecutive
Italian	consecutive
Japanese	consecutive
Portuguese	simultaneous; consecutive
Spanish	simultaneous; consecutive
Swedish	simultaneous; consecutive
Urdu	simultaneous; consecutive

FACILITIES
Language labs: self-access laboratory facilities

NOTES
• has experience of undertaking language training needs analyses for employers
• offers 'Rent a Prof' interpreting and 'Chat Line' language by telephone

89 Coleg Pencraig

Llangefni
Ynys Mon   Telephone   (0248) 750101
LL77 7HY   Fax   (0248) 722097

Contact   Mr J. Griffiths, Head of Business Studies

TRAINING
French   *Type:* institution-based
                 Method: non-intensive
German   *Type:* institution-based
                 Method: non-intensive
Japanese   *Type:* institution-based
                 Method: non-intensive
Welsh   *Type:* institution-based

90   Coleraine Technical College

Union Street
Coleraine   Telephone   (0265) 54717
BT52 1QA   Fax   (0265) 56377

Contact   Dr A. Heaslett, Head of Arts and Social Studies

TRAINING

French   *Type:* institution-based; group (specialism: business)
                     Method: non-intensive
Spanish   *Type:* institution-based; group (specialism: business)
                     Method: non-intensive
Other   German can be offered, with notice

91 Collingham, Brown & Brown Tutorial College

31 St Giles
Oxford   Telephone   (0865) 728280
OX1 3LF   Fax   (0865) 240126

Contact   Mrs C. Llewelyn, Principal

TRAINING

Arabic   *Type:* client-based; institution-based; group; one-to-one; bespoke
                 Method: intensive; non-intensive; open or flexible

Chinese   *Type:* client-based; institution-based; group; one-to-one; bespoke
                 Method: intensive; non-intensive; open or flexible

Danish   *Type:* client-based; institution-based; group; one-to-one; bespoke
                 Method: intensive; non-intensive; open or flexible

Dutch   *Type:* client-based; institution-based; group; one-to-one; bespoke
                 Method: intensive; non-intensive; open or flexible

Farsi   *Type:* client-based; institution-based; group; one-to-one; bespoke
                 Method: intensive; non-intensive; open or flexible

Finnish   *Type:* client-based; institution-based; group; one-to-one; bespoke
                 Method: intensive; non-intensive; open or flexible

French   *Type:* client-based; institution-based; group; one-to-one; bespoke
                 Method: intensive; non-intensive; open or flexible

German   *Type:* client-based; institution-based; group; one-to-one; bespoke
                 Method: intensive; non-intensive; open or flexible

Italian   *Type:* client-based; institution-based; group; one-to-one; bespoke
                 Method: intensive; non-intensive; open or flexible

Japanese   *Type:* client-based; institution-based; group; one-to-one; bespoke
                 Method: intensive; non-intensive; open or flexible

Malay   *Type:* client-based; institution-based; group; one-to-one; bespoke
                 Method: intensive; non-intensive; open or flexible

Norwegian   *Type:* client-based; institution-based; group; one-to-one; bespoke
                 Method: intensive; non-intensive; open or flexible

Polish   *Type:* client-based; institution-based; group; one-to-one; bespoke
                 Method: intensive; non-intensive; open or flexible

Portuguese   *Type:* client-based; institution-based; group; one-to-one; bespoke
                 Method: intensive; non-intensive; open or flexible

Russian   *Type:* client-based; institution-based; group; one-to-one; bespoke
                 Method: intensive; non-intensive; open or flexible

Serbo-Croat   *Type:* client-based; institution-based; group; one-to-one; bespoke
                 Method: intensive; non-intensive; open or flexible

Spanish   *Type:* client-based; institution-based; group; one-to-one; bespoke
                 Method: intensive; non-intensive; open or flexible

Swedish   *Type:* client-based; institution-based; group; one-to-one; bespoke
                 Method: intensive; non-intensive; open or flexible

Welsh	*Type:* client-based; institution-based; group; one-to-one; bespoke
	Method: intensive; non-intensive; open or flexible
Specialisms	commercial; scientific; legal
Other	Additional languages can be offered, with notice

SERVICES
Translating

Arabic	into and out of English
Chinese	into and out of English
Danish	into and out of English
Dutch	into and out of English
Farsi	into and out of English
Finnish	into and out of English
French	into and out of English
German	into and out of English
Italian	into and out of English
Japanese	into and out of English
Malay	into and out of English
Norwegian	into and out of English
Polish	into and out of English
Portuguese	into and out of English
Russian	into and out of English
Serbo-Croat	into and out of English
Spanish	into and out of English
Swedish	into and out of English
Welsh	into and out of English

FACILITIES
Language labs:	under 10 places - 1 fixed
Equipment and	
materials:	audio and videocassettes

NOTES
• has experience of undertaking language training needs analyses for employers

92   Coventry University

Priory Street
Coventry   Telephone   (0203) 838727
CV1 5FB   Fax   (0203) 221396

Contact   Mr C. Leonard, Head of Commercial Development

TRAINING

French	*Type:* client-based; institution-based; group; one-to-one; bespoke
	Method: intensive; non-intensive
German	*Type:* client-based; institution-based; group; one-to-one; bespoke
	Method: intensive; non-intensive
Italian	*Type:* client-based; institution-based; group; one-to-one; bespoke
	Method: intensive; non-intensive
Russian	*Type:* client-based; institution-based; group; one-to-one; bespoke
	Method: intensive; non-intensive
Spanish	*Type:* client-based; institution-based; group; one-to-one; bespoke
	Method: intensive; non-intensive
Specialism	technical
Other	Additional languages can be offered, with notice

SERVICES
Translating

French	into and out of English (specialism: engineering)
German	into and out of English (specialism: engineering)
Russian	into and out of English (specialism: technical)

Interpreting

French	simultaneous; consecutive
German	simultaneous; consecutive
Russian	simultaneous; consecutive

FACILITIES

Language labs:	10–25 places - 4 fixed
Interpreting facilities:	over 100 places - 1 fixed
Equipment and materials:	audio and videocassettes; interactive video; computer-assisted language learning

NOTES
• has experience of undertaking language training needs analyses for employers

93   Cranfield Institute of Technology

Cranfield School of Management
Cranfield
Bedford   Telephone   (0234) 751122
MK43 0AL   Fax   (0234) 751806

Contact   Mr J. Gladkow, Senior Lecturer

TRAINING
French   *Type:* client-based; institution-based; group; one-to-one
                 Method: intensive
German   *Type:* client-based; institution-based; group; one-to-one
                 Method: intensive
Russian   *Type:* institution-based
Spanish   *Type:* institution-based

SERVICES
Translating
French   into and out of English
German   into and out of English
Russian   into and out of English
Interpreting
French   simultaneous; consecutive
German   simultaneous; consecutive
Russian   simultaneous; consecutive

FACILITIES
Language labs: over 25 places - 1 fixed
Interpreting
  facilities: 26–100 places - 1 fixed

NOTES
• provides management development public and in-company courses, for which
  students tend to be of middle management to chief executive level, with an average
  age of 35

94   Crawley College of Technology

College Road
Crawley   Telephone   (0293) 612686
RH10 1NR   Fax   (0293) 522431

Contact   Mr D. J. Edwards, Language Co-ordinator

TRAINING

Arabic   *Type:* client-based; institution-based; group; one-to-one; bespoke
                   Method: intensive; non-intensive
French   *Type:* client-based; institution-based; group; one-to-one; bespoke
                   Method: intensive; non-intensive; open or flexible
German   *Type:* client-based; institution-based; group; one-to-one; bespoke
                   Method: intensive; non-intensive; open or flexible
Italian   *Type:* client-based; institution-based; group; one-to-one; bespoke
                   Method: intensive; non-intensive; open or flexible
Japanese   *Type:* client-based; institution-based; group; one-to-one; bespoke
                   Method: intensive; non-intensive
Portuguese   *Type:* client-based; institution-based; group; one-to-one; bespoke
                   Method: intensive; non-intensive
Russian   *Type:* client-based; institution-based; group; one-to-one; bespoke
                   Method: intensive; non-intensive
Spanish   *Type:* client-based; institution-based; group; one-to-one; bespoke
                   Method: intensive; non-intensive; open or flexible
Urdu   *Type:* institution-based; group; one-to-one; bespoke (specialism:
                   immigration)
                   Method: intensive; non-intensive
Other   Additional languages can be offered, with notice

FACILITIES
Language labs: 10–25 places - 1 fixed

NOTES
• has experience of undertaking language training needs analyses for employers
• has offered tuition by telephone

95   Cricklade College

Charlton Road
Andover   Telephone   (0264) 363311
SP10 1EJ   Fax   (0264) 332088

Contact   Mrs P. Brandon, Consultancy and Training Centre Manager

TRAINING
French   *Type:* client-based; institution-based; group; one-to-one; bespoke
                    Method: non-intensive; open or flexible
German   *Type:* client-based; institution-based; group; one-to-one; bespoke
                    Method: non-intensive; open or flexible
Italian   *Type:* client-based; institution-based; group; one-to-one; bespoke
                    Method: non-intensive; open or flexible
Spanish   *Type:* client-based; institution-based; group; one-to-one; bespoke
                    Method: non-intensive; open or flexible
Other   Additional languages can be offered, with notice

FACILITIES
Language labs: 10–25 places - 1 fixed

NOTES
• has experience of undertaking language training needs analyses for employers

96   Crosskeys College

Risca Road
Crosskeys
NP1 7ZA

Telephone   (0495) 270295
Fax   (0495) 272138

Contact   Mrs H. Beynon, Head of Modern Languages Section

TRAINING

French   *Type:* client-based; institution-based; group; one-to-one; bespoke
             Method: intensive; non-intensive; open or flexible
German   *Type:* client-based; institution-based; group; one-to-one; bespoke
             Method: intensive; non-intensive; open or flexible
Hungarian   *Type:* client-based; one-to-one; group; bespoke
             Method: intensive
Italian   *Type:* client-based; institution-based
             Method: non-intensive
Japanese   *Type:* institution-based; group
             Method: non-intensive
Spanish   *Type:* client-based; institution-based; group; one-to-one; bespoke
             Method: intensive; non-intensive; open or flexible

FACILITIES

Language labs: under 10 places - 4 portable; 10–25 places - 1 portable
Equipment and
  materials: computer room with modern languages software; video sets for
                  individual use; satellite television

NOTES

• has experience of undertaking language training needs analyses for employers

97   Croydon College

Croydon Business School
Fairfield
Croydon   Telephone   081-686 5700
CR9 1DX   Fax   081-760 5921

Contact   Mrs M. C. Belliere-Wilson, Modern Languages Course Director

TRAINING
French   *Type:* client-based; institution-based; group
                    Method: intensive; non-intensive; open or flexible
German   *Type:* client-based; institution-based; group
                    Method: intensive; non-intensive
Spanish   *Type:* client-based; institution-based; group
                    Method: intensive
Other   Portuguese can be offered, with notice

SERVICES
Translating
French   into English
German   into English
Italian   into English
Spanish   into English
Interpreting
French   simultaneous
German   simultaneous
Spanish   simultaneous

FACILITIES
Language labs: 10–25 places - 1 portable
Interpreting
  facilities: under 10 places - 1 portable
Equipment and
  materials: audio and videocassettes

NOTES
• has experience of undertaking language training needs analyses for employers
• specialises in short courses with a modular approach

98   Cumbernauld College

Town Centre
Cumbernauld   Telephone   (0236) 731811
G67 1HU   Fax   (0236) 723416

Contact   Mrs S. Smith, Head of General Education

TRAINING
French   *Type:* client-based; institution-based; group; one-to-one
                     Method: intensive; non-intensive
German   *Type:* client-based; institution-based; group; one-to-one
                     Method: intensive; non-intensive
Italian   *Type:* client-based; institution-based; group; one-to-one
                     Method: intensive; non-intensive
Spanish   *Type:* client-based; institution-based; group; one-to-one
                     Method: intensive; non-intensive

SERVICES
Translating
French   into English
German   into English
Italian   into English
Spanish   into English

FACILITIES
Language labs: 10–25 places - 1 fixed, 1 portable
Interpreting
  facilities: 10–25 places - 1 fixed, 1 portable
Equipment and
  materials: audiocassettes

99 Darlington College of Technology

Cleveland Avenue
Darlington   Telephone   (0325) 467651
DL3 7BB   Fax   (0325) 483843

Contact   Mr L. Baker, Director of Industrial Liaison

TRAINING

Afrikaans	*Type:* client-based; institution-based; group; one-to-one; bespoke
Arabic	*Type:* client-based; institution-based; group; one-to-one; bespoke
Danish	*Type:* client-based; institution-based; group; one-to-one; bespoke
	Method: intensive; non-intensive
Dutch	*Type:* client-based; institution-based; group; one-to-one; bespoke
	Method: intensive; non-intensive
French	*Type:* client-based; institution-based; group; one-to-one; bespoke
	Method: intensive; non-intensive; open or flexible
German	*Type:* client-based; institution-based; group; one-to-one; bespoke
	Method: intensive; non-intensive; open or flexible
Greek	*Type:* client-based; institution-based; group; one-to-one; bespoke
	Method: intensive; non-intensive
Hindi	*Type:* client-based; institution-based; group; one-to-one; bespoke
Italian	*Type:* client-based; institution-based; group; one-to-one; bespoke
	Method: intensive; non-intensive; open or flexible
Japanese	*Type:* client-based; institution-based; group; one-to-one; bespoke
	Method: intensive; non-intensive
Polish	*Type:* client-based; institution-based; group; one-to-one; bespoke
Portuguese	*Type:* client-based; institution-based; group; one-to-one; bespoke
	Method: intensive; non-intensive
Punjabi	*Type:* client-based; institution-based; group; one-to-one; bespoke
Russian	*Type:* client-based; institution-based; group; one-to-one; bespoke
	Method: intensive; non-intensive
Serbo-Croat	*Type:* client-based; institution-based; group; one-to-one; bespoke
Spanish	*Type:* client-based; institution-based; group; one-to-one; bespoke
	Method: intensive; non-intensive; open or flexible
Swahili	*Type:* client-based; institution-based; group; one-to-one; bespoke
Turkish	*Type:* client-based; institution-based; group; one-to-one; bespoke
Zulu	*Type:* client-based; institution-based; group; one-to-one; bespoke
Specialism	business
Other	Czech can be offered, with notice

SERVICES

Translating

| Czech | into and out of English |
| Danish | into and out of English |

French	into and out of English
German	into and out of English
Italian	into and out of English
Japanese	into and out of English
Polish	into and out of English
Russian	into and out of English
Spanish	into and out of English

Interpreting

French	simultaneous; consecutive

FACILITIES

Language labs:	under 10 places - 1 portable
Equipment and materials:	audio and videocassettes

NOTES

• has experience of undertaking language training needs analyses for employers

100 Daventry Tertiary College

Badby Road West
Daventry   Telephone   (0327) 300232
NN11 4HJ   Fax   (0327) 300942

Contact   Mrs L. Emerson, Lecturer in Modern Languages

TRAINING
French   *Type:* client-based; institution-based; group
     Method: intensive
German   *Type:* client-based; institution-based; group
     Method: non-intensive
Italian   *Type:* client-based; institution-based; group
Spanish   *Type:* client-based; institution-based; group
     Method: non-intensive
Specialism   business
Other   Russian can be offered, with notice

SERVICES
Translating
French   into and out of English
German   into and out of English
Italian   into and out of English
Spanish   into and out of English
Specialism   business
Interpreting
French   simultaneous; consecutive
German   simultaneous; consecutive
Italian   simultaneous; consecutive
Spanish   simultaneous; consecutive
Specialism   business

NOTES
• has experience of undertaking language training needs analyses for employers
• does not offer technical translating and interpreting

101   De Montfort University at Leicester

PO Box 143
Leicester   Telephone (0533) 551551
LE3 3HQ   Fax   (0533) 517548

Contact   Mr R. C. O'Brien, Senior Lecturer in German

TRAINING

French	*Type:* client-based; institution-based; group; one-to-one; bespoke (specialism: business)
	Method: intensive; non-intensive; open or flexible
German	*Type:* client-based; institution-based; group; one-to-one; bespoke (specialism: textiles)
	Method: intensive; non-intensive; open or flexible
Italian	*Type:* client-based; institution-based; group; one-to-one; bespoke
	Method: intensive; non-intensive; open or flexible
Spanish	*Type:* client-based; institution-based; group; one-to-one; bespoke
	Method: intensive; non-intensive; open or flexible
Other	Portuguese can be offered, with notice

SERVICES

Translating

Dutch	into and out of English (specialism: business)
French	into and out of English (specialism: business)
German	into and out of English (specialisms: business; textiles)
Italian	into and out of English (specialism: business)
Portuguese	into and out of English (specialism: business)
Spanish	into and out of English (specialism: business)

Interpreting

Dutch	consecutive (specialism: business)
French	consecutive (specialism: business)
German	consecutive (specialisms: business; textiles)
Italian	consecutive (specialism: business)
Portuguese	consecutive (specialism: business)
Spanish	consecutive (specialism: business)

FACILITIES

Language labs: 10–25 places - 1 fixed, 1 portable
Equipment and
 materials: audio and videocassettes; computer-assisted language learning

NOTES

• has experience of undertaking language training needs analyses for employers

102   Derby Tertiary College (Mackworth)

Prince Charles Avenue
Mackworth
Derby   Telephone   (0332) 519951
DE22 4LR   Fax   (0332) 510548

Contact   Mr R. Sfar-Gandoura, Deputy Director

TRAINING
French   *Type:* client-based; institution-based; group; one-to-one (specialism: business)
                Method: intensive; non-intensive; open or flexible
German   *Type:* client-based; institution-based; group; one-to-one (specialism: business)
                Method: intensive; non-intensive; open or flexible
Italian   *Type:* client-based; institution-based; group; one-to-one
                Method: intensive; non-intensive; open or flexible
Spanish   *Type:* client-based; institution-based; group; one-to-one
                Method: intensive; non-intensive; open or flexible
Other   Punjabi, Urdu, Russian and Japanese can be offered, with notice

SERVICES
Translating
French   into and out of English
German   into and out of English
Italian   into and out of English
Spanish   into and out of English
Interpreting
French   simultaneous; consecutive
German   simultaneous; consecutive
Italian   simultaneous; consecutive
Spanish   simultaneous; consecutive

FACILITIES
Language labs: under 10 places - 1 portable; 10–25 places - 2 portable
Equipment and
   materials: audio and videocassettes; satellite television; computer-assisted language learning

NOTES
• has experience of undertaking language training needs analyses for employers

103   Derby Tertiary College (Wilmorton)

Harrow Street
Derby   Telephone   (0332) 757570
DE2 8UG   Fax   (0332) 573149

Contact   Mr G. Doherty, Languages Workshop Co-ordinator

TRAINING
French   *Type:* institution-based
                         Method: open or flexible
German   *Type:* institution-based
                         Method: open or flexible
Spanish   *Type:* institution-based
                         Method: open or flexible

FACILITIES
Language labs: 10–25 places - 1 fixed
Equipment and
  materials: audio and videocassettes; satellite television; computer-assisted
                         language learning

104   Derwentside College

Business Development Centre
Park Road
Consett   Telephone   (0207) 502906
DH8 5EE   Fax   (0207) 502434

Contact   Mr P. Pickard, Manager, Business Development Centre

TRAINING
Dutch   *Type:* client-based; institution-based; group; one-to-one; bespoke
                   Method: intensive; non-intensive
French   *Type:* client-based; institution-based; group; one-to-one; bespoke
                   Method: intensive; non-intensive; open or flexible
German   *Type:* client-based; institution-based; group; one-to-one; bespoke
                   Method: intensive; non-intensive; open or flexible
Hebrew   *Type:* client-based; institution-based; group; one-to-one; bespoke
                   Method: intensive; non-intensive
Italian   *Type:* client-based; institution-based; group; one-to-one; bespoke
                   Method: intensive; non-intensive; open or flexible
Spanish   *Type:* client-based; institution-based; group; one-to-one; bespoke
                   Method: intensive; non-intensive; open or flexible
Other   Additional languages can be offered, with notice

SERVICES
Translating
French   into and out of English
German   into and out of English
Italian   into and out of English
Interpreting
French   consecutive
German   consecutive
Italian   consecutive

NOTES
• has experience of undertaking language training needs analyses for employers

105   Dewsbury College

Yorkshire Enterprise Services
Halifax Road
Dewsbury   Telephone   (0924) 465916
WF13 2AS   Fax   (0924) 457047

Contact   Mr B. Waddington, Yorkshire Enterprise Services Manager

TRAINING
Dutch   *Type:* client-based; institution-based; group; one-to-one; bespoke
                 Method: non-intensive
French   *Type:* client-based; institution-based; group; one-to-one; bespoke
                 Method: intensive; non-intensive; open or flexible
German   *Type:* client-based; institution-based; group; one-to-one; bespoke
                 Method: intensive; non-intensive; open or flexible
Greek   *Type:* client-based; institution-based; group; one-to-one; bespoke
                 Method: non-intensive
Gujarati   *Type:* client-based; institution-based; group; one-to-one; bespoke
                 Method: non-intensive
Italian   *Type:* client-based; institution-based; group; one-to-one; bespoke
                 Method: intensive; non-intensive; open or flexible
Japanese   *Type:* client-based; institution-based; group; one-to-one; bespoke
                 Method: non-intensive
Portuguese   *Type:* client-based; institution-based; group; one-to-one; bespoke
Spanish   *Type:* client-based; institution-based; group; one-to-one; bespoke
                 Method: intensive; non-intensive; open or flexible
Urdu   *Type:* client-based; institution-based; group; one-to-one; bespoke
                 Method: non-intensive
Other   Russian can be offered, with notice

FACILITIES
Language labs: 10–25 places - 1 fixed
Equipment and
  materials: audiocassettes

106　Doncaster College

Waterdale
Doncaster　　　　　　Telephone　　　(0302) 322122
DN1 3EX　　　　　　Fax　　　　　　(0302) 738065

Contact　　　　Mr E. Milner, Senior Lecturer in Modern Foreign Languages

TRAINING
French　　　　*Type:* client-based; institution-based; group; one-to-one; bespoke
　　　　　　　Method: intensive; non-intensive; open or flexible
German　　　　*Type:* client-based; institution-based; group; one-to-one; bespoke
　　　　　　　Method: intensive; non-intensive; open or flexible
Italian　　　　*Type:* client-based; institution-based; group; one-to-one; bespoke
　　　　　　　Method: intensive; non-intensive; open or flexible
Spanish　　　　*Type:* client-based; institution-based; group; one-to-one; bespoke
　　　　　　　Method: intensive; non-intensive; open or flexible

SERVICES
Translating
French　　　　into and out of English
German　　　　into and out of English
Italian　　　　into and out of English
Spanish　　　　into and out of English
Interpreting
French　　　　consecutive
German　　　　consecutive
Italian　　　　consecutive
Spanish　　　　consecutive

FACILITIES
Language labs:　under 10 places - 1 portable; 10–25 places - 1 fixed
Equipment and
　materials:　　videocassettes; computer-assisted language learning; satellite
　　　　　　　television

NOTES
• has experience of undertaking language training needs analyses for employers

107   Dorset Business School

Oxford Road
Bournemouth   Telephone   (0202) 595400
BH8 8EZ   Fax   (0202) 298321

Contact   Mr M. Woodhall, Language Centre Director

TRAINING
French   *Type:* client-based; institution-based; group; one-to-one; bespoke
                     Method: intensive; non-intensive; open or flexible
German   *Type:* client-based; institution-based; group; one-to-one; bespoke
                     Method: intensive; non-intensive; open or flexible
Specialism   business
Other   Spanish and Italian can be offered, with notice

FACILITIES
Language labs: under 10 places - 1 portable
Equipment and
  materials: computer-assisted language learning

NOTES
• has experience of undertaking language training needs analyses for employers
• the business school is part of Bournemouth University

108   Dudley College of Technology

The Broadway
Dudley   Telephone   (0384) 455433
DY1 4AS   Fax   (0384) 455975

Contact   Mr B. Brinkmann, Head of Modern Languages Department

TRAINING

French	*Type:* client-based; group; bespoke (specialism: engineering)
	Method: intensive; non-intensive; open or flexible
German	*Type:* client-based; group; bespoke (specialism: engineering)
	Method: intensive; non-intensive; open or flexible
Italian	*Type:* client-based; one-to-one; bespoke (specialism: engineering)
	Method: non-intensive; open or flexible
Russian	*Type:* client-based
Spanish	*Type:* client-based
	Method: open or flexible
Other	Additional languages can be offered, with notice

SERVICES
Translating

Dutch	into and out of English
French	into and out of English
German	into and out of English
Italian	into and out of English
Portuguese	into and out of English
Russian	into and out of English
Spanish	into and out of English

Interpreting

French	simultaneous; consecutive
German	simultaneous; consecutive
Italian	simultaneous; consecutive
Russian	simultaneous; consecutive
Spanish	simultaneous; consecutive

FACILITIES
Language labs: 10–25 places - 1 fixed
Interpreting
  facilities: over 100 places - 1 fixed

NOTES
• has experience of undertaking language training needs analyses for employers

109   University of Dundee

Dundee	Telephone	(0382) 23181
DD1 4HN	Fax	(0382) 201604

Contact   Dr R. Adamson, Director of Language Unit

TRAINING

French   *Type:* client-based; institution-based; group; one-to-one; bespoke (specialisms: legal; scientific; business; hotel trade; catering; social services)
Method: intensive; non-intensive; open or flexible

German   *Type:* client-based; institution-based; group; one-to-one; bespoke
Method: non-intensive; open or flexible

Italian   *Type:* client-based; institution-based; group; one-to-one; bespoke
Method: non-intensive; open or flexible

Spanish   *Type:* client-based; institution-based; group; one-to-one; bespoke
Method: non-intensive; open or flexible

Other   Russian, Arabic, Japanese, Hindi and Urdu can be offered, with notice

SERVICES
Translating
Arabic   out of English
French   into and out of English
German   into and out of English
Italian   into and out of English
Japanese   out of English
Spanish   into and out of English
Interpreting
French   bilateral
German   bilateral
Spanish   bilateral

FACILITIES
Language labs: 10–25 places - 1 fixed
Equipment and
   materials: computer-assisted language learning; videocassettes

NOTES
* has experience of undertaking language training needs analyses for employers
* has access to French databanks through Minitel, and operates jointly with the University of St Andrews as 'Language Line'

110 Dundee College of Further Education

Old Glamis Road
Dundee
DD3 8LE

Telephone	(0382) 819021
Fax	(0382) 88117

Contact   Mr B. S. Taylor, Section Head, Languages

TRAINING

French   *Type:* client-based; institution-based
              Method: non-intensive; open or flexible
German   *Type:* client-based; institution-based
              Method: non-intensive; open or flexible
Italian   *Type:* client-based; institution-based
              Method: non-intensive; open or flexible
Russian   *Type:* institution-based
              Method: non-intensive; open or flexible
Spanish   *Type:* institution-based
              Method: non-intensive; open or flexible

SERVICES

Translating
French   into and out of English
German   into and out of English
Italian   into and out of English
Russian   into and out of English
Spanish   into and out of English
Interpreting
French   consecutive
German   consecutive
Italian   consecutive
Russian   consecutive
Spanish   consecutive

FACILITIES

Language labs: 10–25 places - 4 portable

111   Dundee Institute of Technology

40 Bell Street
Dundee   Telephone   (0382) 28818
DD1 1HG   Fax   (0382) 308911

Contact   Mrs V. MacKinlay, Technology Transfer Centre Deputy Director

TRAINING
French   *Type:* client-based; institution-based; group; one-to-one
                     Method: open or flexible
German   *Type:* client-based; institution-based; group; one-to-one
                     Method: open or flexible
Russian   *Type:* client-based; institution-based; group; one-to-one
                     Method: open or flexible
Spanish   *Type:* client-based; institution-based; group; one-to-one
                     Method: open or flexible

SERVICES
Translating
French   into and out of English
German   into and out of English
Spanish   into and out of English

FACILITIES
Equipment and
  materials: interactive video

112   Dungannon College of Further Education

Circular Road
Dungannon   Telephone   (08687) 22323
BT71 6BQ   Fax   (08687) 52018

Contact   Mrs J. Clements, Lecturer in Charge of Modern Languages

TRAINING
French   *Type:* institution-based; one-to-one
                   Method: non-intensive
German   *Type:* institution-based; one-to-one
                   Method: non-intensive
Spanish   *Type:* institution-based; one-to-one
                   Method: non-intensive

FACILITIES
Equipment and
   materials: interactive video

113   Dunstable College

Kingsway
Dunstable   Telephone   (0582) 696451
LU5 4HG   Fax   (0582) 472741

Contact   Mr D. Adams, Lecturer in Modern Languages

TRAINING
French   *Type:* client-based; institution-based; group; one-to-one; bespoke
                Method: intensive; non-intensive; open or flexible
German   *Type:* client-based; institution-based; group; one-to-one; bespoke
                Method: intensive; non-intensive; open or flexible
Italian   *Type:* client-based; institution-based; group; one-to-one; bespoke
                Method: intensive; non-intensive; open or flexible
Spanish   *Type:* client-based; institution-based; group; one-to-one; bespoke
                Method: intensive; non-intensive; open or flexible
Other   Polish can be offered, with notice

SERVICES
Translating
French   into English
German   into English
Italian   into English
Polish   into English
Spanish   into English
Interpreting
French   simultaneous; consecutive
German   simultaneous; consecutive
Italian   simultaneous; consecutive
Polish   simultaneous; consecutive
Spanish   simultaneous; consecutive

FACILITIES
Language labs: 10–25 places - 1 portable

NOTES
• offers business know-how training in a European context

114   University of Durham

Language Centre
New Elvet

Durham	Telephone	091-374 3716
DH1 3JT	Fax	091-374 3716

Contact   Dr A. C. Pugh, Language Centre Director

TRAINING

Albanian	*Type:* self-access
Czech	*Type:* self-access
Danish	*Type:* self-access
Dutch	*Type:* self-access
Finnish	*Type:* self-access
French	*Type:* client-based; institution-based; one-to-one; bespoke
	Method: intensive; non-intensive; open or flexible
German	*Type:* institution-based
	Method: intensive; non-intensive; open or flexible
Hungarian	*Type:* self-access
Italian	*Type:* institution-based; bespoke
Japanese	*Type:* institution-based
Norwegian	*Type:* self-access
Portuguese	*Type:* self-access
Russian	*Type:* institution-based; bespoke
	Method: intensive
Serbo-Croat	*Type:* self-access
Spanish	*Type:* institution-based; bespoke
	Method: intensive; non-intensive; open or flexible
Swedish	*Type:* self-access

FACILITIES

Language labs:	under 10 places - 1 fixed; 10–25 places - 3 fixed; over 25 places - 1 fixed
Equipment and materials:	computer-assisted language learning; audio and videocassettes; satellite television

NOTES
• has experience of undertaking language training needs analyses for employers

115 University of East Anglia Language-Export Centre

Norwich	Telephone	(0603) 592802
NR4 7TJ	Fax	(0603) 250035
Contact	Mrs J. Thorp, Director, Short Course Development	

TRAINING

Danish
Type: client-based; institution-based; group; one-to-one; bespoke; self-access
Method: non-intensive

Faroese
Type: client-based; institution-based; group; one-to-one; bespoke; self-access
Method: non-intensive

Finnish
Type: client-based; institution-based; group; one-to-one; bespoke; self-access
Method: non-intensive

French
Type: client-based; institution-based; group; one-to-one; bespoke; self-access (specialism: legal)
Method: non-intensive

German
Type: client-based; institution-based; group; one-to-one; bespoke; self-access (specialism: legal)
Method: non-intensive

Greenlandic
Type: client-based; institution-based; group; one-to-one; bespoke; self-access
Method: non-intensive

Italian
Type: client-based; institution-based; group; one-to-one; bespoke; self-access
Method: non-intensive

Japanese
Type: client-based; institution-based; group; one-to-one; bespoke; self-access
Method: non-intensive

Norwegian
Type: client-based; institution-based; group; one-to-one; bespoke; self access
Method: non-intensive

Russian
Type: client-based; institution-based; group; one-to-one; bespoke; self-access
Method: non-intensive

Spanish
Type: client-based; institution-based; group; one-to-one; bespoke; self-access
Method: non-intensive

Swedish
Type: client-based; institution-based; group; one-to-one; bespoke; self-access
Method: non-intensive

Other
Additional languages can be offered, with notice

FACILITIES

Language labs:	10–25 places - 2 fixed
Interpreting facilities:	10–25 places - 1 fixed
Equipment and materials:	computer-assisted language learning; audio and videocassettes; satellite television; multi-media stations

NOTES

- has experience of undertaking language training needs analyses for employers
- has run tailored courses to cater, for example, for printers, chemical manufacturers and solicitors
- is developing open or flexible learning materials in French

116 East Birmingham College

Garretts Green Lane
Garretts Green
Birmingham   Telephone   021-743 4471
B33 0TS   Fax   021-743 9050

Contact   Ms J. Evans, Lecturer in Modern Languages

TRAINING
French   *Type:* institution-based; group
              Method: non-intensive; open or flexible
German   *Type:* client-based; institution-based; group; bespoke
              Method: non-intensive; open or flexible
Spanish   *Type:* institution-based; group
              Method: non-intensive
Urdu   *Type:* institution-based; group; bespoke
              Method: non-intensive
Other   Dutch can be offered, with notice

SERVICES
Translating
Urdu   into and out of English

FACILITIES
Language labs: 10–25 places - 1 fixed
Equipment and
  materials: audio and videocassettes

117　East Devon College

Bolham Road
Tiverton   Telephone   (0884) 254247
EX16 6SH   Fax   (0884) 259262

Contact   Mr D. Smith, Head of Modern Languages

TRAINING
French   *Type:* client-based; institution-based; group; one-to-one; bespoke
                  (specialism: estate agency)
                  Method: intensive; non-intensive; open or flexible
German   *Type:* client-based; institution-based; group; one-to-one
                  Method: intensive; non-intensive; open or flexible
Italian   *Type:* client-based; institution-based; group; one-to-one
                  Method: intensive; non-intensive; open or flexible
Russian   *Type:* client-based; institution-based; group; one-to-one
                  Method: intensive; non-intensive
Spanish   *Type:* client-based; institution-based; group; one-to-one
                  Method: intensive; non-intensive; open or flexible
Other   Japanese, Danish, Swedish and Portuguese can be offered, with
                  notice

SERVICES
Translating
Danish   into and out of English
French   into and out of English
German   into and out of English
Italian   into and out of English
Russian   into and out of English
Spanish   into and out of English
Swedish   into and out of English
Interpreting
Danish   simultaneous; consecutive
French   simultaneous; consecutive
German   simultaneous; consecutive
Italian   simultaneous; consecutive
Russian   simultaneous; consecutive
Spanish   simultaneous; consecutive

FACILITIES
Language labs: 10–25 places - 1 fixed
Equipment and
  materials: computer-assisted language learning; audio and videocassettes

118   University of East London

Romford Road
London　　　　　Telephone　　　081-590 7722
E15 4LZ　　　　　Fax　　　　　　081-519 3740

Contact　　　　　Ms C. J. Gamble, Head of European Relations

TRAINING
French　　　　　*Type:* client-based; institution-based; bespoke
　　　　　　　　Method: intensive
German　　　　　*Type:* client-based; institution-based; bespoke
　　　　　　　　Method: intensive
Italian　　　　　*Type:* institution-based; bespoke
Spanish　　　　　*Type:* institution-based; bespoke
Specialisms　　　legal; scientific; business
Other　　　　　　Russian can be offered, with notice

SERVICES
Translating
French　　　　　into English (specialism: business)
German　　　　　into English (specialism: business)
Italian　　　　　into English
Spanish　　　　　into English

FACILITIES
Language labs:　　10–25 places - 5 fixed
Equipment and
　materials:　　　satellite distance learning

NOTES
• has experience of undertaking language training needs analyses for employers

119   East Midlands Language-Export Centre

Charles Keene College
Painter Street
Leicester   Telephone   (0533) 516037
LE1 3WA   Fax   (0533) 620592

Contact   Mr T. Gutteridge, Director of Operations

TRAINING
French   *Type:* client-based (specialisms: engineering; textiles; shoe manu-
                     facturing)
                     Method: intensive; non-intensive
German   *Type:* client-based (specialism: engineering)
                     Method: intensive; non-intensive
Italian   *Type:* client-based
Portuguese   *Type:* group
                     Method: non-intensive
Spanish   *Type:* client-based

SERVICES
Translating
Albanian   into and out of English
Arabic   into and out of English
Bulgarian   into and out of English
Chinese   into and out of English
Czech   into and out of English
Danish   into and out of English
Dutch   into and out of English
Finnish   into and out of English
French   into and out of English (specialisms: engineering; textiles; shoe
                     manufacturing)
German   into and out of English (specialisms: engineering; textiles; shoe
                     manufacturing)
Greek   into and out of English
Hungarian   into and out of English
Italian   into and out of English (specialisms: engineering; textiles; shoe
                     manufacturing)
Japanese   into and out of English
Norwegian   into and out of English
Polish   into and out of English
Portuguese   into and out of English
Romanian   into and out of English
Russian   into and out of English
Spanish   into and out of English (specialisms: engineering; textiles; shoe
                     manufacturing)
Swedish   into and out of English

Interpreting

French	simultaneous; consecutive
German	simultaneous; consecutive
Italian	simultaneous; consecutive
Spanish	simultaneous; consecutive

FACILITIES

Language labs:	under 10 places - 1 portable; 10–25 places - 1 fixed
Interpreting facilities:	10–25 places - 1 fixed

NOTES

• has experience of undertaking language training needs analyses for employers
• offers business language taster courses

120   East Surrey College

Gatton Point
London Road
Redhill   Telephone   (0737) 772611
RH1 2JX   Fax   (0737) 770026

Contact   Mr A. Grandhaie, Language Centre Co-ordinator

TRAINING

Arabic   *Type:* client-based; institution-based; group; one-to-one; bespoke
French   *Type:* client-based; institution-based; group; one-to-one; bespoke
              Method: intensive; non-intensive
German   *Type:* client-based; institution-based; group; one-to-one; bespoke
              Method: intensive; non-intensive
Greek   *Type:* client-based; institution-based; group; one-to-one; bespoke
Italian   *Type:* client-based; institution-based; group; one-to-one; bespoke
              Method: intensive; non-intensive
Japanese   *Type:* client-based; institution-based; group; one-to-one; bespoke
              Method: intensive; non-intensive
Portuguese   *Type:* client-based; institution-based; group; one-to-one; bespoke
Russian   *Type:* client-based; institution-based; group; one-to-one; bespoke
              Method: intensive; non-intensive
Spanish   *Type:* client-based; institution-based; group; one-to-one; bespoke
              Method: intensive; non-intensive
Turkish   *Type:* client-based; institution-based; group; one-to-one; bespoke
Specialisms marketing; sales; legal; medical; scientific
Other   Chinese, Swedish, Danish and other languages can be offered, with
              notice

SERVICES

Translating
French   into and out of English
German   into and out of English
Italian   into and out of English
Japanese   into and out of English
Portuguese into and out of English
Russian   into and out of English
Spanish   into and out of English
Specialisms legal; medical; scientific
Interpreting
French   simultaneous; consecutive
German   simultaneous; consecutive
Italian   simultaneous; consecutive

Japanese	simultaneous; consecutive
Russian	simultaneous; consecutive
Spanish	simultaneous; consecutive

NOTES

• has experience of undertaking language training needs analyses for employers

121 East Warwickshire College

Lower Hillmorton Road
Rugby
CV21 3QS

Telephone   (0788) 541666
Fax   (0926) 413514

Contact   Mrs S. Wagg, Business Languages Co-ordinator

TRAINING

French	*Type:* client-based; institution-based; group; one-to-one; bespoke *Method:* intensive; non-intensive; open or flexible
German	*Type:* client-based; institution-based; group; one-to-one; bespoke *Method:* intensive; non-intensive; open or flexible
Italian	*Type:* client-based; institution-based; group; one-to-one; bespoke *Method:* intensive; non-intensive
Japanese	*Type:* client-based; institution-based; group; one-to-one; bespoke
Spanish	*Type:* client-based; institution-based; group; one-to-one; bespoke *Method:* intensive; non-intensive
Specialisms	technical; commercial; secretarial; legal; medical
Other	Additional languages can be offered, with notice

SERVICES

Translating

French	into and out of English (specialisms: technical; medical; legal; computers)
German	into and out of English (specialisms: technical; legal; computers)
Italian	into and out of English (specialisms: technical; commercial)
Spanish	into and out of English (specialism: technical)

Interpreting

French	consecutive
German	consecutive
Italian	consecutive
Spanish	consecutive

FACILITIES

Language labs: 10–25 places - 1 fixed

NOTES

• has experience of undertaking language training needs analyses for employers

122   East Yorkshire College

St Mary's Walk
Bridlington   Telephone   (0262) 672676
YO16 5JW   Fax   (0262) 671719

Contact   Mr G. Rudd, Head of Business

TRAINING
French   *Type:* client-based; institution-based; group; one-to-one bespoke
                Method: intensive; non-intensive; open or flexible
German   *Type:* client-based; institution-based; group; one-to-one; bespoke
                Method: intensive; non-intensive; open or flexible
Spanish   *Type:* client-based; institution-based; group; one-to-one; bespoke
Specialisms   business; industrial; legal; scientific

SERVICES
Translating
French   into and out of English
German   into and out of English
Spanish   into and out of English
Interpreting
French   simultaneous; consecutive
German   simultaneous; consecutive

FACILITIES
Language labs: 10–25 places - 1 fixed, 1 portable
Equipment and
   materials: audio and videocassettes

123   Eastleigh College

Chestnut Avenue
Eastleigh   Telephone   (0703) 613841
SO5 5HT   Fax   (0703) 620654

Contact   Ms S. M. Thomas, Modern Languages Co-ordinator

TRAINING
French   *Type:* client-based; institution-based; group
                  Method: intensive; non-intensive
German   *Type:* institution-based
                  Method: intensive; non-intensive
Italian   *Type:* institution-based
                  Method: intensive; non-intensive
Polish   *Type:* institution-based
                  Method: intensive; non-intensive
Spanish   *Type:* institution-based
                  Method: intensive; non-intensive
Specialism   business
Other   Russian can be offered, with notice

FACILITIES
Equipment and
  materials: videocassettes; computer-assisted language learning

NOTES
• has experience of undertaking language training needs analyses for employers

124   Easton College

Easton
Norwich   Telephone   (0603) 742105
NR9 5DX   Fax   (0603) 741438

Contact   Mr R. N. Percy, Agricultural Part Time Course Manager

TRAINING
French   *Type:* institution-based
German   *Type:* institution-based

NOTES
• all the college's language training is carried out in conjunction with Great Yarmouth
  College, which supplies training packs and staff

125 Edge Hill College of Higher Education

St Helens Road
Ormskirk　　　　　　Telephone　　　(0695) 575171
L39 4QP　　　　　　　Fax　　　　　　(0695) 579997

Contact　　　　　Ms C. N. Shields, Head of French Studies

TRAINING
French　　　　　　*Type:* client-based; institution-based; group; one-to-one
　　　　　　　　　Method: intensive; non-intensive
German　　　　　　*Type:* client-based; institution-based; group; one-to-one
　　　　　　　　　Method: intensive; non-intensive

SERVICES
Translating
French　　　　　　into and out of English
German　　　　　　into and out of English
Italian　　　　　　into and out of English
Spanish　　　　　　into and out of English
Interpreting
French　　　　　　simultaneous; consecutive

FACILITIES
Language labs:　　　over 25 places - 1 fixed
Interpreting
　facilities:　　　　under 10 places - 1 fixed
Equipment and
　materials:　　　　videocassettes; computer-assisted language learning

126   University of Edinburgh

Institute for Applied Language Studies
21 Hill Place

Edinburgh	Telephone	031-650 6200
EH8 9DP	Fax	031-667 5927

Contact   Mrs C. Cooper-Ducancelle, Head of Business and Industry Courses

TRAINING

Arabic
Type: client-based; institution-based; group; one-to-one; bespoke
Method: non-intensive

Chinese
Type: client-based; institution-based; group; one-to-one; bespoke
Method: intensive

Dutch
Type: client-based; institution-based; group; one-to-one; bespoke
Method: intensive

French
Type: client-based; institution-based; group; one-to-one; bespoke
Method: intensive; non-intensive

German
Type: client-based; institution-based; group; one-to-one; bespoke
Method: intensive; non-intensive

Italian
Type: client-based; institution-based; group; one-to-one; bespoke
Method: intensive; non-intensive

Japanese
Type: client-based; institution-based; group; one-to-one; bespoke
Method: intensive; non-intensive

Portuguese
Type: client-based; institution-based; group; one-to-one; bespoke
Method: intensive

Russian
Type: client-based; institution-based; group; one-to-one; bespoke
Method: intensive; non-intensive

Spanish
Type: client-based; institution-based; group; one-to-one; bespoke
Method: intensive; non-intensive

Specialisms
legal; financial; marketing; chemical; pharmaceutical; medical; police; arts; agriculture; computers; education

Other
Additional languages can be offered, with notice

SERVICES

Translating

French	into and out of English
German	into and out of English
Italian	into and out of English
Japanese	into and out of English
Russian	into and out of English
Spanish	into and out of English

Specialisms
legal; financial; marketing; chemical; pharmaceutical; medical; police; arts; agriculture; computers; education

NOTES
• has experience of undertaking language training needs analyses for employers

127　Elmwood Business Training

Elmwood House
Carslogie Road
Cupar　　　　　　　　Telephone　　　(0334) 56500
KY15 4JB　　　　　　Fax　　　　　　(0334) 56795

Contact　　　　Mr T. Black, Director

TRAINING
French　　　　*Type:* client-based; institution-based; group; one-to-one (specialism:
　　　　　　　golf vocabulary)
　　　　　　　Method: intensive; non-intensive; open or flexible
German　　　　*Type:* client-based; institution-based; group; one-to-one
　　　　　　　Method: intensive; non-intensive; open or flexible
Spanish　　　　*Type:* client-based; institution-based; group; one-to-one
　　　　　　　Method: intensive; non-intensive; open or flexible
Other　　　　　Russian can be offered, with notice

SERVICES
Translating
French　　　　　into and out of English
German　　　　　into and out of English
Russian　　　　　into and out of English
Spanish　　　　　into and out of English
Interpreting
French　　　　　consecutive
German　　　　　consecutive
Russian　　　　　consecutive
Spanish　　　　　consecutive

FACILITIES
Equipment and
　materials:　　　interactive video

NOTES
• has experience of undertaking language training needs analyses for employers

128 Enfield College

73 Hertford Road
Enfield   Telephone   081-443 3434
EN3 5HA   Fax   081-804 7028

Contact   Mrs J. Harris, Senior Lecturer in Languages

TRAINING

French   *Type:* client-based; institution-based; group; one-to-one; bespoke
            Method: intensive; non-intensive
German   *Type:* client-based; institution-based; group; one-to-one
            Method: non-intensive
Italian   *Type:* client-based; institution-based; group; one-to-one
            Method: non-intensive
Japanese   *Type:* client-based; institution-based; group; one-to-one
            Method: non-intensive
Russian   *Type:* client-based; institution-based; group; one-to-one
            Method: non-intensive
Spanish   *Type:* client-based; institution-based; group; one-to-one; bespoke
            Method: intensive; non-intensive

NOTES
• has experience of undertaking language training needs analyses for employers

129   Erith College

Tower Road
Belvedere
DA17 6JA

Telephone   (03224) 42331
Fax   (03224) 48403

Contact   Mrs M. C. Fysh, Lecturer in Charge of Languages

TRAINING
French
Type: client-based; institution-based; group (specialisms: business; medical; civil engineering; pharmaceutical)
Method: intensive; non-intensive; open or flexible
German
Type: client-based; institution-based; group
Method: intensive; non-intensive; open or flexible
Italian
Type: client-based; institution-based; group
Method: non-intensive
Spanish
Type: client-based; institution-based; group
Method: intensive; non-intensive;
Other
Russian can be offered, with notice

SERVICES
Translating
French
into and out of English (specialisms: medical; pharmaceutical; business)
German
into and out of English (specialism: business)
Spanish
into and out of English (specialism: business)

FACILITIES
Language labs: 10–25 places - 1 fixed
Equipment and
  materials: interactive video; computer-assisted language learning; satellite television

130   University of Essex

Wivenhoe Park
Colchester   Telephone   (0206) 872239
CO4 3SQ   Fax   (0206) 872198

Contact   Dr R. Bivon, Russian Studies Centre Director

TRAINING
Russian   *Type:* client-based
                   Method: intensive

SERVICES
Translating
Russian   into and out of English
Interpreting
Russian   consecutive

FACILITIES
Language labs: 10–25 places - 3 fixed
Equipment and
  materials: audio and videocassettes; computer-assisted language learning

NOTES
• offers a three week, intensive, residential Russian course, operating at beginner and
  further levels, with advanced levels concentrating on current affairs, politics and
  literature, but capable of being adapted if there are special interest groups

131   Euro-Com Languages for Business

The Cornerstone
42 Church Road
Bolton   Telephone   (0204) 849849
BL1 6HE   Fax   (0204) 849522

Contact   Mrs T. Kitts, Director

TRAINING
Czech   *Type:* institution-based; one-to-one (specialism: financial)
French   *Type:* client-based; institution-based; group; one-to-one (specialism: sales)
German   *Type:* client-based; institution-based; group; one-to-one (specialism: sales)
Italian   *Type:* client-based; one-to-one (specialisms: sales; chemical)
Maltese   *Type:* client-based; group (specialism: management)
Spanish   *Type:* client-based; institution-based; group; one-to-one
Other   Additional languages can be offered, with notice

SERVICES
Translating
Dutch   into and out of English
French   into and out of English
German   into and out of English
Italian   into and out of English
Japanese   into and out of English
Russian   into and out of English
Spanish   into and out of English
Interpreting
Dutch   consecutive
French   consecutive
German   consecutive

FACILITIES
Equipment and
  materials: audio and videocassettes

NOTES
• has experience of undertaking language training needs analyses for employers

132   University of Exeter

Continuing Education and Training
Streatham Rise

Exeter	Telephone	(0392) 411906
EX4 4PE	Fax	(0392) 436082

Contact   Mr C. Nicholas, Continuing Education and Training Officer

TRAINING

Arabic   *Type:* client-based; institution-based; group; one-to-one; bespoke
            Method: intensive; non-intensive; open or flexible

Chinese   *Type:* client-based; institution-based; group; one-to-one; bespoke
            Method: intensive; non-intensive; open or flexible

Czech   *Type:* client-based; institution-based; group; one-to-one; bespoke
            Method: intensive; non-intensive; open or flexible

Dutch   *Type:* client-based; institution-based; group; one-to-one; bespoke
            Method: intensive; non-intensive; open or flexible

French   *Type:* client-based; institution-based; group; one-to-one; bespoke
            Method: intensive; non-intensive; open or flexible

German   *Type:* client-based; institution-based; group; one-to-one; bespoke
            Method: intensive; non-intensive; open or flexible

Greek   *Type:* client-based; institution-based; group; one-to-one; bespoke
            Method: intensive; non-intensive; open or flexible

Italian   *Type:* client-based; institution-based; group; one-to-one; bespoke
            Method: intensive; non-intensive; open or flexible

Japanese   *Type:* client-based; institution-based; group; one-to-one; bespoke
            Method: intensive; non-intensive; open or flexible

Portuguese *Type:* client-based; institution-based; group; one-to-one; bespoke
            Method: intensive; non-intensive; open or flexible

Russian   *Type:* client-based; institution-based; group; one-to-one; bespoke
            Method: intensive; non-intensive; open or flexible

Spanish   *Type:* client-based; institution-based; group; one-to-one; bespoke
            Method: intensive; non-intensive; open or flexible

SERVICES

Translating

Arabic	into and out of English
Chinese	into and out of English
Czech	into and out of English
Dutch	into and out of English
French	into and out of English
German	into and out of English
Greek	into and out of English
Italian	into and out of English
Japanese	into and out of English

Portuguese	into and out of English
Russian	into and out of English
Spanish	into and out of English

FACILITIES

Language labs:	10–25 places - 1 fixed
Equipment and	
materials:	audiocassettes and other support materials

NOTES
- has experience of undertaking language training needs analyses for employers
- for translation services, please telephone Mrs D. Letcher, at Exeter Enterprises, on Exeter (0392) 264376

133   Exeter College

Hele Road
Exeter
EX4 4JS

	Telephone	(0392) 384004
	Fax	(0392) 210282

Contact   Mr J. Needle, Head of Communications and Languages

TRAINING

French   *Type:* client-based; institution-based; group; one-to-one; bespoke (specialism: police)
Method: intensive; non-intensive; open or flexible

German   *Type:* client-based; institution-based; group; one-to-one; bespoke
Method: intensive; non-intensive; open or flexible

Italian   *Type:* client-based; institution-based; group; one-to-one; bespoke
Method: intensive; non-intensive; open or flexible

Russian   *Type:* client-based; institution-based; group; one-to-one; bespoke
Method: intensive; non-intensive; open or flexible

Spanish   *Type:* client-based; institution-based; group; one-to-one; bespoke
Method: intensive; non-intensive; open or flexible

SERVICES

Translating

French   into and out of English
German   into and out of English
Italian   into and out of English
Russian   into and out of English
Spanish   into and out of English

FACILITIES

Language labs: 10–25 places - 4 fixed

134   Falkirk College of Technology

Grangemouth Road
Falkirk   Telephone   (0324) 24981
FK2 9AD   Fax   (0324) 32086

Contact   Mrs E. Speake, Senior Lecturer in Modern Languages

TRAINING
French   *Type:* client-based; institution-based; group; one-to-one
                Method: non-intensive; open or flexible
German   *Type:* client-based; institution-based; group; one-to-one
                Method: non-intensive; open or flexible
Italian   *Type:* client-based; institution-based; group; one-to-one
                Method: non-intensive; open or flexible
Spanish   *Type:* client-based; institution-based; group; one-to-one
                Method: non-intensive; open or flexible
Other   Russian, Dutch and Urdu can be offered, with notice

SERVICES
Translating
French   into and out of English
German   into and out of English
Italian   into and out of English
Spanish   into and out of English
Interpreting
French   consecutive
German   consecutive
Italian   consecutive

FACILITIES
Equipment and
  materials: audio and videocassettes; computer-assisted language learning;
                flexible learning centre; peripheral audio learning equipment

NOTES
• has experience of undertaking language training needs analyses for employers

135   Farnborough College of Technology

Customised Training
Boundary Road
Farnborough   Telephone   (0252) 515511
GU14 6SB   Fax   (0252) 549682

Contact   Mrs D. Barnard, Lecturer and Language Consultant

TRAINING
Dutch   *Type:* client-based; institution-based; group; one-to-one
French   *Type:* client-based; institution-based; group; one-to-one
             Method: intensive; non-intensive
German   *Type:* client-based; institution-based; group; one-to-one
             Method: intensive; non-intensive
Italian   *Type:* client-based; institution-based; group; one-to-one
             Method: intensive; non-intensive
Japanese   *Type:* client-based; institution-based; group; one-to-one
Portuguese   *Type:* institution-based; group; one-to-one
Russian   *Type:* client-based; institution-based; group; one-to-one
Spanish   *Type:* client-based; institution-based; group; one-to-one
             Method: intensive; non-intensive
Specialism   technical

SERVICES
Translating
Dutch   out of English
French   into and out of English
German   into and out of English
Italian   into and out of English
Japanese   out of English
Portuguese   out of English
Russian   out of English
Spanish   into and out of English
Specialism   technical
Interpreting
French   consecutive
German   consecutive
Italian   consecutive
Spanish   consecutive

FACILITIES
Language labs: 10–25 places - 1 portable

NOTES
• has experience of undertaking language training needs analyses for employers

136   Fife College of Technology

St Brycedale Avenue
Kirkcaldy   Telephone   (0592) 268591
KY1 1EX   Fax   (0592) 640225

Contact   Mr N. Hughes, International Services

TRAINING
Dutch   *Type:* client-based; institution-based; group
French   *Type:* client-based; institution-based; group; one-to-one; bespoke
                (specialism: business)
                Method: intensive
German   *Type:* client-based; institution-based; group; one-to-one; bespoke
                (specialism: business)
                Method: intensive
Italian   *Type:* client-based; institution-based; group; one-to-one; bespoke
                (specialisms: business; tourism)
                Method: non-intensive
Spanish   *Type:* client-based; institution-based; group; one-to-one; bespoke
                (specialism: business)
                Method: intensive
Other   Russian can be offered, with notice

SERVICES
Translating
French   into and out of English
German   into and out of English
Italian   into and out of English
Russian   into English
Spanish   into and out of English
Interpreting
French   simultaneous; consecutive
German   simultaneous; consecutive
Italian   simultaneous; consecutive
Spanish   simultaneous; consecutive

FACILITIES
Language labs: 10–25 places - 1 fixed

NOTES
• has experience of undertaking language training needs analyses for employers

137   Filton College

Filton Avenue
Bristol   Telephone   (0272) 694217
BS12 7AT   Fax   (0272) 236450

Contact   Mrs K. Hodge, Co-ordinator of Language Training for Industry

TRAINING

French   *Type:* client-based; institution-based; group; one-to-one; bespoke
               Method: intensive; non-intensive; open or flexible
German   *Type:* client-based; institution-based; group; one-to-one; bespoke
               Method: intensive; non-intensive; open or flexible
Italian   *Type:* client-based; institution-based; group; one-to-one; bespoke
               Method: intensive; non-intensive; open or flexible
Spanish   *Type:* client-based; institution-based; group; one-to-one; bespoke
               Method: intensive; non-intensive; open or flexible

SERVICES

Translating
French   into and out of English
German   into and out of English
Italian   into and out of English
Spanish   into and out of English
Interpreting
French   consecutive
German   consecutive
Italian   consecutive
Spanish   consecutive

FACILITIES

Language labs: 10–25 places - 2 fixed
Interpreting
 facilities: 10–25 places - 2 fixed
Equipment and
 materials: computer-assisted language learning; audiocassettes

NOTES

• has experience of undertaking language training needs analyses for employers

138   French Institute

14 Cromwell Place
London   Telephone   071-581 2701
SW7 2JR   Fax   071-581 2910

Contact   Mr M. Billaudel, Business Course Co-ordinator

TRAINING
French   *Type:* client-based; institution-based; group; one-to-one
                  (specialisms: legal; financial; medical)
                  Method: intensive; non-intensive; open or flexible

SERVICES
Translating
French   into and out of English

FACILITIES
Language labs: 10–25 places - 1 fixed

NOTES
• has experience of undertaking language training needs analyses for employers
• offers a wide range of business courses to prepare students for examinations offered
  by the chambers of commerce of London and Paris
• all teachers are native French speakers

139   Frome Community College

Bath Road
Frome   Telephone   (0373) 465353
BA11 2HQ   Fax   (0373) 452583

Contact   Mr M. Lloyd, Community Education Officer

TRAINING
French   *Type:* client-based (specialism: business)
                         Method: non-intensive
German   *Type:* client-based (specialism: business)
                         Method: non-intensive
Italian   *Type:* institution-based
Spanish   *Type:* institution-based

FACILITIES
Equipment and
  materials: audio and videocassettes; computer-assisted language learning

NOTES
• has experience of undertaking language training needs analyses for employers
• has mainly offered basic training from beginners' level

140   Furness College

Howard Street
Barrow-in-Furness   Telephone   (0229) 825017
LA12 0JW   Fax   (0229) 870964

Contact   Mr J. W. Grantham, Section Leader of General Education and Access

TRAINING
French   *Type:* institution-based; group
   Method: non-intensive; open or flexible
German   *Type:* institution-based; group
   Method: non-intensive; open or flexible
Italian   *Type:* client-based; institution-based
Japanese   *Type:* institution-based; group
   Method: non-intensive
Russian   *Type:* client-based; institution-based
Spanish   *Type:* institution-based; group
   Method: non-intensive; open or flexible

SERVICES
Translating
French   into and out of English
German   into and out of English
Italian   into and out of English
Japanese   into and out of English
Spanish   into and out of English
Interpreting
French   simultaneous
Japanese   simultaneous
Spanish   simultaneous

FACILITIES
Language labs: under 10 places - 1 portable
Equipment and
   materials: audiocassettes

141   Gateshead College

Durham Road
Gateshead   Telephone   091-478 5559
NE9 5BN   Fax   091-477 0630

Contact   Mr G. Heydon, Director of Gateshead Training Consultancy

TRAINING

French   *Type:* client-based; institution-based; group; one-to-one; bespoke
                   (specialisms: business; computers)
                   Method: intensive; non-intensive; open or flexible
German   *Type:* client-based; institution-based; group; one-to-one; bespoke
                   (specialisms: business; computers)
                   Method: intensive; non-intensive; open or flexible
Greek   *Type:* client-based; institution-based; group; one-to-one; bespoke
Italian   *Type:* client-based; institution-based; group; one-to-one; bespoke
                   (specialisms: business; computers)
                   Method: non-intensive
Japanese   *Type:* client-based; institution-based; group; one-to-one; bespoke
Russian   *Type:* client-based; institution-based; group; one-to-one; bespoke
Spanish   *Type:* client-based; institution-based; group; one-to-one; bespoke
                   (specialisms: water and sewage; computers; industrial coatings;
                   police)
                   Method: non-intensive; open or flexible
Other   Portuguese and Swedish can be offered, with notice

FACILITIES

Language labs: 10–25 places - 1 fixed
Equipment and
  materials: computer-assisted language learning

NOTES

• has experience of undertaking language training needs analyses for employers
• has some experience of interpreting, most recently in Italian

142   University of Glamorgan

Pontypridd		Telephone	(0443) 480480
CF37 1DL		Fax	(0443) 480558

Contact   Mr C. Davies, Head of Centre for Language Studies

TRAINING

French   *Type:* client-based; institution-based; group; one-to-one; bespoke
              Method: intensive; non-intensive; open or flexible

German   *Type:* client-based; group
              Method: intensive; non-intensive; open or flexible

Italian   *Type:* client-based; institution-based; group
              Method: intensive; non-intensive; open or flexible

Spanish   *Type:* client-based; group
              Method: intensive; non-intensive; open or flexible

Welsh   *Type:* client-based; institution-based; group; bespoke
              Method: intensive; non-intensive; open or flexible

Other   Portuguese can be offered, with notice

SERVICES

Translating
French   into and out of English
German   into and out of English
Italian   into and out of English
Spanish   into and out of English
Welsh   into and out of English

FACILITIES

Language labs: 10–25 places - 1 fixed

NOTES

• has experience of undertaking language training needs analyses for employers

143   University of Glasgow

Language Centre
Hetherington Building
Glasgow   Telephone   041-339 2211
G12 8RS   Fax   041-339 1119

Contact   Dr D. Bickerton, Director

TRAINING
Danish   *Type:* client-based; institution-based; one-to-one
Dutch   *Type:* client-based; institution-based; one-to-one
French   *Type:* client-based; institution-based; group; one-to-one
            Method: intensive; non-intensive; open or flexible
German   *Type:* client-based; institution-based; group; one-to-one
            Method: intensive; non-intensive; open or flexible
Italian   *Type:* client-based; institution-based; one-to-one
            Method: intensive; non-intensive; open or flexible
Japanese   *Type:* client-based; institution-based; one-to-one
            Method: intensive; open or flexible
Punjabi   *Type:* one-to-one
Russian   *Type:* client-based; institution-based; one-to-one
            Method: intensive; non-intensive; open or flexible
Spanish   *Type:* client-based; institution-based; group; one-to-one
            Method: intensive; non-intensive; open or flexible
Other   Some 35 languages can be offered, with notice

SERVICES
Translating
French   into and out of English
German   into and out of English
Italian   into and out of English
Japanese   into and out of English
Russian   into and out of English
Spanish   into and out of English
Interpreting
French   simultaneous; consecutive
German   simultaneous; consecutive
Italian   simultaneous; consecutive
Japanese   simultaneous; consecutive
Russian   simultaneous; consecutive
Spanish   simultaneous; consecutive

FACILITIES

Language labs: 10–25 places - 2 fixed; over 25 places - 2 fixed

Equipment and
  materials: audio and videocassettes; computer-assisted language learning; satellite television

NOTES

- has experience of undertaking language training needs analyses for employers
- offers translating and interpreting services in more than 50 languages
- offers audio-visual production facilities at broadcast standard
- offers interpreting facilities for up to 2,500 people

144   Glasgow College of Food Technology

230 Cathedral Street
Glasgow   Telephone   041-552 3751
G1 2TG   Fax   041-553 2370

Contact   Mrs M. Goldie, Lecturer in Modern Languages

TRAINING
French   *Type:* client-based; institution-based; group; one-to-one; bespoke
                (specialisms: tourism; commercial)
                Method: intensive; non-intensive; open or flexible
German   *Type:* client-based; institution-based; group; one-to-one; bespoke
                Method: intensive; non-intensive; open or flexible
Italian   *Type:* client-based; institution-based; group; one-to-one; bespoke
                Method: intensive; non-intensive; open or flexible
Japanese   *Type:* client-based; institution-based; group; one-to-one; bespoke
                Method: intensive; non-intensive; open or flexible
Spanish   *Type:* client-based; institution-based; group; one-to-one; bespoke
                Method: intensive; non-intensive; open or flexible

SERVICES
Translating
French   into and out of English
German   into and out of English
Italian   into and out of English
Japanese   into and out of English
Spanish   into and out of English
Interpreting
French   simultaneous; consecutive
German   simultaneous; consecutive
Italian   simultaneous; consecutive
Japanese   simultaneous; consecutive
Spanish   simultaneous; consecutive

FACILITIES
Language labs: 10–25 places - 1 fixed
Interpreting
  facilities: under 10 places - 1 fixed; 10–25 places - 1 fixed; 26–100 places - 1
                 fixed

NOTES
• has experience of undertaking language training needs analyses for employers

145   Glasgow College of Nautical Studies

21 Thistle Street
Glasgow   Telephone   041-429 3201
G5 9XB   Fax   041-420 1690

Contact   Mrs M. Ramsay, Head of Languages

TRAINING
French   *Type:* institution-based
                    Method: non-intensive
German   *Type:* institution-based
                    Method: non-intensive
Spanish   *Type:* institution-based
                    Method: non-intensive

FACILITIES
Language labs: under 10 places - 1 portable

146   Glasgow Caledonian University

70 Cowcaddens Road
Glasgow   Telephone   041-331 3000
G4 0BA   Fax   041-331 3005

Contact   Miss M. Ross, Senior Lecturer in Modern Languages

TRAINING
French   *Type:* client-based; institution-based
                  Method: non-intensive
German   *Type:* client-based
                  Method: non-intensive

SERVICES
Translating
French   into and out of English
German   into and out of English
Italian   out of English
Russian   out of English
Spanish   into and out of English
Interpreting
French   simultaneous; consecutive
German   simultaneous; consecutive
Italian   simultaneous; consecutive
Russian   simultaneous; consecutive
Spanish   simultaneous; consecutive

FACILITIES
Language labs: 10–25 places - 2 fixed
Equipment and
  materials: computer-assisted language learning

147 Glenrothes College Language-Export Centre

Stenton Road
Glenrothes   Telephone   (0592) 772233
KY6 2RA   Fax   (0592) 772758

Contact   Ms B. Beedham, Senior Lecturer in Languages

TRAINING

French	*Type:* client-based; institution-based; group; one-to-one; bespoke
	Method: intensive; non-intensive; open or flexible
German	*Type:* client-based; institution-based; group; one-to-one; bespoke
	Method: intensive; non-intensive; open or flexible
Italian	*Type:* client-based; institution-based; group; one-to-one; bespoke
	Method: intensive; non-intensive
Polish	*Type:* client-based; institution-based; group; one-to-one; bespoke
	Method: intensive; non-intensive
Russian	*Type:* client-based; institution-based; group; one-to-one; bespoke
	Method: intensive; non-intensive
Spanish	*Type:* client-based; institution-based; group; one-to-one; bespoke
	Method: intensive; non-intensive; open or flexible
Specialisms	paper industry; electronics; textiles; engineering; catering; tourism; applied art; occupational therapy; off-shore industries; banking
Other	Dutch and Danish can be offered, with notice

SERVICES

Translating

French	into and out of English
German	into and out of English
Italian	into and out of English
Polish	into and out of English
Russian	into and out of English
Spanish	into and out of English
Specialisms	business; technical; off-shore industries

Interpreting

French	consecutive
German	consecutive
Italian	consecutive
Polish	consecutive
Russian	consecutive
Spanish	consecutive
Specialisms	business; technical; off-shore industries

FACILITIES

Equipment and
materials: computer-assisted language learning; interactive video

NOTES
- has experience of undertaking language training needs analyses for employers
- offers regular business lunches in French and German and monthly social evenings in German to all business clients
- produces promotional or training videos with foreign language voice-overs and graphics, if required

148　Gloucestershire College of Arts and Technology

Language Unit
73 The Park
Cheltenham   Telephone   (0242) 532111
GL50 2RR   Fax   (0242) 532023

Contact   Mr P. R. Arnold, Senior Lecturer in Languages

TRAINING

Chinese	*Type:* client-based; institution-based; group; one-to-one; bespoke
	Method: intensive; non-intensive
Dutch	*Type:* client-based; institution-based; group; one-to-one; bespoke
	Method: intensive; non-intensive
Estonian	*Type:* client-based; institution-based; group; bespoke
	Method: intensive; non-intensive
French	*Type:* client-based; institution-based; group; one-to-one; bespoke
	Method: intensive; non-intensive; open or flexible
German	*Type:* client-based; institution-based; group; one-to-one; bespoke
	Method: intensive; non-intensive; open or flexible
Italian	*Type:* client-based; institution-based; group; one-to-one; bespoke
	Method: intensive; open or flexible
Japanese	*Type:* client-based; institution-based; group; one-to-one; bespoke
	Method: open or flexible
Portuguese	*Type:* client-based; institution-based; group; one-to-one; bespoke
	Method: intensive; non-intensive
Russian	*Type:* client-based; institution-based; group; one-to-one; bespoke
	Method: open or flexible
Spanish	*Type:* client-based; institution-based; group; one-to-one; bespoke
	Method: intensive; open or flexible
Turkish	*Type:* client-based; group; bespoke
	Method: intensive; non-intensive
Specialisms	commercial; industrial
Other	Additional languages can be offered, with notice

FACILITIES

Language labs: 10–25 places - 4 fixed
Equipment and
　materials: audiocassettes; computer-assisted language learning

NOTES
• has experience of undertaking language training needs analyses for employers

149   Gorseinon College

Belgrave Road
Gorseinon
Swansea   Telephone   (0792) 898283
SA4 2RF   Fax   (0792) 898729

Contact   Mrs A. France, Head of Languages

TRAINING
French   *Type:* client-based; institution-based; group; one-to-one; bespoke
                 (specialisms: telephone skills; engineering; hotel trade; business;
                 secretarial)
                 Method: intensive; non-intensive
German   *Type:* client-based; institution-based; group; one-to-one; bespoke
                 (specialisms: engineering; hotel trade; business; telephone skills;
                 secretarial)
                 Method: intensive; non-intensive
Italian   *Type:* client-based; institution-based; group; one-to-one; bespoke
                 (specialisms: hotel trade; business; telephone skills; secretarial)
                 Method: intensive; non-intensive
Russian   *Type:* client-based; institution-based; group; one-to-one; bespoke
                 (specialisms: hotel trade; business)
                 Method: intensive; non-intensive
Spanish   *Type:* client-based; institution-based; group; one-to-one; bespoke
                 (specialisms: hotel trade; business; engineering; telephone skills;
                 secretarial)
                 Method: intensive; non-intensive
Welsh   *Type:* client-based; institution-based; group; one-to-one; bespoke
                 (specialisms: secretarial; nursing; social services)
                 Method: intensive; non-intensive

SERVICES
Translating
French   into and out of English
German   into and out of English
Italian   into and out of English
Russian   into and out of English
Spanish   into and out of English
Welsh   into and out of English
Interpreting
French   simultaneous; consecutive
German   simultaneous; consecutive
Italian   simultaneous; consecutive
Russian   simultaneous; consecutive
Spanish   simultaneous; consecutive
Welsh   simultaneous; consecutive

FACILITIES
Language labs: under 10 places - 1 portable

NOTES
• has experience of undertaking language training needs analyses for employers

150 Great Yarmouth College of Further Education

Southtown
Great Yarmouth   Telephone   (0493) 655261
NR31 0ED   Fax   (0493) 653423

Contact   Mrs J. Tucker, Head of Communications and Languages

TRAINING

Arabic	*Type:* institution-based; bespoke (specialisms: banking; tourism)
	Method: intensive; non-intensive; open or flexible
Dutch	*Type:* institution-based; group; one-to-one
	Method: intensive; non-intensive; open or flexible
French	*Type:* client-based; institution-based; group; one-to-one; bespoke
	(specialisms: agriculture; catering; nursing; secretarial)
	Method: intensive; non-intensive; open or flexible
German	*Type:* client-based; institution-based; group; one-to-one; bespoke
	Method: intensive; non-intensive; open or flexible
Greek	*Type:* institution-based; group
Italian	*Type:* institution-based; group; one-to-one; bespoke
	Method: intensive; non-intensive; open or flexible
Portuguese	*Type:* institution-based; one-to-one; bespoke
	Method: intensive; non-intensive; open or flexible
Russian	*Type:* institution-based; group; one-to-one; bespoke
	Method: intensive; non-intensive; open or flexible
Spanish	*Type:* client-based; institution-based; group; one-to-one; bespoke
	Method: intensive; non-intensive; open or flexible

SERVICES
Translating

Arabic	into and out of English
Dutch	into and out of English
French	into and out of English
German	into and out of English
Italian	into and out of English
Portuguese	into and out of English
Russian	into and out of English
Spanish	into and out of English
Specialism	business

FACILITIES
Language labs: 10–25 places - 1 fixed, 1 portable

NOTES
• has experience of undertaking language training needs analyses for employers
• the language centre can deal with drop-in or phone-in inquiries, and tutorials can be arranged by telephone

151   Greenhill College

Lowlands Road
Harrow
HA1 3AQ

Telephone   081-422 2388
Fax   081-423 5183

Contact   Ms P. Frame, College Manager

TRAINING

French	*Type:* client-based; institution-based; group; one-to-one; bespoke
	Method: non-intensive; open or flexible
German	*Type:* client-based; institution-based; group; one-to-one; bespoke
	Method: non-intensive; open or flexible
Gujarati	*Type:* institution-based; group
Hindi	*Type:* institution-based; group
Italian	*Type:* client-based; institution-based; group; one-to-one
	Method: open or flexible
Russian	*Type:* client-based; institution-based; group; one-to-one
Spanish	*Type:* client-based; institution-based; group; one-to-one
	Method: non-intensive; open or flexible
Urdu	*Type:* institution-based; group
Other	Chinese, Dutch, Portuguese, Greek and Arabic can be offered, with notice

FACILITIES

Language labs: over 25 places - 2 fixed
Equipment and
  materials: computer-assisted language learning; audio and videocassettes

NOTES
• has experience of undertaking language training needs analyses for employers
• offers training for language teachers

152   University of Greenwich

Business School
Beresford Street
London   Telephone   081-316 9000
SE18 6BU   Fax   081-316 9005

Contact   Dr P. Taylor, Head of Modern Languages

TRAINING
French   *Type:* bespoke
                 Method: intensive; non-intensive; open or flexible
German   *Type:* bespoke
                 Method: intensive; non-intensive; open or flexible
Italian   *Type:* bespoke
                 Method: intensive; non-intensive; open or flexible
Spanish   *Type:* bespoke
                 Method: intensive; non-intensive; open or flexible
Specialism   business

FACILITIES
Language labs: 10–25 places - 3 fixed
Equipment and
  materials: computer-assisted language learning

153 Grimsby College of Technology and Arts

Nuns Corner
Grimsby   Telephone   (0472) 79292
DN34 5BQ   Fax   (0472) 79924

Contact   Mrs J. Morris, Deputy Head of Humanities and Science

TRAINING

French   *Type:* client-based; institution-based; group; one-to-one
                 (specialisms: food; textiles; transport)
                 Method: intensive; non-intensive
German   *Type:* client-based; institution-based; group; one-to-one
                 Method: intensive; non-intensive
Spanish   *Type:* client-based; institution-based; group; one-to-one
                 Method: intensive; non-intensive
Other   Italian and Russian can be offered, with notice

SERVICES
Translating
French   into and out of English
German   into and out of English
Spanish   into and out of English
Interpreting
French   simultaneous; consecutive
German   simultaneous; consecutive
Spanish   simultaneous; consecutive

FACILITIES
Language labs: 10–25 places - 1 fixed
Equipment and
  materials: listening stations; computer-assisted language learning; satellite
                 television; videocassettes; study packs

NOTES
• has experience of undertaking language training needs analyses for employers

154   Guildford College of Technology

Stoke Park
Guildford   Telephone   (0483) 31251
GU1 1EZ   Fax   (0483) 63409

Contact   Mr G. Tyas, Senior Lecturer in Modern Languages

TRAINING
French   *Type:* client-based; institution-based; group; bespoke
                   Method: non-intensive; open or flexible
German   *Type:* client-based; institution-based; group; bespoke
                   Method: non-intensive; open or flexible
Spanish   *Type:* client-based; institution-based; group; bespoke
                   Method: non-intensive; open or flexible

FACILITIES
Language labs: 10–25 places - 1 fixed

155   Gwynedd Technical College

Ffriddoedd Road
Bangor   Telephone   (0248) 370125
LL57 2TP   Fax   (0248) 370052

Contact   Mrs M. Hughes, Languages Lecturer

TRAINING
French   *Type:* client-based; institution-based; group; one-to-one; bespoke
                (specialisms: business; catering; tourism)
                Method: intensive; non-intensive; open or flexible
German   *Type:* client-based; institution-based; group; one-to-one; bespoke
                (specialisms: business; catering; tourism)
                Method: intensive; non-intensive; open or flexible
Greek   *Type:* institution-based
                Method: open or flexible
Italian   *Type:* client-based; institution-based; group; one-to-one; bespoke
                Method: open or flexible
Japanese   *Type:* client-based; institution-based; group; one-to-one; bespoke
                Method: open or flexible
Russian   *Type:* client-based; institution-based; group; one-to-one; bespoke
                Method: open or flexible
Spanish   *Type:* client-based; institution-based; group; one-to-one; bespoke
                (specialisms: business; catering; tourism)
                Method: open or flexible
Welsh   *Type:* client-based; institution-based; group; one-to-one; bespoke
                (specialisms: business; catering; tourism)
                Method: open or flexible
Other   Arabic, Czech, Chinese, Dutch, Finnish and Portuguese can be
                offered, with notice

SERVICES
Translating
French   into and out of English
German   into and out of English
Spanish   into and out of English
Welsh   into and out of English
Interpreting
French   simultaneous; consecutive
German   simultaneous; consecutive
Spanish   simultaneous; consecutive
Welsh   simultaneous; consecutive

FACILITIES

Interpreting
  facilities: 10–25 places - 1 portable
Equipment and
  materials: audio and videocassettes; computer-assisted language learning

NOTES
- can, with notice, arrange translating and interpreting in Italian, Japanese and Russian
- conference interpreting for groups of more than 22 can be arranged at short notice
- language training needs analyses can be offered on request

156　Hackney College

Brooke House
Kenninghall Road
London　　　　　　Telephone　　　081-986 5708
E8 4RG　　　　　　Fax　　　　　　081-985 4845

Contact　　　　Ms C. Kane, Language Co-ordinator

TRAINING

Amharic　　　　*Type:* client-based; institution-based; group; one-to-one; bespoke
Arabic　　　　　*Type:* client-based; institution-based; group; one-to-one; bespoke
Bengali　　　　 *Type:* client-based; institution-based; group; one-to-one; bespoke
　　　　　　　　Method: intensive; non-intensive
Chinese　　　　*Type:* client-based; institution-based; group; one-to-one; bespoke
　　　　　　　　Method: intensive; non-intensive
French　　　　　*Type:* client-based; institution-based; group; one-to-one; bespoke
　　　　　　　　(specialism: police)
　　　　　　　　Method: intensive; non-intensive; open or flexible
German　　　　 *Type:* client-based; institution-based; group; one-to-one; bespoke
　　　　　　　　(specialism: police)
　　　　　　　　Method: intensive; non-intensive; open or flexible
Gujarati　　　　*Type:* client-based; institution-based; group; one-to-one; bespoke
Hausa　　　　　*Type:* client-based; institution-based; group; one-to-one; bespoke
Hindi　　　　　*Type:* client-based; institution-based; group; one-to-one; bespoke
Ibo　　　　　　*Type:* client-based; institution-based; group; one-to-one; bespoke
Italian　　　　　*Type:* client-based; institution-based; group; one-to-one; bespoke
　　　　　　　　(specialism: police)
　　　　　　　　Method: intensive; non-intensive; open or flexible
Japanese　　　 *Type:* client-based; institution-based; group; one-to-one; bespoke
Polish　　　　　*Type:* client-based; institution-based; group; one-to-one; bespoke
Punjabi　　　　*Type:* client-based; institution-based; group; one-to-one; bespoke
Russian　　　　*Type:* client-based; institution-based; group; one-to-one; bespoke
Somali　　　　 *Type:* client-based; institution-based; group; one-to-one; bespoke
Spanish　　　　*Type:* client-based; institution-based; group; one-to-one; bespoke
　　　　　　　　(specialism: police)
　　　　　　　　Method: intensive; non-intensive; open or flexible
Swahili　　　　 *Type:* client-based; institution-based; group; one-to-one; bespoke
Tigrean　　　　*Type:* client-based; institution-based; group; one-to-one; bespoke
Turkish　　　　*Type:* client-based; institution-based; group; one-to-one; bespoke
　　　　　　　　(specialism: housing)
　　　　　　　　Method: intensive; non-intensive
Urdu　　　　　*Type:* client-based; institution-based; group; one-to-one; bespoke
　　　　　　　　(specialism: legal)
Vietnamese　　 *Type:* client-based; institution-based; group; one-to-one; bespoke
　　　　　　　　Method: intensive; non-intensive

Yoruba	*Type:* client-based; institution-based; group; one-to-one; bespoke (specialisms: legal; computers)
Other	Additional languages can be offered, with notice

FACILITIES

Language labs:	under 10 places - 1 fixed
Equipment and materials:	computer-assisted language learning; satellite television

NOTES

• has experience of undertaking language training needs analyses for employers

157 Hall Green College

Cole Bank Road
Birmingham Telephone 021-778 2311
B28 8ES Fax 021-702 2441

Contact Mr N. Pachler, European Languages Co-ordinator

TRAINING
Arabic *Type:* institution-based
Farsi *Type:* institution-based
French *Type:* client-based; institution-based; group; one-to-one (specialism: business)
Method: intensive; non-intensive
German *Type:* client-based; institution-based; group; one-to-one (specialism: business)
Method: intensive; non-intensive
Gujarati *Type:* institution-based
Italian *Type:* client-based; institution-based; group
Method: non-intensive
Japanese *Type:* client-based; institution-based; group
Method: non-intensive
Punjabi *Type:* client-based; institution-based
Pushtu *Type:* institution-based
Spanish *Type:* client-based; institution-based; group
Method: non-intensive
Urdu *Type:* client-based; institution-based

SERVICES
Translating
Arabic into and out of English
Farsi into and out of English
French into and out of English
German into and out of English
Gujarati into and out of English
Punjabi into and out of English
Pushtu into and out of English
Spanish into and out of English
Urdu into and out of English

FACILITIES
Language labs: 10–25 places - 1 fixed, 1 portable
Equipment and materials: computer-assisted language learning; audio and videocassettes

NOTES
• Mr D. Tatla, Asian Languages Co-ordinator, is a further contact at the institution

158   Halton College of Further Education

Kingsway
Widnes   Telephone   051-423 1391
WA8 7QQ   Fax   051-495 2483

Contact   Mr C. Proudfoot, Lecturer in Modern Languages

TRAINING

French   *Type:* client-based; institution-based; group; one-to-one; bespoke
                Method: intensive; non-intensive; open or flexible
German   *Type:* client-based; institution-based; group; one-to-one; bespoke
                Method: intensive; non-intensive; open or flexible
Italian   *Type:* client-based; institution-based; group; one-to-one; bespoke
                Method: intensive; non-intensive; open or flexible
Portuguese   *Type:* client-based; institution-based; group; one-to-one; bespoke
                Method: non-intensive
Spanish   *Type:* client-based; institution-based; group; one-to-one; bespoke
                (specialism: commercial)
                Method: intensive; non-intensive; open or flexible
Swedish   *Type:* client-based; institution-based; group; one-to-one; bespoke
                Method: non-intensive

NOTES
• has experience of undertaking language training needs analyses for employers

159   Hammersmith and West London College

Gliddon Road
Barons Court
London   Telephone   081-741 1688
W14 9BL   Fax   081-741 2491

Contact   Mr R. Perry, Programme Area Leader, Modern Languages

TRAINING
French   *Type:* client-based; institution-based; group; one-to-one
                Method: non-intensive
German   *Type:* client-based; institution-based; group; one-to-one
                Method: non-intensive
Spanish   *Type:* client-based; institution-based; group; one-to-one
                Method: non-intensive

FACILITIES
Language labs: over 25 places - 2 fixed
Equipment and
  materials: audio and videocassettes

NOTES
• has experience of undertaking language training needs analyses for employers

160   Handsworth College

The Council House
Soho Road
Handsworth   Telephone   021-551 6031
B21 9DP   Fax   021-523 4447

Contact   Mr G. A. Twinn, Section Head, Language Development

TRAINING

French   *Type:* client-based; institution-based; group; one-to-one; bespoke
                    Method: non-intensive
German   *Type:* client-based; institution-based; group; one-to-one; bespoke
                    Method: non-intensive
Hindi   *Type:* client-based; institution-based; group; one-to-one; bespoke
Punjabi   *Type:* client-based; institution-based; group; one-to-one; bespoke
Spanish   *Type:* client-based; institution-based; group; one-to-one; bespoke
                    Method: non-intensive
Urdu   *Type:* client-based; institution-based; group; one-to-one; bespoke
Vietnamese   *Type:* client-based; institution-based; group; one-to-one; bespoke

SERVICES

Translating
French   into English
German   into English
Hindi   into and out of English
Punjabi   into and out of English
Spanish   into English
Urdu   into and out of English
Vietnamese   into and out of English
Interpreting
Punjabi   consecutive

NOTES
• has experience of undertaking language training needs analyses for employers

161   Harlow College

College Square
The High
Harlow   Telephone   (0279) 441288
CM20 1LT   Fax   (0279) 420139

Contact   Mr D. Briggs, Open Learning Client Manager

TRAINING

French	*Type:* client-based; institution-based; group; one-to-one
	Method: intensive; non-intensive; open or flexible
German	*Type:* client-based; institution-based; group; one-to-one
	Method: intensive; non-intensive; open or flexible
Italian	*Type:* client-based; institution-based; group; one-to-one
	Method: intensive; non-intensive; open or flexible
Japanese	*Type:* client-based; institution-based; group; one-to-one
	Method: intensive; non-intensive; open or flexible
Russian	*Type:* institution-based
Spanish	*Type:* client-based; institution-based; group; one-to-one
	Method: intensive; non-intensive; open or flexible

FACILITIES

Language labs: under 10 places - 1 portable; 10–25 places - 1 fixed

162   Harper Adams Agricultural College

Newport	Telephone	(0952) 820280
TF10 8NB	Fax	(0952) 814783

Contact	Mr I. Barnard, Professional Development Unit Manager

TRAINING

French	*Type:* client-based; institution-based; group; one-to-one; bespoke
	Method: intensive; non-intensive; open or flexible
Spanish	*Type:* client-based; institution-based; group; one-to-one; bespoke
Specialism	agriculture

SERVICES
Translating

French	into and out of English (specialism: agriculture)

Interpreting

French	consecutive (specialism: agriculture)

FACILITIES
Equipment and
  materials: audiocassettes

NOTES
• has experience of undertaking language training needs analyses for employers

163   Harrogate College of Arts and Technology

Hornbeam Park
Hookstone Drive
Harrogate   Telephone   (0423) 879466
HG2 8QT   Fax   (0423) 879829

Contact   Mrs E. Winship, Lecturer in Languages

TRAINING

French   *Type:* client-based; institution-based; group; one-to-one
           Method: intensive; non-intensive; open or flexible

German   *Type:* client-based; institution-based; group; one-to-one
           Method: intensive; non-intensive; open or flexible

Italian   *Type:* client-based; institution-based; group; one-to-one
           Method: intensive; non-intensive; open or flexible

Spanish   *Type:* client-based; institution-based; group; one-to-one
           Method: intensive; non-intensive; open or flexible

Other   Russian and Portuguese can be offered, with notice

FACILITIES

Language labs: 10–25 places - 1 fixed

NOTES

• has experience of undertaking language training needs analyses for employers

164   Hartlepool College of Further Education

Stockton Street
Hartlepool   Telephone   (0429) 275453
TS24 7NT   Fax   (0429) 863328

Contact   Mr S. Barton, Lecturer (PICKUP Unit)

TRAINING
French   *Type:* client-based; group
                       Method: non-intensive; open or flexible
German   *Type:* client-based; group
                       Method: non-intensive; open or flexible
Other   Russian and Dutch can be offered, with notice

SERVICES
Translating
Dutch   into English
German   into English

FACILITIES
Language labs: under 10 places - 1 fixed
Equipment and
  materials: independent learning centre and mediatheque where students have
                       access to audio equipment and independent television monitors

165   Hastings College of Arts and Technology

Archery Road
St Leonards-on-Sea   Telephone   (0424) 442222
TN38 0HX   Fax   (0424) 721763

Contact   Mrs S. Longfield, Lecturer in Charge of Languages

TRAINING

Dutch	*Type:* institution-based
French	*Type:* client-based; institution-based
	Method: non-intensive
German	*Type:* institution-based
	Method: non-intensive
Italian	*Type:* institution-based
Russian	*Type:* institution-based
	Method: non-intensive
Spanish	*Type:* institution-based
	Method: non-intensive
Other	Arabic can be offered, with notice

FACILITIES

Language labs: 10–25 places - 1 fixed
Equipment and
    materials: computer-assisted language learning

166   Havering College of Further and Higher Education

Ardleigh Green Road
Hornchurch   Telephone   (0708) 455011
RM11 2LL   Fax   (0708) 477961

Contact   Ms H. Wood, Languages Co-ordinator

TRAINING

Arabic   *Type:* client-based; institution-based; group; one-to-one; bespoke
             Method: intensive; non-intensive
French   *Type:* client-based; institution-based; group; one-to-one; bespoke
             Method: intensive; non-intensive
German   *Type:* client-based; institution-based; group; one-to-one; bespoke
             Method: intensive; non-intensive
Italian   *Type:* client-based; institution-based; group; one-to-one; bespoke
             Method: intensive; non-intensive
Japanese   *Type:* client-based; institution-based; group; one-to-one; bespoke
             Method: intensive; non-intensive
Portuguese   *Type:* client-based; institution-based; group; one-to-one; bespoke
             Method: intensive; non-intensive
Spanish   *Type:* client-based; institution-based; group; one-to-one; bespoke
             Method: intensive; non-intensive
Turkish   *Type:* client-based; institution-based; group; one-to-one; bespoke

SERVICES

Translating
Arabic   into and out of English
French   into and out of English
German   into and out of English
Italian   into and out of English
Japanese   into and out of English
Portuguese   into and out of English
Russian   into and out of English
Spanish   into and out of English
Interpreting
Arabic   simultaneous; consecutive
French   consecutive
German   consecutive
Italian   consecutive
Japanese   consecutive
Portuguese   simultaneous; consecutive
Russian   consecutive
Spanish   consecutive

238

FACILITIES

Language labs: 10–25 places - 1 fixed
Equipment and
  materials: computer-assisted language learning; satellite television

167   Hendon College of Further Education

Corner Mead
Grahame Park Way
London   Telephone   081-200 8300
NW9 5RA   Fax   081-205 7177

Contact   Mrs M. Hay, Business Training Advisory Service Unit

TRAINING
French   *Type:* client-based; institution-based; group; one-to-one; bespoke
                Method: intensive; non-intensive; open or flexible
German   *Type:* client-based; institution-based; group; one-to-one; bespoke
                Method: intensive; non-intensive; open or flexible
Italian   *Type:* client-based; institution-based; group; one-to-one; bespoke
                Method: intensive; non-intensive; open or flexible
Spanish   *Type:* client-based; institution-based; group; one-to-one; bespoke
                Method: intensive; non-intensive; open or flexible
Specialisms   business; financial; tourism; hotel trade; catering; engineering
Other   Urdu, Gujarati, Japanese, Greek, Hungarian, Arabic and Russian
                can be offered, with notice

FACILITIES
Language labs: under 10 places - 1 portable
Equipment and
  materials: audiocassettes

NOTES
• has experience of undertaking language training needs analyses for employers

168   Henley College

Deanfield Avenue
Henley-on-Thames   Telephone   (0491) 579988
RG9 1UH   Fax   (0491) 410099

Contact   Miss A. Giovanazzi, Head of Modern Languages

TRAINING

Chinese	*Type:* client-based; institution-based; group; one-to-one; bespoke
French	*Type:* client-based; institution-based; group; one-to-one; bespoke
	Method: intensive; non-intensive; open or flexible
German	*Type:* client-based; institution-based; group; one-to-one; bespoke
	(specialism: marketing)
	Method: intensive; non-intensive; open or flexible
Italian	*Type:* client-based; institution-based; group; one-to-one; bespoke
	(specialism: scientific)
	Method: intensive; non-intensive; open or flexible
Russian	*Type:* client-based; institution-based; group; one-to-one; bespoke
	Method: non-intensive
Spanish	*Type:* client-based; institution-based; group; one-to-one; bespoke
	Method: intensive; non-intensive; open or flexible
Other	Arabic can be offered, with notice

SERVICES

Translating

French	into English (specialisms: medical; legal)
German	into English
Italian	into and out of English (specialism: scientific)
Spanish	into English

Interpreting

French	consecutive
German	consecutive
Italian	consecutive
Spanish	consecutive

FACILITIES

Language labs:	10–25 places - 1 fixed
Interpreting facilities:	26–100 places - 1 fixed
Equipment and materials:	audio and videocassettes

NOTES

• has experience of undertaking language training needs analyses for employers

169 Henley College (Coventry)

Henley Road
Bell Green
Coventry   Telephone   (0203) 611021
CV2 1ED   Fax   (0203) 611837

Contact   Mr N. Adair, General Manager, Planning and Marketing

TRAINING
French   *Type:* institution-based
                    Method: open or flexible
German   *Type:* institution-based
                    Method: open or flexible
Spanish   *Type:* institution-based
                    Method: open or flexible

FACILITIES
Language labs: 10–25 places - 1 fixed

170   Herefordshire College of Technology

Folly Lane
Hereford   Telephone   (0432) 352235
HR1 1LS   Fax   (0432) 353449

Contact   Mr C. Scott, Head of Business and Management Studies

TRAINING
French   *Type:* client-based; institution-based; group; one-to-one
                     Method: intensive; non-intensive; open or flexible
German   *Type:* client-based; group
                     Method: intensive; non-intensive; open or flexible
Italian   *Type:* client-based; group
                     Method: intensive; non-intensive
Spanish   *Type:* client-based; group; one-to-one
                     Method: intensive; non-intensive; open or flexible

FACILITIES
Language labs: 10–25 places - 1 fixed
Equipment and
  materials: interactive video; computer-assisted language learning

NOTES
• has experience of undertaking language training needs analyses for employers

171   Heriot-Watt University

Integrated Language Services
Riccarton
Edinburgh   Telephone   031-451 3159
EH14 4AS   Fax   031-451 3160

Contact   Miss A. Sutherland, Administrator

SERVICES
Translating
Czech   into and out of English
Danish   into and out of English
Finnish   into and out of English
French   into and out of English
German   into and out of English
Hungarian   into and out of English
Italian   into and out of English
Norwegian   into and out of English
Portuguese   into and out of English
Russian   into and out of English
Spanish   into and out of English
Swedish   into and out of English
Interpreting
French   simultaneous; consecutive
German   simultaneous; consecutive
Italian   simultaneous; consecutive
Russian   simultaneous; consecutive
Spanish   simultaneous; consecutive

FACILITIES
Interpreting
  facilities: over 100 places - 2 portable

NOTES
• uses a pool of freelance translators and interpreters, and matches their specialisms to
  customer requirements, while academic staff assure quality control

172   Hertford Regional College (Broxbourne Centre)

Turnford
Broxbrourne   Telephone   (0992) 466451
EN10 6AF   Fax   (0992) 451096

Contact   Mrs M. C. Bremont, Lecturer in Charge of Languages

TRAINING

French	*Type:* client-based; group; one-to-one (specialism: legal)
	Method: intensive; non-intensive
German	*Type:* client-based; group (specialisms: technical; scientific)
	Method: intensive; non-intensive
Italian	*Type:* client-based; institution-based; group; one-to-one; bespoke
Russian	*Type:* client-based; institution-based; group; one-to-one; bespoke
Spanish	*Type:* client-based; group; one-to-one (specialism: commercial)
	Method: intensive; non-intensive
Other	Japanese can be offered, with notice

SERVICES

Translating

French	into and out of English
German	into and out of English
Italian	into and out of English
Spanish	into and out of English

FACILITIES

Interpreting
  facilities: 10–25 places - 1 portable

NOTES

• has experience of undertaking language training needs analyses for employers

173 Hertford Regional College (Ware Centre)

Scotts Road
Ware   Telephone   (0920) 465441
SG12 9JF   Fax   (0920) 462772

Contact   Mr J. Grisbrooke, Senior Lecturer

TRAINING

Dutch   *Type:* institution-based; group
                 Method: intensive; non-intensive; open or flexible
French   *Type:* client-based; institution-based; group; one-to-one
                 (specialisms: legal; catering)
                 Method: intensive; non-intensive; open or flexible
German   *Type:* client-based; institution-based; group (specialisms: technical;
                 scientific)
                 Method: intensive; non-intensive; open or flexible
Greek   *Type:* institution-based; group; one-to-one
                 Method: intensive; non-intensive; open or flexible
Italian   *Type:* client-based; institution-based; group; one-to-one; bespoke
                 Method: intensive; non-intensive; open or flexible
Japanese   *Type:* client-based; institution-based; group; one-to-one
                 Method: intensive; non-intensive; open or flexible
Portuguese   *Type:* institution-based; group; one-to-one
                 Method: intensive; non-intensive; open or flexible
Russian   *Type:* institution-based; group
                 Method: intensive; non-intensive; open or flexible
Spanish   *Type:* client-based; institution-based; group; one-to-one (specialism:
                 commercial)
                 Method: intensive; non-intensive; open or flexible
Welsh   *Type:* institution-based; group

SERVICES

Translating
Dutch   into and out of English
French   into and out of English
German   into and out of English
Greek   into and out of English
Italian   into and out of English
Japanese   into and out of English
Portuguese   into and out of English
Russian   into and out of English
Spanish   into and out of English
Interpreting
Dutch   simultaneous; consecutive
French   simultaneous; consecutive

German	simultaneous; consecutive
Greek	simultaneous; consecutive
Italian	simultaneous; consecutive
Japanese	simultaneous; consecutive
Portuguese	simultaneous; consecutive
Russian	simultaneous; consecutive
Spanish	simultaneous; consecutive

FACILITIES

Language labs:	10–25 places - 1 portable
Equipment and materials:	computer-assisted language learning; audio and videocassettes

NOTES

• has experience of undertaking language training needs analyses for employers

174　University of Hertfordshire

College Lane
Hatfield　　　　　　Telephone　　(0707) 279640
AL10 9AB　　　　　Fax　　　　　(0707) 279415

Contact　　　　　Mrs G. Holt, Marketing Officer

TRAINING

French　　　　　*Type:* client-based; institution-based; group; one-to-one; bespoke
　　　　　　　Method: intensive; non-intensive; open or flexible
German　　　　　*Type:* client-based; institution-based; group; one-to-one; bespoke
　　　　　　　Method: intensive; non-intensive; open or flexible
Greek　　　　　*Type:* client-based; institution-based; group; one-to-one; bespoke
Italian　　　　　*Type:* client-based; institution-based; group; one-to-one; bespoke
　　　　　　　Method: intensive; non-intensive
Japanese　　　　*Type:* client-based; institution-based; group; one-to-one; bespoke
　　　　　　　Method: intensive; non-intensive
Russian　　　　　*Type:* client-based; institution-based; group; one-to-one; bespoke
　　　　　　　Method: intensive; non-intensive
Spanish　　　　　*Type:* client-based; institution-based; group; one-to-one; bespoke
　　　　　　　Method: intensive; non-intensive
Specialisms　　　engineering; banking; business; social; marketing; computers;
　　　　　　　scientific; cultural; environment
Other　　　　　Portuguese can be offered, with notice

SERVICES
Translating
French　　　　　into and out of English
German　　　　　into and out of English
Italian　　　　　into and out of English
Russian　　　　　into and out of English
Spanish　　　　　into and out of English
Specialisms　　　technical; legal; advertising; scientific
Interpreting
French　　　　　simultaneous; consecutive
German　　　　　simultaneous; consecutive
Specialisms　　　technical; scientific

FACILITIES
Language labs:　　10–25 places - 4 fixed
Equipment and
　materials:　　computer-assisted language learning; audio and videocassettes

NOTES
• has experience of undertaking language training needs analyses for employers

175   High Peak College

Harpur Hill
Buxton   Telephone   (0298) 71100
SK17 9JZ   Fax   (0298) 27261

Contact   Mrs M. Ward, Marketing Officer

TRAINING
French   *Type:* client-based; institution-based; group; one-to-one
                 Method: non-intensive; open or flexible
German   *Type:* client-based; institution-based; group; one-to-one
                 Method: non-intensive; open or flexible
Greek   *Type:* client-based; institution-based; group; one-to-one
                 Method: non-intensive; open or flexible
Italian   *Type:* client-based; institution-based; group; one-to-one
                 Method: non-intensive; open or flexible
Russian   *Type:* client-based; institution-based; group; one-to-one
                 Method: non-intensive; open or flexible
Spanish   *Type:* client-based; institution-based; group; one-to-one
                 Method: non-intensive; open or flexible

FACILITIES
Language labs: 10–25 places - 1 fixed
Equipment and
  materials: individual video booths

176   Hopwood Hall College

Hopwood Campus
Rochdale Road
Middleton   Telephone   061-643 7560
M24 3XH   Fax   061-643 2114

Contact   Ms P. Sanchez, Senior Lecturer in Languages

TRAINING
French   *Type:* client-based; institution-based; group; one-to-one
                     Method: intensive; non-intensive; open or flexible
German   *Type:* client-based; institution-based; group; one-to-one
                     Method: intensive; non-intensive; open or flexible
Italian   *Type:* client-based; institution-based; group; one-to-one
                     Method: non-intensive; open or flexible
Russian   *Type:* client-based; institution-based; group; one-to-one
Spanish   *Type:* client-based; institution-based; group; one-to-one
                     Method: intensive; non-intensive; open or flexible
Urdu   *Type:* client-based; institution-based; group; one-to-one

FACILITIES
Language labs: under 10 places - 1 portable
Equipment and
  materials: audio and videocassettes; computer-assisted language learning

NOTES
• has experience of undertaking language training needs analyses for employers

177　Hounslow Borough College

London Road
Isleworth　　　　　Telephone　　081-568 0244
TW7 4HS　　　　　Fax　　　　　081-569 7787

Contact　　　Ms B. Worms, Programme Co-ordinator, Modern Languages

TRAINING

Dutch　　　*Type:* client-based; institution-based; group; one-to-one; bespoke
　　　　　Method: intensive; non-intensive; open or flexible

French　　　*Type:* client-based; institution-based; group; one-to-one; bespoke
　　　　　(specialisms: computers; engineering; marketing; financial)
　　　　　Method: intensive; non-intensive; open or flexible

German　　　*Type:* client-based; institution-based; group; one-to-one; bespoke
　　　　　(specialisms: computers; engineering; marketing; financial)
　　　　　Method: intensive; non-intensive; open or flexible

Italian　　　*Type:* client-based; institution-based; group; one-to-one; bespoke
　　　　　(specialisms: computers; engineering; marketing; financial)
　　　　　Method: intensive; non-intensive; open or flexible

Japanese　　　*Type:* client-based; institution-based; group; one-to-one; bespoke
　　　　　Method: intensive; non-intensive; open or flexible

Polish　　　*Type:* client-based; institution-based; group; one-to-one; bespoke
　　　　　Method: intensive; non-intensive; open or flexible

Portuguese　　　*Type:* client-based; institution-based; group; one-to-one; bespoke
　　　　　Method: intensive; non-intensive; open or flexible

Russian　　　*Type:* client-based; institution-based; group; one-to-one; bespoke
　　　　　Method: intensive; non-intensive; open or flexible

Serbo-Croat　　　*Type:* client-based; institution-based; group; one-to-one; bespoke
　　　　　Method: intensive; non-intensive; open or flexible

Spanish　　　*Type:* client-based; institution-based; group; one-to-one; bespoke
　　　　　(specialisms: computers; engineering; marketing; financial)
　　　　　Method: intensive; non-intensive; open or flexible

SERVICES

Translating
Dutch　　　　into and out of English
French　　　　into and out of English
German　　　　into and out of English
Italian　　　　into and out of English
Japanese　　　into and out of English
Polish　　　　into and out of English
Portuguese　　into and out of English
Russian　　　　into and out of English
Serbo-Croat　　into and out of English
Spanish　　　　into and out of English

Interpreting

French	simultaneous; consecutive
German	simultaneous; consecutive
Italian	simultaneous; consecutive
Japanese	simultaneous; consecutive
Russian	simultaneous; consecutive
Spanish	simultaneous; consecutive

FACILITIES

Language labs: 10–25 places - 1 fixed; over 25 places - 1 fixed

Interpreting
  facilities: 26–100 places - 1 fixed

Equipment and
  materials: interactive video; computer-assisted language learning; satellite television

NOTES

- has experience of undertaking language training needs analyses for employers
- specialises in tailor made courses
- took part in the 1991 Thames Valley Business Language Project, which involved defining language need in specialist areas of computing, engineering and petro-chemicals

178   University of Huddersfield

Queensgate
Huddersfield   Telephone   (0484) 422288
HD1 3DH   Fax   (0484) 516151

Contact   Mr J. Arragon, Senior Lecturer in Charge of Language Services

TRAINING

Arabic   *Type:* client-based; institution-based; group; one-to-one; bespoke
Chinese   *Type:* client-based; institution-based; group; one-to-one; bespoke
              Method: intensive; non-intensive
Dutch   *Type:* client-based; institution-based; group; one-to-one; bespoke
              Method: intensive; non-intensive
French   *Type:* client-based; institution-based; group; one-to-one; bespoke
              (specialisms: scientific; technical)
              Method: intensive; non-intensive; open or flexible
German   *Type:* client-based; institution-based; group; one-to-one; bespoke
              (specialisms: scientific; technical)
              Method: intensive; non-intensive; open or flexible
Greek   *Type:* client-based; institution-based; group; one-to-one; bespoke
              Method: non-intensive
Italian   *Type:* client-based; institution-based; group; one-to-one; bespoke
              (specialisms: scientific; technical)
              Method: intensive; non-intensive; open or flexible
Japanese   *Type:* client-based; institution-based; group; one-to-one; bespoke
              Method: intensive; non-intensive; open or flexible
Polish   *Type:* client-based; institution-based; group; one-to-one; bespoke
Portuguese   *Type:* client-based; institution-based; group; one-to-one; bespoke
              (specialisms: scientific; technical)
              Method: non-intensive
Russian   *Type:* client-based; institution-based; group; one-to-one; bespoke
              Method: intensive; non-intensive
Spanish   *Type:* client-based; institution-based; group; one-to-one; bespoke
              (specialisms: scientific; technical)
              Method: intensive; non-intensive; open or flexible

SERVICES
Translating
Arabic   into and out of English
Chinese   into and out of English
Danish   into and out of English
Dutch   into and out of English
Finnish   into and out of English
French   into and out of English (specialisms: scientific; technical)
German   into and out of English (specialisms: scientific; technical)

Italian	into and out of English (specialisms: scientific; technical)
Japanese	into and out of English
Norwegian	into and out of English
Polish	into and out of English
Portuguese	into and out of English
Russian	into and out of English
Spanish	into and out of English (specialisms: scientific; technical)
Swedish	into and out of English

Interpreting

Arabic	consecutive
Chinese	consecutive
Dutch	consecutive
French	consecutive (specialisms: scientific; technical)
German	consecutive (specialisms: scientific; technical)
Greek	consecutive
Italian	consecutive (specialisms: scientific; technical)
Japanese	consecutive
Polish	consecutive
Portuguese	consecutive (specialisms: scientific; technical)
Russian	consecutive
Spanish	consecutive (specialisms: scientific; technical)

FACILITIES

Language labs:	10–25 places - 3 fixed
Interpreting facilities:	10–25 places - 3 fixed
Equipment and materials:	computer-assisted language learning

NOTES
- has experience of undertaking language training needs analyses for employers
- offers help to firms which encounter language problems when dealing with businesses abroad
- offers hire of language learning facilities such as mini-labs
- offers voice-overs for commercial videos
- offers proofing of 'in house' translations

179 Huddersfield Technical College

New North Road
Huddersfield   Telephone   (0484) 536521
HD1 5NN   Fax   (0484) 511885

Contact   Mrs E. Griffin, Marketing Co-ordinator

TRAINING
French   *Type:* client-based; institution-based; group; one-to-one; bespoke
                 Method: intensive; non-intensive; open or flexible
German   *Type:* client-based; institution-based; group; one-to-one; bespoke
                 Method: intensive; non-intensive; open or flexible; learning packs
Italian   *Type:* client-based; institution-based; group; one-to-one; bespoke
                 Method: intensive; non-intensive; open or flexible
Japanese   *Type:* client-based; institution-based; group; one-to-one; bespoke
                 Method: intensive; non-intensive; open or flexible; learning packs
Russian   *Type:* client-based; institution-based; group; one-to-one; bespoke
                 Method: intensive; non-intensive; open or flexible
Spanish   *Type:* client-based; institution-based; group; one-to-one; bespoke
                 Method: intensive; non-intensive; open or flexible
Other   Arabic can be offered, with notice

SERVICES
Translating
French   into and out of English
German   into and out of English
Italian   into and out of English
Japanese   into and out of English
Russian   into and out of English
Spanish   into and out of English
Interpreting
French   simultaneous; consecutive
German   simultaneous; consecutive
Japanese   simultaneous; consecutive
Russian   simultaneous; consecutive
Spanish   simultaneous; consecutive

FACILITIES
Language labs: under 10 places - 1 portable; 10–25 places - 1 fixed
Equipment and
  materials: computer-assisted language learning; audio and videocassettes

NOTES
• has experience of undertaking language training needs analyses for employers
• has learning packs available in Greek and Portuguese

180   University of Hull

Languages for Industry and Foreign Trade (LIFT)
Cottingham Road

Hull	Telephone	(0482) 465162
HU6 7RX	Fax	(0482) 465991

Contact   Dr C. Greensmith, Director of Languages for Industry and Foreign Trade

TRAINING

Arabic
Type: client-based; institution-based; group; one-to-one
Method: intensive; non-intensive; open or flexible

Danish
Type: client-based; institution-based; group; one-to-one
Method: intensive; non-intensive; open or flexible

Dutch
Type: client-based; institution-based; group; one-to-one
Method: intensive; non-intensive; open or flexible

French
Type: client-based; institution-based; group; one-to-one
Method: intensive; non-intensive; open or flexible

German
Type: client-based; institution-based; group; one-to-one
Method: intensive; non-intensive; open or flexible

Greek
Type: client-based; institution-based; group; one-to-one
Method: intensive; non-intensive; open or flexible

Italian
Type: client-based; institution-based; group; one-to-one
Method: intensive; non-intensive; open or flexible

Japanese
Type: client-based; institution-based; group; one-to-one
Method: intensive; non-intensive; open or flexible

Malay
Type: client-based; institution-based; group; one-to-one
Method: intensive; non-intensive; open or flexible

Portuguese
Type: client-based; institution-based; group; one-to-one
Method: intensive; non-intensive; open or flexible

Spanish
Type: client-based; institution-based; group; one-to-one
Method: intensive; non-intensive; open or flexible

Swedish
Type: client-based; institution-based; group; one-to-one
Method: intensive; non-intensive; open or flexible

Thai
Type: client-based; institution-based; group; one-to-one
Method: intensive; non-intensive; open or flexible

SERVICES
Translating

Danish	into and out of English
Dutch	into and out of English
French	into and out of English
German	into and out of English
Greek	into and out of English
Italian	into and out of English

Japanese	into and out of English
Malay	into English
Norwegian	into and out of English
Portuguese	into and out of English
Russian	into and out of English
Spanish	into and out of English
Swedish	into and out of English
Thai	into English
Specialisms	technical; legal; advertising

Interpreting

Arabic	simultaneous; consecutive
Danish	simultaneous; consecutive
Dutch	simultaneous; consecutive
French	simultaneous; consecutive
German	simultaneous; consecutive
Greek	simultaneous; consecutive
Italian	simultaneous; consecutive
Malay	simultaneous; consecutive
Norwegian	simultaneous; consecutive
Portuguese	simultaneous; consecutive
Spanish	simultaneous; consecutive
Swedish	simultaneous; consecutive
Thai	simultaneous; consecutive
Specialisms	technical; legal

FACILITIES

Language labs:	under 10 places - 1 fixed; 10–25 places - 1 fixed
Equipment and materials:	computer-assisted language learning; audio and videocassettes; satellite television

NOTES
- has experience of undertaking language training needs analyses for employers
- holds telephone courses, cultural awareness seminars and correspondence courses
- prepares candidates for Paris Chamber of Commerce and Institute of Linguists examinations

181   Hull College of Further Education

Queens Gardens
Hull   Telephone   (0482) 29943
HU1 3DG   Fax   (0482) 219079

Contact   Mr A. Escasany, Senior Lecturer

TRAINING

French   *Type:* client-based; institution-based; group; one-to-one; bespoke
                Method: intensive; non-intensive
German   *Type:* client-based; institution-based; group; one-to-one; bespoke
                Method: intensive; non-intensive
Italian   *Type:* client-based; institution-based; group; one-to-one; bespoke
                Method: intensive; non-intensive
Spanish   *Type:* client-based; institution-based; group; one-to-one; bespoke
                Method: intensive; non-intensive
Swedish   *Type:* client-based; institution-based; group; one-to-one; bespoke
                Method: non-intensive
Specialisms   business; secretarial; public administration; engineering; tourism;
                construction
Other   Additional languages can be offered, with notice

FACILITIES
Language labs: 10–25 places - 1 fixed

NOTES
• has experience of undertaking language training needs analyses for employers

182   Huntingdonshire College

California Road
Huntingdon   Telephone   (0480) 52346
PE18 7BL   Fax   (0480) 450129

Contact   Mrs A. Zimmerman, Languages Co-ordinator

TRAINING

Chinese   *Type:* institution-based
                 Method: non-intensive
Dutch   *Type:* institution-based
                 Method: non-intensive
French   *Type:* client-based; institution-based; group; one-to-one
                 Method: intensive; non-intensive; open or flexible
German   *Type:* institution-based
                 Method: non-intensive; open or flexible
Greek   *Type:* institution-based
                 Method: non-intensive
Italian   *Type:* institution-based
                 Method: non-intensive
Japanese   *Type:* institution-based
                 Method: non-intensive
Russian   *Type:* institution-based
                 Method: non-intensive
Spanish   *Type:* institution-based
                 Method: non-intensive
Other   Additional languages can be offered, with notice

FACILITIES
Equipment and
   materials: audio and videocassettes; satellite television

NOTES
• has experience of undertaking language training needs analyses for employers
• offers specialised language training in the medical, legal and business sectors in
  French and German, provided time is given for preparation

183 International Business and Export Services (IBEX)

North East Surrey College of Technology
Longmead Road

Epsom	Telephone	081-394 3267
KT19 9BH	Fax	081-394 3232

Contact   Mrs W. Gill, Language-Export Centre Operational Director

TRAINING

Bulgarian	*Type:* client-based; institution-based; group; one-to-one; bespoke
French	*Type:* client-based; institution-based; group; one-to-one; bespoke
	Method: intensive; non-intensive; open or flexible
German	*Type:* client-based; institution-based; group; one-to-one; bespoke
	Method: intensive; non-intensive; open or flexible
Greek	*Type:* client-based; institution-based; group; one-to-one; bespoke
Italian	*Type:* client-based; institution-based; group; one-to-one; bespoke
	Method: non-intensive; open or flexible
Japanese	*Type:* client-based; institution-based; group; one-to-one; bespoke
	Method: intensive; non-intensive; open or flexible
Polish	*Type:* client-based; institution-based; group; one-to-one; bespoke
Portuguese	*Type:* client-based; institution-based; group; one-to-one; bespoke
Russian	*Type:* client-based; institution-based; group; one-to-one; bespoke
	Method: intensive; non-intensive
Spanish	*Type:* client-based; institution-based; group; one-to-one; bespoke
	Method: intensive; non-intensive; open or flexible
Swedish	*Type:* client-based; institution-based; group; one-to-one; bespoke
Other	Additional languages can be offered, with notice

SERVICES

Translating

Bulgarian	into and out of English
French	into and out of English
German	into and out of English
Greek	into and out of English
Italian	into and out of English
Japanese	into and out of English
Polish	into and out of English
Portuguese	into and out of English
Russian	into and out of English
Spanish	into and out of English
Swedish	into and out of English

Interpreting

Bulgarian	simultaneous; consecutive
French	simultaneous; consecutive

German	simultaneous; consecutive
Greek	simultaneous; consecutive
Italian	simultaneous; consecutive
Japanese	simultaneous; consecutive
Polish	simultaneous; consecutive
Portuguese	simultaneous; consecutive
Russian	simultaneous; consecutive
Spanish	simultaneous; consecutive
Swedish	simultaneous; consecutive

FACILITIES

Language labs:	10–25 places - 1 fixed
Equipment and materials:	audio and videocassettes; computer-assisted language learning

NOTES

- has experience of undertaking language training needs analyses for employers
- can offer training, translating and interpreting services in any language, and any specialism, with notice

184 International Business and Export Services (IBEX)

Varley Lodge
Bereweeke Road
Winchester   Telephone   (0962) 842533
SO23 8XY   Fax   (0962) 842533

Contact   Ms M. Edwards, IBEX Language-Export Centre Co-ordinator

TRAINING
French   *Type:* client-based; institution-based; group; one-to-one; bespoke
              (specialisms: food; electronics)
              Method: intensive
German   *Type:* client-based; institution-based; group; one-to-one; bespoke
              (specialism: electronics)
              Method: intensive
Italian   *Type:* client-based; group; one-to-one; bespoke
              Method: intensive
Japanese   *Type:* group; one-to-one; bespoke
              Method: intensive
Russian   *Type:* one-to-one; bespoke
              Method: intensive
Spanish   *Type:* client-based; institution-based; group; one-to-one; bespoke
              Method: intensive
Other   Additional languages can be offered, with notice

SERVICES
Translating
Dutch   into and out of English (specialism: advertising)
French   into and out of English
German   into and out of English
Italian   into and out of English
Japanese   into and out of English
Polish   into and out of English
Portuguese   into and out of English
Russian   into and out of English
Spanish   into and out of English
Interpreting
French   consecutive
Italian   consecutive
Specialism   oil industry

FACILITIES

Equipment and
   materials: computer-assisted language learning; videocassettes

NOTES

• has experience of undertaking language training needs analyses for employers

185 International House

Marketing Department
106 Piccadilly
London   Telephone   071-491 2598
W1V 9FL   Fax   071-409 0959

Contact   Mrs K. Naameh, Marketing Director

TRAINING

French   *Type:* client-based; institution-based; group; one-to-one; bespoke
                (specialism: teacher training)
                Method: intensive; non-intensive
German   *Type:* client-based; institution-based; group; one-to-one; bespoke
                (specialism: teacher training)
                Method: intensive; non-intensive
Italian   *Type:* client-based; institution-based; group; one-to-one; bespoke
                (specialisms: legal; teacher training)
                Method: intensive; non-intensive
Japanese   *Type:* client-based; institution-based; group; one-to-one; bespoke
                (specialism: teacher training)
                Method: intensive; non-intensive
Spanish   *Type:* client-based; institution-based; group; one-to-one; bespoke
                (specialisms: legal; teacher training)
                Method: intensive; non-intensive

FACILITIES

Language labs: 10–25 places - 2 fixed
Equipment and
  materials: computer-assisted language learning; audio and videocassettes

NOTES
• has experience of undertaking language training needs analyses for employers
• has served as a consultant for employers, by checking the language level of job
  applicants through interviews and written tests

186   Inverness College of Further and Higher Education

3 Longman Road
Inverness   Telephone   (0463) 236681
IV1 1SA   Fax   (0463) 711977

Contact   Mrs S. Whyte, Head of Commercial Activities

TRAINING

French   *Type:* client-based; institution-based; group; one-to-one; bespoke
                    (specialism: legal)
                    Method: intensive; non-intensive
Gaelic (Scottish)   *Type:* institution-based; group
German   *Type:* client-based; institution-based; group; one-to-one
                    Method: intensive; non-intensive
Hungarian   *Type:* one-to-one; bespoke
                    Method: intensive
Italian   *Type:* client-based; institution-based; group; one-to-one; bespoke
                    Method: intensive; non-intensive
Japanese   *Type:* client-based; institution-based; one-to-one; bespoke
                    Method: intensive; non-intensive
Russian   *Type:* client-based; institution-based; group; one-to-one
                    Method: intensive; non-intensive
Spanish   *Type:* client-based; institution-based; group; one-to-one
                    Method: intensive; non-intensive
Other   Dutch can be offered, with notice

SERVICES

Translating
French   into and out of English
German   into and out of English
Hungarian   into and out of English
Italian   into and out of English
Japanese   into and out of English
Polish   into and out of English
Russian   into and out of English
Spanish   into and out of English
Interpreting
French   simultaneous; consecutive
German   simultaneous; consecutive
Hungarian   consecutive
Italian   simultaneous; consecutive
Japanese   simultaneous; consecutive

Polish	consecutive
Russian	consecutive
Spanish	simultaneous; consecutive

FACILITIES

Language labs:	under 10 places - 1 fixed, 1 portable
Interpreting facilities:	under 10 places - 1 fixed, 1 portable
Equipment and materials:	interactive video

187 Isle College

Ramnoth Road
Wisbech   Telephone   (0945) 582561
PE13 0HY   Fax   (0945) 582706

Contact   Mr A. L. Jones, Head of Division, Humanities and Social Science

TRAINING

Dutch	*Type:* institution-based
	Method: non-intensive
French	*Type:* institution-based
	Method: non-intensive
German	*Type:* institution-based
	Method: non-intensive
Italian	*Type:* institution-based
	Method: non-intensive
Spanish	*Type:* institution-based
	Method: non-intensive
Other	Additional languages can be offered, with notice

SERVICES

Translating

Dutch	into and out of English
French	into and out of English
German	into and out of English
Italian	into and out of English
Japanese	into and out of English
Russian	into and out of English
Spanish	into and out of English

FACILITIES

Language labs: 10–25 places - 1 fixed

188 Isle of Man College of Further Education

Homefield Road
Douglas   Telephone   (0624) 623113
Isle of Man   Fax   (0624) 661432

Contact   Mr S. Colvin, Lecturer in Charge of Languages

TRAINING
French   *Type:* client-based; institution-based; group; one-to-one; bespoke
                Method: intensive; non-intensive; open or flexible
German   *Type:* institution-based; group; one-to-one; bespoke
                Method: intensive; non-intensive; open or flexible
Italian   *Type:* institution-based; group; bespoke
                Method: non-intensive; open or flexible
Spanish   *Type:* client-based; institution-based; group; bespoke
                Method: non-intensive; open or flexible
Other   Russian and possibly other languages can be offered, with notice

FACILITIES
Equipment and
  materials: audio and videocassettes; computer-assisted language learning

189   James Watt College

Finnart Street
Greenock   Telephone   (0475) 24433
PA16 8HF   Fax   (0475) 888079

Contact   Ms A. Campbell, Head of General Education and Languages

TRAINING
French   *Type:* client-based; institution-based; group; one-to-one
                   Method: non-intensive; open or flexible
German   *Type:* client-based; institution-based; group; one-to-one
                   Method: non-intensive; open or flexible
Spanish   *Type:* client-based; institution-based; group; one-to-one

FACILITIES
Language labs: 10–25 places - 1 portable; over 25 places - 1 fixed
Equipment and
   materials: computer-assisted language learning; audiocassettes

190　University of Keele

Language Services Unit
Keele　　　　　　　Telephone　　　(0782) 713036
ST5 5BG　　　　　　Fax　　　　　　(0782) 713036

Contact　　　　Dr S. Levy, Language Services Unit Co-ordinator

TRAINING

Chinese　　　　*Type:* institution-based; group; one-to-one
　　　　　　　Method: intensive; non-intensive
French　　　　*Type:* client-based; institution-based; group; one-to-one; bespoke
　　　　　　　(specialism: computers)
　　　　　　　Method: intensive; non-intensive; open or flexible
German　　　　*Type:* client-based; institution-based; group; one-to-one
　　　　　　　Method: intensive; non-intensive; open or flexible
Japanese　　　*Type:* client-based; institution-based; group; one-to-one
　　　　　　　Method: intensive; non-intensive
Russian　　　　*Type:* institution-based; group; one-to-one
　　　　　　　Method: intensive; non-intensive
Spanish　　　　*Type:* client-based; institution-based; group; one-to-one
　　　　　　　Method: intensive; non-intensive

SERVICES
Translating
French　　　　into and out of English
German　　　　into and out of English
Japanese　　　into and out of English
Russian　　　　into and out of English
Spanish　　　　into and out of English
Interpreting
French　　　　consecutive
Japanese　　　consecutive
Russian　　　　consecutive

FACILITIES
Language labs:　　over 25 places - 1 fixed

191   Keighley College

Cavendish Street
Keighley
BD21 3DF

Telephone   (0535) 618555
Fax   (0535) 618539

Contact   Mr T. Tarpy, European Cross-College Co-ordinator

TRAINING

French	*Type:* client-based; institution-based; group; one-to-one; bespoke (specialism: engineering) *Method:* non-intensive
German	*Type:* client-based; institution-based; group; one-to-one; bespoke (specialism: plastics) *Method:* non-intensive
Italian	*Type:* client-based; institution-based; group; one-to-one; bespoke *Method:* non-intensive
Japanese	*Type:* client-based; institution-based; group; one-to-one; bespoke (specialism: tourism) *Method:* non-intensive
Portuguese	*Type:* client-based; institution-based; group; one-to-one; bespoke (specialism: textiles) *Method:* non-intensive
Russian	*Type:* client-based; institution-based; group; one-to-one; bespoke
Spanish	*Type:* client-based; institution-based; group; one-to-one; bespoke *Method:* non-intensive
Urdu	*Type:* institution-based; group *Method:* non-intensive
Other	Additional languages can be offered, with notice

NOTES
• has experience of undertaking language training needs analyses for employers

192   Kendal College

Milnthorpe Road
Kendal   Telephone   (0539) 724313
LA9 5AY ·   Fax   (0539) 733714

Contact   Mr M. Cawthorn, Languages Co-ordinator

TRAINING
French   *Type:* client-based; institution-based; one-to-one
                 Method: intensive; non-intensive; open or flexible
German   *Type:* client-based; institution-based; one-to-one
                 Method: intensive; non-intensive; open or flexible
Italian   *Type:* institution-based
                 Method: intensive; non-intensive; open or flexible
Spanish   *Type:* institution-based
                 Method: intensive; non-intensive; open or flexible

SERVICES
Translating
French   into and out of English
German   into and out of English
Italian   into and out of English
Spanish   into and out of English

NOTES
• also offers 20 week courses in Japanese for beginners, and basic Portuguese

193   University of Kent at Canterbury

Centre for Language and Business in Europe
161 Cornwallis West

Canterbury	Telephone	(0227) 475479
CT2 7NF	Fax	(0227) 475476

Contact   Professor A. Stevens, Director of the Centre for Language and Business in Europe

TRAINING

Arabic
Type: client-based; institution-based; group; one-to-one; bespoke
Method: intensive; non-intensive; open or flexible

French
Type: client-based; institution-based; group; one-to-one; bespoke (specialisms: legal; chemical; marketing)
Method: intensive; non-intensive; open or flexible

German
Type: client-based; institution-based; group; one-to-one; bespoke (specialisms: legal; chemical; marketing)
Method: intensive; non-intensive; open or flexible

Greek
Type: client-based; institution-based; group; one-to-one; bespoke
Method: intensive; non-intensive; open or flexible

Italian
Type: client-based; institution-based; group; one-to-one; bespoke (specialisms: legal; chemical; marketing)
Method: intensive; non-intensive; open or flexible

Japanese
Type: client-based; institution-based; group; one-to-one; bespoke (specialisms: chemical; marketing; medical)
Method: intensive; non-intensive; open or flexible

Portuguese
Type: client-based; institution-based; group; one-to-one; bespoke
Method: intensive; non-intensive; open or flexible

Russian
Type: client-based; institution-based; group; one-to-one; bespoke
Method: intensive; non-intensive; open or flexible

Spanish
Type: client-based; institution-based; group; one-to-one; bespoke (specialisms: legal; chemical; marketing)
Method: intensive; non-intensive; open or flexible

Swedish
Type: client-based; institution-based; group; one-to-one; bespoke

Turkish
Type: client-based; institution-based; group; one-to-one; bespoke
Method: intensive; non-intensive; open or flexible

SERVICES
Translating

Arabic	into and out of English
French	into and out of English
German	into and out of English
Italian	into and out of English
Japanese	into and out of English
Portuguese	into and out of English

Russian	into and out of English
Spanish	into and out of English
Turkish	into and out of English
Specialisms	legal; scientific; marketing
Interpreting	
French	consecutive (specialisms: legal; medical)
German	consecutive (specialism: business)
Italian	consecutive (specialism: marketing)
Japanese	consecutive (specialism: business)
Portuguese	consecutive (specialism: business)
Russian	consecutive (specialism: business)
Spanish	consecutive (specialism: business)

FACILITIES

Language labs:	under 10 places - 1 fixed; 10–25 places - 2 fixed
Interpreting facilities:	10–25 places - 1 fixed
Equipment and materials:	computer-assisted language learning; satellite television; video laboratory; audiocassettes

NOTES
- has experience of undertaking language training needs analyses for employers
- holds intensive weekend courses in legal French
- organises cultural briefings covering European countries and Japan

194   Kilmarnock College

Holehouse Road
Kilmarnock   Telephone   (0563) 23501
KA3 7AT   Fax   (0563) 38182

Contact   Mr D. Wilcock, Industrial Liaison Officer

TRAINING
French   *Type:* client-based; institution-based; group; one-to-one; bespoke
                  Method: non-intensive
German   *Type:* client-based; institution-based; group; one-to-one; bespoke
                  Method: non-intensive
Italian   *Type:* client-based; institution-based; group; one-to-one; bespoke
Spanish   *Type:* client-based; institution-based; group; one-to-one; bespoke
                  Method: non-intensive

FACILITIES
Language labs: under 10 places - 1 fixed

195 King Alfred's College

Sparkford Road
Winchester   Telephone   (0962) 870731
SO22 4NR   Fax   (0962) 842280

Contact   Mr C. Stephens, Business Services Manager

TRAINING

French   *Type:* client-based; institution-based; group; one-to-one; bespoke
(specialisms: food; electronics)
Method: intensive

German   *Type:* client-based; institution-based; group; one-to-one; bespoke
(specialism: electronics)
Method: intensive

Italian   *Type:* client-based; group; one-to-one; bespoke
Method: intensive

Japanese   *Type:* group; one-to-one; bespoke
Method: intensive

Russian   *Type:* one-to-one; bespoke
Method: intensive

Spanish   *Type:* client-based; institution-based; group; one-to-one; bespoke
Method: intensive

Other   Additional languages can be offered, with notice

SERVICES

Translating
Dutch   into and out of English (specialism: advertising)
French   into and out of English
German   into and out of English
Italian   into and out of English
Japanese   into and out of English
Polish   into and out of English
Portuguese   into and out of English
Russian   into and out of English
Spanish   into and out of English
Interpreting
French   consecutive
Italian   consecutive
Specialism   oil industry

FACILITIES

Equipment and
   materials: computer-assisted language learning; videocassettes

NOTES

- has experience of undertaking language training needs analyses for employers
- acts as a marketing support agency for International Business and Export Services (IBEX) Language-Export Centre, and sub-contracts to it any language work which comes to the college

196   King's College (London)

Language and Communication Centre
The Strand

London	Telephone	071-873 2890
WC2R 2LS	Fax	071-240 0035

Contact   Dr V. Davies, Director

TRAINING

French
Type: client-based; institution-based; group; one-to-one; bespoke (specialisms: legal; commercial; scientific; cultural; insurance; medical)
Method: intensive; non-intensive; open or flexible

German
Type: client-based; institution-based; group; one-to-one; bespoke (specialisms: legal; commercial; scientific; cultural)
Method: intensive; non-intensive; open or flexible

Greek
Type: client-based; institution-based; group; one-to-one; bespoke (specialism: commercial)
Method: intensive; non-intensive; open or flexible

Italian
Type: client-based; institution-based; group; one-to-one; bespoke (specialisms: commercial; cultural)
Method: intensive; non-intensive; open or flexible

Japanese
Type: client-based; institution-based; group; one-to-one; bespoke (specialisms: commercial; cultural)
Method: intensive; non-intensive; open or flexible

Portuguese
Type: client-based; institution-based; group; one-to-one; bespoke (specialism: commercial)
Method: intensive; non-intensive; open or flexible

Russian
Type: client-based; institution-based; group; one-to-one; bespoke (specialism: commercial)
Method: intensive; non-intensive; open or flexible

Spanish
Type: client-based; institution-based; group; one-to-one; bespoke (specialisms: legal; commercial; scientific; cultural)
Method: intensive; non-intensive; open or flexible

Other
Additional languages can be offered, with notice

FACILITIES

Language labs: under 10 places - 1 portable; 10–25 places - 1 fixed
Equipment and
  materials: computer-assisted language learning; satellite television

NOTES

- has experience of undertaking language training needs analyses for employers
- provides all the language training on the London Business School MBA programme and graduate non-MBA students may apply to join these classes

197   Kingston College of Further Education

Kingston Hall Road
Kingston upon Thames   Telephone   081-546 2151
KT1 2AQ   Fax   081-547 2292

Contact   Mr P. Dennis, European Liaison Officer

TRAINING
French   *Type:* client-based; institution-based; group; bespoke
                 Method: non-intensive
German   *Type:* client-based; institution-based; group; bespoke
                 Method: non-intensive
Italian   *Type:* client-based; institution-based; group; bespoke
                 Method: non-intensive
Spanish   *Type:* client-based; institution-based; group; bespoke
                 Method: non-intensive
Specialism   business

FACILITIES
Language labs: 10–25 places - 2 fixed

NOTES
• has experience of undertaking language training needs analyses for employers
• offers intensive language training for business during college vacations

198   Kingston Language-Export Centre

Kingston University
21 Eden Street
Kingston upon Thames   Telephone   081-547 2623
KT1 1BL   Fax   081-546 5776

Contact   Ms P. Lane, Manager of Kingston Language-Export Centre

TRAINING

Czech   *Type:* institution-based; group; bespoke
           Method: intensive; non-intensive
French   *Type:* client-based; institution-based; group; one-to-one; bespoke
           (specialism: financial)
           Method: intensive; non-intensive; open or flexible
German   *Type:* client-based; institution-based; group; one-to-one; bespoke
           Method: intensive; non-intensive; open or flexible
Japanese   *Type:* client-based; group; one-to-one
           Method: intensive; non-intensive; open or flexible
Russian   *Type:* client-based; one-to-one
           Method: intensive; non-intensive; open or flexible
Spanish   *Type:* client-based; institution-based; group; one-to-one
           Method: intensive; non-intensive; open or flexible
Other   Additional languages can be offered, with notice

SERVICES

Translating
Czech   into and out of English
French   into and out of English
German   into and out of English
Italian   into and out of English
Japanese   into and out of English
Russian   into and out of English
Spanish   into and out of English
Interpreting
Czech   consecutive
French   consecutive
German   consecutive
Russian   consecutive

FACILITIES

Language labs: 10–25 places - 3 fixed
Equipment and
  materials: audio and videocassettes; computer-assisted language learning;
                  interactive video; satellite television

NOTES
- has experience of undertaking language training needs analyses for employers
- operates a language consultancy service for help with foreign language business meetings and in-house language courses, and can meet almost all translation needs

199   Kingston University

21 Eden Street
Kingston upon Thames   Telephone   081-547 2623
KT1 1BL   Fax   081-546 5776

Contact   Ms P. Lane, Manager of Kingston Language-Export Centre

NOTES
• see entry for Kingston Language-Export Centre

200   Kirby College

Training and Management Enterprises
Orchard Road

Middlesborough	Telephone	(0642) 850885
TS5 5PN	Fax	(0642) 850686

Contact   Mr T. Bishop, Training and Management Enterprises Manager

TRAINING

Arabic
Type: client-based; institution-based; group; one-to-one; bespoke
Method: intensive; non-intensive

Czech
Type: client-based; institution-based; group; one-to-one; bespoke
Method: intensive; non-intensive

Dutch
Type: client-based; institution-based; group; one-to-one; bespoke
Method: intensive; non-intensive

French
Type: client-based; institution-based; group; one-to-one; bespoke
(specialism: exporting)
Method: intensive; non-intensive; open or flexible

German
Type: client-based; institution-based; group; one-to-one; bespoke
(specialisms: exporting; pharmaceutical)
Method: intensive; non-intensive; open or flexible

Greek
Type: client-based; institution-based; group; one-to-one; bespoke
Method: non-intensive

Italian
Type: client-based; institution-based; group; one-to-one; bespoke
Method: intensive; non-intensive; open or flexible

Japanese
Type: client-based; institution-based; group; one-to-one; bespoke
Method: intensive; non-intensive

Malay
Type: client-based; institution-based; group; one-to-one; bespoke
Method: intensive; non-intensive

Portuguese
Type: client-based; institution-based; group; one-to-one; bespoke
Method: intensive; non-intensive

Russian
Type: client-based; institution-based; group; one-to-one; bespoke
Method: intensive; non-intensive

Spanish
Type: client-based; institution-based; group; one-to-one; bespoke
Method: intensive; non-intensive; open or flexible

Swedish
Type: client-based; institution-based; group; one-to-one; bespoke
Method: intensive; non-intensive

FACILITIES

Language labs: 10–25 places - 1 fixed
Equipment and
  materials: computer-assisted language learning; audio and videocassettes

NOTES
- has experience of undertaking language training needs analyses for employers
- offers short courses for telephonists, receptionists and trade fair exhibitors

201   Kitson College

Cookridge Street
Leeds   Telephone   (0532) 430381
LS2 8BL   Fax   (0532) 340365

Contact   Ms S. Brooksbank, Director of Faculty

TRAINING

French	*Type:* client-based; institution-based; group; one-to-one; bespoke (specialisms: printing; auto engineering)
	Method: open or flexible
German	*Type:* client-based; institution-based; group; one-to-one; bespoke (specialism: printing; auto engineering)
	Method: open or flexible
Italian	*Type:* client-based; institution-based; group; one-to-one; bespoke
Polish	*Type:* client-based; institution-based; group; one-to-one; bespoke (specialism: scientific)
Russian	*Type:* client-based; institution-based; group; one-to-one; bespoke
Spanish	*Type:* client-based; institution-based; group; one-to-one; bespoke
	Method: open or flexible
Other	Bengali, Urdu and Gujarati can be offered, with notice

SERVICES
Translating

Polish	into and out of English (specialism: scientific)
Portuguese	into and out of English

Interpreting

Polish	simultaneous; consecutive (specialism: scientific)
Portuguese	simultaneous; consecutive

FACILITIES

Language labs:	under 10 places - 1 fixed
Interpreting facilities:	under 10 places - 1 fixed

202   Knowsley Community College

Rupert Road
Roby   Telephone   051-443 2600
L36 9TD   Fax   051-449 2352

Contact   Mr G. Williams, Lecturer in Modern Languages

TRAINING
French   *Type:* client-based; institution-based; group (specialisms: business; technical; tourism)
                Method: intensive; non-intensive
German   *Type:* client-based; institution-based; group
                Method: intensive; non-intensive
Spanish   *Type:* client-based; institution-based
                Method: intensive; non-intensive

SERVICES
Translating
French   into and out of English
German   into and out of English
Spanish   into and out of English
Specialism   building
Interpreting
French   simultaneous; consecutive
German   simultaneous; consecutive
Specialisms   building; public administration

FACILITIES
Language labs: 10–25 places - 1 portable
Equipment and
   materials: computer-assisted language learning; videocassettes; interactive video

NOTES
• has experience of undertaking language training needs analyses for employers

203   Knuston Hall Adult Residential College

Irchester
Wellingborough   Telephone   (0933) 312104
NN9 7EU   Fax   (0933) 57596

Contact   Mr J. Herrick, Warden

TRAINING

Chinese   *Type:* institution-based; group
                     Method: non-intensive
French   *Type:* institution-based; group
                     Method: non-intensive
German   *Type:* institution-based; group
                     Method: non-intensive
Italian   *Type:* institution-based; group
                     Method: non-intensive
Portuguese   *Type:* institution-based; group
                     Method: non-intensive
Russian   *Type:* institution-based; group
                     Method: non-intensive
Spanish   *Type:* institution-based; group
                     Method: non-intensive
Other   Additional languages can be offered, with notice

204 Lancashire and Cumbria Language-Export Centre

University of Central Lancashire
Preston   Telephone   (0772) 893132
PR1 2TQ   Fax   (0772) 892900

Contact   Mrs J. Davies, Language-Export Centre Manager

TRAINING

Chinese	*Type:* client-based; institution-based; group; one-to-one; bespoke
Dutch	*Type:* client-based; institution-based; group; one-to-one; bespoke
	Method: intensive; non-intensive
French	*Type:* client-based; institution-based; group; one-to-one; bespoke
	(specialism: technical)
	Method: intensive; non-intensive; open or flexible
German	*Type:* client-based; institution-based; group; one-to-one; bespoke
	(specialism: technical)
	Method: intensive; non-intensive; open or flexible
Italian	*Type:* client-based; institution-based; group; one-to-one; bespoke
	(specialism: technical)
	Method: intensive; non-intensive
Japanese	*Type:* client-based; institution-based; group; one-to-one; bespoke
	Method: intensive; non-intensive
Portuguese	*Type:* client-based; institution-based; group; one-to-one; bespoke
	Method: intensive; non-intensive
Russian	*Type:* client-based; institution-based; group; one-to-one; bespoke
	Method: intensive; non-intensive
Spanish	*Type:* client-based; institution-based; group; one-to-one; bespoke
	Method: intensive; non-intensive
Swedish	*Type:* client-based; institution-based; group; one-to-one; bespoke
Other	Additional languages can be offered, with notice

SERVICES

Translating

Dutch	into and out of English
Finnish	into and out of English
French	into and out of English
German	into and out of English
Italian	into and out of English
Japanese	into and out of English
Norwegian	into and out of English
Polish	into and out of English
Portuguese	into and out of English

Russian	into and out of English
Spanish	into and out of English
Swedish	into and out of English
Interpreting	
Dutch	consecutive
French	consecutive
German	consecutive
Italian	consecutive
Japanese	consecutive
Portuguese	consecutive
Russian	consecutive
Spanish	consecutive

FACILITIES

Language labs:	10–25 places - 3 fixed
Equipment and materials:	computer-assisted language learning

NOTES

- has experience of undertaking language training needs analyses for employers
- simultaneous interpreting can be arranged

205   Lancashire College

Southport Road
Chorley   Telephone   (0257) 276719
PR7 1NB   Fax   (0257) 241370

Contact   Mr D. Garcia Lucas, Principal

TRAINING

Arabic   *Type:* institution-based; one-to-one; bespoke
                Method: intensive; non-intensive; open or flexible
Bengali   *Type:* institution-based; group
                Method: intensive; non-intensive; open or flexible
Chinese   *Type:* institution-based; group; one-to-one; bespoke
                Method: intensive; non-intensive; open or flexible
Danish   *Type:* institution-based; one-to-one; bespoke
                Method: intensive; open or flexible
Dutch   *Type:* institution-based; one-to-one; bespoke
                Method: intensive; non-intensive; open or flexible
Farsi   *Type:* institution-based
                Method: intensive; non-intensive; open or flexible
Finnish   *Type:* institution-based
                Method: intensive
French   *Type:* client-based; institution-based; group; one-to-one; bespoke
                Method: intensive; non-intensive; open or flexible
German   *Type:* client-based; institution-based; group; one-to-one; bespoke
                Method: intensive; non-intensive; open or flexible
Greek   *Type:* institution-based; one-to-one; bespoke
                Method: intensive; non-intensive
Gujarati   *Type:* institution-based; group
                Method: intensive; non-intensive; open or flexible
Hungarian   *Type:* institution-based; one-to-one; bespoke
                Method: intensive; open or flexible
Italian   *Type:* institution-based; group; one-to-one; bespoke
                Method: intensive; non-intensive; open or flexible
Japanese   *Type:* institution-based; group; one-to-one; bespoke
                Method: intensive; non-intensive; open or flexible
Norwegian   *Type:* institution-based; one-to-one; bespoke
                Method: intensive; open or flexible
Polish   *Type:* institution-based; one-to-one; bespoke
                Method: intensive; non-intensive
Portuguese   *Type:* institution-based; group; one-to-one; bespoke
                Method: intensive; non-intensive; open or flexible
Punjabi   *Type:* institution-based; group
                Method: intensive; non-intensive; open or flexible

Romanian	*Type:* institution-based
	Method: intensive; non-intensive
Russian	*Type:* client-based; institution-based; group; one-to-one; bespoke
	Method: intensive; non-intensive; open or flexible
Spanish	*Type:* client-based; institution-based; group; one-to-one; bespoke
	Method: intensive; non-intensive; open or flexible
Swahili	*Type:* institution-based
	Method: intensive; non-intensive; open or flexible
Swedish	*Type:* institution-based; one-to-one; bespoke
	Method: intensive
Thai	*Type:* institution-based; one-to-one; bespoke
	Method: intensive
Turkish	*Type:* institution-based; group; one-to-one; bespoke
	Method: intensive; non-intensive; open or flexible
Urdu	*Type:* institution-based; group; one-to-one; bespoke
	Method: intensive; non-intensive; open or flexible
Specialisms	legal; industrial; commercial; scientific
Other	Additional languages can be offered, with notice

SERVICES
Translating

Chinese	into and out of English
Dutch	into and out of English
French	into and out of English (specialism: technical)
German	into and out of English (specialism: technical)
Greek	into and out of English
Hungarian	out of English
Italian	into and out of English (specialism: technical)
Japanese	into and out of English
Portuguese	into and out of English
Russian	into and out of English (specialism: technical)
Spanish	into and out of English

Interpreting

French	consecutive
German	consecutive
Hungarian	consecutive
Italian	consecutive
Japanese	consecutive
Polish	consecutive
Russian	consecutive
Spanish	consecutive

FACILITIES

Language labs:	10–25 places - 1 fixed
Interpreting facilities:	under 10 places - 1 fixed; 10–25 places - 1 fixed; 26–100 places - 1 fixed

Equipment and
  materials: interactive video; audio and videocassettes; computer-assisted
                language learning

NOTES
- has experience of undertaking language training needs analyses for employers

206　Adult College (Lancaster)

White Cross Education Centre
Quarry Road
Lancaster　　　　　　　Telephone　　　(0524) 60141
LA1 3SE　　　　　　　　Fax　　　　　　(0524) 844347

Contact　　　　Mr D. Noonan, Principal

TRAINING
French　　　　*Type:* client-based; institution-based; group; one-to-one
　　　　　　　Method: intensive; non-intensive
German　　　　*Type:* client-based; institution-based; group; one-to-one
　　　　　　　Method: intensive; non-intensive
Italian　　　　*Type:* client-based; institution-based; group; one-to-one
　　　　　　　Method: intensive; non-intensive
Russian　　　　*Type:* client-based; institution-based; group; one-to-one
　　　　　　　Method: intensive; non-intensive
Spanish　　　　*Type:* client-based; institution-based; group; one-to-one
　　　　　　　Method: intensive; non-intensive

NOTES
• has experience of undertaking language training needs analyses for employers

207   Lancaster and Morecambe College

Morecambe Road
Lancaster   Telephone   (0524) 66215
LA1 2TY   Fax   (0524) 843078

Contact   Miss A. Styles, Lecturer in Charge of Modern Languages

TRAINING

French
Type: client-based; institution-based; group; bespoke (specialisms: tourism; hotel trade; catering; business; secretarial; receptionists)
Method: intensive; non-intensive; open or flexible

German
Type: client-based; institution-based; group; bespoke (specialisms: tourism; hotel trade; catering; business; secretarial; receptionists)
Method: intensive; non-intensive; open or flexible

Italian
Type: institution-based; group
Method: intensive; non-intensive

Russian
Type: institution-based; group
Method: intensive; non-intensive

Spanish
Type: institution-based; group; bespoke
Method: intensive; non-intensive; open or flexible

Other
Additional languages can be offered, with notice

SERVICES
Translating
French   into and out of English
German   into and out of English
Russian   into and out of English
Spanish   into and out of English

FACILITIES
Language labs: 10–25 places - 1 fixed
Equipment and
  materials: computer-assisted language learning; audio and videocassettes

NOTES
• has experience of undertaking language training needs analyses for employers

208   Langley College

Langcet Limited
Lascelles Road
Slough   Telephone   (0753) 511626
SL3 7PP   Fax   (0753) 551102

Contact   Ms A. Evans, Commercial Manager, Langcet Ltd

TRAINING
French   *Type:* client-based; institution-based; group; one-to-one; bespoke
                    (specialism: secretarial)
                    Method: intensive; non-intensive; open or flexible
German   *Type:* client-based; institution-based; group; one-to-one; bespoke
                    (specialism: secretarial)
                    Method: intensive; non-intensive; open or flexible
Italian   *Type:* client-based; institution-based; group; one-to-one; bespoke
                    Method: intensive; non-intensive; open or flexible
Russian   *Type:* client-based; institution-based; group; one-to-one; bespoke
Spanish   *Type:* client-based; institution-based; group; one-to-one; bespoke
                    Method: intensive; non-intensive; open or flexible

SERVICES
Translating
French   into and out of English
German   into and out of English
Italian   into and out of English
Russian   into and out of English
Spanish   into and out of English
Interpreting
French   simultaneous; consecutive
German   simultaneous; consecutive
Russian   simultaneous; consecutive
Spanish   simultaneous; consecutive

NOTES
• has experience of undertaking language training needs analyses for employers

209　Lauder College

North Fod
Halbeath
Dunfermline　　　　Telephone　　　(0383) 726201
KY11 5DY　　　　　Fax　　　　　　(0383) 621449

Contact　　　Ms C. Law, Senior Lecturer, European Initiatives

TRAINING
French　　　　*Type:* client-based; institution-based; group; one-to-one; bespoke
　　　　　　　(specialisms: legal; medical)
　　　　　　　Method: intensive; non-intensive
German　　　　*Type:* client-based; institution-based; group; one-to-one; bespoke
　　　　　　　(specialisms: legal; medical)
　　　　　　　Method: intensive; non-intensive
Italian　　　　*Type:* client-based; institution-based; one-to-one; bespoke
　　　　　　　Method: intensive; non-intensive
Norwegian　　*Type:* institution-based; one-to-one; bespoke (specialism: military)
Polish　　　　*Type:* client-based; institution-based; one-to-one; bespoke
Portuguese　　*Type:* client-based; institution-based; group; one-to-one; bespoke
Spanish　　　　*Type:* client-based; institution-based; group; one-to-one; bespoke
　　　　　　　Method: intensive; non-intensive
Other　　　　Japanese and Danish can be offered, with notice

SERVICES
Translating
French　　　　into and out of English
German　　　　into and out of English
Italian　　　　into and out of English
Portuguese　　into and out of English
Spanish　　　　into and out of English
Interpreting
French　　　　simultaneous; consecutive
German　　　　simultaneous; consecutive
Italian　　　　simultaneous; consecutive
Portuguese　　simultaneous; consecutive
Spanish　　　　simultaneous; consecutive

FACILITIES
Language labs:　　under 10 places - 1 fixed

NOTES
• has experience of undertaking language training needs analyses for employers

210 University of Leeds

Woodhouse Lane
Leeds   Telephone   (0532) 431751
LS2 9JT   Fax   (0532) 336017

Contact   Dr F. Todd, Director of Continuing Professional Education

TRAINING

Arabic	*Type:* client-based; institution-based; group; one-to-one; bespoke
	Method: intensive; non-intensive; open or flexible
Bulgarian	*Type:* client-based; institution-based; group; one-to-one; bespoke
	Method: intensive; non-intensive; open or flexible
Chinese	*Type:* client-based; institution-based; group; one-to-one
	Method: intensive; non-intensive; open or flexible
Czech	*Type:* client-based; institution-based; group; one-to-one; bespoke
	Method: intensive; non-intensive; open or flexible
French	*Type:* client-based; institution-based; group; one-to-one; bespoke (specialisms: legal; technical; engineering; scientific; social services)
	Method: intensive; non-intensive
Hebrew	*Type:* client-based; institution-based; group; one-to-one; bespoke
	Method: intensive; non-intensive; open or flexible
Japanese	*Type:* client-based; institution-based; group; one-to-one
	Method: intensive; non-intensive; open or flexible
Mongolian	*Type:* client-based; institution-based; group; one-to-one
	Method: intensive; non-intensive; open or flexible
Portuguese	*Type:* client-based; institution-based; group
Russian	*Type:* client-based; institution-based; group; one-to-one; bespoke (specialisms: business; commercial; media)
	Method: intensive; non-intensive; open or flexible
Spanish	*Type:* client-based; institution-based; group (specialism: economics)
Other	Ukrainian can be offered, with notice

SERVICES
Translating

Arabic	into and out of English
Bulgarian	into and out of English
Chinese	into and out of English
Czech	into and out of English
French	into and out of English
Hebrew	into and out of English
Japanese	into and out of English
Mongolian	into and out of English
Portuguese	into and out of English
Russian	into and out of English
Spanish	into and out of English

Interpreting

Arabic	consecutive (specialism: legal)
Bulgarian	simultaneous; consecutive
Chinese	consecutive
Czech	simultaneous; consecutive
French	consecutive
Hebrew	consecutive (specialism: legal)
Japanese	consecutive
Mongolian	consecutive
Portuguese	consecutive
Russian	simultaneous; consecutive

FACILITIES

Language labs:	10–25 places - 2 fixed, 1 portable; over 25 places - 1 fixed
Equipment and materials:	computer-assisted language learning; audio and videocassettes; satellite television

NOTES
- has experience of undertaking language training needs analyses for employers
- is preparing a self-teaching course in Bulgarian
- offers voice-overs in Bulgarian, Russian and Czech

211   Leeds Metropolitan University

The Language Centre
Beckett Park Campus
Leeds   Telephone   (0532) 832600
LS6 3QS   Fax   (0532) 745966

Contact   Ms E. Jones, Language Consultant

TRAINING

Arabic	*Type:* client-based; institution-based; group; one-to-one; bespoke
	Method: intensive; non-intensive
Chinese	*Type:* client-based; institution-based; group; one-to-one; bespoke
	Method: intensive; non-intensive
Danish	*Type:* client-based; institution-based; group; one-to-one; bespoke
	Method: intensive; non-intensive
Dutch	*Type:* client-based; institution-based; group; one-to-one; bespoke
	Method: intensive; non-intensive
French	*Type:* client-based; institution-based; group; one-to-one; bespoke
	Method: intensive; non-intensive; open or flexible
German	*Type:* client-based; institution-based; group; one-to-one; bespoke
	Method: intensive; non-intensive; open or flexible
Greek	*Type:* client-based; institution-based; group; one-to-one; bespoke
	Method: intensive; non-intensive
Irish	*Type:* client-based; institution-based; group; one-to-one; bespoke
	Method: intensive; non-intensive
Italian	*Type:* client-based; institution-based; group; one-to-one; bespoke
	Method: intensive; non-intensive; open or flexible
Japanese	*Type:* client-based; institution-based; group; one-to-one; bespoke
	Method: intensive; non-intensive
Norwegian	*Type:* client-based; institution-based; group; one-to-one; bespoke
	Method: non-intensive
Polish	*Type:* client-based; institution-based; group; one-to-one; bespoke
	Method: intensive; non-intensive
Portuguese	*Type:* client-based; institution-based; group; one-to-one; bespoke
	Method: intensive; non-intensive
Russian	*Type:* client-based; institution-based; group; one-to-one; bespoke
	Method: intensive; non-intensive
Spanish	*Type:* client-based; institution-based; group; one-to-one; bespoke
	Method: intensive; non-intensive; open or flexible
Swedish	*Type:* client-based; institution-based; group; one-to-one; bespoke
	Method: intensive; non-intensive
Other	Additional languages can be offered, with notice

SERVICES
Translating

Afrikaans	into and out of English
Arabic	into and out of English
Bengali	into and out of English
Bulgarian	into and out of English
Chinese	into and out of English
Czech	into and out of English
Danish	into and out of English
Dutch	into and out of English
Finnish	into and out of English
French	into and out of English
German	into and out of English
Greek	into and out of English
Gujarati	into and out of English
Hungarian	into and out of English
Icelandic	into and out of English
Indonesian	into and out of English
Irish	into and out of English
Italian	into and out of English
Japanese	into and out of English
Korean	into and out of English
Malay	into and out of English
Norwegian	into and out of English
Polish	into and out of English
Portuguese	into and out of English
Punjabi	into and out of English
Romanian	into and out of English
Russian	into and out of English
Serbo-Croat	into and out of English
Spanish	into and out of English
Swedish	into and out of English
Thai	into and out of English
Turkish	into and out of English
Ukrainian	into and out of English
Urdu	into and out of English
Vietnamese	into and out of English

Interpreting

Arabic	consecutive
Chinese	consecutive
Danish	consecutive
Dutch	consecutive
French	consecutive
German	consecutive
Greek	consecutive
Irish	consecutive
Italian	consecutive
Japanese	consecutive

Norwegian	consecutive
Polish	consecutive
Portuguese	consecutive
Russian	consecutive
Spanish	consecutive
Swedish	consecutive

FACILITIES

Language labs:	10–25 places - 6 fixed
Equipment and materials:	computer-assisted language learning; audio and videocassettes; satellite television; CD-ROM

NOTES

- has experience of undertaking language training needs analyses for employers
- runs around 200 tailored courses a year for business clients, ranging from shop-floor workers and receptionists, to managing directors
- is applying for BS5750 registration

212 Leek College of Further Education

Stockwell Street
Leek   Telephone   (0538) 382506
ST13 6DP   Fax   (0538) 399506

Contact   Mrs R. Harris, Director of Marketing

TRAINING
French   *Type:* client-based; institution-based; group
                Method: non-intensive; open or flexible
German   *Type:* institution-based
                Method: non-intensive; open or flexible
Greek   *Type:* institution-based
                Method: non-intensive; open or flexible

SERVICES
Translating
French   into English
German   into English

FACILITIES
Language labs: under 10 places - 1 portable
Interpreting
   facilities: under 10 places - 1 portable

213 Leicester South Fields College

Aylestone Road
Leicester
LE2 7LW

Telephone	(0533) 541818
Fax	(0533) 653147

Contact   Mr I. Lathom, Academic Courses Co-ordinator

TRAINING

French   *Type:* institution-based
                Method: open or flexible
German   *Type:* institution-based
                Method: open or flexible
Gujarati   *Type:* institution-based
Italian   *Type:* institution-based
                Method: open or flexible
Russian   *Type:* institution-based
Spanish   *Type:* institution-based
                Method: open or flexible

FACILITIES
Language labs: under 10 places - 1 portable; 10–25 places - 1 fixed

NOTES
• has experience of undertaking language training needs analyses for employers
• has given training in Gujarati for Leicestershire Fire Brigade

214   Leigh College

Marshall Street
Leigh   Telephone   (0942) 608811
WN7 4HR   Fax   (0942) 260041

Contact   Mrs C. Doublet-Stewart, Head of Modern Languages

TRAINING
French   *Type:* client-based; institution-based; group; one-to-one
                 Method: intensive
German   *Type:* client-based; institution-based; group; one-to-one
                 Method: intensive
Italian   *Type:* client-based; group
                 Method: intensive
Russian   *Type:* client-based; institution-based; group; one-to-one
Spanish   *Type:* client-based; institution-based; group; one-to-one

SERVICES
Translating
French   into and out of English
German   into and out of English
Italian   into and out of English
Russian   into and out of English
Spanish   into and out of English
Interpreting
French   simultaneous; consecutive
German   simultaneous; consecutive
Italian   simultaneous; consecutive
Spanish   simultaneous; consecutive

FACILITIES
Language labs: under 10 places - 1 portable; 10–25 places - 1 fixed
Interpreting
  facilities: 10–25 places - 1 fixed

215 Lews Castle College

Stornoway
Isle of Lewis
PA86 0XR

Telephone	(0851) 703311
Fax	(0851) 705449

Contact   Miss C. Aitken, Lecturer

TRAINING

French   *Type:* client-based; institution-based; group; one-to-one; bespoke
               Method: intensive; non-intensive
Gaelic (Scottish) *Type:* client-based; institution-based; group; one-to-one; bespoke
               Method: non-intensive; open or flexible
Russian   *Type:* client-based; institution-based; group; one-to-one
               Method: non-intensive

SERVICES
Translating
French   into and out of English
Gaelic (Scottish) into and out of English
Russian   into English
Interpreting
French   simultaneous; consecutive

FACILITIES
Equipment and
  materials: computer-assisted language learning

NOTES
• offers Scottish Gaelic television training course and Scottish Gaelic open learning
  pack for beginners

216   Limavady College of Further Education

Main Street
Limavady   Telephone   (05047) 62334
BT49 0EX   Fax   (05047) 22229

Contact   Mrs M. Talbot, Head of Business and Secretarial Studies

TRAINING
French   *Type:* client-based; institution-based; group; one-to-one
German   *Type:* client-based; institution-based; group; one-to-one
                     Method: intensive; non-intensive
Spanish   *Type:* client-based; institution-based; group; one-to-one

217 Lincolnshire College of Agriculture and Horticulture

Caythorpe Court
Caythorpe
Grantham   Telephone   (0400) 72521
NG32 3EP   Fax   (0400) 72722

Contact   Mr J. Fane, Head of Special Projects

TRAINING
French   *Type:* client-based; institution-based; group
                     Method: intensive; non-intensive
Spanish   *Type:* client-based; institution-based; group
                     Method: intensive; non-intensive
Specialisms   agriculture; business

SERVICES
Translating
French   into and out of English
Spanish   into and out of English
Specialisms   agriculture; business
Interpreting
French   consecutive
Spanish   consecutive
Specialisms   agriculture; business

FACILITIES
Equipment and
  materials: computer-assisted language learning; videocassettes

NOTES
• has experience of undertaking language training needs analyses for employers

218   Lincolnshire College of Art and Design

Lindum Road
Lincoln   Telephone   (0522) 512912
LN2 1NP   Fax   (0522) 524167

Contact   Mrs L. Staley-Brookes, Assistant Principal

TRAINING
French   *Type:* client-based; institution-based; group; one-to-one; bespoke
                        Method: intensive; non-intensive; open or flexible
German   *Type:* client-based; institution-based; group; one-to-one; bespoke
                        Method: intensive; non-intensive; open or flexible
Italian   *Type:* client-based; institution-based; group; one-to-one; bespoke
                        Method: intensive; non-intensive; open or flexible
Spanish   *Type:* client-based; institution-based; group; one-to-one; bespoke
                        Method: intensive; non-intensive; open or flexible

SERVICES
Translating
French   into and out of English (specialisms: art; design)
German   into and out of English
Spanish   into and out of English

FACILITIES
Equipment and
   materials: computer-assisted language learning

219 University of Liverpool

4 Cambridge Street
Liverpool   Telephone   051-794 2796
L69 3BX   Fax   051-794 2827

Contact   Mrs S. O'Connell, Language Training Adviser

NOTES
• see entry for Merseyside Language-Export Centre

220   City of Liverpool Community College

Bankfield Centre
Bankfield Road
Liverpool   Telephone   051-259 1124
L13 0BQ   Fax   051-228 9055

Contact   Mr N. Hannah, Foreign Languages Co-ordinator

TRAINING

French
Type: client-based; institution-based; group; one-to-one; bespoke (specialisms: business; tourism)
Method: intensive; non-intensive; open or flexible

German
Type: client-based; institution-based; group; one-to-one; bespoke (specialism: business)
Method: intensive; non-intensive; open or flexible

Italian
Type: client-based; institution-based; group; one-to-one; bespoke (specialism: business)
Method: intensive; non-intensive; open or flexible

Spanish
Type: client-based; institution-based; group; one-to-one; bespoke (specialisms: business; technical)
Method: intensive; non-intensive; open or flexible

Other
Russian, Chinese, Arabic, Swedish, Dutch, Portuguese, Greek and Japanese can be offered, with notice

FACILITIES

Language labs: under 10 places - 1 portable; 10–25 places - 1 fixed
Equipment and
  materials: audio and videocassettes; satellite television; computer-assisted language learning

NOTES

• has experience of undertaking language training needs analyses for employers

221 Liverpool Institute of Higher Education

Stand Park Road
Liverpool
L16 8ND

Telephone   051-737 3000
Fax   051-737 3664

Contact   Dr K. Paterson, Head of European Studies

TRAINING

French   *Type:* institution-based
             Method: intensive; non-intensive
German   *Type:* institution-based
             Method: non-intensive
Spanish   *Type:* institution-based
             Method: non-intensive

FACILITIES

Language labs: under 10 places - 1 portable; 10–25 places - 1 fixed
Equipment and
  materials: computer-assisted language learning

NOTES
• has experience of undertaking language training needs analyses for employers

222 Liverpool John Moores University

School of Modern Languages
98 Mount Pleasant

| Liverpool | Telephone | 051-231 2121 |
| L3 5UZ | Fax | 051-707 0423 |

Contact   Dr L. Archibald, Director

TRAINING

Chinese   *Type:* client-based; institution-based
              Method: intensive; non-intensive; open or flexible
Czech   *Type:* client-based; institution-based
              Method: intensive; non-intensive; open or flexible
Dutch   *Type:* client-based; institution-based
              Method: intensive; non-intensive; open or flexible
Finnish   *Type:* client-based; institution-based
              Method: intensive; non-intensive; open or flexible
French   *Type:* client-based; institution-based
              Method: intensive; non-intensive; open or flexible
German   *Type:* client-based; institution-based (specialism: technical)
              Method: intensive; non-intensive; open or flexible
Italian   *Type:* institution-based
              Method: open or flexible
Japanese   *Type:* client-based; institution-based
              Method: intensive; non-intensive; open or flexible
Russian   *Type:* client-based; institution-based
              Method: intensive; non-intensive; open or flexible
Spanish   *Type:* client-based; institution-based
              Method: intensive; non-intensive; open or flexible
Swedish   *Type:* client-based; institution-based
              Method: intensive; non-intensive; open or flexible
Other   Additional languages can be offered, with notice

FACILITIES

Language labs: under 10 places - 1 portable; 10–25 places - 2 fixed, 1 portable; over
                 25 places - 1 fixed
Equipment and
  materials: computer-assisted language learning; satellite television; audio and
                 videocassettes

NOTES
• has experience of undertaking language training needs analyses for employers

223 Llandrillo Technical College

Llandudno Road
Colwyn Bay   Telephone   (0492) 546666
LL28 4HZ   Fax   (0492) 543052

Contact   Mrs M. Monteith, Languages Co-ordinator, Commercial Courses

TRAINING

French   *Type:* client-based; institution-based; group; one-to-one; bespoke
             (specialism: commercial)
             Method: intensive; non-intensive; open or flexible
German   *Type:* client-based; institution-based; group; one-to-one; bespoke
             (specialism: manufacturing)
             Method: intensive; non-intensive; open or flexible
Greek   *Type:* client-based; institution-based; group; one-to-one; bespoke
             Method: intensive; non-intensive
Italian   *Type:* client-based; institution-based; group; one-to-one; bespoke
             Method: intensive; non-intensive; open or flexible
Japanese   *Type:* client-based; institution-based; group; one-to-one; bespoke
             Method: intensive; non-intensive; open or flexible
Russian   *Type:* client-based; institution-based; group; one-to-one; bespoke
             (specialism: commercial)
             Method: intensive; non-intensive; open or flexible
Spanish   *Type:* client-based; institution-based; group; one-to-one; bespoke
             Method: intensive; non-intensive; open or flexible
Welsh   *Type:* client-based; institution-based; group; one-to-one; bespoke
             (specialism: commercial)
             Method: intensive; non-intensive
Other   Chinese can be offered, with notice

SERVICES

Translating
French   into and out of English (specialisms: commercial; legal)
German   into and out of English
Greek   into and out of English
Italian   into and out of English
Russian   into and out of English (specialism: commercial)
Spanish   into English
Welsh   into and out of English
Interpreting
French   simultaneous; consecutive
German   simultaneous
Greek   simultaneous; consecutive
Russian   simultaneous

| Spanish | consecutive |
| Welsh | simultaneous; consecutive |

FACILITIES

Language labs: 10–25 places - 1 fixed, 1 portable

NOTES

• has experience of undertaking language training needs analyses for employers

224   Llysfasi College

Ruthin	Telephone	(097 888) 263
LL15 2LB	Fax	(097 888) 468

Contact   Mrs C. P. Jones, Business Unit Co-ordinator

TRAINING

French	*Type:* client-based; institution-based; group; one-to-one; bespoke
	Method: intensive; non-intensive; open or flexible
German	*Type:* institution-based; group; one-to-one; bespoke
	Method: intensive; non-intensive; open or flexible
Italian	*Type:* client-based; institution-based; group; one-to-one; bespoke
	Method: intensive; non-intensive; open or flexible
Welsh	*Type:* client-based; institution-based; group; one-to-one; bespoke
	Method: intensive; non-intensive; open or flexible
Specialisms	business; rural studies
Other	Spanish can be offered, with notice

SERVICES

Translating

French	into and out of English
German	into and out of English
Welsh	into and out of English
Specialisms	business; rural studies

Interpreting

French	consecutive
Welsh	simultaneous; consecutive

NOTES

• has experience of undertaking language training needs analyses for employers

225   London Guildhall University

Language Services Centre
Old Castle Street
London   Telephone   071-320 1000
E1 7NT   Fax   071-320 1117

Contact   Mr D. Scarbrough, Director, Language Services Centre

TRAINING

French   *Type:* client-based; institution-based; group; one-to-one; bespoke
             (specialisms: financial; legal)
             Method: intensive; non-intensive
German   *Type:* client-based; institution-based; group; bespoke (specialisms:
             business; legal)
             Method: intensive; non-intensive
Italian   *Type:* client-based; group; bespoke (specialism: legal)
             Method: intensive; non-intensive
Spanish   *Type:* client-based; institution-based; group; bespoke (specialism:
             business)
             Method: intensive; non-intensive
Other   Additional languages can be offered, with notice

FACILITIES

Language labs: 10–25 places - 3 fixed
Equipment and
  materials: computer-assisted language learning

NOTES

• has experience of undertaking language training needs analyses for employers

226   University College London

134-136 Gower Street
London   Telephone   071-380 7722
WC1E 6BT   Fax   071-383 3577

Contact   Mrs D. Ditner, Language Centre Director

TRAINING

Danish   *Type:* client-based; institution-based; group; one-to-one; bespoke
                Method: intensive; non-intensive; open or flexible
Dutch   *Type:* client-based; institution-based; group; one-to-one; bespoke
                (specialisms: legal; medical; scientific; business)
                Method: intensive; non-intensive; open or flexible
Finnish   *Type:* client-based; institution-based; group; one-to-one; bespoke
                Method: intensive; non-intensive; open or flexible
French   *Type:* client-based; institution-based; group; one-to-one; bespoke
                (specialisms: legal; medical; scientific; business)
                Method: intensive; non-intensive; open or flexible
German   *Type:* client-based; institution-based; group; one-to-one; bespoke
                (specialisms: legal; medical; scientific; business)
                Method: intensive; non-intensive; open or flexible
Italian   *Type:* client-based; institution-based; group; one-to-one; bespoke
                (specialisms: legal; medical; scientific; business)
                Method: intensive; non-intensive; open or flexible
Japanese   *Type:* client-based; institution-based; group; one-to-one; bespoke
                Method: intensive; non-intensive; open or flexible
Norwegian   *Type:* client-based; institution-based; group; one-to-one; bespoke
                Method: intensive; non-intensive; open or flexible
Russian   *Type:* client-based; institution-based; group; one-to-one; bespoke
                Method: intensive; non-intensive; open or flexible
Spanish   *Type:* client-based; institution-based; group; one-to-one; bespoke
                (specialisms: legal; medical; scientific; business)
                Method: intensive; non-intensive; open or flexible
Swedish   *Type:* client-based; institution-based; group; one-to-one; bespoke
                Method: intensive; non-intensive; open or flexible
Other   Additional languages can be offered, with notice

FACILITIES

Language labs: under 10 places - 3 portable; 10–25 places - 1 fixed
Equipment and
  materials: computer-assisted language learning; satellite television; interactive
                 video

NOTES
• has experience of undertaking language training needs analyses for employers
• offers distance learning via satellite

227 University of London

Central and Eastern Europe Liaison Office
Senate House
London   Telephone   071-636 8000
WC1E 7HU   Fax   071-436 0970

Contact   Ms P. Cross, Central and East European Liaison Officer of the University of London

TRAINING

Albanian
Type: institution-based; group; one-to-one; bespoke
Method: intensive; non-intensive; open or flexible

Bulgarian
Type: institution-based; group; bespoke
Method: intensive; non-intensive; open or flexible

Czech
Type: client-based; institution-based; group; one-to-one; bespoke (specialism: technical)
Method: intensive; non-intensive; open or flexible

Estonian
Type: institution-based; group; one-to-one; bespoke
Method: intensive; non-intensive; open or flexible

Finnish
Type: institution-based; group; one-to-one; bespoke
Method: intensive; non-intensive; open or flexible

Hungarian
Type: institution-based; group; one-to-one; bespoke
Method: intensive; non-intensive; open or flexible

Polish
Type: institution-based; group; one-to-one; bespoke
Method: intensive; non-intensive; open or flexible

Romanian
Type: institution-based; group; one-to-one; bespoke
Method: intensive; non-intensive; open or flexible

Russian
Type: institution-based; group; one-to-one; bespoke (specialism: technical)
Method: intensive; non-intensive; open or flexible

Serbo-Croat
Type: institution-based; group; one-to-one; bespoke
Method: intensive; non-intensive; open or flexible

Slovak
Type: institution-based; group; one-to-one; bespoke
Method: intensive; non-intensive; open or flexible

Ukrainian
Type: institution-based; group; one-to-one; bespoke
Method: intensive; non-intensive; open or flexible

SERVICES
Translating
Albanian   into and out of English
Bulgarian   into and out of English
Czech   into and out of English
Estonian   into and out of English
Finnish   into and out of English
Hungarian   into and out of English
Polish   into and out of English

Romanian	into and out of English
Russian	into and out of English (specialism: medical)
Serbo-Croat	into and out of English
Slovak	into and out of English
Ukrainian	into and out of English
Interpreting	
Albanian	simultaneous; consecutive
Bulgarian	simultaneous; consecutive
Czech	simultaneous; consecutive
Estonian	simultaneous; consecutive
Finnish	simultaneous; consecutive
Hungarian	simultaneous; consecutive
Polish	simultaneous; consecutive
Romanian	simultaneous; consecutive
Russian	simultaneous; consecutive
Serbo-Croat	simultaneous; consecutive
Slovak	simultaneous; consecutive
Ukrainian	simultaneous; consecutive

FACILITIES
Language labs: 10–25 places - 1 fixed

NOTES
• can provide background briefings on the countries whose languages it teaches

228 University of London

Federal Centre for Continuing Education
14 St Donatt's Road

| London | Telephone | 081-694 1356 |
| SE14 6NR | Fax | 081-694 2009 |

Contact   Ms M. Halvorson, Director of Professional Training

TRAINING

Arabic   *Type:* client-based; institution-based; group; one-to-one
                Method: intensive; non-intensive
Chinese   *Type:* client-based; institution-based; group; one-to-one
                Method: intensive; non-intensive
French   *Type:* client-based; institution-based; group; one-to-one; bespoke
                Method: intensive; non-intensive; open or flexible
German   *Type:* client-based; institution-based; group; one-to-one; bespoke
                Method: intensive; non-intensive; open or flexible
Italian   *Type:* client-based; institution-based; group; one-to-one; bespoke
                Method: intensive; non-intensive; open or flexible
Japanese   *Type:* client-based; institution-based; group; one-to-one; bespoke
                Method: intensive; non-intensive; open or flexible
Portuguese   *Type:* client-based; institution-based; group; one-to-one
                Method: intensive; non-intensive
Russian   *Type:* client-based; institution-based; group; one-to-one; bespoke
                Method: intensive; non-intensive; open or flexible
Spanish   *Type:* client-based; institution-based; group; one-to-one; bespoke
                Method: intensive; non-intensive; open or flexible

SERVICES
Translating
French   into and out of English
German   into and out of English
Italian   into and out of English
Japanese   into and out of English
Russian   into and out of English
Spanish   into and out of English
Interpreting
French   simultaneous; consecutive
German   simultaneous; consecutive
Italian   simultaneous; consecutive
Japanese   simultaneous; consecutive
Russian   simultaneous; consecutive
Spanish   simultaneous; consecutive

FACILITIES

Language labs:	over 25 places - 1 fixed
Interpreting facilities:	26–100 places - 1 fixed
Equipment and materials:	audiocassettes

NOTES
• has experience of undertaking language training needs analyses for employers

229   London Language-Export Centre (LEXCEL)

50-52 Putney Hill
London   Telephone 081-780 0543
SW15 6QX   Fax   081-785 2070

Contact   Ms M. Nicholls, Manager

TRAINING

French	*Type:* client-based; institution-based; group; one-to-one; bespoke (specialisms: insurance; engineering; legal; computers; construction)
	Method: intensive; non-intensive; open or flexible
German	*Type:* client-based; institution-based; group; one-to-one; bespoke (specialisms: engineering; construction)
	Method: intensive; non-intensive; open or flexible
Italian	*Type:* client-based; institution-based; group; one-to-one; bespoke
	Method: intensive; non-intensive; open or flexible
Russian	*Type:* client-based; institution-based; group; one-to-one; bespoke
	Method: intensive; non-intensive; open or flexible
Spanish	*Type:* client-based; institution-based; group; one-to-one; bespoke (specialisms: engineering; construction; medical)
	Method: intensive; non-intensive; open or flexible
Other	Additional languages can be offered, with notice

SERVICES
Translating

French	into and out of English (specialisms: technical; insurance)
German	into and out of English (specialism: engineering)
Italian	into and out of English
Russian	into English
Spanish	into and out of English (specialism: medical)

Interpreting

French	consecutive
German	consecutive
Italian	consecutive
Russian	consecutive
Spanish	consecutive

FACILITIES

Language labs: 10–25 places - 2 fixed

Equipment and
 materials: associate providers have audio and videocassettes, satellite television and computer-assisted language learning

NOTES
• has experience of undertaking language training needs analyses for employers
• runs monthly language clubs, as a 'maintenance' programme

230 Longlands College of Further Education

Douglas Street
Middlesborough
TS4 2JW

Telephone	(0642) 248351
Fax	(0642) 245313

Contact   Mrs L. Dixon, Lecturer

TRAINING

Dutch   *Type:* client-based; institution-based; group; one-to-one; bespoke
            Method: non-intensive

French   *Type:* client-based; institution-based; group; one-to-one; bespoke
            Method: non-intensive

German   *Type:* client-based; institution-based; group; one-to-one; bespoke
            Method: non-intensive

Italian   *Type:* client-based; institution-based; group; one-to-one; bespoke

Spanish   *Type:* client-based; institution-based; group; one-to-one; bespoke
            Method: non-intensive

Urdu   *Type:* client-based; institution-based; group; one-to-one; bespoke

SERVICES
Translating
Dutch   into and out of English
French   into and out of English
German   into and out of English
Spanish   into and out of English
Interpreting
Dutch   simultaneous; consecutive
French   simultaneous; consecutive
German   simultaneous; consecutive
Italian   simultaneous; consecutive
Spanish   simultaneous; consecutive

NOTES
• has experience of undertaking language training needs analyses for employers

231   Loughborough College

Radmoor
Loughborough   Telephone   (0509) 215831
LE11 3BT   Fax   (0509) 232310

Contact   Ms J. Spavin, Head of Languages Division

TRAINING
Catalan   *Type:* client-based; institution-based; group; one-to-one; bespoke
                 Method: intensive; non-intensive; open or flexible
French   *Type:* client-based; institution-based; group; one-to-one; bespoke
                 Method: intensive; non-intensive; open or flexible
German   *Type:* client-based; institution-based; group; one-to-one; bespoke
                 Method: intensive; non-intensive; open or flexible
Greek   *Type:* institution-based; group
                 Method: intensive; non-intensive; open or flexible
Italian   *Type:* client-based; institution-based; group; one-to-one; bespoke
                 Method: intensive; non-intensive; open or flexible
Russian   *Type:* client-based; institution-based; group; one-to-one; bespoke
                 Method: intensive; non-intensive
Spanish   *Type:* client-based; institution-based; group; one-to-one; bespoke
                 Method: intensive; non-intensive; open or flexible
Specialisms   engineering; construction; textiles; travel; business
Other   Portuguese, Dutch, Swedish, Norwegian, Danish, Bengali, Hindi,
                 Gujarati, Punjabi, Japanese and Polish can be offered, with notice

SERVICES
Translating
Catalan   into English
French   into and out of English
German   into and out of English
Greek   into and out of English
Italian   into and out of English
Russian   into English
Spanish   into and out of English
Specialisms   engineering; manufacturing; education; textiles; tourism; business
Interpreting
Catalan   consecutive
French   consecutive
German   consecutive
Greek   consecutive
Italian   consecutive
Spanish   consecutive
Specialisms   engineering; manufacturing; education; textiles; tourism; business

FACILITIES

Language labs: 10–25 places - 4 fixed
Equipment and
  materials: interactive video; computer-assisted language learning;
            audiocassettes

NOTES
• has experience of undertaking language training needs analyses for employers

232   Loughborough University of Technology

Department of European Studies
Loughborough   Telephone   (0509) 222991
LE11 3TU   Fax   (0509) 269395

Contact   Professor L. Hantrais, Professor of Modern Languages

FACILITIES
Language labs: 10–25 places - 3 fixed
Equipment and
 materials: audio and videocassettes; computer-assisted language learning;
                   satellite television

NOTES
• does not run language courses on a commercial basis for business, but its self-study
  facilities are open to the public

233 Lowestoft College

St Peter's Street
Lowestoft
NR32 2NB

Telephone   (0502) 583521
Fax   (0502) 500031

Contact   Ms E. Gwyther, Language Co-ordinator

TRAINING

French
: *Type:* client-based; institution-based; group; one-to-one (specialisms: commercial; business)
Method: intensive; non-intensive

German
: *Type:* client-based; institution-based; group; one-to-one (specialisms: commercial; business)
Method: intensive; non-intensive

Russian
: *Type:* client-based; institution-based; group; one-to-one (specialisms: commercial; business)
Method: intensive; non-intensive

Spanish
: *Type:* client-based; institution-based; group; one-to-one (specialisms: legal; commercial; business)
Method: intensive; non-intensive

Other
: Italian and Dutch can be offered, with notice

FACILITIES

Language labs: 10–25 places - 1 fixed

Equipment and
  materials: audio and videocassettes; computer-assisted language learning

234 Loxley College

Myers Grove Lane
Sheffield   Telephone   (0742) 323163
S6 5JL   Fax   (0742) 852387

Contact   Ms K. Austin, Consultant

TRAINING
French	*Type:* client-based; institution-based; group; one-to-one; bespoke
	Method: intensive; non-intensive; open or flexible
German	*Type:* client-based; institution-based; group; one-to-one; bespoke
	Method: intensive; non-intensive; open or flexible
Italian	*Type:* client-based; institution-based; group; one-to-one; bespoke
	Method: intensive; non-intensive; open or flexible
Spanish	*Type:* client-based; institution-based; group; one-to-one; bespoke
	Method: intensive; non-intensive; open or flexible
Specialism	business

SERVICES
Translating
French	into and out of English
German	into and out of English
Italian	into and out of English
Spanish	into and out of English
Specialism	business

FACILITIES
Language labs: 10–25 places - 1 fixed

NOTES
• has experience of undertaking language training needs analyses for employers

235   LSU College of Higher Education

The Avenue
Southampton   Telephone   (0703) 228761
SO9 5HB   Fax   (0703) 230944

Contact   Mrs E. Bell, Director of European Developments

TRAINING

French	*Type:* client-based; institution-based; group; one-to-one; bespoke (specialisms: business; machine tool industry; para-medical; scientific) *Method:* intensive; non-intensive; open or flexible
German	*Type:* client-based; institution-based; group; one-to-one; bespoke (specialisms: legal; business; scientific) *Method:* intensive; non-intensive; open or flexible
Italian	*Type:* client-based; institution-based; group; one-to-one (specialism: business) *Method:* non-intensive
Russian	*Type:* client-based; institution-based; group; one-to-one; bespoke (specialisms: business; scientific; legal) *Method:* intensive; non-intensive; open or flexible
Spanish	*Type:* client-based; institution-based; group; one-to-one; (specialisms: business; machine tool industry) *Method:* non-intensive
Other	Additional languages can be offered, with notice

SERVICES

Translating

French	into and out of English (specialisms: business; machine tool industry; para-medical; scientific)
German	into and out of English (specialisms: scientific; legal; business)
Italian	into English
Russian	into and out of English (specialisms: business; legal; scientific)
Spanish	into English (specialisms: business; machine tool industry)

Interpreting

French	simultaneous; consecutive
German	simultaneous; consecutive
Italian	consecutive
Russian	simultaneous; consecutive
Spanish	consecutive

FACILITIES

Language labs: under 10 places - 1 portable; 10–25 places - 2 fixed

| Equipment and materials: | computer-assisted language learning; multi-lingual dictionary facility on CD-ROM; audio and videocassettes |

NOTES

• has experience of undertaking language training needs analyses for employers

236   Lurgan College of Further Education

Kitchen Hill
Lurgan   Telephone   (0762) 326135
BT66 6AZ   Fax   (0762) 322762

Contact   Mrs D. Hanna, Head of Continuing Education

TRAINING

French	*Type:* client-based (specialisms: accountancy; business)
	Method: intensive; non-intensive; open or flexible
German	*Type:* institution-based; one-to-one
	Method: intensive; non-intensive; open or flexible
Spanish	*Type:* one-to-one
	Method: intensive; non-intensive; open or flexible
Other	Italian and Portuguese can be offered, with notice

SERVICES
Translating

French	into and out of English
German	into and out of English

Interpreting

French	simultaneous; consecutive
German	simultaneous; consecutive

FACILITIES

Equipment and materials:	audio and videocassettes

NOTES
• has experience of undertaking language training needs analyses for employers

237   Lydbury English Centre

The Old Vicarage
Lydbury North   Telephone   (05888) 233
SY7 8AU   Fax   (05888) 334

Contact   Mr D. J. Baker, Principal

TRAINING
French   *Type:* institution-based; group; one-to-one; bespoke
                Method: intensive
German   *Type:* institution-based; group; one-to-one
                Method: intensive
Italian   *Type:* institution-based; group; one-to-one
                Method: intensive
Spanish   *Type:* institution-based; group; one-to-one
                Method: intensive
Turkish   *Type:* institution-based; group; bespoke (specialism: financial)
Other   Additional languages can be offered, with notice

FACILITIES
Language labs: under 10 places - 1 portable
Equipment and
  materials: computer-assisted language learning

NOTES
• has experience of undertaking language training needs analyses for employers

238   Macclesfield College

Park Lane
Macclesfield
SK11 8LF

Contact

Telephone	(0625) 511923
Fax	(0625) 501084

Miss J. Varley, Section Head, Foreign Languages

TRAINING

French
: *Type:* client-based; institution-based; group; one-to-one; bespoke
Method: intensive; non-intensive; open or flexible

German
: *Type:* client-based; institution-based; group; one-to-one; bespoke
Method: intensive; non-intensive; open or flexible

Italian
: *Type:* client-based; institution-based; group; one-to-one; bespoke
Method: intensive; non-intensive; open or flexible

Japanese
: *Type:* client-based; institution-based; group; one-to-one; bespoke
Method: intensive; non-intensive

Russian
: *Type:* client-based; institution-based; group; one-to-one; bespoke
Method: intensive; non-intensive

Spanish
: *Type:* client-based; institution-based; group; one-to-one; bespoke
Method: intensive; non-intensive; open or flexible

Other
: Dutch and Portuguese can be offered, with notice

SERVICES

Translating

Dutch	into and out of English
French	into and out of English
German	into and out of English
Italian	into and out of English
Japanese	into and out of English
Portuguese	into and out of English
Russian	into and out of English
Spanish	into and out of English

Interpreting

Dutch	simultaneous; consecutive
French	simultaneous; consecutive
German	simultaneous; consecutive
Italian	simultaneous; consecutive
Japanese	simultaneous; consecutive
Portuguese	simultaneous; consecutive
Russian	simultaneous; consecutive
Spanish	simultaneous; consecutive

FACILITIES

Language labs:
: under 10 places - 1 portable

Equipment and	
materials:	interactive video; computer-assisted language learning; satellite television

NOTES
• has experience of undertaking language training needs analyses for employers

239   Magherafelt College of Further Education

22 Moneymore Road
Magherafelt   Telephone   (0648) 32462
BT45 6AE   Fax   (0648) 33501

Contact   Mrs E. Rowan, Lecturer in Modern Languages

TRAINING
French   *Type:* client-based; institution-based; group
                     Method: intensive; non-intensive; open or flexible
German   *Type:* client-based; institution-based; group
                     Method: intensive; non-intensive; open or flexible
Other   Spanish can be offered, with notice

FACILITIES
Language labs: 10–25 places - 1 fixed
Equipment and
  materials: computer-assisted language learning

240   Managed Learning

Harcourt Hill
North Hinksey
Oxford   Telephone   (0865) 798188
OX2 9AS   Fax   (0865) 727425

Contact   Ms J. Millar, Language Training Director

TRAINING
French   *Type:* client-based; institution-based; group; one-to-one; bespoke
German   *Type:* client-based; institution-based; group; one-to-one; bespoke
Italian   *Type:* client-based; institution-based; group; one-to-one; bespoke
Japanese *Type:* client-based; institution-based; group; one-to-one; bespoke
Korean   *Type:* client-based; group
Russian   *Type:* client-based; institution-based; group; one-to-one; bespoke
Spanish   *Type:* client-based; institution-based; group; one-to-one; bespoke
Other   Additional languages can be offered, with notice

NOTES
- has experience of undertaking language training needs analyses for employers
- specialises in the design and implementation of large scale training programmes, including materials design and writing, and in open or flexible learning

241   University of Manchester

Department of Extra-Mural Studies
Oxford Road
Manchester
M13 9PL

Telephone	061-275 2101
Fax	061-275 3300

Contact   Dr S. M. Truscott, Staff Tutor in Languages

TRAINING

Arabic
Type: client-based; institution-based; group; one-to-one; bespoke (specialisms: religious; politics)
Method: intensive; non-intensive; open or flexible

Aramaic *Type:* client-based; institution-based; group; one-to-one; bespoke

Azeri *Type:* client-based; institution-based; group; one-to-one; bespoke

Farsi *Type:* client-based; institution-based; group; one-to-one; bespoke
Method: intensive; non-intensive; open or flexible

French *Type:* client-based; institution-based; group; one-to-one
Method: intensive; non-intensive; open or flexible

German *Type:* client-based; institution-based; group; one-to-one

Greek *Type:* client-based; institution-based; group; one-to-one

Hebrew *Type:* client-based; institution-based; group; one-to-one; bespoke (specialisms: religious; social sciences)
Method: intensive; non-intensive; open or flexible

Italian *Type:* client-based; institution-based; group; one-to-one

Japanese *Type:* client-based; institution-based; group; one-to-one

Russian *Type:* client-based; institution-based; group; one-to-one

Spanish *Type:* client-based; institution-based; group; one-to-one
Method: intensive; non-intensive; open or flexible

Tajik *Type:* client-based; institution-based; group; one-to-one; bespoke

Turkish *Type:* client-based; institution-based; group; one-to-one; bespoke (specialisms: business; social sciences)
Method: intensive; non-intensive; open or flexible

Uighur *Type:* client-based; institution-based; group; one-to-one; bespoke

Uzbek *Type:* client-based; institution-based; one-to-one; bespoke

Other Kazakh, Kurdish, Armenian and Yiddish can be offered, with notice

SERVICES

Translating

Arabic into and out of English (specialisms: technical; legal; business)

Farsi into and out of English

Hebrew into and out of English (specialisms: legal; medical)

Turkish into and out of English (specialisms: business; technical)

Interpreting

Arabic consecutive

Farsi consecutive

| Hebrew | consecutive |
| Turkish | consecutive |

FACILITIES
Language labs: over 25 places - 1 fixed
Equipment and
  materials: audio and videocassettes; satellite television (by arrangement);
computer-assisted language learning

NOTES
- has experience of undertaking language training needs analyses for employers
- has residential accommodation available
- language testing of potential employees can be arranged
- the contact for Middle Eastern languages is Dr Cigdem Balim, on 061-275 3073

242   Manchester Business School

Language Centre
Booth Street West
Manchester
M15 6PB

Telephone	061-275 6560
Fax	061-273 7732

Contact   Mr H. Ward, Language Centre Director

TRAINING

Arabic
: *Type:* client-based; institution-based; group; one-to-one; bespoke
Method: intensive; non-intensive

Chinese
: *Type:* client-based; institution-based; group; one-to-one; bespoke
Method: intensive; non-intensive

Danish
: *Type:* client-based; institution-based; group; one-to-one; bespoke

Dutch
: *Type:* client-based; institution-based; group; one-to-one; bespoke
Method: intensive; non-intensive

French
: *Type:* client-based; institution-based; group; one-to-one; bespoke
Method: intensive; non-intensive; open or flexible

German
: *Type:* client-based; institution-based; group; one-to-one; bespoke
Method: intensive; non-intensive; open or flexible

Italian
: *Type:* client-based; institution-based; group; one-to-one; bespoke
Method: intensive; non-intensive; open or flexible

Japanese
: *Type:* client-based; institution-based; group; one-to-one; bespoke
Method: intensive; non-intensive

Korean
: *Type:* client-based; institution-based; group; one-to-one; bespoke

Portuguese
: *Type:* client-based; institution-based; group; one-to-one; bespoke
Method: intensive; non-intensive

Romanian
: *Type:* client-based; institution-based; group; one-to-one; bespoke
Method: intensive; non-intensive

Russian
: *Type:* client-based; institution-based; group; one-to-one; bespoke
Method: intensive; non-intensive

Serbo-Croat
: *Type:* client-based; institution-based; group; one-to-one; bespoke

Spanish
: *Type:* client-based; institution-based; group; one-to-one; bespoke
Method: intensive; non-intensive; open or flexible

Swedish
: *Type:* client-based; institution-based; group; one-to-one; bespoke

Turkish
: *Type:* client-based; institution-based; group; one-to-one; bespoke

Specialism   business

SERVICES

Interpreting

French	consecutive
German	consecutive
Italian	consecutive
Japanese	consecutive
Russian	consecutive
Spanish	consecutive

FACILITIES

Language labs: over 25 places - 1 portable
Equipment and
  materials: audio and videocassettes

NOTES
- has experience of undertaking language training needs analyses for employers
- instruction in business and social culture accompanies language courses
- weekend programmes and telephone tutorials available

243 Manchester College of Arts and Technology

Lower Hardman Street
Manchester   Telephone   061-953 5995
M3 3ER   Fax   061-953 2259

Contact   Mr R. Barrett, Head of European and International Studies

TRAINING

Arabic
Type: client-based; institution-based; group; one-to-one; bespoke
Method: intensive; non-intensive; open or flexible

Chinese
Type: client-based; institution-based; group; one-to-one; bespoke
Method: intensive; non-intensive; open or flexible

Dutch
Type: client-based; institution-based; group; one-to-one; bespoke
Method: intensive; non-intensive; open or flexible

French
Type: client-based; institution-based; group; one-to-one; bespoke
Method: intensive; non-intensive; open or flexible

German
Type: client-based; institution-based; group; one-to-one; bespoke
Method: intensive; non-intensive; open or flexible

Italian
Type: client-based; institution-based; group; one-to-one; bespoke
Method: intensive; non-intensive; open or flexible

Japanese
Type: client-based; institution-based; group; one-to-one; bespoke
Method: intensive; non-intensive; open or flexible

Portuguese
Type: client-based; institution-based; group; one-to-one; bespoke
Method: intensive; non-intensive; open or flexible

Russian
Type: client-based; institution-based; group; one-to-one; bespoke
Method: intensive; non-intensive; open or flexible

Spanish
Type: client-based; institution-based; group; one-to-one; bespoke
Method: intensive; non-intensive; open or flexible

Urdu
Type: client-based; institution-based; group; one-to-one; bespoke
Method: intensive; non-intensive; open or flexible

Other   Additional languages can be offered, with notice

SERVICES

Translating

Arabic   into and out of English
Chinese   into and out of English
Dutch   into and out of English
French   into and out of English
German   into and out of English
Italian   into and out of English
Japanese   into and out of English
Portuguese   into and out of English
Russian   into and out of English
Spanish   into and out of English
Urdu   into and out of English

FACILITIES

Language labs: 10–25 places - 1 portable

Equipment and
  materials: computer-assisted language learning; interactive video

NOTES
• has experience of undertaking language training needs analyses for employers

244 University of Manchester Institute of Science and Technology

PO Box 88
Sackville Street
Manchester
M60 1QD

Telephone	061-236 3311
Fax	061-228 7040

Contact   Dr J. Walters, Director of Continuing Education and Training

TRAINING

French
Type: institution-based; group
Method: non-intensive; open or flexible

German
Type: institution-based; group (specialism: scientific)
Method: intensive; non-intensive; open or flexible

Japanese
Type: institution-based; group
Method: non-intensive

Spanish
Type: institution-based; group
Method: non-intensive; open or flexible

SERVICES
Translating

French	into and out of English
German	into and out of English
Japanese	into and out of English
Spanish	into and out of English

FACILITIES

Language labs: 10–25 places - 2 fixed
Equipment and
  materials: 20 seat computer-assisted language learning laboratory

NOTES
• runs a one week intensive German course for civil servants and managers, which is a refresher course for language graduates

245   Manchester Language-Export Centre

Tatton Buildings
6 Old Hall Road
Cheadle   Telephone   061-491 3330
SK8 4BE   Fax   061-491 5002

Contact   Mr M. Ducasse, Managing Director

TRAINING

Dutch	*Type:* client-based; institution-based; group; one-to-one
	Method: intensive; non-intensive; open or flexible
Farsi	*Type:* client-based; institution-based; group; one-to-one
French	*Type:* client-based; institution-based; group; one-to-one
	Method: intensive; non-intensive; open or flexible
German	*Type:* client-based; institution-based; group; one-to-one
	Method: intensive; non-intensive; open or flexible
Italian	*Type:* client-based; institution-based; group; one-to-one
	Method: intensive; non-intensive; open or flexible
Japanese	*Type:* client-based; institution-based; group; one-to-one
	Method: intensive; non-intensive; open or flexible
Portuguese	*Type:* client-based; institution-based; group; one-to-one
	Method: intensive; non-intensive; open or flexible
Russian	*Type:* client-based; institution-based; group; one-to-one
Spanish	*Type:* client-based; institution-based; group; one-to-one
	Method: intensive; non-intensive; open or flexible
Specialisms	business; exporting; accountancy; air cabin crew; airline ticket assistants; legal; textiles; fashion; construction; transport; freight; telephone skills; marketing
Other	Additional languages can be offered, with notice

SERVICES

Translating

French	into and out of English
German	into and out of English
Italian	into and out of English
Japanese	into and out of English
Russian	into and out of English
Spanish	into and out of English

Interpreting

French	simultaneous; consecutive
German	simultaneous; consecutive
Italian	simultaneous; consecutive
Japanese	simultaneous; consecutive
Russian	simultaneous; consecutive
Spanish	simultaneous; consecutive

FACILITIES

Equipment and
   materials: audiocassettes and work books published by the language-export
                    centre

NOTES

- has experience of undertaking language training needs analyses for employers
- can offer interpreting and translating in any language, and 'training the tutor' seminars and conferences

246   Matthew Boulton College

Sherlock Street
Birmingham   Telephone   021-446 4545
B5 7DB   Fax   021-446 4699

Contact   Ms C. Sewell, Senior Lecturer for Foreign and Community Languages

TRAINING
French   *Type:* client-based; institution-based; group; bespoke (specialisms: engineering; business)
                    Method: non-intensive; open or flexible
German   *Type:* client-based; institution-based; group (specialism: business)
                    Method: non-intensive; open or flexible
Italian   *Type:* client-based; institution-based; group (specialism: business)
                    Method: non-intensive
Spanish   *Type:* client-based; institution-based; group (specialism: business)
                    Method: non-intensive; open or flexible
Urdu   *Type:* institution-based; group
                    Method: non-intensive

SERVICES
Translating
Gujarati   out of English
Urdu   out of English
Specialism   engineering

FACILITIES
Language labs: under 10 places - 1 fixed; 10–25 places - 1 fixed
Equipment and
  materials: satellite television; computer-assisted language learning; audiocassettes

NOTES
- has experience of undertaking language training needs analyses for employers
- offers a range of early evening courses in six languages at four levels, for London Chamber of Commerce, Institute of Linguists, GCSE and A-Level qualifications

247 Merseyside Language-Export Centre

University of Liverpool
4 Cambridge Street
Liverpool   Telephone   051-794 2796
L69 3BX   Fax   051-794 2827

Contact   Mrs S. O'Connell, Languages Training Adviser

TRAINING

Arabic	*Type:* client-based; institution-based; group; one-to-one; bespoke
Chinese	*Type:* client-based; institution-based; group; one-to-one; bespoke (specialisms: scientific; engineering) *Method:* non-intensive
Dutch	*Type:* client-based
French	*Type:* client-based; institution-based; group; one-to-one; bespoke (specialisms: telecommunications; health and safety; telephone skills) *Method:* non-intensive; open or flexible
German	*Type:* client-based; institution-based; group; one-to-one; bespoke (specialisms: telecommunications; health and safety; telephone skills) *Method:* non-intensive; open or flexible
Greek	*Type:* institution-based; one-to-one; bespoke (specialism: telecommunications)
Italian	*Type:* client-based; institution-based; group; one-to-one; bespoke (specialisms: telecommunications; health and safety; telephone skills) *Method:* non-intensive; open or flexible
Japanese	*Type:* institution-based; group *Method:* non-intensive
Portuguese	*Type:* client-based; institution-based; group; one-to-one; bespoke (specialism: shoe manufacturing) *Method:* non-intensive
Russian	*Type:* client-based; institution-based; group; one-to-one; bespoke (specialisms: telecommunications; health and safety) *Method:* non-intensive
Spanish	*Type:* client-based; institution-based; group; one-to-one; bespoke (specialisms: telecommunications; health and safety; telephone skills) *Method:* intensive; non-intensive; open or flexible
Other	Hungarian, Polish and Czech can be offered, with notice

SERVICES
Translating

French	into and out of English
German	into and out of English

Italian	into and out of English
Japanese	into and out of English
Russian	into and out of English
Spanish	into and out of English
Interpreting	
French	simultaneous; consecutive
German	simultaneous; consecutive
Italian	simultaneous; consecutive
Japanese	simultaneous; consecutive
Russian	simultaneous; consecutive
Spanish	simultaneous; consecutive

FACILITIES

Language labs:	under 10 places - 1 fixed; over 25 places - 1 fixed
Equipment and materials:	computer-assisted language learning; access to satellite television

NOTES
- has experience of undertaking language training needs analyses for employers
- can offer translating and interpreting services in all languages
- includes cultural briefings and instruction in local business customs in all language training

248 Merthyr Tydfil Technical College

Ynysfach
Merthyr Tydfil   Telephone   (0685) 723663
CF48 1AR   Fax   (0685) 721782

Contact   Mr D. Byles, Director of Marketing

TRAINING

French   *Type:* client-based; institution-based; group; one-to-one; bespoke
                (specialism: legal)
                Method: intensive; non-intensive; open or flexible
German   *Type:* client-based; institution-based; group; one-to-one; bespoke
                (specialism: accountancy)
                Method: intensive; non-intensive; open or flexible
Italian   *Type:* institution-based
                Method: non-intensive
Japanese   *Type:* client-based; institution-based; bespoke
                Method: non-intensive
Spanish   *Type:* institution-based
                Method: intensive; non-intensive; open or flexible
Other   Dutch can be offered, with notice

SERVICES

Translating
French   into and out of English
German   into and out of English
Italian   into and out of English
Japanese   into and out of English
Spanish   into and out of English
Interpreting
French   simultaneous; consecutive
German   simultaneous; consecutive
Italian   simultaneous; consecutive
Japanese   simultaneous; consecutive

FACILITIES

Language labs: 10–25 places - 1 fixed, 1 portable
Equipment and
  materials: audio and videocassettes

NOTES

• has experience of undertaking language training needs analyses for employers

249 Mid-Cheshire College of Further Education

Hartford Campus
Northwich   Telephone   (0606) 75281
CW8 1LJ   Fax   (0606) 75281 ext. 269

Contact   Mr P. Main, Senior Lecturer in Charge of Languages

TRAINING

Chinese   *Type:* client-based; institution-based; group; one-to-one; bespoke
              Method: intensive; non-intensive; open or flexible

Dutch   *Type:* client-based; institution-based; group; one-to-one; bespoke
              Method: intensive; non-intensive; open or flexible

French   *Type:* client-based; institution-based; group; one-to-one; bespoke
              Method: intensive; non-intensive; open or flexible

German   *Type:* client-based; institution-based; group; one-to-one; bespoke
              Method: intensive; non-intensive; open or flexible

Italian   *Type:* client-based; institution-based; group; one-to-one; bespoke
              Method: intensive; non-intensive; open or flexible

Japanese   *Type:* client-based; institution-based; group; one-to-one; bespoke
              Method: intensive; non-intensive; open or flexible

Portuguese   *Type:* client-based; institution-based; group; one-to-one; bespoke
              Method: intensive; non-intensive; open or flexible

Russian   *Type:* client-based; institution-based; group; one-to-one; bespoke
              Method: intensive; non-intensive; open or flexible

Spanish   *Type:* client-based; institution-based; group; one-to-one; bespoke
              Method: intensive; non-intensive; open or flexible

Turkish   *Type:* client-based; institution-based; group; one-to-one; bespoke
              Method: intensive; non-intensive; open or flexible

Specialisms   business; scientific; legal; technical; commercial
Other   Additional languages can be offered, with notice

SERVICES

Translating
French   into and out of English
German   into and out of English
Italian   into and out of English
Japanese   into and out of English
Russian   into and out of English
Spanish   into and out of English
Specialisms   business; commercial; scientific; legal

Interpreting
French   simultaneous; consecutive
German   simultaneous; consecutive
Italian   simultaneous; consecutive
Japanese   simultaneous; consecutive

Russian	simultaneous; consecutive
Spanish	simultaneous; consecutive
Specialisms	business; commercial; scientific; legal

FACILITIES

Language labs:	10–25 places - 2 fixed
Interpreting facilities:	10–25 places - 2 fixed
Equipment and materials:	computer-assisted language learning; audio and videocassettes

NOTES

- has experience of undertaking language training needs analyses for employers
- can offer translating and interpreting in other languages, on request

250   Mid-Cornwall College

Palace Road
St Austell   Telephone   (0726) 67911
PL25 4BW   Fax   (0726) 68499

Contact   Mr K. Andrews, Head of Liberal and Communication Studies

TRAINING
French   *Type:* institution-based
                   Method: intensive; non-intensive; open or flexible
German   *Type:* institution-based
                   Method: intensive; non-intensive; open or flexible
Italian   *Type:* institution-based
Spanish   *Type:* institution-based
                   Method: intensive; non-intensive; open or flexible

FACILITIES
Language labs: 10–25 places - 1 fixed

251 Mid-Kent College of Higher and Further Education

Oakwood Park
Tonbridge Road
Maidstone
ME16 8AQ

Telephone   (0622) 691555
Fax   (0622) 695049

Contact   Mrs M. Noel, Manager, Modern Language Services

TRAINING

Dutch	*Type:* client-based; one-to-one
	Method: non-intensive
Finnish	*Type:* client-based; one-to-one
French	*Type:* client-based; institution-based; group; one-to-one; bespoke (specialisms: trading standards; business; secretarial; local government; police; civil engineering; education; electronics; computers)
	Method: intensive; non-intensive; open or flexible
German	*Type:* client-based; institution-based; group; one-to-one (specialism: business)
	Method: intensive; non-intensive
Greek	*Type:* institution-based; group
Hungarian	*Type:* client-based; institution-based; group; one-to-one
Italian	*Type:* client-based; institution-based; group; one-to-one
	Method: intensive; non-intensive
Japanese	*Type:* client-based; institution-based; group; one-to-one
	Method: intensive; non-intensive
Portuguese	*Type:* client-based; institution-based; group; one-to-one
Russian	*Type:* client-based; institution-based; group; one-to-one; bespoke
	Method: intensive; non-intensive
Spanish	*Type:* client-based; institution-based; group; one-to-one (specialism: business)
	Method: intensive; non-intensive

SERVICES
Translating

French	into and out of English (specialisms: education; local government; trading standards; civil engineering; police)
German	into and out of English (specialisms: education; local government; trading standards; civil engineering; police)
Hungarian	out of English
Italian	out of English
Japanese	out of English
Portuguese	out of English
Russian	out of English
Spanish	into and out of English

Interpreting

French	simultaneous (specialisms: education; local government; trading standards; civil engineering; police)
German	simultaneous (specialisms: education; local government; trading standards; civil engineering; police)
Hungarian	simultaneous
Italian	simultaneous
Russian	simultaneous

FACILITIES

Language labs:	10–25 places - 1 fixed
Equipment and materials:	computer-assisted language learning; audio and videocassettes

NOTES

• has experience of undertaking language training needs analyses for employers

252 Mid-Warwickshire College of Further Education

Warwick New Road
Leamington Spa   Telephone   (0926) 311711
CV32 5JE   Fax   (0926) 426910

Contact   Mr K. Jones, Head of Languages

TRAINING

French   *Type:* client-based; institution-based; group; one-to-one; bespoke
                Method: intensive; non-intensive
German   *Type:* client-based; institution-based; group; one-to-one; bespoke
                Method: intensive; non-intensive
Hungarian   *Type:* client-based; institution-based; group; one-to-one; bespoke
                Method: non-intensive
Italian   *Type:* client-based; institution-based; group; one-to-one; bespoke
                Method: intensive; non-intensive
Portuguese   *Type:* client-based; institution-based; group; one-to-one; bespoke
                Method: non-intensive
Spanish   *Type:* client-based; institution-based; group; one-to-one; bespoke
                Method: intensive; non-intensive
Other   Japanese and Russian can be offered, with notice

SERVICES
Translating
French   into and out of English
German   into and out of English
Hungarian   into and out of English
Italian   into and out of English
Spanish   into and out of English

FACILITIES
Language labs: under 10 places - 1 portable; 10–25 places - 1 fixed
Equipment and
 materials: audio and videocassettes; computer-assisted language learning

NOTES
• has experience of undertaking language training needs analyses for employers
• provides short, 'off the peg' twilight modules to which companies can send individuals to join a small group

253　Middlesex University

The Burroughs
Hendon
London   Telephone   081-362 5965
NW4 4BT   Fax   081-202 1539

Contact   Dr J. Rees-Smith, Head of Middlesex Language Centres

TRAINING

Arabic	*Type:* client-based; institution-based; group; one-to-one; bespoke
French	*Type:* client-based; institution-based; group; one-to-one; bespoke (specialisms: banking; hotel trade; engineering) *Method:* intensive; non-intensive; open or flexible
German	*Type:* client-based; institution-based; group; one-to-one; bespoke (specialism: engineering) *Method:* intensive; non-intensive; open or flexible
Italian	*Type:* client-based; institution-based; group; bespoke *Method:* intensive; non-intensive; open or flexible
Japanese	*Type:* client-based; institution-based; group; one-to-one; bespoke *Method:* non-intensive
Portuguese	*Type:* client-based; institution-based; group; one-to-one; bespoke
Russian	*Type:* client-based; institution-based; group; one-to-one; bespoke
Spanish	*Type:* client-based; institution-based; group; one-to-one; bespoke (specialism: computers) *Method:* intensive; non-intensive; open or flexible
Other	Greek and Turkish can be offered, with notice

SERVICES

Translating

Arabic	into and out of English
French	into and out of English (specialisms: architecture; scientific)
German	into and out of English (specialisms: architecture; scientific)
Portuguese	into and out of English
Spanish	into and out of English

Interpreting

Arabic	consecutive
French	consecutive (specialism: engineering)
German	consecutive (specialism: engineering)
Italian	consecutive
Japanese	consecutive
Portuguese	consecutive
Spanish	consecutive

FACILITIES

Language labs: 10–25 places - 5 fixed

Equipment and
   materials: computer-assisted language learning; audio and videocassettes;
                   satellite television

NOTES
- has experience of undertaking language training needs analyses for employers
- runs eleven week 'Languages for Business and Pleasure' courses in French, German, Spanish, Italian, Arabic and Japanese

254   Milton Keynes College

Sherwood Drive
Bletchley
Milton Keynes   Telephone   (0908) 668998
MK3 6DR   Fax   (0908) 3222

Contact   Mrs C. Cruz, Business Languages Co-ordinator

TRAINING

Arabic   *Type:* client-based; institution-based; group; one-to-one
French   *Type:* client-based; institution-based; group; one-to-one (specialism: telephone skills)
          Method: non-intensive; open or flexible
German   *Type:* client-based; institution-based; group; one-to-one; bespoke (specialism: secretarial)
          Method: non-intensive; open or flexible
Greek   *Type:* client-based; institution-based; group; one-to-one
Italian   *Type:* client-based; institution-based; group; one-to-one
          Method: non-intensive
Spanish   *Type:* client-based; institution-based; group; one-to-one
          Method: non-intensive; open or flexible

FACILITIES

Language labs: under 10 places - 1 portable
Equipment and
  materials: computer-assisted language learning; audiocassettes

NOTES
• has experience of undertaking language training needs analyses for employers

255 Milton Keynes Language Centre

7 Bradbury Close
Bradwell
Milton Keynes   Telephone   (0908) 225870
MK13 9EX   Fax   (0908) 225871

Contact   Mrs J. McKeon, Principal

TRAINING

French	*Type:* client-based; institution-based; group; one-to-one; bespoke *Method:* intensive; non-intensive
German	*Type:* client-based; institution-based; group; one-to-one; bespoke *Method:* intensive; non-intensive
Italian	*Type:* client-based; institution-based; group; one-to-one; bespoke *Method:* intensive; non-intensive
Japanese	*Type:* institution-based; one-to-one
Spanish	*Type:* client-based; institution-based; group; one-to-one; bespoke *Method:* intensive; non-intensive
Other	Swedish, Finnish, Russian, Arabic and Portuguese can be offered, with notice

SERVICES
Translating

Arabic	into and out of English (specialism: technical)
French	into and out of English (specialisms: technical; legal)
German	into and out of English (specialisms: technical; legal)
Italian	into and out of English (specialism: technical)
Japanese	into and out of English
Portuguese	into and out of English
Russian	into and out of English
Spanish	into and out of English (specialism: technical)
Swedish	into and out of English (specialism: technical)

Interpreting

French	consecutive
German	simultaneous; consecutive (specialism: motor industry)
Italian	consecutive (specialism: motor industry)
Spanish	consecutive

FACILITIES
Equipment and
  materials: audio and videocassettes

NOTES
• has experience of undertaking language training needs analyses for employers
• holds breakfast session courses over 18 weeks, at a local hotel

256   Monkwearmouth College

Swan Street Centre
Sunderland   Telephone   091-548 7119
SR5 1EB   Fax   091-516 0871

Contact   Mr J. E. Rutter, Business Development Centre Manager

TRAINING

Danish   *Type:* client-based; institution-based; group; one-to-one; bespoke
Dutch   *Type:* client-based; institution-based; group; one-to-one; bespoke
                    Method: non-intensive; open or flexible
French   *Type:* client-based; institution-based; group; one-to-one; bespoke
                    (specialism: secretarial)
                    Method: intensive; non-intensive; open or flexible
German   *Type:* client-based; institution-based; group; one-to-one; bespoke
                    Method: intensive; non-intensive; open or flexible
Greek   *Type:* client-based; institution-based; group; one-to-one; bespoke
Japanese   *Type:* client-based; one-to-one
                    Method: non-intensive; open or flexible
Norwegian *Type:* client-based; institution-based; group; one-to-one; bespoke
                    Method: non-intensive; open or flexible
Spanish   *Type:* client-based; institution-based; group; one-to-one; bespoke
                    Method: non-intensive; open or flexible
Other   Chinese can be offered, with notice

FACILITIES

Language labs: under 10 places - 1 portable; 10–25 places - 1 portable
Equipment and
  materials: audiocassettes

NOTES
• has experience of undertaking language training needs analyses for employers

257　Moray College of Further Education

Hay Street
Elgin   Telephone   (0343) 543425
IV30 2NN   Fax   (0343) 540830

Contact   Mr G. Biggs, Senior Lecturer

TRAINING
French   *Type:* client-based; institution-based; group; one-to-one; bespoke
            (specialism: business)
            Method: intensive; non-intensive; open or flexible
German   *Type:* client-based; institution-based; group; one-to-one; bespoke
            (specialism: business)
            Method: intensive; non-intensive; open or flexible
Italian   *Type:* institution-based
Spanish   *Type:* institution-based; one-to-one
            Method: non-intensive; open or flexible

FACILITIES
Equipment and
  materials: satellite television; audio and videocassettes

NOTES
• has experience of undertaking language training needs analyses for employers

258   Motherwell College

Dalzell Drive
Motherwell   Telephone   (0698) 59641
ML1 2DD   Fax   (0698) 75430

Contact   Mrs M. Sutherland, Senior Lecturer in Languages

TRAINING
French   *Type:* client-based; institution-based; group; bespoke (specialism: business)
                    Method: non-intensive
German   *Type:* client-based; institution-based; group
                    Method: non-intensive
Spanish   *Type:* client-based; institution-based; group
                    Method: non-intensive

SERVICES
Translating
French   into and out of English
German   into and out of English
Spanish   into and out of English
Specialism   business

FACILITIES
Language labs: 10–25 places - 1 fixed

259   Nailsea and Clevedon Adult Education

Nailsea Training Services
Nailsea School
Nailsea   Telephone   (0275) 810659
BS19 2HL   Fax   (0275) 857137

Contact   Ms E. Hein, Tutor Organiser

TRAINING
French   *Type:* client-based; institution-based; group; one-to-one; bespoke
                 Method: intensive; non-intensive; open or flexible
German   *Type:* client-based; institution-based; group; one-to-one; bespoke
                 Method: intensive; non-intensive; open or flexible
Italian   *Type:* client-based; institution-based; group; one-to-one; bespoke
                 Method: intensive; non-intensive; open or flexible
Spanish   *Type:* client-based; institution-based; group; one-to-one; bespoke
                 Method: intensive; non-intensive; open or flexible
Specialism   business
Other   Additional languages can be offered, with notice

FACILITIES
Language labs: 10–25 places - 1 portable
Equipment and
  materials: audio and videocassettes; computer-assisted language learning

NOTES
• has experience of undertaking language training needs analyses for employers
• offers French, German and Spanish for beginners
• provides courses in French telephone, facsimile and letter writing skills and German
  for telephonists, receptionists and front office staff

260　Napier University

Language Unit
18 Blantyre Terrace
Edinburgh　　　　　Telephone　　　031-455 2209
EH10 5AE　　　　　Fax　　　　　　031-447 9900

Contact　　　　　Mrs E. Mitchell, Language Unit Manager

TRAINING

Arabic
: *Type:* institution-based; group; one-to-one; bespoke
Method: open or flexible

French
: *Type:* client-based; institution-based; group; one-to-one; bespoke
Method: intensive; non-intensive; open or flexible

German
: *Type:* client-based; institution-based; group; one-to-one; bespoke
Method: intensive; non-intensive; open or flexible

Italian
: *Type:* client-based; institution-based; group; one-to-one; bespoke
Method: intensive; non-intensive; open or flexible

Japanese
: *Type:* client-based; institution-based; group; one-to-one; bespoke
Method: intensive; non-intensive; open or flexible

Spanish
: *Type:* client-based; institution-based; group; one-to-one; bespoke
Method: intensive; non-intensive; open or flexible

Specialisms
: construction; science; engineering; tourism; business

Other
: Chinese, Dutch and Greek can be offered, with notice

SERVICES

Translating

Arabic	into and out of English
Chinese	into and out of English
Czech	into and out of English
Dutch	into and out of English
French	into and out of English
German	into and out of English
Italian	into and out of English
Japanese	into and out of English
Polish	into and out of English
Portuguese	into and out of English
Russian	into and out of English
Spanish	into and out of English

Interpreting

French	consecutive
German	consecutive
Italian	consecutive
Japanese	consecutive
Spanish	consecutive

FACILITIES

Language labs:	10–25 places - 6 fixed
Equipment and materials:	audio and videocassettes

NOTES
• has experience of undertaking language training needs analyses for employers

261　Neath College

Dwr y Felin Road
Neath　　　　　　　Telephone　　　(0639) 646377
SA10 7RF　　　　　Fax　　　　　　(0639) 637453

Contact　　　　Mrs R. Stephens, Industry and Business Centre Manager

TRAINING
French　　　　　*Type:* client-based; institution-based; group; one-to-one; bespoke
　　　　　　　　Method: intensive; non-intensive
German　　　　　*Type:* client-based; institution-based; group; one-to-one; bespoke
　　　　　　　　Method: intensive; non-intensive
Italian　　　　　*Type:* client-based; institution-based; group; one-to-one; bespoke
　　　　　　　　Method: intensive; non-intensive
Spanish　　　　　*Type:* client-based; institution-based; group; one-to-one; bespoke
　　　　　　　　Method: intensive; non-intensive
Welsh　　　　　　*Type:* client-based; institution-based; group; one-to-one; bespoke
Other　　　　　　Irish can be offered, with notice

SERVICES
Translating
German　　　　　into English (specialism: motor industry)
Spanish　　　　　into English (specialisms: police; legal)

FACILITIES
Language labs:　　10–25 places - 1 fixed

NOTES
• has experience of undertaking language training needs analyses for employers

262　Nelson and Colne College

Scotland Road
Nelson
BB9 7YT

Telephone　(0282) 603151
Fax　(0282) 602588

Contact　　Mr R. Oliver, Head of Languages

TRAINING

French　　　*Type:* client-based; institution-based; group; one-to-one
　　　　　　Method: non-intensive; open or flexible
German　　　*Type:* client-based; institution-based; group; one-to-one
　　　　　　Method: non-intensive; open or flexible
Italian　　　*Type:* client-based; institution-based; group; one-to-one
　　　　　　Method: non-intensive; open or flexible
Romanian　　*Type:* client-based; institution-based; group; one-to-one
　　　　　　Method: non-intensive; open or flexible
Spanish　　　*Type:* client-based; institution-based; group; one-to-one
　　　　　　Method: non-intensive; open or flexible
Urdu　　　　*Type:* client-based; institution-based; group; one-to-one
　　　　　　Method: non-intensive; open or flexible

SERVICES

Translating
French　　　into and out of English
German　　　into and out of English
Italian　　　into and out of English
Romanian　　into and out of English
Spanish　　　into and out of English
Urdu　　　　into and out of English
Interpreting
French　　　consecutive
German　　　consecutive
Italian　　　consecutive
Romanian　　consecutive
Spanish　　　consecutive
Urdu　　　　consecutive

FACILITIES
Language labs:　　10–25 places - 1 fixed

NOTES
• has experience of undertaking language training needs analyses for employers

263　New College

Helston Road
Park North
Swindon　　　　　Telephone　　　(0793) 611470
SN3 2LA　　　　　Fax　　　　　　(0793) 496355

Contact　　　　Mr C. Watson, Director, Development

TRAINING
French　　　*Type:* client-based; institution-based; group; one-to-one; bespoke
　　　　　　Method: intensive; non-intensive
German　　　*Type:* institution-based; group; one-to-one; bespoke
　　　　　　Method: intensive; non-intensive
Italian　　　*Type:* client-based; institution-based; group; one-to-one; bespoke
　　　　　　Method: intensive; non-intensive
Japanese　　*Type:* client-based; institution-based; group; one-to-one; bespoke
　　　　　　Method: intensive; non-intensive
Spanish　　　*Type:* client-based; institution-based; group; one-to-one; bespoke
　　　　　　Method: intensive; non-intensive

SERVICES
Translating
French　　　into and out of English
German　　　into and out of English
Japanese　　into and out of English
Spanish　　　into and out of English

FACILITIES
Language labs:　　10–25 places - 2 fixed

NOTES
• has experience of undertaking language training needs analyses for employers
• has established a Euro-Shop to provide support for business people who wish to initiate or develop links with Europe

264 New College (Durham)

Framwellgate Moor Centre
Durham   Telephone   091-386 2421
DH1 5ES   Fax   091-386 0303

Contact   Mrs M. Pearson, Modern Languages Lecturer

TRAINING

Arabic
: *Type:* institution-based; one-to-one
Method: intensive

Dutch
: *Type:* client-based; institution-based; group; one-to-one; bespoke
Method: non-intensive

French
: *Type:* institution-based; group; bespoke (specialism: engineering)
Method: intensive; non-intensive

German
: *Type:* client-based; institution-based; group; one-to-one; bespoke
(specialism: light engineering)
Method: intensive; non-intensive

Greek
: *Type:* client-based; institution-based; group; one-to-one; bespoke

Italian
: *Type:* institution-based; group; one-to-one; bespoke (specialism:
engineering)
Method: intensive; non-intensive

Japanese
: *Type:* institution-based; group
Method: intensive

Spanish
: *Type:* group; one-to-one; bespoke (specialism: engineering)
Method: intensive; non-intensive

Other
: Swedish can be offered, with notice

SERVICES

Translating

Danish	into and out of English
Dutch	into and out of English
French	into and out of English
German	into and out of English
Greek	into and out of English
Italian	into and out of English
Japanese	out of English
Spanish	into and out of English
Swedish	into and out of English

FACILITIES

Language labs: 10–25 places - 3 fixed

NOTES

• has experience of undertaking language training needs analyses for employers
• runs limited-objective courses, helping people to communicate in foreign languages
over the telephone, at exhibition stands or reception desks

265   Newark and Sherwood College

Friary Road
Newark
NG24 1PB

Telephone   (0636) 705921
Fax   (0636) 701990

Contact   Mr M. Hunt, NEWSTEP Manager

TRAINING

French
Type: client-based; institution-based; group; one-to-one; bespoke
Method: intensive; non-intensive; open or flexible

German
Type: client-based; institution-based; group; one-to-one; bespoke
Method: intensive; non-intensive; open or flexible

Italian
Type: institution-based; group

Japanese
Type: client-based; institution-based; group

Spanish
Type: institution-based; group

Specialisms
business; engineering; transport

SERVICES

Translating

Czech   into and out of English
French   into and out of English
German   into and out of English
Hebrew   into and out of English
Italian   into and out of English
Japanese   into and out of English
Polish   into and out of English
Russian   into and out of English
Slovak   into and out of English
Spanish   into and out of English
Specialisms   business; engineering; transport

Interpreting

French   simultaneous; consecutive
German   simultaneous; consecutive
Spanish   simultaneous; consecutive

FACILITIES

Language labs: 10–25 places - 1 fixed
Interpreting
  facilities: 10–25 places - 1 fixed

NOTES

• has experience of undertaking language training needs analyses for employers

266　Newbury College

Oxford Road
Newbury   Telephone   (0635) 42824
RG13 1PQ   Fax   (0635) 41812

Contact   Mrs A. Cuff, Manager, Language Services

TRAINING
French   *Type:* client-based; institution-based; group; one-to-one; bespoke
                 (specialism: scientific)
                 Method: intensive; non-intensive
German   *Type:* client-based; institution-based; group; one-to-one; bespoke
                 (specialism: scientific)
                 Method: intensive; non-intensive
Italian   *Type:* client-based; group; bespoke
                 Method: intensive; non-intensive
Japanese   *Type:* client-based; institution-based; group; one-to-one; bespoke
                 Method: intensive; non-intensive
Russian   *Type:* client-based; group; bespoke
                 Method: intensive; non-intensive
Spanish   *Type:* client-based; group; bespoke
                 Method: intensive; non-intensive

FACILITIES
Language labs: under 10 places - 1 fixed, 1 portable
Equipment and
　materials: interactive video

NOTES
• has experience of undertaking language training needs analyses for employers
• open and flexible learning may be offered on a one-off basis

267   Newcastle College

Maple Terrace
Newcastle upon Tyne   Telephone   091-226 0066
NE4 7SA   Fax   091-272 4297

Contact   Mr P. Latham, Head of Languages

TRAINING
French   *Type:* client-based; institution-based
                 Method: non-intensive
German   *Type:* client-based
                 Method: non-intensive
Spanish   *Type:* client-based
                 Method: non-intensive
Swahili   *Type:* one-to-one
Other   Chinese, Hindi, Russian, Arabic and Urdu can be offered, with
                 notice

FACILITIES
Language labs: 10–25 places - 1 fixed

NOTES
• has experience of undertaking language training needs analyses for employers

268   Newcastle College of Further Education

Donard Street
Newcastle   Telephone   (03967) 22451
BT33 0AP   Fax   (03967) 26203

Contact   Mrs A. O'Donoghue, Lecturer

TRAINING
French   *Type:* institution-based; group; one-to-one
                    Method: intensive; non-intensive; open or flexible
German   *Type:* institution-based; group
                    Method: intensive; non-intensive; open or flexible
Spanish   *Type:* institution-based; group
                    Method: intensive; non-intensive; open or flexible

FACILITIES
Language labs: over 25 places - 1 fixed
Equipment and
  materials: audio and videocassettes; satellite television

269 University of Newcastle upon Tyne

Business Language School
Newcastle upon Tyne Telephone 091-222 7098
NE1 7RU Fax 091-261 1182

Contact Dr M. Ogden, Manager

TRAINING

Chinese	*Type:* client-based; institution-based; group; one-to-one; bespoke
	Method: intensive; non-intensive;
French	*Type:* client-based; institution-based; group; one-to-one; bespoke
	(specialism: secretarial)
	Method: intensive; non-intensive; open or flexible
German	*Type:* client-based; institution-based; group; one-to-one; bespoke
	Method: intensive; non-intensive; open or flexible
Italian	*Type:* client-based; institution-based; group; one-to-one; bespoke
	Method: intensive; non-intensive; open or flexible
Japanese	*Type:* client-based; institution-based; group; one-to-one
	Method: intensive; non-intensive
Korean	*Type:* client-based; institution-based; group; one-to-one; bespoke
	Method: intensive; non-intensive
Russian	*Type:* client-based; institution-based; group; one-to-one; bespoke
	Method: intensive; non-intensive
Spanish	*Type:* client-based; institution-based; group; one-to-one; bespoke
	Method: intensive; non-intensive; open or flexible

FACILITIES

Language labs: 10–25 places - 1 portable; over 25 places - 1 fixed
Equipment and
  materials: audio and videocassettes; satellite television; computer-assisted
  language learning

NOTES

• has experience of undertaking language training needs analyses for employers
• offers taster courses in Chinese
• offers residential weekend courses

270 Newcastle-under-Lyme College

Liverpool Road
Newcastle-under-Lyme   Telephone   (0782) 715111
ST5 2DF   Fax   (0782) 717396

Contact   Mr A. M. Lucas, Manager, Business Language Services

TRAINING

French	*Type:* client-based; institution-based; group; one-to-one; bespoke (specialisms: legal; insurance; technical)
	Method: intensive; non-intensive
German	*Type:* client-based; institution-based; group; one-to-one; bespoke (specialisms: technical; insurance)
	Method: intensive; non-intensive
Italian	*Type:* client-based; institution-based; group; one-to-one; bespoke
	Method: intensive; non-intensive
Japanese	*Type:* client-based; institution-based; group; one-to-one; bespoke
	Method: intensive; non-intensive
Portuguese	*Type:* client-based; institution-based; group; one-to-one; bespoke
	Method: intensive; non-intensive
Russian	*Type:* client-based; institution-based; group; one-to-one; bespoke
	Method: intensive; non-intensive
Spanish	*Type:* client-based; institution-based; group; one-to-one; bespoke
	Method: intensive; non-intensive

SERVICES
Translating

French	into and out of English
German	into and out of English
Italian	into and out of English
Japanese	into and out of English
Portuguese	into and out of English
Russian	into and out of English
Spanish	into and out of English

Interpreting

French	consecutive
German	consecutive
Spanish	consecutive

FACILITIES

Language labs:	10–25 places - 2 fixed
Equipment and materials:	computer-assisted language learning; audio and videocassettes

374

NOTES
- has experience of undertaking language training needs analyses for employers
- offers twilight classes in languages for business

271   Newport College

Nash Road
Newport   Telephone   (0633) 274861
NP9 0TS   Fax   (0633) 273045

Contact   Ms S. Coady, Language Courses Adviser

TRAINING
Bengali	*Type:* institution-based; group; one-to-one; bespoke
Dutch	*Type:* institution-based; group; one-to-one (specialism: exporting)
French	*Type:* client-based; institution-based; group; one-to-one; bespoke (specialisms: social work; tourism; exporting)
	Method: intensive; open or flexible
German	*Type:* client-based; institution-based; group; one-to-one; bespoke (specialisms: social work; tourism; exporting)
	Method: intensive; open or flexible
Italian	*Type:* client-based; institution-based; bespoke
	Method: intensive
Japanese	*Type:* client-based; one-to-one
	Method: intensive
Portuguese	*Type:* institution-based; group; one-to-one
Russian	*Type:* client-based; institution-based; group; one-to-one; bespoke
Somali	*Type:* institution-based; group; one-to-one; bespoke
	Method: intensive
Spanish	*Type:* client-based; institution-based; group; one-to-one; bespoke (specialisms: social work; tourism; exporting)
	Method: intensive
Swedish	*Type:* client-based; institution-based; one-to-one; bespoke
	Method: intensive
Urdu	*Type:* institution-based; group; one-to-one; bespoke
	Method: intensive
Welsh	*Type:* institution-based; group
Other	Additional languages can be offered, with notice

SERVICES
Translating
French	into and out of English
German	into and out of English
Italian	into and out of English
Japanese	into and out of English
Somali	into and out of English
Spanish	into and out of English
Swedish	into and out of English
Urdu	into and out of English
Welsh	into and out of English

FACILITIES

Language labs: under 10 places - 1 fixed
Equipment and
  materials: computer-assisted language learning

NOTES
• has experience of undertaking language training needs analyses for employers

272   Norfolk College of Arts and Technology

Tennyson Avenue
King's Lynn   Telephone   (0553) 761144
PE30 2QW   Fax   (0553) 764902

Contact   Mr R. Withers, Head of Business Development Unit

TRAINING
Dutch   *Type:* client-based; institution-based; group; one-to-one
French   *Type:* client-based; institution-based; group; one-to-one
                      Method: non-intensive; open or flexible
German   *Type:* client-based; institution-based; group; one-to-one
                      Method: non-intensive; open or flexible
Italian   *Type:* client-based; institution-based; group; one-to-one
                      Method: non-intensive; open or flexible
Spanish   *Type:* client-based; institution-based; group; one-to-one
                      Method: non-intensive; open or flexible
Other   Russian can be offered, with notice

SERVICES
Translating
French   into and out of English
German   into and out of English
Italian   into and out of English
Russian   into and out of English
Spanish   into and out of English
Interpreting
French   simultaneous; consecutive
German   simultaneous; consecutive

273 North Antrim College of Further Education

2 Coleraine Road
Ballymoney   Telephone   (02656) 62258
BT53 6BP   Fax   (02656) 64529

Contact   Mrs J. E. Hanna, Lecturer in Business Studies

TRAINING
French   *Type:* client-based; institution-based; group; one-to-one; bespoke
      Method: intensive; non-intensive; open or flexible
German   *Type:* client-based; institution-based; group; one-to-one; bespoke
      Method: intensive; non-intensive; open or flexible
Other   Spanish can be offered, with notice

SERVICES
Translating
French   into and out of English
Interpreting
French   simultaneous; consecutive

FACILITIES
Language labs: over 25 places - 1 fixed
Equipment and
   materials: audio and videocassettes

NOTES
• has access to satellite television facilities at the University of Ulster, Coleraine

274   North Cheshire College

Company Plus
Fearnhead
Warrington   Telephone   (0925) 824082
WA2 0NY   Fax   (0925) 823119

Contact   Mrs S. Sims, Company Plus

TRAINING
French   *Type:* client-based; institution-based; group; one-to-one; bespoke
            Method: intensive; non-intensive; open or flexible
German   *Type:* client-based; institution-based; group; one-to-one; bespoke
            Method: intensive; non-intensive; open or flexible
Italian   *Type:* client-based; institution-based; group; one-to-one; bespoke
            Method: intensive; non-intensive; open or flexible
Japanese   *Type:* client-based; institution-based; group; one-to-one; bespoke
            Method: intensive; non-intensive; open or flexible
Portuguese *Type:* client-based; institution-based; group; one-to-one; bespoke
Russian   *Type:* client-based; institution-based; group; one-to-one; bespoke
Spanish   *Type:* client-based; institution-based; group; one-to-one; bespoke
            Method: intensive; non-intensive; open or flexible
Other   Catalan can be offered, with notice

NOTES
• has experience of undertaking language training needs analyses for employers

275   North Devon College

Old Sticklepath Hill
Barnstaple   Telephone   (0271) 45291
EX31 2BQ   Fax   (0271) 42130

Contact   Mr J. Kelland, Senior Lecturer in Languages

TRAINING
French   *Type:* institution-based; group
              Method: non-intensive
German   *Type:* institution-based; group
              Method: non-intensive; open or flexible
Russian   *Type:* institution-based; group
Spanish   *Type:* institution-based; group
              Method: non-intensive; open or flexible

SERVICES
Translating
French   into and out of English
German   into and out of English
Spanish   into and out of English
Interpreting
French   consecutive
German   consecutive
Spanish   consecutive

FACILITIES
Language labs: 10–25 places - 1 fixed
Equipment and
  materials: audiocassettes

NOTES
• has experience of undertaking language training needs analyses for employers
• does not have specialist translators or interpreters, but can deal with ad-hoc requests

276 North East Export Associates

University of Northumbria at Newcastle
Ellison Place
Newcastle upon Tyne   Telephone   091-261 0190
NE1 8ST   Fax   091-261 0190

Contact   Mrs C Arkless, Marketing Manager

TRAINING

Bulgarian   *Type:* client-based; institution-based; group; one-to-one; bespoke
                (specialism: business)
                Method: intensive; non-intensive

Chinese   *Type:* client-based; institution-based; group; one-to-one; bespoke
                (specialism: business)
                Method: intensive; non-intensive

Czech   *Type:* client-based; institution-based; group; one-to-one; bespoke
                (specialism: business)
                Method: intensive; non-intensive

Danish   *Type:* client-based; institution-based; group; one-to-one; bespoke
                (specialism: business)
                Method: intensive; non-intensive

Dutch   *Type:* client-based; institution-based; group; one-to-one; bespoke
                (specialism: business)
                Method: intensive; non-intensive

French   *Type:* client-based; institution-based; group; one-to-one; bespoke
                (specialisms: business; water industry; museums)
                Method: intensive; non-intensive; open or flexible

German   *Type:* client-based; institution-based; group; one-to-one; bespoke
                (specialisms: business; engineering; paint industry; museums)
                Method: intensive; non-intensive; open or flexible

Greek   *Type:* client-based; institution-based; group; one-to-one; bespoke
                (specialism: business)
                Method: intensive; non-intensive

Italian   *Type:* client-based; institution-based; group; one-to-one; bespoke
                (specialism: business)
                Method: intensive; non-intensive; open or flexible

Japanese   *Type:* client-based; institution-based; group; one-to-one; bespoke
                (specialism: business)
                Method: intensive; non-intensive; open or flexible

Malay   *Type:* client-based; institution-based; group; one-to-one; bespoke
                (specialism: business)
                Method: intensive; non-intensive

Norwegian   *Type:* client-based; institution-based; group; one-to-one; bespoke
                (specialisms: business; retailers)
                Method: intensive; non-intensive

Polish	*Type:* client-based; institution-based; group; one-to-one; bespoke (specialism: business)
	Method: intensive; non-intensive
Portuguese	*Type:* client-based; institution-based; group; one-to-one; bespoke (specialisms: business; water industry)
	Method: intensive; non-intensive
Romanian	*Type:* client-based; institution-based; group; one-to-one; bespoke (specialism: business)
	Method: intensive; non-intensive
Russian	*Type:* client-based; institution-based; group; one-to-one; bespoke (specialism: business)
	Method: intensive; non-intensive; open or flexible
Serbo-Croat	*Type:* client-based; institution-based; group; one-to-one; bespoke (specialism: business)
	Method: intensive; non-intensive
Spanish	*Type:* client-based; institution-based; group; one-to-one; bespoke (specialisms: business; water industry)
	Method: intensive; non-intensive; open or flexible
Swedish	*Type:* client-based; institution-based; group; one-to-one; bespoke (specialism: business)
	Method: intensive; non-intensive
Other	Slovak can be offered, with notice

SERVICES

Translating

Bulgarian	into and out of English
Chinese	into and out of English
Czech	into and out of English
Danish	into and out of English
Dutch	into and out of English
French	into and out of English
German	into and out of English
Greek	into and out of English
Italian	into and out of English
Japanese	into and out of English
Malay	into and out of English
Norwegian	into and out of English
Polish	into and out of English
Portuguese	into and out of English
Romanian	into and out of English
Russian	into and out of English
Serbo-Croat	into and out of English
Spanish	into and out of English
Swedish	into and out of English

Interpreting

Bulgarian	simultaneous; consecutive
Chinese	simultaneous; consecutive
Czech	simultaneous; consecutive
Danish	simultaneous; consecutive
Dutch	simultaneous; consecutive
French	simultaneous; consecutive
German	simultaneous; consecutive
Greek	simultaneous; consecutive
Italian	simultaneous; consecutive
Japanese	simultaneous; consecutive
Malay	simultaneous; consecutive
Norwegian	simultaneous; consecutive
Polish	simultaneous; consecutive
Portuguese	simultaneous; consecutive
Romanian	simultaneous; consecutive
Russian	simultaneous; consecutive
Serbo-Croat	simultaneous; consecutive
Spanish	simultaneous; consecutive
Swedish	simultaneous; consecutive

FACILITIES

Language labs:	10–25 places - 1 portable, 3 fixed; over 25 places - 1 fixed
Equipment and materials:	satellite television; computer-assisted language learning; audio and videocassettes

NOTES

• has experience of undertaking language training needs analyses for employers
• runs a telephone course for receptionists

277   North East Worcestershire College

Blackwood Drive
Bromsgrove   Telephone   (0527) 570020
B60 1PQ   Fax   (0527) 572900

Contact   Mrs F. Hancock, Senior Lecturer in the Department of Adult and
                 Continuing Education

TRAINING
French   *Type:* client-based; institution-based; group; one-to-one
                 Method: intensive; non-intensive; open or flexible
German   *Type:* client-based; institution-based; group; one-to-one
                 Method: intensive; non-intensive; open or flexible
Italian   *Type:* client-based; institution-based; group; one-to-one
                 Method: intensive; non-intensive; open or flexible
Spanish   *Type:* client-based; institution-based; group; one-to-one
                 Method: non-intensive; open or flexible
Specialisms   business; sales; exporting; engineering

SERVICES
Translating
French   into and out of English
German   into and out of English
Italian   into and out of English
Japanese   into and out of English
Russian   into and out of English
Spanish   into and out of English
Specialism   business
Interpreting
French   simultaneous; consecutive
German   simultaneous; consecutive
Italian   simultaneous; consecutive
Spanish   simultaneous; consecutive
Specialism   business

FACILITIES
Language labs: under 10 places - 1 portable; 10–25 places - 1 fixed
Equipment and
  materials: audio and videocassettes; satellite television

NOTES
• has experience of undertaking language training needs analyses for employers

278　North Glasgow College

186 Rye Road
Glasgow　　　　　　　Telephone　　041-558 2857
G21 3JY　　　　　　　Fax　　　　　041-558 9744

Contact　　　　　Mr G. Stewart, PICKUP Project Director

TRAINING

Catalan　　　*Type:* client-based; institution-based; group; one-to-one; bespoke
　　　　　　Method: intensive; non-intensive; open or flexible
French　　　*Type:* client-based; institution-based; group; one-to-one; bespoke
　　　　　　Method: intensive; non-intensive; open or flexible
German　　　*Type:* client-based; institution-based; group; one-to-one; bespoke
　　　　　　Method: intensive; non-intensive; open or flexible
Italian　　　*Type:* client-based; institution-based; group; one-to-one; bespoke
　　　　　　Method: intensive; non-intensive; open or flexible
Japanese　　*Type:* client-based; institution-based group; one-to-one; bespoke
　　　　　　Method: intensive; non-intensive; open or flexible
Russian　　　*Type:* client-based; institution-based; group; one-to-one; bespoke
　　　　　　Method: intensive; non-intensive; open or flexible
Spanish　　　*Type:* client-based; institution-based; group; one-to-one; bespoke
　　　　　　Method: intensive; non-intensive; open or flexible
Specialism　business
Other　　　　Additional languages can be offered, with notice

SERVICES

Translating
French　　　into and out of English
German　　　into and out of English
Italian　　　into and out of English
Spanish　　　into and out of English
Interpreting
French　　　simultaneous; consecutive
German　　　simultaneous; consecutive
Italian　　　simultaneous; consecutive
Spanish　　　simultaneous; consecutive

FACILITIES

Language labs:　under 10 places - 3 fixed, 2 portable; 10–25 places - 3 fixed, 2
　　　　　　　portable

NOTES

• has experience of undertaking language training needs analyses for employers

279   North Hertfordshire College

Hitchin Centre
Cambridge Road
Hitchin   Telephone   (0462) 422882
SG4 0JD   Fax   (0462) 421720

Contact   Mr A. Drewery, Team Leader, Business Languages

TRAINING

Arabic	*Type:* institution-based; group; one-to-one
Bengali	*Type:* institution-based; group; one-to-one
	Method: intensive; non-intensive
Chinese	*Type:* institution-based; group; one-to-one
	Method: intensive; non-intensive
Dutch	*Type:* institution-based; group; one-to-one
	Method: intensive; non-intensive
French	*Type:* client-based; institution-based; group; one-to-one
	Method: intensive; non-intensive; open or flexible
German	*Type:* client-based; institution-based; group; one-to-one
	Method: intensive; non-intensive; open or flexible
Greek	*Type:* client-based; institution-based; group; one-to-one
	Method: intensive; non-intensive
Gujarati	*Type:* institution-based; group; one-to-one
	Method: intensive; non-intensive
Italian	*Type:* client-based; institution-based; group; one-to-one
	Method: intensive; non-intensive
Japanese	*Type:* client-based; institution-based; group; one-to-one
	Method: intensive; non-intensive
Portuguese	*Type:* client-based; institution-based; group; one-to-one
	Method: intensive; non-intensive
Punjabi	*Type:* institution-based; group; one-to-one
	Method: intensive; non-intensive
Russian	*Type:* client-based; institution-based; group; one-to-one
	Method: intensive; non-intensive
Spanish	*Type:* client-based; institution-based; group; one-to-one
	Method: intensive; non-intensive
Urdu	*Type:* institution-based; group; one-to-one
	Method: intensive; non-intensive

SERVICES
Translating

Bengali	into and out of English
Chinese	into and out of English
French	into and out of English
German	into and out of English

Gujarati	into and out of English
Hindi	into and out of English
Italian	into and out of English
Punjabi	into and out of English
Russian	into and out of English
Spanish	into and out of English
Tamil	into and out of English
Urdu	into and out of English

Interpreting

Dutch	consecutive
French	consecutive
German	consecutive
Italian	consecutive
Portuguese	consecutive
Russian	consecutive
Spanish	consecutive

FACILITIES
Language labs: under 10 places - 1 portable

280   North Lindsey College

Kingsway
Scunthorpe   Telephone   (0724) 281111
DN17 1AJ   Fax   (0724) 281308

Contact   Ms B. MacDougall, European Languages Co-ordinator

TRAINING

Bengali	*Type:* institution-based; group
French	*Type:* client-based; institution-based; group; one-to-one (specialism: computers)
	Method: intensive; non-intensive; open or flexible
German	*Type:* client-based; institution-based; group; one-to-one
	Method: intensive; non-intensive; open or flexible
Italian	*Type:* institution-based; group; one-to-one
Japanese	*Type:* client-based; institution-based; group; one-to-one
Punjabi	*Type:* institution-based; group
Russian	*Type:* client-based; institution-based; group; one-to-one
Spanish	*Type:* institution-based; group; one-to-one
Urdu	*Type:* institution-based; group
Other	Greek and Arabic can be offered, with notice

SERVICES
Translating

French	into and out of English
German	into and out of English (specialism: steel industry)
Russian	into English
Spanish	into English

Interpreting

French	simultaneous; consecutive
German	simultaneous; consecutive
Russian	consecutive

FACILITIES

Language labs:	10–25 places - 1 portable
Equipment and materials:	satellite television; computer-assisted language learning; audio and videocassettes

NOTES
• has experience of undertaking language training needs analyses for employers

281 University of North London

European and Language Services
383 Holloway Road

London	Telephone	071-753 5106
N7 0RN	Fax	071-753 5112

Contact   Ms A. Carlisle, Marketing Manager

TRAINING

French	*Type:* client-based; institution-based; group; one-to-one; bespoke *Method:* intensive; non-intensive; open or flexible
German	*Type:* client-based; institution-based; group; one-to-one; bespoke *Method:* intensive; non-intensive; open or flexible
Italian	*Type:* client-based; institution-based; group; one-to-one; bespoke *Method:* intensive; non-intensive; open or flexible
Spanish	*Type:* client-based; institution-based; group; one-to-one; bespoke *Method:* intensive; non-intensive; open or flexible
Other	Additional languages can be offered, with notice

SERVICES
Translating

Danish	into and out of English
Dutch	into and out of English
French	into and out of English
German	into and out of English
Italian	into and out of English
Spanish	into and out of English

FACILITIES

Language labs:	10–25 places - 6 fixed
Equipment and materials:	computer-assisted language learning; satellite television; audio and videocassettes

NOTES
• has developed specialist course materials, such as a French training programme for British Rail drivers

282 North Trafford College

Talbot Road
Stretford
Manchester   Telephone   061-872 3731
M32 0XH   Fax   061-872 7921

Contact   Mr A. Griffiths, Language Co-ordinator

TRAINING

Arabic
Type: institution-based
Method: non-intensive; open or flexible

Chinese
Type: client-based; institution-based; one-to-one; bespoke
Method: open or flexible

Danish
Type: client-based; institution-based; one-to-one; bespoke
Method: open or flexible

Dutch
Type: client-based; institution-based; group; one-to-one; bespoke (specialism: legal)
Method: intensive; open or flexible

French
Type: client-based; institution-based; group; one-to-one; bespoke (specialism: legal)
Method: intensive; non-intensive; open or flexible

German
Type: client-based; institution-based; group; one-to-one; bespoke (specialism: legal)
Method: intensive; non-intensive; open or flexible

Greek
Type: institution-based; group
Method: non-intensive

Hebrew
Type: one-to-one; bespoke (specialism: legal)
Method: intensive; non-intensive

Hungarian
Type: client-based; institution-based; one-to-one; bespoke
Method: open or flexible

Italian
Type: client-based; institution-based; group; one-to-one; bespoke (specialism: legal)
Method: intensive; non-intensive; open or flexible

Japanese
Type: bespoke
Method: open or flexible

Norwegian
Type: client-based; institution-based; one-to-one; bespoke
Method: open or flexible

Portuguese
Type: client-based; institution-based; one-to-one; bespoke
Method: open or flexible

Russian
Type: client-based; institution-based; one-to-one; bespoke
Method: non-intensive

Spanish
Type: client-based; institution-based; group; one-to-one; bespoke
Method: intensive; non-intensive; open or flexible

Welsh
Type: institution-based
Method: non-intensive

Other
Additional languages can be offered, with notice

SERVICES
Translating
French	into and out of English
German	into and out of English
Italian	into and out of English
Russian	into and out of English
Spanish	into and out of English
Specialism	technical

Interpreting
French	simultaneous
German	simultaneous
Italian	consecutive

FACILITIES
Equipment and
  materials: audio and videocassettes

NOTES
• has experience of undertaking language training needs analyses for employers

283 North Tyneside College

Embleton Avenue
Wallsend   Telephone   091-262 4081
NE28 9NJ   Fax   091-295 0301

Contact   Mrs J. Donjon, Course Tutor, Commercial Languages

TRAINING

Arabic	*Type:* institution-based; group
	Method: intensive
French	*Type:* client-based; institution-based; group; one-to-one; bespoke
	Method: intensive; non-intensive
German	*Type:* client-based; institution-based; group; one-to-one; bespoke
	Method: intensive; non-intensive
Italian	*Type:* client-based; institution-based; group; one-to-one; bespoke
	Method: intensive; non-intensive
Norwegian	*Type:* client-based; institution-based; group; one-to-one; bespoke
	Method: intensive; non-intensive
Spanish	*Type:* client-based; institution-based; group; one-to-one; bespoke
	Method: intensive; non-intensive
Other	Greek can be offered, with notice

FACILITIES

Language labs: 10–25 places - 1 fixed
Equipment and
   materials: audio and videocassettes

NOTES
• has experience of undertaking language training needs analyses for employers

284 North Warwickshire College of Technology and Art

Hinckley Road
Nuneaton
CV11 6BH

Telephone   (0203) 349321
Fax   (0203) 329056

Contact   Mrs D. Dale, Lecturer in Business Studies

TRAINING

French   *Type:* client-based; institution-based; group; one-to-one; bespoke
Method: intensive; non-intensive; open or flexible

German   *Type:* client-based; institution-based; group; one-to-one; bespoke
Method: intensive; non-intensive; open or flexible

Italian   *Type:* client-based; institution-based; group; one-to-one; bespoke
Method: intensive; non-intensive; open or flexible

Spanish   *Type:* client-based; institution-based; group; one-to-one; bespoke
Method: intensive; non-intensive; open or flexible

FACILITIES

Language labs: 10–25 places - 1 fixed
Equipment and
materials: computer-assisted language learning; satellite television

NOTES

• has experience of undertaking language training needs analyses for employers

285   North West Kent College of Technology

The Business Language Centre
Miskin Road

Dartford	Telephone	(0322) 289676
DA1 2LU	Fax	(0322) 288683

Contact   Miss P. Aubert, Language Centre Manager

TRAINING

Arabic	*Type:* client-based; institution-based; group; one-to-one; bespoke (specialism: business)
French	*Type:* client-based; institution-based; group; one-to-one; bespoke (specialisms: business; legal; technical) *Method:* intensive; non-intensive; open or flexible
German	*Type:* client-based; institution-based; group; one-to-one; bespoke (specialisms: business; legal; technical) *Method:* intensive; non-intensive; open or flexible
Italian	*Type:* client-based; institution-based; group; one-to-one; bespoke (specialisms: business; legal; technical) *Method:* intensive; non-intensive; open or flexible
Japanese	*Type:* client-based; institution-based; group; one-to-one; bespoke (specialism: business)
Portuguese	*Type:* client-based; institution-based; group; one-to-one; bespoke (specialism: business)
Russian	*Type:* client-based; institution-based; group; one-to-one; bespoke (specialisms: business; technical) *Method:* intensive; non-intensive; open or flexible
Spanish	*Type:* client-based; institution-based; group; one-to-one; bespoke (specialisms: business; legal; technical) *Method:* intensive; non-intensive; open or flexible
Other	Additional languages can be offered, with notice

SERVICES

Translating

Arabic	into and out of English (specialisms: business; tourism)
French	into and out of English (specialisms: commercial; technical; legal; scientific)
German	into and out of English (specialisms: commercial; technical; legal; scientific)
Italian	into and out of English (specialisms: commercial; technical; legal; scientific)
Japanese	into and out of English (specialism: business)
Portuguese	into and out of English (specialisms: commercial; technical)
Russian	into and out of English (specialisms: business; technical)
Spanish	into and out of English (specialisms: commercial; technical; legal; scientific)

Interpreting

Arabic	consecutive (specialism: technical)
French	simultaneous; consecutive (specialisms: commercial; legal; scientific)
German	simultaneous; consecutive (specialisms: commercial; legal; scientific)
Italian	simultaneous; consecutive (specialisms: commercial; legal; scientific)
Japanese	simultaneous; consecutive (specialisms: commercial; legal; scientific)
Portuguese	consecutive (specialisms: commercial; technical)
Russian	simultaneous; consecutive (specialisms: commercial; legal; scientific)
Spanish	simultaneous; consecutive (specialisms: commercial; legal; scientific)

FACILITIES

Language labs:	10–25 places - 1 fixed
Equipment and materials:	computer-assisted language learning; audio and videocassettes; satellite television

NOTES
• has experience of undertaking language training needs analyses for employers
• has designed a language survival course for receptionists, available in French and being developed in Spanish, Italian and German

286　College of North West London

Priory Park Road
London
NW6 7UJ

Telephone	071-328 8241
Fax	071-624 3051

Contact　　　Mr A. Rix, Business Studies Programme Team Leader

TRAINING

French	*Type:* institution-based
	Method: non-intensive
German	*Type:* institution-based
	Method: non-intensive
Spanish	*Type:* institution-based
	Method: non-intensive
Other	Greek, Bengali, Gujarati, Hindi, Punjabi and Urdu can be offered, with notice

FACILITIES

Language labs:　　10–25 places - 1 fixed

287   Northampton College of Further Education

Booth Lane
Northampton   Telephone   (0604) 403322
NN3 3RF   Fax   (0604) 784625

Contact   Ms C. Devaney, Head of Languages and English as a Foreign
                     Language

TRAINING

French   *Type:* client-based; institution-based; group; one-to-one; bespoke
                     Method: intensive; non-intensive
German   *Type:* client-based; institution-based; group; one-to-one; bespoke
                     Method: intensive; non-intensive
Italian   *Type:* client-based; institution-based; group; one-to-one; bespoke
                     Method: intensive; non-intensive
Spanish   *Type:* client-based; institution-based; group; one-to-one; bespoke
                     Method: intensive; non-intensive

FACILITIES

Language labs: 10–25 places - 1 fixed
Equipment and
  materials: audio and videocassettes

NOTES

• has experience of undertaking language training needs analyses for employers
• self-study packs developed for French, German, Spanish and Italian, to support
  beginners-to-intermediate course

288 Northern Ireland Hotel and Catering College

Ballywillan Road
Portrush   Telephone   (0265) 823768
BT56 8JL   Fax   (0265) 824733

Contact   Mrs L. Campbell, Assistant to Principal

TRAINING

French   *Type:* institution-based
                  Method: intensive; open or flexible
Japanese   *Type:* institution-based
                  Method: non-intensive
Spanish   *Type:* institution-based
                  Method: intensive; open or flexible

FACILITIES

Equipment and
  materials: audio and videocassettes

289 Northumberland College of Arts and Technology

College Road
Ashington   Telephone   (0670) 813248
NE63 9RG   Fax   (0670) 520255

Contact   Mr H. Nowicki, Communications and European Studies Network
                   Leader

TRAINING
French   *Type:* client-based; institution-based; group; one-to-one; bespoke
                   (specialism: business)
                   Method: non-intensive; open or flexible
German   *Type:* client-based; institution-based; group; one-to-one; bespoke
                   (specialism: business)
                   Method: non-intensive; open or flexible
Italian   *Type:* client-based; institution-based; group; one-to-one
                   Method: non-intensive; open or flexible
Polish   *Type:* client-based; institution-based; group; one-to-one; bespoke
                   (specialisms: business; technical; education)
Portuguese   *Type:* client-based; institution-based; group; one-to-one
Spanish   *Type:* client-based; institution-based; group;
                   Method: non-intensive; open or flexible

SERVICES
Translating
French   into and out of English (specialism: business)
German   into and out of English (specialism: business)
Italian   into and out of English (specialism: business)
Polish   into and out of English (specialisms: technical; business; education)
Portuguese   into and out of English
Spanish   into and out of English (specialism: business)
Interpreting
French   simultaneous; consecutive (specialism: business)
German   simultaneous; consecutive (specialism: business)
Italian   simultaneous; consecutive (specialism: business)
Polish   simultaneous; consecutive (specialisms: business; education; technical)
Spanish   consecutive (specialism: business)

FACILITIES
Language labs: 10–25 places - 1 portable
Equipment and
  materials: computer-assisted language learning; satellite television; audio and
                   videocassettes

NOTES
• has experience of undertaking language training needs analyses for employers

290 University of Northumbria at Newcastle

Ellison Place
Newcastle upon Tyne   Telephone   091-261 0190
NE1 8ST   Fax   091-261 0190

Contact   Mrs C. Arkless, Marketing Manager

NOTES
- see entry for North East Export Associates

291 Norton College

Dyche Lane
Sheffield
S8 8BR

Contact

Telephone   (0742) 372741
Fax   (0742) 373161

Mr J. Higgins, Senior Lecturer, Modern Languages

TRAINING

French	*Type:* client-based; institution-based; group; one-to-one
German	*Type:* client-based; institution-based; group; one-to-one
Greek	*Type:* client-based; institution-based; group; one-to-one
Italian	*Type:* client-based; institution-based; group; one-to-one
Spanish	*Type:* client-based; institution-based; group; one-to-one

FACILITIES

Equipment and
  materials: audio and videocassettes; computer-assisted language learning

292   Norton Radstock College

South Hill Park
Radstock   Telephone   (0761) 433161
BA3 3RW   Fax   (0761) 436173

Contact   Mr J. Crawley, Co-ordinator, Communications

TRAINING
French   *Type:* client-based; institution-based; group; one-to-one; bespoke
                 (specialisms: scientific; business)
                 Method: intensive; non-intensive; open or flexible
German   *Type:* client-based; institution-based; group; one-to-one; bespoke
                 (specialisms: scientific; business)
                 Method: intensive; non-intensive; open or flexible
Italian   *Type:* client-based; institution-based; group; one-to-one; bespoke
                 Method: intensive; non-intensive
Romanian   *Type:* bespoke (specialism: medical)
Spanish   *Type:* client-based; institution-based; group; one-to-one; bespoke
                 Method: intensive; non-intensive; open or flexible
Other   Russian can be offered, with notice

SERVICES
Translating
French   into and out of English
German   into and out of English
Italian   into and out of English
Spanish   into and out of English
Specialisms   legal; medical; scientific; transport

FACILITIES
Language labs: 10–25 places - 1 fixed
Equipment and
  materials: audio and videocassettes

NOTES
• has experience of undertaking language training needs analyses for employers

293 University of Nottingham

Language Centre
University Park
Nottingham   Telephone   (0602) 791283
NG7 2RD   Fax   (0602) 420825

Contact   Mr T. Norcross, University Language Centre Director

TRAINING

Chinese   *Type:* client-based; institution-based; group; one-to-one; bespoke
Method: open or flexible

Dutch   *Type:* client-based; institution-based; group; one-to-one; bespoke
Method: open or flexible

French   *Type:* client-based; institution-based; group; one-to-one; bespoke
Method: open or flexible

German   *Type:* client-based; institution-based; group; one-to-one; bespoke
Method: open or flexible

Italian   *Type:* client-based; institution-based; group; one-to-one; bespoke
Method: open or flexible

Japanese   *Type:* client-based; institution-based; group; one-to-one; bespoke
Method: open or flexible

Portuguese   *Type:* institution-based; group; one-to-one; bespoke
Method: open or flexible

Russian   *Type:* client-based; institution-based; group; one-to-one; bespoke
Method: open or flexible

Spanish   *Type:* one-to-one; bespoke
Method: open or flexible

Other   Additional languages can be offered, with notice

SERVICES
Translating
Chinese   into and out of English
French   into and out of English
German   into and out of English
Italian   into and out of English
Japanese   into and out of English
Portuguese   into and out of English
Russian   into and out of English
Spanish   into and out of English
Interpreting
Chinese   consecutive
French   simultaneous; consecutive
German   simultaneous; consecutive
Italian   consecutive
Japanese   consecutive

Portuguese	consecutive
Russian	consecutive
Spanish	simultaneous; consecutive

FACILITIES
| Language labs: | 10–25 places - 4 fixed |
| Equipment and materials: | audio and videocassettes; satellite television; self-access centre |

NOTES
- has experience of undertaking language training needs analyses for employers
- offers a full programme of evening classes, usually three, ten week sessions a year, beginning in September, with more popular languages offered at four different levels, leading to examinations of the Institute of Linguists in May

294　Nottingham Trent University

Burton Street
Nottingham　　　　　Telephone　　　(0602) 486526
NG1 4BU　　　　　　Fax　　　　　　(0602) 486513

Contact　　　　　Mrs S. Maurel-Healey, Head of Nottingham Language Centre

TRAINING

Arabic
Type: client-based; institution-based; group; one-to-one; bespoke
Method: non-intensive; open or flexible

Bulgarian
Type: client-based; institution-based; group; one-to-one; bespoke
Method: non-intensive; open or flexible

Chinese
Type: client-based; institution-based; group; one-to-one; bespoke
(specialisms: business; telecommunications)
Method: intensive; non-intensive; open or flexible

Czech
Type: institution-based; one-to-one (specialisms: art; design)
Method: non-intensive; open or flexible

Dutch
Type: client-based; institution-based; group; one-to-one; bespoke
Method: intensive; non-intensive; open or flexible

French
Type: client-based; institution-based; group; one-to-one; bespoke
(specialisms: business; telecommunications)
Method: intensive; non-intensive; open or flexible

German
Type: client-based; institution-based; group; one-to-one; bespoke
(specialisms: business; telecommunications)
Method: intensive; non-intensive; open or flexible

Greek
Type: client-based; institution-based; group; one-to-one; bespoke
Method: non-intensive; open or flexible

Hungarian
Type: client-based; institution-based; group; one-to-one; bespoke
Method: non-intensive; open or flexible

Italian
Type: client-based; institution-based; group; one-to-one; bespoke
(specialisms: art; design; telecommunications)
Method: intensive; non-intensive; open or flexible

Japanese
Type: client-based; institution-based; group; one-to-one; bespoke
(specialism: business)
Method: non-intensive; open or flexible

Polish
Type: client-based; institution-based; group; one-to-one; bespoke
Method: non-intensive; open or flexible

Portuguese
Type: client-based; institution-based; group; one-to-one; bespoke
Method: non-intensive; open or flexible

Russian
Type: client-based; institution-based; group; one-to-one; bespoke
(specialism: art)
Method: non-intensive; open or flexible

Spanish
Type: client-based; institution-based; group; one-to-one; bespoke
(specialisms: business; telecommunications)
Method: intensive; non-intensive; open or flexible

Swedish	*Type:* client-based; institution-based; group; one-to-one; bespoke
	Method: non-intensive; open or flexible
Other	Serbo-Croat, Slovak, Kiribatese, Afrikaans, Finnish, Icelandic,
	Norwegian, Romanian, Swahili, Turkish and Urdu can be offered,
	with notice

SERVICES

Translating

Czech	out of English
French	into and out of English (specialisms: medical; religious)
German	into and out of English (specialism: computers)
Hungarian	out of English
Italian	into and out of English
Japanese	out of English
Russian	out of English
Spanish	into and out of English

Interpreting

Arabic	simultaneous; consecutive
Czech	simultaneous; consecutive
French	simultaneous; consecutive
German	simultaneous; consecutive
Hungarian	simultaneous; consecutive
Italian	simultaneous; consecutive
Japanese	simultaneous; consecutive
Polish	simultaneous; consecutive
Russian	simultaneous; consecutive
Spanish	simultaneous; consecutive

FACILITIES

Language labs:	over 25 places - 5 fixed
Equipment and	
materials:	satellite television; audio and videocassettes

NOTES

- has experience of undertaking language training needs analyses for employers
- has visiting scholars from China, eastern Europe, the Middle East and Far East
- can arrange simultaneous interpreting facilities on request

295   Oaklands College (Oaklands Campus)

Hatfield Road
St Albans
AL4 0JA

Telephone   (0727) 50651
Fax   (0727) 47987

Contact   Mr S. Carter, Head of Modern Languages

TRAINING

Arabic   *Type:* client-based; institution-based; group; one-to-one; bespoke
            Method: non-intensive; open or flexible
French   *Type:* client-based; institution-based; group; one-to-one; bespoke
            Method: non-intensive; open or flexible
German   *Type:* client-based; institution-based; group; bespoke
            Method: non-intensive; open or flexible
Greek   *Type:* client-based; institution-based; group; one-to-one; bespoke
            Method: non-intensive; open or flexible
Italian   *Type:* client-based; institution-based; group; one-to-one; bespoke
            Method: non-intensive; open or flexible
Japanese   *Type:* client-based; group; bespoke
            Method: non-intensive; open or flexible
Spanish   *Type:* client-based; institution-based; group; one-to-one; bespoke
            Method: non-intensive; open or flexible
Other   Additional languages can be offered, with notice

SERVICES
Translating
Arabic   into and out of English
French   into and out of English
German   into and out of English
Greek   into and out of English
Italian   into and out of English
Spanish   into and out of English
Interpreting
French   consecutive
German   consecutive
Japanese   consecutive

FACILITIES
Language labs: 10–25 places - 1 fixed, 3 portable
Equipment and
  materials: computer-assisted language learning

NOTES
• has experience of undertaking language training needs analyses for employers

296   Oaklands College (St Albans City Campus)

St Peters Road
St Albans   Telephone   (0727) 47070
AL1 3RX   Fax   (0727) 47071

Contact   Mrs L. Boereboom, Senior Lecturer

TRAINING

French	*Type:* client-based; institution-based; group; one-to-one
	Method: non-intensive
German	*Type:* client-based; institution-based; group; one-to-one
	Method: non-intensive
Italian	*Type:* institution-based
Spanish	*Type:* client-based; institution-based; group; one-to-one
	Method: non-intensive
Specialism	receptionists
Other	Japanese and Russian can be offered, with notice

SERVICES

Translating

French	into and out of English
German	into and out of English
Italian	into and out of English
Japanese	into and out of English
Russian	into and out of English
Spanish	into and out of English

Interpreting

French	consecutive
German	consecutive
Spanish	simultaneous; consecutive

FACILITIES

Language labs: 10–25 places - 1 fixed

297   Oldham College

Rochdale Road
Oldham   Telephone   061-624 5241
OL9 6AA   Fax   061-627 3635

Contact   Ms W. Cooke, Foreign Language Training Co-ordinator

TRAINING

French   *Type:* client-based; institution-based; group; one-to-one
              Method: intensive; non-intensive; open or flexible
German   *Type:* client-based; institution-based; group; one-to-one
              Method: intensive; non-intensive; open or flexible
Italian   *Type:* client-based; institution-based; group; one-to-one
              Method: open or flexible
Spanish   *Type:* client-based; institution-based; group; one-to-one
              Method: intensive; non-intensive; open or flexible
Urdu   *Type:* client-based; institution-based; group; one-to-one (specialism: medical)
              Method: intensive; non-intensive
Other   Bengali can be offered, with notice

FACILITIES
Language labs: 10–25 places - 1 fixed

NOTES
• has experience of undertaking language training needs analyses for employers

298 University of Oxford

Language Training Centre
Woodstock Road
Oxford   Telephone   (0865) 283360
OX2 6HT   Fax   (0865) 283366

Contact   Mr T. Stableford, Language Teaching Centre Deputy Director

TRAINING
French   *Type:* client-based; institution-based; group; one-to-one; bespoke
                Method: intensive; non-intensive; open or flexible
German   *Type:* client-based; institution-based; group; one-to-one; bespoke
                Method: intensive; non-intensive; open or flexible
Greek   *Type:* client-based; institution-based; group; one-to-one; bespoke
                Method: intensive; non-intensive; open or flexible
Italian   *Type:* client-based; institution-based; group; one-to-one; bespoke
                Method: intensive; non-intensive; open or flexible
Portuguese   *Type:* client-based; institution-based; group; one-to-one; bespoke
                Method: intensive; non-intensive; open or flexible
Russian   *Type:* client-based; institution-based; group; one-to-one; bespoke
                Method: intensive; non-intensive; open or flexible
Spanish   *Type:* client-based; institution-based; group; one-to-one; bespoke
                Method: intensive; non-intensive; open or flexible
Other   Additional languages can be offered, with notice

FACILITIES
Language labs: 10–25 places - 1 fixed
Equipment and
  materials: audio and videocassettes; satellite television

NOTES
• has materials available in 85 languages

299 Oxford Brookes University

Gipsy Lane
Headington
Oxford   Telephone   (0865) 819720
OX3 0BP   Fax   (0865) 819791

Contact   Ms A. Proudfoot, Head of Oxford Polyglot

TRAINING

Arabic   *Type:* client-based; institution-based; group; one-to-one; bespoke
Danish   *Type:* client-based; institution-based; group; one-to-one; bespoke
Dutch   *Type:* client-based; institution-based; group; one-to-one; bespoke
French   *Type:* client-based; institution-based; group; one-to-one; bespoke
              Method: intensive; non-intensive; open or flexible
German   *Type:* client-based; institution-based; group; one-to-one; bespoke
              Method: intensive; non-intensive; open or flexible
Italian   *Type:* client-based; institution-based; group; one-to-one; bespoke
              Method: intensive; non-intensive; open or flexible
Japanese   *Type:* client-based; institution-based; group; one-to-one; bespoke
              Method: non-intensive
Malay   *Type:* client-based; one-to-one
              Method: non-intensive
Portuguese   *Type:* client-based; institution-based; group; one-to-one; bespoke
Russian   *Type:* client-based; institution-based; group; one-to-one; bespoke
Spanish   *Type:* client-based; institution-based; group; one-to-one; bespoke
              Method: intensive; non-intensive; open or flexible
Other   Additional languages can be offered, with notice

SERVICES
Translating
Danish   into and out of English
French   into and out of English
German   into and out of English
Greek   into and out of English
Italian   into and out of English
Japanese   into and out of English
Russian   into and out of English
Spanish   into and out of English
Specialisms   commercial; technical
Interpreting
French   consecutive
German   consecutive
Italian   consecutive
Spanish   consecutive
Specialisms   commercial; marketing; legal; police; technical

FACILITIES

Language labs: under 10 places - 1 fixed; 10–25 places - 1 fixed
Equipment and
  materials: computer-assisted language learning; audio and videocassettes; satellite television

NOTES

* has experience of undertaking language training needs analyses for employers
* provides native speakers for video voice-overs, proof-reading and recordings
* can record course participants on videotape
* keeps a register of translators and interpreters for many languages

300　Oxford College of Further Education

Oxpens Road
Oxford　　　　　Telephone　　(0865) 245871
OX1 1SA　　　　Fax　　　　　(0865) 248871

Contact　　　Mr D. Ansell, Head of Arts and Languages

TRAINING

Arabic　　　*Type:* institution-based
　　　　　　Method: non-intensive
Chinese　　　*Type:* institution-based
　　　　　　Method: non-intensive
Danish　　　*Type:* institution-based
　　　　　　Method: non-intensive
Dutch　　　*Type:* institution-based
　　　　　　Method: non-intensive
French　　　*Type:* client-based; institution-based
　　　　　　Method: intensive; non-intensive
German　　　*Type:* institution-based
　　　　　　Method: intensive; non-intensive
Greek　　　*Type:* institution-based
　　　　　　Method: non-intensive
Italian　　　*Type:* institution-based
　　　　　　Method: intensive; non-intensive
Japanese　　*Type:* client-based; institution-based (specialism: computers)
　　　　　　Method: intensive; non-intensive
Polish　　　*Type:* institution-based
　　　　　　Method: non-intensive
Portuguese　*Type:* institution-based
　　　　　　Method: non-intensive
Russian　　　*Type:* institution-based
　　　　　　Method: non-intensive
Spanish　　　*Type:* client-based; institution-based
　　　　　　Method: intensive; non-intensive
Swedish　　　*Type:* institution-based
　　　　　　Method: non-intensive
Urdu　　　　*Type:* institution-based
　　　　　　Method: non-intensive

FACILITIES

Language labs:　10–25 places - 4 fixed
Equipment and
　materials:　　audio and videocassettes; computer-assisted language learning

301   University of Paisley

High Street
Paisley
PA1 2BE

Telephone   041-848 3000
Fax   041-848 3395

Contact   Mrs D. Finlay, Lecturer

TRAINING

French
: *Type:* client-based; institution-based; group; one-to-one (specialisms: mechanical engineering; electronic engineering; information technology; legal; medical; technical)
Method: intensive; non-intensive; open or flexible

German
: *Type:* client-based; institution-based; group; one-to-one (specialisms: mechanical engineering; electronic engineering; information technology; legal; medical; technical)
Method: intensive; non-intensive; open or flexible

Italian
: *Type:* client-based; institution-based; group; one-to-one
Method: non-intensive

Japanese
: *Type:* client-based; institution-based; group; one-to-one (specialism: technical)

Portuguese
: *Type:* client-based; institution-based; group; one-to-one

Russian
: *Type:* client-based; institution-based; group; one-to-one (specialisms: mechanical engineering; electronic engineering; information technology; legal; medical; technical)
Method: intensive; non-intensive

Spanish
: *Type:* client-based; institution-based; group; one-to-one (specialisms: mechanical engineering; electronic engineering; information technology; legal; medical; technical)
Method: intensive; non-intensive; open or flexible

Other
: Additional languages can be offered, with notice

SERVICES

Translating

French   into and out of English
German   into and out of English
Italian   out of English
Russian   into and out of English
Spanish   into and out of English
Specialisms   mechanical engineering; electronic engineering; legal; medical; technical

Interpreting

French   simultaneous; consecutive
German   simultaneous; consecutive
Russian   simultaneous; consecutive

415

| Spanish | simultaneous; consecutive |
| Specialisms | mechanical engineering; electronic engineering; legal; medical; technical; information technology |

FACILITIES

Language labs:	10–25 places - 2 fixed, 1 portable
Interpreting facilities:	10–25 places - 2 fixed, 2 portable
Equipment and materials:	audio and videocassettes; interactive video

NOTES

• has experience of undertaking language training needs analyses for employers
• is preparing Italian and Russian flexible learning resources

302   Park Lane College

Park Lane
Leeds   Telephone   (0532) 443011
LS3 1AA   Fax   (0532) 446372

Contact   Mrs P. Waterhouse, Director, Communication Studies Department

TRAINING
French   *Type:* client-based; institution-based; group; one-to-one; bespoke
                     Method: intensive; non-intensive; open or flexible
German   *Type:* client-based; institution-based; group; one-to-one; bespoke
                     Method: intensive; non-intensive; open or flexible
Italian   *Type:* client-based; institution-based; group; one-to-one; bespoke
                     Method: intensive; non-intensive; open or flexible
Spanish   *Type:* client-based; institution-based; group; one-to-one; bespoke
                     Method: intensive; non-intensive; open or flexible
Specialism   business
Other   Japanese, Chinese, Portuguese, Greek, Polish, Urdu, Russian, Dutch
                     and Punjabi can be offered, with notice

SERVICES
Interpreting
French   consecutive
German   consecutive
Italian   consecutive
Spanish   consecutive

FACILITIES
Language labs: 10–25 places - 1 fixed
Equipment and
  materials: audiocassettes

NOTES
• has experience of undertaking language training needs analyses for employers
• modern languages drop-in workshop open at lunchtimes and evenings, when a
  qualified teacher can guide and support students using language laboratory on self-
  access or open-learning basis
• offers cultural briefings

303 Parkwood College

Shirecliffe Road
Sheffield   Telephone   (0742) 768301
S5 8XZ   Fax   (0742) 728148

Contact   Ms L. Charlton, Short Course Manager

TRAINING
French   *Type:* client-based; institution-based; group; one-to-one
                     Method: intensive; non-intensive; open or flexible
German   *Type:* client-based; institution-based; group; one-to-one
Other   Spanish, Punjabi and Urdu can be offered, with notice

FACILITIES
Language labs: 10–25 places - 1 fixed
Interpreting
  facilities: 10–25 places - 1 fixed
Equipment and
  materials: computer-assisted language learning; listening stations and console

NOTES
• has experience of undertaking language training needs analyses for employers

304   Parson Cross College

Remington Road
Sheffield   Telephone   (0742) 322841
S5 9PB   Fax   (0742) 852643

Contact   Mr R. Williams, Parson Cross Training Manager

TRAINING
French   *Type:* client-based; institution-based; group; one-to-one; bespoke
          Method: intensive; non-intensive
German   *Type:* client-based; institution-based; group; one-to-one; bespoke
          Method: intensive; non-intensive

SERVICES
Translating
French   into and out of English
German   into and out of English

FACILITIES
Equipment and
   materials: computer-assisted language learning

305   Pembrokeshire College

Dew Street
Haverfordwest   Telephone   (0437) 765427
SA61 1SZ   Fax   (0437) 767279

Contact   Mrs S. Leonard, Programme Area Leader

TRAINING

French   *Type:* institution-based; group
                       Method: intensive; non-intensive
German   *Type:* institution-based; group
                       Method: intensive; non-intensive
Russian   *Type:* institution-based; group
                       Method: non-intensive
Spanish   *Type:* institution-based; group
                       Method: non-intensive

SERVICES
Translating
French   into and out of English
German   into and out of English
Italian   into and out of English
Russian   into and out of English
Spanish   into and out of English
Interpreting
French   consecutive
German   consecutive
Italian   consecutive
Spanish   consecutive

FACILITIES

Language labs: 10–25 places - 1 portable
Interpreting
  facilities: 10–25 places - 1 portable
Equipment and
  materials: audio and videocassettes

NOTES
• has experience of undertaking language training needs analyses for employers

306 People's College of Tertiary Education

Maid Marian Way
Nottingham
NG1 6AB

Telephone (0602) 417721
Fax (0602) 483749

Contact   Mr M. Stringer, Assistant Principal

TRAINING

French   *Type:* client-based; institution-based; group; bespoke
            Method: intensive; non-intensive; open or flexible
German   *Type:* client-based; institution-based; group; bespoke
            Method: intensive; non-intensive
Italian   *Type:* institution-based; group; bespoke
            Method: intensive; non-intensive
Spanish   *Type:* institution-based; group; bespoke
            Method: intensive; non-intensive
Urdu   *Type:* institution-based; group
            Method: non-intensive

307　Perth College of Further Education

Brahan Estate
Crieff Road
Perth　　　　　　　　Telephone　　　(0738) 21171
PH1 2NX　　　　　　Fax　　　　　　(0738) 31364

Contact　　　　　Mrs P. Walton, Lecturer in Languages

TRAINING
French　　　　　　*Type:* client-based; institution-based; group; one-to-one; bespoke
　　　　　　　　　Method: intensive; non-intensive; open or flexible
German　　　　　　*Type:* client-based; institution-based; group; bespoke
　　　　　　　　　Method: intensive; non-intensive; open or flexible
Specialism　　　　business

SERVICES
Translating
French　　　　　　into and out of English
German　　　　　　into and out of English
Specialisms　　　business; legal
Interpreting
French　　　　　　consecutive
German　　　　　　consecutive

FACILITIES
Language labs:　　under 10 places - 1 portable; 10–25 places - 1 fixed

NOTES
• has experience of undertaking language training needs analyses for employers

308   College of Further Education (Plymouth)

Kings Road
Devonport
Plymouth   Telephone   (0752) 385391
PL14 6NG   Fax   (0752) 385343

Contact   Dr A. Thompson, Head of General Education

TRAINING
French   *Type:* client-based; institution-based; group; one-to-one; bespoke
                (specialism: engineering)
                Method: intensive; non-intensive; open or flexible
German   *Type:* client-based; institution-based; group; one-to-one; bespoke
                (specialisms: engineering; distribution)
                Method: intensive; non-intensive; open or flexible
Italian   *Type:* client-based; institution-based; group; one-to-one; bespoke
                Method: intensive; non-intensive; open or flexible
Russian   *Type:* client-based; institution-based; group; one-to-one; bespoke
                Method: intensive; non-intensive; open or flexible
Spanish   *Type:* client-based; institution-based; group; one-to-one; bespoke
                Method: intensive; non-intensive; open or flexible
Other   Portuguese, Dutch and Czech can be offered, with notice

SERVICES
Translating
French   into and out of English
German   into and out of English
Russian   into and out of English
Spanish   into and out of English

FACILITIES
Language labs: under 10 places - 1 portable; 10–25 places - 2 fixed
Equipment and
  materials: interactive video; computer-assisted language learning; audio and
                videocassettes

NOTES
• has experience of undertaking language training needs analyses for employers

309 University of Plymouth

Plymouth Business School
Drake Circus

Plymouth	Telephone	(0752) 232803
PL4 8AA	Fax	(0752) 232853

Contact   Dr A. Cornell, Head of Modern Languages Unit

TRAINING

French	*Type:* client-based; institution-based; group; one-to-one
	Method: intensive; non-intensive; open or flexible
German	*Type:* client-based; institution-based; group; one-to-one
	Method: intensive; non-intensive; open or flexible
Italian	*Type:* client-based; institution-based; group; one-to-one
	Method: intensive; non-intensive; open or flexible
Spanish	*Type:* client-based; institution-based; group; one-to-one
	Method: intensive; non-intensive; open or flexible
Specialism	business

FACILITIES

Language labs: 10–25 places - 2 fixed

310   Pontypool and Usk College

Blaendare Road
Pontypool   Telephone   (0495) 755141
NP4 5YE   Fax   (0495) 751040

Contact   Mr G. Jones, Lecturer

TRAINING
French   *Type:* client-based; institution-based; group; one-to-one
               Method: non-intensive; open or flexible
German   *Type:* client-based; institution-based; group; one-to-one
               Method: non-intensive; open or flexible
Spanish   *Type:* client-based; institution-based; group; one-to-one
               Method: non-intensive; open or flexible

FACILITIES
Language labs: under 10 places - 1 portable

NOTES
• has experience of undertaking language training needs analyses for employers

311   Pontypridd Technical College

Ynys Terrace
Rhydyfelin
Pontypridd   Telephone   (0443) 486121
CF37 5RN   Fax   (0443) 409345

Contact   Mr J. Payne, Languages Co-ordinator

TRAINING
French   *Type:* client-based; institution-based; group; one-to-one; bespoke
                  Method: intensive; non-intensive; open or flexible
German   *Type:* client-based; institution-based; group; one-to-one; bespoke
Italian   *Type:* client-based; institution-based; group; one-to-one; bespoke
Japanese   *Type:* client-based; institution-based; group; one-to-one; bespoke
Spanish   *Type:* client-based; institution-based; group; one-to-one; bespoke
Welsh   *Type:* client-based; institution-based; group; one-to-one; bespoke
Other   Russian can be offered, with notice

SERVICES
Translating
French   into and out of English
German   into and out of English
Italian   into and out of English
Japanese   into and out of English
Spanish   into and out of English
Welsh   into and out of English
Interpreting
French   consecutive
German   consecutive
Italian   consecutive
Spanish   consecutive
Welsh   consecutive

FACILITIES
Equipment and
  materials: audio and videocassettes; computer-assisted language learning

NOTES
• has experience of undertaking language training analyses for employers

312 Portadown College of Further Education

26-44 Lurgan Road
Portadown   Telephone   (0762) 337111
BT63 5BL   Fax   (0762) 350490

Contact   Dr J. R. Wright, Head of Department

TRAINING
French   *Type:* institution-based
                      Method: non-intensive
German   *Type:* institution-based
                      Method: non-intensive
Spanish   *Type:* institution-based
Other   Additional languages can be offered, with notice

313   University of Portsmouth

University House
Winston Churchill Avenue

Portsmouth	Telephone	(0705) 843047
PO1 2EG	Fax	(0705) 295124

Contact   Mrs E. Aldridge, Director, Language Centre

TRAINING

Arabic
: *Type:* client-based; institution-based; group; one-to-one
: *Method:* intensive; non-intensive

Danish
: *Type:* client-based; one-to-one
: *Method:* intensive; non-intensive

Dutch
: *Type:* client-based; institution-based; group
: *Method:* intensive; non-intensive

French
: *Type:* client-based; institution-based; group; one-to-one
: *Method:* intensive; non-intensive

German
: *Type:* client-based; institution-based; group; one-to-one
: *Method:* intensive; non-intensive

Italian
: *Type:* client-based; institution-based; group; one-to-one
: *Method:* intensive; non-intensive

Japanese
: *Type:* client-based; institution-based; group; one-to-one
: *Method:* intensive; non-intensive

Portuguese
: *Type:* client-based; institution-based; group
: *Method:* intensive; non-intensive

Russian
: *Type:* client-based; institution-based; group; one-to-one
: *Method:* intensive; non-intensive

Spanish
: *Type:* client-based; institution-based; group; one-to-one
: *Method:* intensive; non-intensive

SERVICES

Translating

French	into and out of English
German	into and out of English
Italian	into and out of English
Japanese	into and out of English
Spanish	into and out of English
Specialisms	engineering; legal; business; music

Interpreting

French	consecutive
German	consecutive
Russian	consecutive

FACILITIES
Language labs: 10–25 places - 4 fixed

NOTES
• has experience of undertaking language training needs analyses for employers

314   Preston College

St Vincent's Road
Fulwood
Preston   Telephone   (0772) 716511
PR2 4UR   Fax   (0772) 712530

Contact   Mrs H. Powell, Senior Tutor, Employer Liaison

TRAINING
Dutch   *Type:* client-based; institution-based; group; one-to-one; bespoke
               Method: intensive; non-intensive
French   *Type:* client-based; institution-based; group; one-to-one; bespoke
               Method: intensive; non-intensive; open or flexible
German   *Type:* client-based; institution-based; group; one-to-one; bespoke
               Method: intensive; non-intensive; open or flexible
Greek   *Type:* client-based; institution-based; group; one-to-one; bespoke
               Method: intensive; non-intensive; open or flexible
Italian   *Type:* client-based; institution-based; group; one-to-one; bespoke
               Method: intensive; non-intensive; open or flexible
Japanese   *Type:* client-based; institution-based; group; one-to-one; bespoke
               Method: intensive; non-intensive; open or flexible
Portuguese   *Type:* client-based; institution-based; group; one-to-one; bespoke
               Method: intensive; non-intensive; open or flexible
Russian   *Type:* client-based; institution-based; group; one-to-one; bespoke
               Method: intensive; non-intensive; open or flexible
Spanish   *Type:* client-based; institution-based; group; one-to-one; bespoke
               Method: intensive; non-intensive; open or flexible
Turkish   *Type:* client-based; institution-based; group; one-to-one; bespoke
               Method: intensive; non-intensive
Specialisms   technical; tourism; transport; telecommunications
Other   Urdu, Gujarati and Arabic can be offered, with notice

SERVICES
Translating
Dutch   into and out of English (specialism: tourism)
French   into and out of English (specialisms: agriculture; engineering;
               commercial)
German   into and out of English (specialism: chemical engineering)
Greek   into and out of English
Italian   into and out of English
Japanese   into and out of English
Portuguese   into and out of English
Russian   into and out of English
Spanish   into and out of English

Interpreting

Dutch	simultaneous; consecutive (specialism: tourism)
French	simultaneous; consecutive (specialisms: agriculture; engineering; commercial)
German	simultaneous; consecutive (specialism: chemical engineering)
Greek	simultaneous; consecutive
Italian	simultaneous; consecutive
Japanese	simultaneous; consecutive
Portuguese	simultaneous; consecutive
Russian	simultaneous; consecutive
Spanish	simultaneous; consecutive

FACILITIES

Language labs:	10–25 places - 3 fixed
Equipment and materials:	audio and videocassettes

NOTES

- has experience of undertaking language training needs analyses for employers
- promotes languages for business through its college company, Preston Training
- throughout the courses there are opportunities to extend or modify objectives to ensure that training fits the needs of students and of the company

315   Queen's College (Glasgow)

1 Park Drive
Glasgow   Telephone   041-337 4000
G3 6LP   Fax   041-337 4500

Contact   Miss C. Leroy, Lecturer in Applied French

TRAINING
French   *Type:* institution-based; group
                        Method: intensive; open or flexible
German   *Type:* client-based; institution-based; group; one-to-one

NOTES
• hopes to develop language courses for business, although efforts so far have concentrated on language courses for full time students

316   Queen's University of Belfast

University Road
Belfast
BT7 1NN

Telephone   (0232) 245133
Fax   (0232) 247895

Contact   Dr P. Tame, Lecturer in French

TRAINING

Arabic	*Type:* institution-based; group
	Method: non-intensive
Dutch	*Type:* institution-based; group
	Method: non-intensive
French	*Type:* client-based; institution-based; group; one-to-one (specialism: commercial)
	Method: intensive; non-intensive
German	*Type:* client-based; institution-based; group; one-to-one (specialism: commercial)
	Method: intensive; non-intensive
Greek	*Type:* institution-based; group
	Method: non-intensive
Irish	*Type:* institution-based; group
	Method: non-intensive
Italian	*Type:* institution-based; group
	Method: non-intensive
Japanese	*Type:* institution-based; group
	Method: non-intensive
Portuguese	*Type:* institution-based; group
	Method: non-intensive
Russian	*Type:* institution-based; group
	Method: intensive; non-intensive
Spanish	*Type:* institution-based; group
	Method: non-intensive
Swedish	*Type:* institution-based; group
	Method: non-intensive

SERVICES

Translating

Dutch	into and out of English
French	into and out of English
German	into and out of English
Greek	into and out of English
Hungarian	into and out of English
Italian	into and out of English
Japanese	into and out of English
Polish	into and out of English

Portuguese	into and out of English
Russian	into and out of English
Spanish	into and out of English
Swedish	into and out of English
Specialisms	scientific; legal; medical
Interpreting	
French	simultaneous; consecutive
German	simultaneous; consecutive
Russian	simultaneous; consecutive
Spanish	simultaneous; consecutive

FACILITIES

Language labs:	10–25 places - 3 fixed
Equipment and materials:	computer-assisted language learning; audio and videocassettes

NOTES
• could offer interpreting and translating services in most languages, if required

317   University of Reading

Centre for Applied Language Studies
Whiteknights

Reading	Telephone	(0734) 318514
RG6 2AA	Fax	(0734) 756506

Contact   Dr S. Yuksel, Language Access Development Officer

TRAINING

French	*Type:* institution-based; group; one-to-one
	Method: intensive; non-intensive; open or flexible
German	*Type:* institution-based; group; one-to-one
	Method: intensive; non-intensive; open or flexible
Italian	*Type:* institution-based; group; one-to-one
	Method: intensive; non-intensive; open or flexible
Spanish	*Type:* institution-based; group; one-to-one
	Method: intensive; non-intensive; open or flexible
Turkish	*Type:* client-based; institution-based; group; one-to-one
Other	Japanese can be offered, with notice

SERVICES
Translating

French	into and out of English
German	into and out of English
Italian	into and out of English
Spanish	into and out of English
Turkish	into English

Interpreting

French	simultaneous; consecutive
German	simultaneous; consecutive
Italian	simultaneous; consecutive
Spanish	simultaneous; consecutive
Turkish	simultaneous; consecutive

FACILITIES

Language labs:	10–25 places - 1 fixed
Equipment and materials:	computer-assisted language learning

NOTES
• has experience of undertaking language training needs analyses for employers

318 Reading Adult College

Wilson Centre
Wilson Road
Reading   Telephone   (0734) 575575
RG3 2RW   Fax   (0734) 393914

Contact   Mrs L. Waites, Open Learning Organiser

TRAINING

Arabic	*Type:* client-based; institution-based; group; one-to-one; bespoke (specialism: legal) *Method:* non-intensive
Dutch	*Type:* client-based; institution-based; group; one-to-one; bespoke *Method:* non-intensive
French	*Type:* client-based; institution-based; group; one-to-one; bespoke *Method:* intensive; non-intensive
German	*Type:* client-based; institution-based; group; one-to-one; bespoke *Method:* intensive; non-intensive
Italian	*Type:* client-based; institution-based; group; one-to-one; bespoke *Method:* intensive; non-intensive
Japanese	*Type:* client-based; institution-based; group; one-to-one; bespoke *Method:* non-intensive
Russian	*Type:* client-based; institution-based; group; one-to-one; bespoke *Method:* non-intensive
Spanish	*Type:* client-based; institution-based; group; one-to-one; bespoke *Method:* intensive; non-intensive
Other	Greek, Thai, Portuguese, Urdu, Hindi and Punjabi can be offered, with notice

FACILITIES

Language labs: under 10 places - 1 fixed
Equipment and
   materials: audio and videocassettes; computer-assisted language learning

NOTES
- has experience of undertaking language training needs analyses for employers
- regularly teaches 15 modern languages to adult learners

319 Redbridge College of Further Education

Little Heath
Romford   Telephone   081-598 2412
RM6 4XT   Fax   081-599 8224

Contact   Mrs P. Wildman, Manager, Enterprise Unit

TRAINING
French   *Type:* client-based; institution-based
                  Method: intensive; non-intensive
German   *Type:* client-based; institution-based
                  Method: intensive; non-intensive
Italian   *Type:* institution-based
                  Method: non-intensive
Russian   *Type:* institution-based; bespoke
                  Method: non-intensive
Spanish   *Type:* institution-based
                  Method: non-intensive

SERVICES
Translating
French   into and out of English
German   into and out of English
Italian   into and out of English
Russian   into and out of English
Spanish   into and out of English

FACILITIES
Language labs: 10–25 places - 1 fixed

NOTES
• has experience of undertaking language training needs analyses for employers

320   Reid Kerr College

Renfrew Road
Paisley   Telephone   041-889 4225
PA3 4DR   Fax   041-889 3958

Contact   Mrs A. Osborne, PICKUP Development Officer

TRAINING
French   *Type:* client-based; institution-based; group
                     Method: non-intensive
German   *Type:* client-based; institution-based; group
                     Method: non-intensive
Spanish   *Type:* institution-based; group
                     Method: non-intensive
Other   Italian can be offered, with notice

FACILITIES
Language labs: 10–25 places - 4 portable

321 Rhondda College

Llwynpia
Tonypandy   Telephone   (0443) 432187
CF40 2TQ   Fax   (0443) 438786

Contact   Mr E. Baldascino, Marketing Manager

German, French, Italian and Spanish can be offered, with notice

FACILITIES
Language labs: 10–25 places - 5 portable
Equipment and
  materials: computer-assisted language learning; audio and videocassettes

NOTES
• has experience of undertaking language training needs analyses for employers

322   Richmond Adult and Community College

Clifden Road
Twickenham   Telephone   081-891 5907
TW1 4LT   Fax   081-892 6354

Contact   Mr M. Rogers, Head of Business Studies and Languages

TRAINING

Arabic   *Type:* institution-based
French   *Type:* client-based; institution-based; group; one-to-one
               Method: intensive; non-intensive; open or flexible
German   *Type:* institution-based; one-to-one
               Method: intensive; non-intensive; open or flexible
Italian   *Type:* one-to-one
               Method: intensive; non-intensive; open or flexible
Japanese   *Type:* institution-based
               Method: non-intensive
Russian   *Type:* one-to-one
               Method: intensive; non-intensive
Spanish   *Type:* institution-based
               Method: intensive; non-intensive; open or flexible
Other   Dutch, Turkish and Portuguese can be offered, with notice

FACILITIES

Equipment and
  materials: audiocassettes

NOTES

• has experience of undertaking language training needs analyses for employers

323 Richmond upon Thames College

Egerton Road
Twickenham   Telephone   081-892 6656
TW2 7SJ   Fax   081-744 1148

Contact   Mr D. Rubin, Senior Lecturer in Modern Languages

TRAINING

French
Type: client-based; institution-based; group; one-to-one; bespoke
Method: intensive; non-intensive; open or flexible

German
Type: client-based; institution-based; group; one-to-one; bespoke
Method: intensive; non-intensive; open or flexible

Italian
Type: client-based; institution-based; group; bespoke
Method: intensive; non-intensive; open or flexible

Russian
Type: client-based; institution-based; group; one-to-one; bespoke
Method: intensive; non-intensive; open or flexible

Spanish
Type: institution-based; group; one-to-one; bespoke
Method: intensive; non-intensive; open or flexible

Specialisms   business; airline industry; motor industry

Other   Additional languages can be offered, with notice

FACILITIES

Language labs: over 25 places - 1 fixed
Equipment and
  materials: audio and videocassettes; computer-assisted language learning

NOTES
• has experience of undertaking language training needs analyses for employers
• offers translating services in any language, on demand

324   University College of Ripon and York St John

International Language and Short Courses Unit
Lord Mayor's Walk

York	Telephone	(0904) 625072
YO3 7EX	Fax	(0904) 612512

Contact — Ms J. Moody, International Language and Short Courses Unit Manager

TRAINING

French — *Type:* client-based; institution-based; group; one-to-one; bespoke
Method: intensive; non-intensive

German — *Type:* client-based; institution-based; group; one-to-one; bespoke
Method: intensive; non-intensive

Italian — *Type:* client-based; institution-based; group; one-to-one; bespoke

Norwegian — *Type:* client-based; institution-based; group; one-to-one; bespoke

Spanish — *Type:* client-based; institution-based; group; one-to-one; bespoke

Swedish — *Type:* client-based; institution-based; group; one-to-one; bespoke
Method: intensive; non-intensive

SERVICES

Translating

French	into and out of English
German	into and out of English
Italian	into and out of English
Norwegian	into and out of English
Spanish	into and out of English
Swedish	into and out of English

Interpreting

French	consecutive
German	consecutive
Italian	consecutive
Norwegian	consecutive
Spanish	consecutive
Swedish	consecutive

FACILITIES

Language labs: 10–25 places - 1 fixed, 1 portable

NOTES

• has experience of undertaking language training needs analyses for employers

325   Robert Gordon University

Schoolhill
Aberdeen
AB9 1FR

Telephone   (0224) 633611
Fax   (0224) 642003

Contact   Dr M. Hill, Senior Lecturer

TRAINING
French   *Type:* client-based; institution-based; group; one-to-one; bespoke
                 Method: intensive; non-intensive
German   *Type:* client-based; institution-based; group; one-to-one; bespoke

FACILITIES
Language labs: 10–25 places - 2 fixed

NOTES
• has experience of undertaking language training needs analyses for employers
• hopes to expand its languages for business provision, concentrating initially on French and German

326 Rockingham College

Rockingham Business Training Centre
West Street
Wath-upon-Dearne   Telephone   (0709) 760310
S63 6PX   Fax   (0709) 874513

Contact   Mrs S. Corns, Lecturer in French and Spanish

TRAINING

French   *Type:* client-based; institution-based; group; one-to-one
           (specialisms: water sport; tourism; catering; telephone skills)
           Method: non-intensive; open or flexible
German   *Type:* client-based; institution-based; group; one-to-one
           (specialisms: tourism; telephone skills)
           Method: non-intensive; open or flexible
Italian   *Type:* client-based; institution-based; group; one-to-one
           (specialisms: tourism; telephone skills)
           Method: non-intensive; open or flexible
Spanish   *Type:* client-based; institution-based; group; one-to-one
           (specialisms: tourism; telephone skills)
           Method: non-intensive; open or flexible

SERVICES
Translating
Afrikaans   into and out of English
Arabic   into and out of English
Bulgarian   into and out of English
Catalan   into and out of English
Czech   into and out of English
Danish   into and out of English
Dutch   into and out of English
Farsi   into and out of English
French   into and out of English
German   into and out of English
Greek   into and out of English
Italian   into and out of English
Japanese   into and out of English
Maltese   into and out of English
Polish   into and out of English
Portuguese   into and out of English
Romanian   into and out of English
Russian   into and out of English
Serbo-Croat   into and out of English
Slovak   into and out of English
Spanish   into and out of English

Swahili	into and out of English
Turkish	into and out of English
Ukrainian	into and out of English

FACILITIES
Language labs: under 10 places - 1 portable; 10–25 places - 1 portable

NOTES
• has experience of undertaking language training needs analyses for employers

327 Rotherham College of Arts and Technology

Eastwood Lane
Rotherham   Telephone   (0709) 362111
S65 1EG   Fax   (0709) 360765

Contact   Mrs A. Plant, Lecturer

TRAINING
French   *Type:* client-based; institution-based; group; one-to-one
                     Method: non-intensive; open or flexible
German   *Type:* client-based; institution-based; group; one-to-one
                     Method: non-intensive; open or flexible
Spanish   *Type:* client-based; institution-based; group; one-to-one
                     Method: non-intensive; open or flexible
Other   Swedish, Italian and Russian can be offered, with notice

FACILITIES
Language labs: 10–25 places - 1 fixed

328 Royal Agricultural College

Cirencester	Telephone	(0285) 652531
GL7 6JS	Fax	(0285) 650219

Contact   Mrs N. White, Head of Languages

TRAINING

French
Type: client-based; institution-based; group; one-to-one; bespoke
Method: intensive; non-intensive

German
Type: client-based; institution-based; group; one-to-one; bespoke
Method: intensive; non-intensive

Italian
Type: client-based; one-to-one; bespoke
Method: intensive; non-intensive

Japanese
Type: client-based; one-to-one
Method: intensive; non-intensive

Russian
Type: client-based; institution-based; group; one-to-one
Method: intensive; non-intensive

Spanish
Type: client-based; institution-based; group; one-to-one; bespoke
Method: intensive; non-intensive

Specialisms   agriculture; business; commercial

Other   Additional languages can be offered, with notice

NOTES
• has experience of undertaking language training needs analyses for employers

329   Royal Forest of Dean College

Five Acres Campus
Berry Hill
Coleford   Telephone   (0594) 833416
GL16 7JT   Fax   (0594) 837497

Contact   Mrs M. Stephens, Division Manager, Modern Languages

TRAINING

French   *Type:* client-based; institution-based; group; one-to-one; bespoke
                 (specialism: business)
                 Method: intensive; non-intensive; open or flexible
German   *Type:* client-based; institution-based; group; one-to-one; bespoke
                 (specialism: business)
                 Method: intensive; non-intensive
Italian   *Type:* client-based; institution-based; group; one-to-one; bespoke
                 Method: intensive; non-intensive
Russian   *Type:* client-based; institution-based; group; one-to-one; bespoke
Spanish   *Type:* client-based; institution-based; group; one-to-one; bespoke
                 (specialism: business)
                 Method: intensive; non-intensive

SERVICES
Translating
French   into English
German   into English
Spanish   into English
Interpreting
French   consecutive
German   consecutive
Spanish   consecutive

FACILITIES
Language labs: under 10 places - 1 portable; 10–25 places - 1 portable
Equipment and
   materials: computer-assisted language learning

NOTES
• has experience of undertaking language training needs analyses for employers
• is part of an international consortium funded under the European Community Lingua
  programme to develop new language learning materials for people in work

330   Royal Holloway

Egham Hill
Egham
TW20 0EX

Telephone	(0784) 434455
Fax	(0784) 437520

Contact   Mr D. White, Head of External Affairs

TRAINING

French	*Type:* client-based; institution-based; group; one-to-one; bespoke
	Method: intensive; non-intensive; open or flexible
German	*Type:* institution-based
	Method: intensive
Italian	*Type:* institution-based
Spanish	*Type:* institution-based
Other	Japanese can be offered, with notice

SERVICES
Translating

French	into and out of English
German	into and out of English
Italian	into and out of English
Japanese	into and out of English

FACILITIES

Language labs:	over 25 places - 2 fixed
Equipment and materials:	computer-assisted language learning

NOTES
• language departments are responsible for University of London external degrees in French, German and Italian

331   Runshaw College

Langdale Road
Leyland
Preston   Telephone   (0772) 432511
PR5 2DQ   Fax   (0772) 622295

Contact   Mr A. Pegge, Assistant Principal, Head of Languages

TRAINING
French   *Type:* client-based; institution-based; group; one-to-one; bespoke
                   Method: intensive; non-intensive; open or flexible
German   *Type:* client-based; institution-based; group; one-to-one; bespoke
                   Method: intensive; non-intensive; open or flexible
Italian   *Type:* client-based; one-to-one; bespoke
                   Method: intensive; non-intensive; open or flexible
Spanish   *Type:* institution-based; one-to-one; bespoke
                   Method: intensive; non-intensive; open or flexible
Other   Japanese, Russian, Greek, Turkish and Dutch can be offered, with
                   notice

SERVICES
Translating
Dutch   into and out of English
French   into and out of English
German   into and out of English
Italian   into and out of English
Japanese   into and out of English
Russian   into and out of English
Spanish   into and out of English
Turkish   into and out of English
Interpreting
Dutch   consecutive
French   consecutive
German   consecutive
Italian   consecutive
Japanese   consecutive
Russian   consecutive
Spanish   consecutive
Turkish   consecutive

FACILITIES
Language labs: under 10 places - 1 portable; 10–25 places - 2 fixed
Equipment and
  materials: audio and videocassettes; satellite television

332 Ruskin College

Walton Street
Oxford   Telephone   (0865) 54331
OX1 2HE   Fax   (0865) 54372

Contact   Mrs E. Barnes, Head of Languages

TRAINING

French	*Type:* institution-based; group; one-to-one; bespoke (specialisms: industrial relations; French government and institutions) *Method:* non-intensive; open or flexible
German	*Type:* institution-based; group; one-to-one; bespoke

SERVICES

Translating

French	into English (specialisms: industrial relations; social and economic organisation)
German	into English
Russian	into English
Spanish	into English

Interpreting

French	consecutive (specialisms: industrial relations; social and economic organisation)
German	consecutive
Russian	consecutive
Spanish	consecutive

FACILITIES

Equipment and
  materials: computer-assisted language learning

NOTES

- has experience of undertaking language training needs analyses for employers
- specialises on language programmes for trade union organisations
- language laboratory places are contracted from an institution near by

333   Rycotewood College

Priest End
Thame   Telephone   (084421) 2501
OX9 2AF   Fax   (084421) 8809

Contact   Mrs Z. Schmidt, German Language Tutor

TRAINING
French   *Type:* client-based; institution-based; group
                      Method: intensive; non-intensive; open or flexible
German   *Type:* client-based; institution-based; group
                      Method: intensive; non-intensive; open or flexible

SERVICES
Translating
French   into and out of English
German   into and out of English
Specialisms   engineering; furniture design
Interpreting
French   consecutive
German   consecutive
Specialisms   engineering; furniture design

FACILITIES
Interpreting
 facilities: 26–100 places - 1 fixed, 1 portable

334 S. Martin's College

Languages Development Centre
Bowerham Road

Lancaster	Telephone	(0524) 63446
LA1 3JD	Fax	(0524) 68943

Contact   Mr M. Pickles, Manager

TRAINING

Danish	*Type:* institution-based; group
	Method: non-intensive; open or flexible
Dutch	*Type:* institution-based; group
	Method: non-intensive; open or flexible
French	*Type:* institution-based; group
	Method: non-intensive; open or flexible
German	*Type:* institution-based; group
	Method: non-intensive; open or flexible
Greek	*Type:* institution-based; group
	Method: non-intensive; open or flexible
Italian	*Type:* institution-based; group
	Method: non-intensive; open or flexible
Portuguese	*Type:* institution-based; group
	Method: non-intensive; open or flexible
Russian	*Type:* institution-based; group
	Method: non-intensive; open or flexible
Spanish	*Type:* institution-based; group
	Method: non-intensive; open or flexible
Other	Japanese can be offered, with notice

335   University College Salford

Frederick Road
Salford
M6 6PU

Telephone	061-736 6541
Fax	061-736 8386

Contact   Mr S. Fletcher, Head of Foreign Languages

TRAINING

French   *Type:* client-based; institution-based; group; one-to-one; bespoke
              Method: intensive; non-intensive; open or flexible
German   *Type:* client-based; institution-based; group; one-to-one; bespoke
              Method: intensive; non-intensive; open or flexible
Italian   *Type:* client-based; institution-based; group; one-to-one; bespoke
              Method: intensive; non-intensive; open or flexible
Spanish   *Type:* client-based; institution-based; group; one-to-one; bespoke
              Method: intensive; non-intensive; open or flexible
Specialism   exporting
Other   Arabic and Portuguese can be offered, with notice

SERVICES
Translating
French   into and out of English
German   into and out of English
Italian   into and out of English
Spanish   into and out of English
Interpreting
French   simultaneous; consecutive
German   simultaneous; consecutive
Italian   simultaneous; consecutive
Spanish   simultaneous; consecutive

FACILITIES
Language labs: under 10 places - 1 fixed; 10–25 places - 1 fixed

NOTES
• has experience of undertaking language training needs analyses for employers

336 University of Salford

Services for Export and Language
Crescent House

Manchester	Telephone	061-745 7480
M5 4WT	Fax	061-745 5110

Contact   Mr G. McLeish, Training Manager

TRAINING

Arabic
Type: client-based; institution-based; group; one-to-one; bespoke (specialism: journalism)
Method: intensive; non-intensive

Chinese
Type: client-based; group; bespoke (specialism: commercial)
Method: intensive; non-intensive

Dutch
Type: client-based; institution-based; group; one-to-one; bespoke
Method: intensive; non-intensive

French
Type: client-based; institution-based; group; one-to-one; bespoke (specialisms: commercial; technical; financial)
Method: intensive; non-intensive; open or flexible

German
Type: client-based; institution-based; group; one-to-one; bespoke (specialisms: commercial; technical; financial)
Method: intensive; non-intensive; open or flexible

Italian
Type: client-based; institution-based; group; one-to-one; bespoke (specialisms: commercial; technical; financial)
Method: intensive; non-intensive; open or flexible

Japanese
Type: client-based; institution-based; group; one-to-one; bespoke (specialisms: commercial; technical; financial)
Method: intensive; non-intensive

Korean
Type: client-based; group; bespoke (specialism: commercial)
Method: intensive; non-intensive

Portuguese
Type: client-based; one-to-one (specialisms: social services; commercial)
Method: intensive; non-intensive

Romanian
Type: client-based; institution-based; group; one-to-one; bespoke
Method: intensive; non-intensive

Russian
Type: client-based; institution-based; group; one-to-one; bespoke (specialisms: commercial; technical; financial)
Method: intensive; non-intensive

Spanish
Type: client-based; institution-based; group; one-to-one; bespoke (specialisms: commercial; technical; financial)
Method: intensive; non-intensive; open or flexible

Swedish
Type: institution-based; one-to-one; bespoke (specialism: aeronautical)
Method: intensive; non-intensive

Turkish	*Type:* client-based; institution-based; group; one-to-one; bespoke (specialism: technical)
	Method: intensive; non-intensive
Other	Some east European languages, and Greek, can be offered, with notice

SERVICES

Translating

French	into and out of English
German	into and out of English
Italian	into and out of English
Japanese	into and out of English
Russian	into and out of English
Spanish	into and out of English
Specialisms	mechanical engineering; electrical engineering; computers; commercial

Interpreting

Chinese	simultaneous; consecutive
French	simultaneous; consecutive
German	simultaneous; consecutive
Italian	simultaneous; consecutive
Japanese	simultaneous; consecutive
Russian	simultaneous; consecutive
Spanish	simultaneous; consecutive

FACILITIES

Language labs:	10–25 places - 3 fixed
Interpreting facilities:	under 10 places - 1 fixed
Equipment and materials:	audiocassettes; computer-assisted language learning

NOTES

• has experience of undertaking language training needs analyses for employers
• offers translating services in most European and Far Eastern languages, and interpreting services in most west European languages
• cultural briefings often accompany language training

337 Salford College of Further Education

Walkden Road
Worsley
Salford   Telephone   061-872 3466
M28 4QD   Fax   061-703 8716

Contact   Ms C. Barnett, Language Co-ordinator

TRAINING
Arabic   *Type:* client-based; institution-based; group; one-to-one; bespoke
French   *Type:* client-based; institution-based; group; one-to-one; bespoke
            Method: intensive; non-intensive; open or flexible
German   *Type:* client-based; institution-based; group; one-to-one; bespoke
            Method: intensive; non-intensive; open or flexible
Italian   *Type:* client-based; institution-based; group; one-to-one; bespoke
            Method: intensive; non-intensive; open or flexible
Russian   *Type:* institution-based
Spanish   *Type:* client-based; institution-based; group; one-to-one; bespoke
            Method: intensive; non-intensive; open or flexible
Other   Additional languages can be offered, with notice

FACILITIES
Language labs: 10–25 places - 1 fixed

NOTES
• has experience of undertaking language training needs analyses for employers

338　Salisbury College

Southampton Road
Salisbury　　　　　　　Telephone　　　(0722) 323711
SP1 2LW　　　　　　　Fax　　　　　　(0722) 326006

Contact　　　　　Mr D. Richardson, Head of Languages

TRAINING
Arabic　　　　　*Type:* client-based; institution-based; group; one-to-one; bespoke
Danish　　　　　*Type:* client-based; institution-based; group; one-to-one; bespoke
　　　　　　　　Method: non-intensive
French　　　　　*Type:* client-based; institution-based; group; one-to-one; bespoke
　　　　　　　　Method: intensive; non-intensive; open or flexible
German　　　　　*Type:* client-based; institution-based; group; one-to-one; bespoke
　　　　　　　　Method: intensive; non-intensive; open or flexible
Italian　　　　　*Type:* client-based; institution-based; group; one-to-one; bespoke
　　　　　　　　Method: intensive; non-intensive
Japanese　　　　*Type:* client-based; institution-based; group; one-to-one; bespoke
　　　　　　　　Method: intensive; non-intensive
Russian　　　　　*Type:* client-based; institution-based; group; one-to-one; bespoke
　　　　　　　　Method: intensive; non-intensive
Spanish　　　　　*Type:* client-based; institution-based; group; one-to-one; bespoke
　　　　　　　　Method: intensive; non-intensive; open or flexible
Other　　　　　　Portuguese, Dutch and Greek can be offered, with notice

SERVICES
Translating
French　　　　　into and out of English
German　　　　　into and out of English
Italian　　　　　into and out of English
Japanese　　　　into and out of English
Russian　　　　　into and out of English
Spanish　　　　　into and out of English
Interpreting
French　　　　　consecutive
German　　　　　consecutive
Italian　　　　　consecutive
Japanese　　　　consecutive
Russian　　　　　consecutive
Spanish　　　　　consecutive

FACILITIES
Language labs:　　under 10 places - 1 portable; 10–25 places - 1 fixed, 1 portable

Equipment and
   materials: computer-assisted language learning; audio and videocassettes

NOTES
- has experience of undertaking language training needs analyses for employers

339 Sandwell College of Further and Higher Education

Woden Road South
Wednesbury
Sandwell
WS10 0PE

Telephone 021-556 6000
Fax 021-556 6069

Contact Ms R. Patel, Head of Languages and Language Links

TRAINING

Arabic	*Type:* client-based; institution-based; group; one-to-one; bespoke
Bengali	*Type:* client-based; institution-based; group; one-to-one; bespoke
Chinese	*Type:* client-based; group (specialism: police)
Czech	*Type:* client-based; institution-based; group; one-to-one; bespoke
French	*Type:* client-based; institution-based; group; one-to-one; bespoke (specialisms: engineering; motor industry; chemical) *Method:* intensive; non-intensive
German	*Type:* client-based; institution-based; group; one-to-one; bespoke (specialisms: engineering; motor industry; chemical) *Method:* intensive; non-intensive
Gujarati	*Type:* client-based; institution-based; group; one-to-one; bespoke
Hindi	*Type:* client-based; institution-based; group; one-to-one; bespoke
Italian	*Type:* client-based; institution-based; group; one-to-one; bespoke (specialisms: engineering; motor industry; chemical) *Method:* intensive; non-intensive
Polish	*Type:* client-based; institution-based; group; one-to-one; bespoke
Punjabi	*Type:* client-based; institution-based; group; one-to-one; bespoke (specialisms: police; medical)
Spanish	*Type:* client-based; institution-based; group; one-to-one; bespoke (specialisms: engineering; motor industry; chemical) *Method:* intensive; non-intensive
Ukrainian	*Type:* client-based; institution-based; group; one-to-one; bespoke
Urdu	*Type:* client-based; institution-based; group; one-to-one; bespoke
Other	Romanian can be offered, with notice

SERVICES

Translating

Bengali	into and out of English
Czech	into and out of English
French	into and out of English
German	into and out of English
Gujarati	into and out of English
Hindi	into and out of English
Italian	into and out of English
Japanese	into and out of English

Polish	into and out of English
Punjabi	into and out of English
Russian	into and out of English
Spanish	into and out of English
Urdu	into and out of English
Interpreting	
Bengali	consecutive
Czech	consecutive
French	consecutive
German	consecutive
Gujarati	consecutive
Hindi	consecutive
Italian	consecutive
Japanese	consecutive
Polish	consecutive
Punjabi	consecutive
Russian	consecutive
Spanish	consecutive
Urdu	consecutive

FACILITIES

Language labs:	10–25 places - 1 fixed
Equipment and materials:	computer-assisted language learning; audiocassettes; satellite television

NOTES
- has experience of undertaking language training needs analyses for employers
- provides voice-overs in foreign languages for corporate videos, help with recruiting foreign language speakers and help with business and protocol problems
- has produced business language training materials in several languages

340 School of Oriental and African Studies

Thornhaugh Street
London   Telephone   071-637 2388
WC1H 0XG   Fax   071-637 7355

Contact   Mr T. Osborn-Jones, Director, External Services Division

TRAINING

Arabic   *Type:* client-based; institution-based; group; one-to-one; bespoke
                Method: intensive; non-intensive
Chinese   *Type:* client-based; institution-based; group; one-to-one; bespoke
                Method: intensive; non-intensive
Indonesian   *Type:* institution-based; group; one-to-one; bespoke
                Method: intensive; non-intensive
Japanese   *Type:* client-based; institution-based; group; one-to-one; bespoke
                (specialisms: legal; art; economics)
                Method: intensive; non-intensive
Korean   *Type:* institution-based; group; one-to-one; bespoke
                Method: intensive; non-intensive
Swahili   *Type:* institution-based; group; one-to-one; bespoke
                Method: intensive; non-intensive
Thai   *Type:* institution-based; group; one-to-one; bespoke
                Method: intensive; non-intensive
Turkish   *Type:* institution-based; group; one-to-one; bespoke
                Method: intensive; non-intensive
Other   Additional Asian and African languages can be offered, with notice

SERVICES
Translating
Arabic   into and out of English
Chinese   into and out of English
Indonesian   into and out of English
Japanese   into and out of English
Korean   into and out of English
Swahili   into and out of English
Thai   into and out of English
Interpreting
Arabic   simultaneous; consecutive
Chinese   simultaneous; consecutive
Japanese   simultaneous; consecutive

FACILITIES
Language labs: 10–25 places - 2 fixed
Equipment and
  materials: computer-assisted language learning; audio and videocassettes

NOTES
- has experience of undertaking language training needs analyses for employers
- offers individual tuition and related services in most of the languages of Asia and Africa

341   Scottish College of Textiles

Netherdale
Galashiels
TD1 3HF

Telephone   (0896) 3351
Fax   (0896) 58965

Contact   Mrs J. L. Rees, Head of Management Studies

TRAINING

French	*Type:* institution-based
	Method: non-intensive
German	*Type:* institution-based
	Method: non-intensive
Italian	*Type:* institution-based
	Method: non-intensive
Spanish	*Type:* institution-based

SERVICES

Translating

French	into and out of English
German	into and out of English
Italian	into and out of English

FACILITIES

Language labs:	10–25 places - 1 fixed
Equipment and materials:	computer-assisted language learning; audiocassettes

NOTES

- is the Faculty of Textiles of Heriot-Watt University, Edinburgh, which has a Department of Languages with interpreting and translating facilities

342   University of Sheffield

Japan Business Services
317 Glossop Road
Sheffield   Telephone   (0742) 824004
S10 2HP   Fax   (0742) 728028

Contact   Mrs Y. McLeod, Assistant Manager, Japan Business Services

TRAINING
Japanese   *Type:* client-based; institution-based; group; one-to-one; bespoke
                 Method: intensive
Korean   *Type:* client-based; institution-based; group; one-to-one; bespoke
                 Method: intensive
Other   Chinese can be offered, with notice

SERVICES
Translating
Chinese   into and out of English
French   into and out of English
German   into and out of English
Italian   into and out of English
Japanese   into and out of English
Korean   into and out of English
Malay   into and out of English
Spanish   into and out of English
Interpreting
Chinese   simultaneous; consecutive
Japanese   simultaneous; consecutive
Korean   simultaneous; consecutive

FACILITIES
Language labs: under 10 places - 1 portable; 10–25 places - 1 fixed
Interpreting
  facilities: under 10 places - 1 portable
Equipment and
  materials: audiocassettes

NOTES
• has experience of undertaking language training needs analyses for employers
• Japan Business Services aims to provide clients with advice and practical help when
  dealing with the Japanese and Asia-Pacific market, both in Europe and overseas

343   Sheffield Hallam University

Pond Street
Sheffield
S1 1WB

Telephone	(0742) 533362
Fax	(0742) 533628

Contact   Ms M. Hanna, Head of Business Language Centre

TRAINING

Arabic   *Type:* client-based; institution-based; group; one-to-one; bespoke
                Method: intensive; non-intensive; open or flexible

Chinese   *Type:* client-based; institution-based; group; one-to-one; bespoke
                Method: intensive; non-intensive; open or flexible

Czech   *Type:* client-based; institution-based; group; one-to-one; bespoke
                Method: intensive; non-intensive; open or flexible

Danish   *Type:* client-based; institution-based; group; one-to-one; bespoke
                Method: intensive; non-intensive; open or flexible

Dutch   *Type:* client-based; institution-based; group; one-to-one; bespoke
                Method: intensive; non-intensive; open or flexible

Farsi   *Type:* client-based; institution-based; group; one-to-one; bespoke
                Method: intensive; non-intensive; open or flexible

French   *Type:* client-based; institution-based; group; one-to-one; bespoke
                (specialism: business)
                Method: intensive; non-intensive; open or flexible

German   *Type:* client-based; institution-based; group; one-to-one; bespoke
                (specialism: technical)
                Method: intensive; non-intensive; open or flexible

Greek   *Type:* client-based; institution-based; group; one-to-one; bespoke
                Method: intensive; non-intensive; open or flexible

Hungarian   *Type:* client-based; bespoke
                Method: intensive; non-intensive; open or flexible

Italian   *Type:* client-based; institution-based; group (specialism: scientific)
                Method: intensive; non-intensive; open or flexible

Japanese   *Type:* client-based; institution-based; group; one-to-one
                Method: intensive; non-intensive; open or flexible

Norwegian   *Type:* client-based; institution-based; group; one-to-one; bespoke
                Method: intensive; non-intensive; open or flexible

Polish   *Type:* client-based; institution-based; group; one-to-one; bespoke
                Method: intensive; non-intensive; open or flexible

Portuguese   *Type:* institution-based; group
                Method: intensive; non-intensive; open or flexible

Romanian   *Type:* client-based; institution-based; group; one-to-one; bespoke
                Method: intensive; non-intensive; open or flexible

Russian   *Type:* institution-based; one-to-one
                Method: intensive; non-intensive; open or flexible

Spanish	*Type:* client-based; institution-based; group; one-to-one; bespoke (specialism: computers)
	Method: intensive; non-intensive; open or flexible
Swedish	*Type:* institution-based; group; bespoke
	Method: intensive; non-intensive; open or flexible
Turkish	*Type:* client-based; one-to-one
	Method: intensive; non-intensive; open or flexible

SERVICES

Translating

Arabic	into and out of English
Chinese	into and out of English
Czech	into and out of English
Danish	into and out of English
Dutch	into and out of English
Farsi	into and out of English
French	into and out of English
German	into and out of English
Greek	into and out of English
Hungarian	into and out of English
Italian	into and out of English
Japanese	into and out of English
Norwegian	into and out of English
Polish	into and out of English
Portuguese	into and out of English
Romanian	into and out of English
Russian	into and out of English
Spanish	into and out of English
Swedish	into and out of English
Turkish	into and out of English

Interpreting

Arabic	consecutive
Chinese	consecutive
Czech	consecutive
Danish	consecutive
Dutch	consecutive
Farsi	consecutive
French	consecutive
German	consecutive
Greek	consecutive
Hungarian	consecutive
Italian	consecutive
Japanese	consecutive
Norwegian	consecutive
Polish	consecutive
Portuguese	consecutive

Romanian	consecutive
Russian	consecutive
Spanish	consecutive
Swedish	consecutive
Turkish	consecutive

FACILITIES

Language labs: 10–25 places - 4 fixed
Equipment and
  materials: computer-assisted language learning; satellite television; interactive video; audio and videocassettes

NOTES

• has experience of undertaking language training needs analyses for employers

344   Shipley College

Business and Professional Services (SalTEC)
Exhibition Road

Shipley	Telephone	(0274) 757200
BD18 3JW	Fax	(0274) 757201

Contact   Ms J. Lynch, Marketing Co-ordinator

TRAINING

Arabic	*Type:* client-based; institution-based; group; one-to-one; bespoke
Bengali	*Type:* group
French	*Type:* client-based; institution-based; group; one-to-one; bespoke *Method:* intensive; non-intensive
German	*Type:* client-based; institution-based; group; one-to-one; bespoke *Method:* non-intensive
Italian	*Type:* client-based; institution-based; group; one-to-one; bespoke
Japanese	*Type:* client-based; institution-based; group; one-to-one; bespoke *Method:* intensive; non-intensive
Russian	*Type:* client-based; institution-based; group; one-to-one; bespoke
Spanish	*Type:* client-based; institution-based; group; one-to-one; bespoke
Urdu	*Type:* group

NOTES
• co-ordinates a network of three colleges currently developing language materials for use in a range of contexts

345 Shrewsbury College of Arts and Technology

London Road
Shrewsbury   Telephone   (0743) 232686
SY2 6PR   Fax   (0743) 271563

Contact   Mr B. T. Goodwin, Head of Market Research and Development

TRAINING

Arabic   *Type:* client-based; institution-based; group; one-to-one; bespoke
             (specialism: cultural)
             Method: intensive; non-intensive

Chinese   *Type:* client-based; institution-based; group; one-to-one; bespoke
             (specialism: cultural)
             Method: intensive; non-intensive

Dutch   *Type:* client-based; institution-based; group; one-to-one; bespoke
             (specialisms: business; legal)
             Method: intensive; non-intensive; open or flexible

French   *Type:* client-based; institution-based; group; one-to-one; bespoke
             (specialisms: business; legal)
             Method: intensive; non-intensive; open or flexible

German   *Type:* client-based; institution-based; group; one-to-one; bespoke
             (specialisms: business; legal)
             Method: intensive; non-intensive; open or flexible

Greek   *Type:* client-based; institution-based; group; one-to-one; bespoke
             (specialism: cultural)
             Method: intensive; non-intensive

Italian   *Type:* client-based; institution-based; group; one-to-one; bespoke
             (specialisms: business; legal)
             Method: intensive; non-intensive; open or flexible

Japanese   *Type:* client-based; institution-based; group; one-to-one; bespoke
             (specialism: cultural)
             Method: intensive; non-intensive

Polish   *Type:* client-based; institution-based; group; one-to-one
Portuguese   *Type:* client-based; institution-based; group; one-to-one; bespoke
             (specialisms: business; legal)
             Method: intensive; non-intensive

Russian   *Type:* client-based; institution-based; group; one-to-one; bespoke
             (specialisms: business; legal)
             Method: intensive; non-intensive

Spanish   *Type:* client-based; institution-based; group; one-to-one; bespoke
             (specialisms: business; legal)
             Method: intensive; non-intensive; open or flexible

Swedish   *Type:* client-based; institution-based; group; one-to-one; bespoke
             (specialism: business)
             Method: intensive; non-intensive

| Welsh | *Type:* client-based; institution-based; group; one-to-one; bespoke (specialisms: business; legal) |
| | *Method:* intensive; non-intensive; open or flexible |

SERVICES

Translating

Arabic	into and out of English
Chinese	into and out of English
Dutch	into and out of English
French	into and out of English
German	into and out of English
Greek	into and out of English
Italian	into and out of English
Japanese	into and out of English
Polish	into and out of English
Portuguese	into and out of English
Russian	into and out of English
Spanish	into and out of English
Welsh	into and out of English

Interpreting

Arabic	simultaneous; consecutive
Chinese	simultaneous; consecutive
Dutch	simultaneous; consecutive
French	simultaneous; consecutive
German	simultaneous; consecutive
Greek	simultaneous; consecutive
Italian	simultaneous; consecutive
Japanese	simultaneous; consecutive
Polish	simultaneous; consecutive
Portuguese	simultaneous; consecutive
Russian	simultaneous; consecutive
Spanish	simultaneous; consecutive
Welsh	simultaneous; consecutive

FACILITIES

| Language labs: | 10–25 places - 1 fixed, 1 portable |
| Equipment and materials: | computer-assisted language learning; audio and videocassettes |

NOTES

- has experience of undertaking language training needs analyses for employers
- Mr I. Hacking, Business Language Unit Manager, is a further languages for business contact at the college

346   Solihull College of Technology

Blossomfield Road
Solihull   Telephone   021-711 2111
B91 1SB   Fax   021-711 2316

Contact   Ms H. McCartney, Curriculum Manager

TRAINING
French   *Type:* client-based; institution-based; group; one-to-one
                 Method: intensive; non-intensive; open or flexible
German   *Type:* client-based; institution-based; group; one-to-one
                 Method: intensive; non-intensive; open or flexible
Italian   *Type:* client-based; institution-based; group; one-to-one
                 Method: intensive; non-intensive
Japanese   *Type:* client-based; institution-based; group; one-to-one
                 Method: intensive; non-intensive
Spanish   *Type:* client-based; institution-based; group; one-to-one
                 Method: intensive; non-intensive; open or flexible
Other   Greek, Polish and Dutch can be offered, with notice

FACILITIES
Language labs: 10–25 places - 1 fixed, 1 portable
Equipment and
  materials: audio and videocassettes; Minitel; satellite television

NOTES
• has experience of undertaking language training needs analyses for employers

347   Somerset College of Arts and Technology

Wellington Road
Taunton   Telephone   (0823) 274307
TA1 5AX   Fax   (0823) 274307

Contact   Mr D. Tilley, Director of Training Services

TRAINING
French   *Type:* client-based; institution-based; group; one-to-one; bespoke
                 Method: intensive; non-intensive; open or flexible
German   *Type:* client-based; institution-based; group; one-to-one; bespoke
                 Method: intensive; non-intensive; open or flexible
Italian   *Type:* client-based; institution-based; group; one-to-one; bespoke
                 Method: intensive; non-intensive; open or flexible
Spanish   *Type:* client-based; institution-based; group; one-to-one; bespoke
                 Method: intensive; non-intensive; open or flexible
Other   Additional languages can be offered, with notice

SERVICES
Translating
French   into and out of English
German   into and out of English
Italian   into and out of English
Spanish   into and out of English

FACILITIES
Language labs: under 10 places - 1 fixed; 10–25 places - 1 fixed

NOTES
• has experience of undertaking language training needs analyses for employers
• is part of Somerset Language Training, a consortium of Somerset colleges

348   Soundwell College

St Stephen's Road
Soundwell
Bristol   Telephone   (0272) 675101
BS16 4RL   Fax   (0272) 352753

Contact   Ms T. Thorpe, Head of Modern Languages

TRAINING
French   *Type:* client-based; institution-based; group; one-to-one; bespoke
                (specialism: business)
                Method: intensive; non-intensive; open or flexible
German   *Type:* client-based; institution-based; group; one-to-one; bespoke
                Method: intensive; non-intensive; open or flexible
Italian   *Type:* client-based; institution-based; group; one-to-one; bespoke
                Method: intensive; non-intensive; open or flexible
Spanish   *Type:* client-based; institution-based; group; one-to-one; bespoke
                Method: intensive; non-intensive; open or flexible
Other   Additional languages can be offered, with notice

FACILITIES
Language labs: under 10 places - 1 portable
Equipment and
  materials: audiocassettes; computer-assisted language learning facilities
                planned

NOTES
• has experience of undertaking language training needs analyses for employers

349   South Bank University

Language Centre
103 Borough Road
London   Telephone   071-334 3434
SE1 0AA   Fax   071-334 3441

Contact   Dr P. Bangs, Head of Language Centre

TRAINING

Chinese	*Type:* institution-based; group; one-to-one (specialisms: Chinese medicine; food hygiene)
French	*Type:* client-based; institution-based; group; one-to-one; bespoke (specialisms: train drivers; tourism)
	Method: intensive; non-intensive; open or flexible
German	*Type:* client-based; institution-based; group; one-to-one; bespoke (specialisms: engineering; tourism)
	Method: intensive; non-intensive; open or flexible
Italian	*Type:* client-based; institution-based; group; one-to-one; bespoke
	Method: intensive; non-intensive; open or flexible
Japanese	*Type:* client-based; institution-based; group; one-to-one; bespoke (specialism: tourism)
	Method: intensive; non-intensive; open or flexible
Portuguese	*Type:* institution-based; one-to-one
Russian	*Type:* client-based; institution-based; group; one-to-one; bespoke (specialisms: financial; business)
	Method: intensive; non-intensive; open or flexible
Spanish	*Type:* client-based; institution-based; group; one-to-one; bespoke (specialism: tourism)
	Method: intensive; non-intensive; open or flexible
Other	More than 50 languages can be offered, with notice

FACILITIES

Language labs:	10–25 places - 6 fixed; over 25 places - 1 fixed
Equipment and materials:	two open access laboratories, with more than 40 computers; seven satellite dishes; six interactive video stations; audio and videocassettes; voice input-output available on many computers

NOTES
• has experience of undertaking language training needs analyses for employers
• a speciality of the institution is materials creation, especially video and software

350   South Bristol College

Marksbury Road
Bedminster
Bristol   Telephone   (0272) 639033
BS3 5JL   Fax   (0272) 636682

Contact   Mr P. Johnson, Head of Languages

TRAINING

French   *Type:* client-based; institution-based; group
                Method: non-intensive; open or flexible
German   *Type:* client-based; institution-based; group
                Method: non-intensive; open or flexible
Italian   *Type:* client-based
                Method: non-intensive
Russian   *Type:* client-based; institution-based; group
                Method: non-intensive
Spanish   *Type:* client-based; institution-based; group
                Method: non-intensive; open or flexible
Urdu   *Type:* institution-based; group
Other   Additional major European and Oriental languages can be offered,
                with notice

FACILITIES

Equipment and
  materials: audiocassettes

351　South Cheshire College Language-Export Centre

Dane Bank Avenue
Crewe   Telephone   (0270) 665596
CW2 8AB   Fax   (0270) 67923

Contact   Mr A. Loffill, Language-Export Centre Manager

TRAINING

Chinese   *Type:* client-based; institution-based; group; one-to-one; bespoke
                 Method: non-intensive; open or flexible
Dutch   *Type:* client-based; institution-based; group; one-to-one; bespoke
                 Method: non-intensive; open or flexible
French   *Type:* client-based; institution-based; group; one-to-one; bespoke
                 Method: intensive; non-intensive; open or flexible
German   *Type:* client-based; institution-based; group; one-to-one; bespoke
                 Method: intensive; non-intensive; open or flexible
Hungarian   *Type:* institution-based
                 Method: non-intensive; open or flexible
Italian   *Type:* client-based; institution-based; group; one-to-one; bespoke
                 Method: intensive; non-intensive; open or flexible
Japanese   *Type:* client-based; institution-based; group; one-to-one; bespoke
                 Method: intensive; non-intensive; open or flexible
Polish   *Type:* institution-based
                 Method: non-intensive; open or flexible
Portuguese   *Type:* client-based; institution-based; group; one-to-one; bespoke
                 Method: non-intensive; open or flexible
Russian   *Type:* client-based; institution-based; group; one-to-one; bespoke
                 Method: intensive; non-intensive; open or flexible
Spanish   *Type:* client-based; institution-based; group; one-to-one; bespoke
                 Method: intensive; non-intensive; open or flexible
Other   Additional languages can be offered, with notice

SERVICES

Translating
Arabic   into and out of English
Chinese   into and out of English
French   into and out of English
German   into and out of English
Italian   into and out of English
Japanese   into and out of English
Portuguese   into and out of English
Russian   into and out of English
Spanish   into and out of English

Interpreting

Arabic	simultaneous; consecutive
Chinese	simultaneous; consecutive
French	simultaneous; consecutive
German	simultaneous; consecutive
Italian	simultaneous; consecutive
Japanese	simultaneous; consecutive
Portuguese	simultaneous; consecutive
Russian	simultaneous; consecutive
Spanish	simultaneous; consecutive

FACILITIES

Language labs:	10–25 places - 1 fixed
Interpreting facilities:	over 100 places - 1 fixed
Equipment and materials:	audiocassettes; satellite television

NOTES

• has experience of undertaking language training needs analyses for employers

352   South Devon College

Newton Road
Torquay   Telephone   (0803) 217474
TQ2 5BY   Fax   (0803) 211135

Contact   Mrs C. Smale, European Liaison Officer

TRAINING
Arabic   *Type:* client-based; one-to-one
              Method: non-intensive
French   *Type:* client-based; institution-based; group; bespoke
              Method: intensive; non-intensive
German   *Type:* client-based; group
              Method: intensive; non-intensive
Japanese   *Type:* client-based; one-to-one
              Method: non-intensive
Spanish   *Type:* client-based; group; one-to-one; bespoke
              Method: intensive

SERVICES
Translating
French   into English
German   into English
Italian   into English
Spanish   into English
Interpreting
French   consecutive
German   consecutive
Italian   consecutive
Spanish   consecutive

FACILITIES
Language labs: 10–25 places - 2 fixed
Equipment and
  materials: computer-assisted language learning

NOTES
- has experience of undertaking language training needs analyses for employers
- organises one to one 'crash' training for technical and sales managers, immersion programmes, a two day course for teams of sales managers, and special interest workshops, e.g. for the regional law association

353   South Downs College

College Road
Havant   Telephone   (0705) 257011
PO7 8AA   Fax   (0705) 263930

Contact   Mr P. Syson, Head of Department, Marketing and Short Course Unit

TRAINING
Arabic   *Type:* client-based; institution-based; group; one-to-one; bespoke
                Method: intensive; non-intensive; open or flexible
Dutch   *Type:* client-based; institution-based; group; one-to-one; bespoke
                Method: intensive; non-intensive; open or flexible
French   *Type:* client-based; institution-based; group; one-to-one; bespoke
                Method: intensive; non-intensive; open or flexible
German   *Type:* client-based; institution-based; group; one-to-one; bespoke
                Method: intensive; non-intensive; open or flexible
Greek   *Type:* client-based; institution-based; group; one-to-one; bespoke
                Method: intensive; non-intensive; open or flexible
Italian   *Type:* client-based; institution-based; group; one-to-one; bespoke
                Method: intensive; non-intensive; open or flexible
Japanese   *Type:* client-based; institution-based; group; one-to-one; bespoke
                Method: intensive; non-intensive; open or flexible
Norwegian   *Type:* client-based; institution-based; group; one-to-one; bespoke
                Method: intensive; non-intensive; open or flexible
Portuguese   *Type:* client-based; institution-based; group; one-to-one; bespoke
                Method: intensive; non-intensive; open or flexible
Russian   *Type:* client-based; institution-based; group; one-to-one; bespoke
                Method: intensive; non-intensive; open or flexible
Spanish   *Type:* client-based; institution-based; group; one-to-one; bespoke
                Method: intensive; non-intensive; open or flexible
Swedish   *Type:* client-based; institution-based; group; one-to-one; bespoke
                Method: intensive; non-intensive; open or flexible
Turkish   *Type:* client-based; institution-based; group; one-to-one; bespoke
                Method: intensive; non-intensive; open or flexible
Other   Chinese can be offered, with notice

SERVICES
Translating
French   into and out of English
German   into and out of English
Italian   into and out of English
Japanese   into and out of English
Russian   into and out of English
Spanish   into and out of English

FACILITIES

Language labs: 10–25 places - 2 fixed

Equipment and
materials: audio and videocassettes

NOTES

• has experience of undertaking language training needs analyses for employers

354   South East Derbyshire College

Field Road
Ilkeston   Telephone   (0602) 324212
DE7 5RS   Fax   (0602) 306553

Contact   Mr J. Reilly, Marketing Officer

TRAINING
French   *Type:* client-based; institution-based; group; one-to-one; bespoke
                  Method: intensive; non-intensive; open or flexible
German   *Type:* client-based; institution-based; group; one-to-one; bespoke
                  Method: intensive; non-intensive; open or flexible
Spanish   *Type:* client-based; institution-based; group; one-to-one; bespoke
                  Method: intensive; non-intensive; open or flexible
Specialism   business
Other   Russian and Italian can be offered, with notice

SERVICES
Translating
French   into and out of English
German   into and out of English
Spanish   into and out of English
Specialism   business
Interpreting
French   consecutive
German   consecutive
Specialism   business

FACILITIES
Equipment and
  materials: audio and videocassettes; satellite television

NOTES
• has experience of undertaking language training needs analyses for employers
• has a French, German and Spanish database offering a weekly news service written
  by college staff

355　South East Essex College of Arts and Technology

Carnarvon Road
Southend-on-Sea　　　Telephone　　(0702) 220400
SS2 6LS　　　　　　 Fax　　　　　　(0702) 432320

Contact　　　　　Mr R. Hopkins, Head of Communications Studies

TRAINING

French　　　*Type:* client-based; institution-based; group; one-to-one; bespoke
　　　　　　(specialisms: scientific; technical)
　　　　　　Method: intensive; non-intensive; open or flexible
German　　　*Type:* client-based; institution-based; group; one-to-one; bespoke
　　　　　　(specialisms: scientific; technical)
　　　　　　Method: intensive; non-intensive; open or flexible
Italian　　　*Type:* client-based; institution-based; group; one-to-one; bespoke
　　　　　　(specialisms: scientific; technical)
　　　　　　Method: intensive; non-intensive; open or flexible
Japanese　　*Type:* client-based; institution-based; group; one-to-one; bespoke
　　　　　　Method: non-intensive; open or flexible
Spanish　　 *Type:* client-based; institution-based; group; one-to-one; bespoke
　　　　　　Method: intensive; non-intensive; open or flexible
Other　　　Russian, Turkish and Arabic can be offered, with notice

SERVICES

Translating
Arabic　　　into English
Finnish　　　into and out of English
French　　　into and out of English (specialisms: scientific; technical)
German　　　into and out of English (specialisms: scientific; technical; engineer-
　　　　　　ing)
Italian　　　into and out of English (specialisms: scientific; technical)
Japanese　　into and out of English
Romanian　　into English
Russian　　　into and out of English
Spanish　　　into and out of English
Swedish　　　into and out of English
Turkish　　　into English
Interpreting
French　　　consecutive (specialisms: scientific; technical)
German　　　consecutive (specialisms: scientific; technical; engineering)
Italian　　　consecutive (specialisms: scientific; technical)
Spanish　　　consecutive

FACILITIES

Language labs: under 10 places - 1 portable; 10–25 places - 1 fixed
Equipment and
  materials: computer-assisted language learning; audio and videocassettes

NOTES

• has experience of undertaking language training needs analyses for employers

356   South Kent College

European Business and Language Centre
Maison Dieu Road

Dover	Telephone	(0304) 214830
CT16 1DH	Fax	(0304) 215621

Contact   Mr C. Beckett, European Business and Language Centre Manager

TRAINING

Dutch	*Type:* client-based; institution-based; group; one-to-one; bespoke
French	*Type:* client-based; institution-based; group; one-to-one; bespoke (specialism: receptionists)
	Method: intensive; non-intensive; open or flexible
German	*Type:* client-based; institution-based; group
	Method: intensive; non-intensive
Italian	*Type:* client-based; institution-based; group; one-to-one; bespoke
Russian	*Type:* client-based; institution-based; group; one-to-one; bespoke
Spanish	*Type:* client-based; group
	Method: intensive; non-intensive
Swedish	*Type:* client-based; institution-based; group; one-to-one; bespoke
Other	Portuguese, Serbo-Croat, Greek and Danish can be offered, with notice

SERVICES

Translating

French	into and out of English
German	into and out of English
Italian	into English
Spanish	into English

Interpreting

French	consecutive
German	consecutive

FACILITIES

Language labs:	10–25 places - 1 fixed
Equipment and materials:	computer-assisted language learning

NOTES
• has experience of undertaking language training needs analyses for employers

357   South Thames College

50-52 Putney Hill
London   Telephone   081-788 2150
SW15 6QX   Fax   081-785 2070

Contact   Ms M. Semple, Language Training Consultant

NOTES
• see entry for London Language-Export Centre (LEXCEL)

358 South Trafford College of Further Education

Manchester Road
Altrincham
WA14 5PQ

Telephone   061-973 7064
Fax   061-969 6099

Contact   Mrs C. Mainwaring, Lecturer in Modern Languages

TRAINING

French   *Type:* client-based; institution-based; group; one-to-one; bespoke
            Method: intensive; non-intensive; open or flexible

German   *Type:* client-based; institution-based; group; one-to-one; bespoke
            Method: intensive; non-intensive; open or flexible

Greek   *Type:* client-based; institution-based
            Method: non-intensive

Italian   *Type:* client-based; institution-based; group; one-to-one; bespoke
            Method: non-intensive

Japanese   *Type:* client-based; institution-based; group; one-to-one; bespoke
            Method: intensive; non-intensive; open or flexible

Portuguese *Type:* client-based; institution-based
            Method: non-intensive

Russian   *Type:* client-based; institution-based; group; one-to-one; bespoke
            Method: intensive; non-intensive; open or flexible

Spanish   *Type:* client-based; institution-based; group; one-to-one; bespoke
            Method: intensive; non-intensive; open or flexible

SERVICES

Translating
French   out of English
Japanese   into English
Russian   out of English
Spanish   out of English (specialisms: commercial; business)

Interpreting
French   consecutive
German   consecutive
Japanese   consecutive
Russian   consecutive
Spanish   consecutive

FACILITIES

Language labs: 10–25 places - 2 fixed
Equipment and
  materials: computer-assisted language learning; audio and videocassettes;
                    foreign news on Prestel

NOTES

• has experience of undertaking language training needs analyses for employers

359 South Tyneside College

St George's Avenue
South Shields
NE34 6ET

Telephone   091-456 0403
Fax   091-427 0267

Contact   Mrs P. A. Millward, Lecturer in Modern Languages

TRAINING

French	*Type:* client-based; institution-based; group; one-to-one; bespoke *Method:* intensive; non-intensive
German	*Type:* client-based; institution-based; group; one-to-one; bespoke *Method:* intensive; non-intensive
Italian	*Type:* client-based; institution-based; group; one-to-one *Method:* intensive; non-intensive
Russian	*Type:* client-based; institution-based; group; one-to-one; bespoke *Method:* intensive; non-intensive
Spanish	*Type:* client-based; institution-based; group; one-to-one; bespoke *Method:* intensive; non-intensive

SERVICES

Translating

French   into and out of English
German   into and out of English
Spanish   into and out of English

Interpreting

French   simultaneous; consecutive
German   simultaneous; consecutive
Spanish   simultaneous; consecutive

FACILITIES

Language labs: under 10 places - 1 portable; 10–25 places - 1 fixed
Equipment and
  materials: computer-assisted language learning; audio and videocassettes

360   South Wales Language-Export Centre

University College of Swansea
Singleton Park

| Swansea | Telephone | (0792) 295621 |
| SA2 8PP | Fax | (0792) 295718 |

Contact   Mrs S. Jones, Assistant Manager

TRAINING

French	*Type:* client-based; institution-based; group; one-to-one
	Method: intensive; non-intensive
German	*Type:* client-based; institution-based; group; one-to-one
	Method: intensive; non-intensive
Italian	*Type:* client-based; institution-based; group; one-to-one
	Method: intensive; non-intensive
Japanese	*Type:* client-based; institution-based; group; one-to-one
	Method: intensive; non-intensive
Russian	*Type:* client-based; institution-based; group; one-to-one
	Method: intensive; non-intensive
Spanish	*Type:* client-based; institution-based; group; one-to-one
	Method: intensive; non-intensive
Specialism	business
Other	Additional languages can be offered, with notice

SERVICES

Interpreting

French	simultaneous; consecutive
German	simultaneous; consecutive
Italian	simultaneous; consecutive
Japanese	consecutive
Russian	consecutive
Spanish	simultaneous; consecutive

FACILITIES

Language labs: under 10 places - 1 fixed; 10–25 places - 2 fixed

NOTES

• has experience of undertaking language training needs analyses for employers
• offers translating services in all languages and specialisms

361   University of Southampton

Languages International
University Road

Southampton	Telephone	(0703) 592250
SO9 5NH	Fax	(0703) 593288

Contact   Dr W. Brooks, Co-ordinator of Languages International

TRAINING

Catalan	*Type:* client-based; institution-based; group; one-to-one; bespoke
French	*Type:* client-based; institution-based; group; one-to-one; bespoke
	Method: intensive; non-intensive; open or flexible
German	*Type:* client-based; institution-based; group; one-to-one; bespoke
	Method: intensive; non-intensive; open or flexible
Hungarian	*Type:* client-based; institution-based; group; one-to-one; bespoke
Portuguese	*Type:* client-based; institution-based; group; one-to-one; bespoke
Russian	*Type:* client-based; institution-based; group; one-to-one; bespoke
Spanish	*Type:* client-based; institution-based; group; one-to-one; bespoke
	Method: intensive; non-intensive; open or flexible

SERVICES

Translating

Catalan	into and out of English
French	into and out of English
German	into and out of English
Hungarian	into and out of English
Italian	into and out of English
Japanese	into and out of English
Portuguese	into and out of English
Russian	into and out of English
Spanish	into and out of English

Interpreting

French	simultaneous; consecutive
German	simultaneous; consecutive
Italian	simultaneous; consecutive
Spanish	simultaneous; consecutive

FACILITIES

Language labs:	10–25 places - 1 fixed
Equipment and materials:	computer-assisted language learning; interactive video; audio and videocassettes

NOTES
- has experience of undertaking language training needs analyses for employers
- courses are aimed at executives and senior executives in large companies
- classes are never larger than eight and courses are tailored to particular needs

362   Southampton Institute of Higher Education

East Park Terrace
Southampton   Telephone   (0703) 229381
SO9 4WW   Fax   (0703) 222259

Contact   Mr C. Beaven, Head of Languages

TRAINING
French   *Type:* client-based; institution-based; group; one-to-one; bespoke
                     Method: intensive; non-intensive
German   *Type:* client-based; institution-based; group; one-to-one; bespoke
                     Method: intensive; non-intensive
Italian   *Type:* client-based; institution-based; group; one-to-one; bespoke
                     Method: intensive; non-intensive
Russian   *Type:* client-based; institution-based; group; one-to-one; bespoke
                     Method: intensive; non-intensive
Spanish   *Type:* client-based; institution-based; group; one-to-one; bespoke
                     Method: intensive; non-intensive

SERVICES
Translating
Bulgarian   out of English
Danish   into and out of English
French   into and out of English
German   into and out of English
Italian   into and out of English
Russian   into and out of English
Spanish   into and out of English
Interpreting
Bulgarian   consecutive
French   consecutive
German   consecutive
Italian   consecutive
Russian   consecutive
Spanish   consecutive

FACILITIES
Language labs: 10–25 places - 4 fixed

NOTES
• has experience of undertaking language training needs analyses for employers
• offers a programme of language training to members of the local chamber of commerce, as a member of the chamber's language training consortium

363 Southampton Technical College

St Mary Street
Southampton
SO9 4WX

Telephone	(0703) 635222
Fax	(0703) 636728

Contact   Mrs M. Avison, Lecturer in Charge of Modern Languages

TRAINING
French   *Type:* client-based; one-to-one; bespoke (specialism: customs)

German   *Type:* client-based; institution-based; one-to-one; bespoke (specialism: customs)

Italian   *Type:* client-based; one-to-one; bespoke

Spanish   *Type:* client-based; one-to-one; bespoke

FACILITIES
Language labs: 10–25 places - 1 fixed

NOTES
• has experience of undertaking language training needs analyses for employers

364   Southgate College

High Street
Southgate
London   Telephone   081-886 6521
N14 6BS   Fax   081-982 5420

Contact   Ms P. Alexander, Head of Social Sciences

TRAINING
French   *Type:* client-based; institution-based; group
                    Method: non-intensive
German   *Type:* client-based; institution-based; group
                    Method: non-intensive
Greek   *Type:* client-based; institution-based; group
                    Method: non-intensive
Italian   *Type:* client-based; institution-based; group
                    Method: non-intensive
Spanish   *Type:* client-based; institution-based; group
                    Method: non-intensive
Other   Additional languages can be offered, with notice

SERVICES
Translating
French   into and out of English
German   into and out of English
Greek   into and out of English
Italian   into and out of English
Spanish   into and out of English
Interpreting
French   consecutive
Greek   simultaneous; consecutive
Spanish   consecutive

FACILITIES
Language labs: 10–25 places - 1 fixed
Equipment and
  materials: satellite television

365   Southwark College

The Cut
London   Telephone   071-928 9561
SE1 8LE   Fax   071-261 1301

Contact   Ms T. Scott, Senior Lecturer in Languages

TRAINING
Chinese   *Type:* client-based; institution-based; group; one-to-one
French   *Type:* client-based; institution-based; group; one-to-one
                 Method: non-intensive
German   *Type:* client-based; institution-based; group; one-to-one
                 Method: non-intensive
Italian   *Type:* client-based; institution-based; group; one-to-one
                 Method: non-intensive
Spanish   *Type:* client-based; institution-based; group; one-to-one
                 Method: non-intensive
Other   Bengali can be offered, with notice

NOTES
• has experience of undertaking language training needs analyses for employers

School of Modern Languages
St Andrews   Telephone   (0334) 76161
KY16 9PH   Fax   (0334) 74674

Contact   Mr J. Devereux, Director, Foreign Language Teaching Services

TRAINING

Arabic	*Type:* client-based; institution-based; group; one-to-one; bespoke *Method:* non-intensive; open or flexible
Danish	*Type:* client-based; institution-based; group; one-to-one; bespoke (specialism: commercial) *Method:* non-intensive; open or flexible
Dutch	*Type:* client-based; institution-based; group; one-to-one; bespoke *Method:* non-intensive; open or flexible
French	*Type:* client-based; institution-based; group; one-to-one; bespoke (specialisms: computers; paper industry; tourism; commercial; industrial) *Method:* intensive; non-intensive; open or flexible
German	*Type:* client-based; institution-based; group; one-to-one; bespoke (specialisms: architecture; medical; financial; banking; commercial) *Method:* intensive; non-intensive; open or flexible
Greek	*Type:* client-based; institution-based; group; one-to-one; bespoke *Method:* non-intensive; open or flexible
Italian	*Type:* client-based; institution-based; group; one-to-one; bespoke (specialisms: commercial; industrial; scientific) *Method:* intensive; non-intensive; open or flexible
Japanese	*Type:* client-based; institution-based; group; one-to-one; bespoke *Method:* intensive; non-intensive; open or flexible
Norwegian	*Type:* client-based; institution-based; group; one-to-one; bespoke *Method:* intensive; non-intensive; open or flexible
Portuguese	*Type:* client-based; institution-based; group; one-to-one; bespoke (specialism: scientific) *Method:* non-intensive; open or flexible
Russian	*Type:* client-based; institution-based; group; one-to-one; bespoke *Method:* intensive; non-intensive; open or flexible
Spanish	*Type:* client-based; institution-based; group; one-to-one; bespoke (specialisms: commercial; industrial) *Method:* intensive; non-intensive; open or flexible
Turkish	*Type:* client-based; institution-based; group; one-to-one; bespoke *Method:* intensive; non-intensive; open or flexible
Other	Chinese and Polish can be offered, with notice

SERVICES
Translating

Arabic	into and out of English
Danish	into and out of English (specialisms: business; technical)
French	into and out of English (specialisms: business; legal; agriculture)
German	into and out of English (specialisms: medical; pharmaceutical; scientific; technical; transport; business)
Greek	into and out of English (specialisms: business; technical)
Hungarian	into and out of English
Italian	into and out of English (specialism: biochemistry)
Japanese	into and out of English (specialisms: engineering; electronics; technology; fuel; steel industry)
Portuguese	into and out of English (specialism: scientific)
Russian	into and out of English
Spanish	into and out of English (specialisms: paper industry; technical)

FACILITIES

Language labs:	10–25 places - 1 fixed
Equipment and materials:	audio and videocassettes; satellite television

NOTES
- has experience of undertaking language training needs analyses for employers
- is involved in 'Language Line', with Dundee University, offering three day, mid week immersion, two weekend intensive and evening courses, workshops, and customised, small group or one to one training in French, German and Spanish

367 College of St Mark and St John

Derriford Road
Plymouth   Telephone   (0752) 777188
PL6 8BH   Fax   (0752) 761120

Contact   Ms R. Lynn, Senior Lecturer

TRAINING

French	*Type:* client-based; institution-based; group; one-to-one; bespoke *Method:* intensive; non-intensive
German	*Type:* client-based; institution-based; group; one-to-one; bespoke *Method:* intensive; non-intensive
Italian	*Type:* client-based; institution-based; group; one-to-one; bespoke *Method:* intensive; non-intensive
Spanish	*Type:* client-based; institution-based; group; one-to-one; bespoke *Method:* intensive; non-intensive
Other	Japanese, Dutch and Arabic can be offered, with notice

FACILITIES

Language labs: 10–25 places - 1 fixed

368   Stafford College

Earl Street
Stafford
ST16 2QR

Telephone   (0785) 223800
Fax   (0785) 59953

Contact   Mr R. Lemon, Senior Lecturer in Languages

TRAINING

French
: *Type:* client-based; institution-based; group; one-to-one (specialism: tourism)
Method: intensive; non-intensive

German
: *Type:* client-based; institution-based; group; one-to-one
Method: intensive; non-intensive

Italian
: *Type:* client-based; institution-based; group; one-to-one
Method: non-intensive

Russian
: *Type:* client-based; institution-based; group; one-to-one
Method: non-intensive

Spanish
: *Type:* client-based; institution-based; group; one-to-one
Method: intensive; non-intensive

FACILITIES

Language labs: 10–25 places - 2 fixed
Equipment and
  materials: audio and videocassettes; computer-assisted language learning

369   Staffordshire Language-Export Centre

Staffordshire University
Leek Road
Stoke-on-Trent   Telephone   (0782) 412515
ST4 2DF   Fax   (0782) 747112

Contact   Mrs M. Atkinson, Marketing Manager for the Schools of Law, Business and Social Sciences

TRAINING

French	*Type:* client-based; institution-based; group; one-to-one; bespoke (specialisms: power generation; engineering) *Method:* intensive; non-intensive
German	*Type:* client-based; institution-based; group; bespoke (specialisms: power generation; engineering) *Method:* intensive; non-intensive
Italian	*Type:* institution-based; group *Method:* intensive; non-intensive
Spanish	*Type:* client-based; institution-based; group; one-to-one; bespoke *Method:* intensive; non-intensive
Other	Additional languages can be offered, with notice

SERVICES

Translating

French	into and out of English
German	into and out of English
Italian	into and out of English
Japanese	into and out of English
Russian	into and out of English
Spanish	into and out of English

Interpreting

French	consecutive
German	consecutive
Italian	consecutive
Japanese	consecutive
Russian	consecutive
Spanish	consecutive

FACILITIES

Language labs: 10–25 places - 1 fixed
Equipment and
  materials: computer-assisted language learning

NOTES

• has experience of undertaking language training needs analyses for employers
• can offer translating and interpreting services in most languages and specialisms

370   Staffordshire University

College Road
Stoke-on-Trent   Telephone   (0782) 412515
ST4 2DE   Fax   (0782) 747112

Contact   Mrs M. Atkinson, Marketing Manager for the Schools of Law,
                        Business and Social Sciences

NOTES
• see entry for Staffordshire Language-Export Centre

371   Stevenson College of Further Education

Bankhead Avenue
Sighthill
Edinburgh   Telephone   031-453 6161
EH11 4DE   Fax   031-458 5067

Contact   Mrs R. Leishman, Business Languages Co-ordinator

TRAINING
French   *Type:* client-based; institution-based; group; one-to-one; bespoke
                Method: non-intensive
German   *Type:* client-based; institution-based; group; one-to-one; bespoke
Italian   *Type:* client-based; institution-based; group; one-to-one; bespoke
                Method: non-intensive; open or flexible
Japanese   *Type:* client-based; bespoke (specialism: tourism)
                Method: non-intensive; open or flexible
Spanish   *Type:* client-based; institution-based; group; one-to-one; bespoke
                (specialism: tourism)
                Method: non-intensive; open or flexible
Other   Additional languages can be offered, with notice

FACILITIES
Language labs: 10–25 places - 2 fixed
Equipment and
  materials: audio and videocassettes; satellite television

NOTES
• has experience of undertaking language training needs analyses for employers

372   University of Stirling

Stirling Telephone (0786) 73171
FK9 4LA Fax (0786) 63000

Contact Ms C. Stewart, Educational Development Officer

TRAINING
French *Type:* client-based; institution-based; group; bespoke
  Method: non-intensive
German *Type:* client-based; institution-based; group; bespoke
  Method: non-intensive
Italian *Type:* client-based; group; one-to-one; bespoke
  Method: non-intensive
Japanese *Type:* client-based; institution-based; group; bespoke
  Method: non-intensive
Spanish *Type:* institution-based; group
  Method: non-intensive

SERVICES
Translating
French into and out of English
German into and out of English
Italian into and out of English
Japanese into and out of English
Spanish into and out of English
Interpreting
French consecutive
German consecutive
Italian consecutive
Japanese consecutive

FACILITIES
Equipment and
  materials: audio and videocassettes; computer-assisted language learning

NOTES
• has experience of undertaking language training needs analyses for employers

373   Stockport College of Further and Higher Education

Wellington Road South
Stockport   Telephone   061-480 3897
SK1 3UQ   Fax   061-480 6636

Contact   Mrs P. Coull, Business Language Co-ordinator

TRAINING

Arabic	*Type:* client-based; institution-based; group; one-to-one; bespoke
Chinese	*Type:* client-based; institution-based; group; one-to-one; bespoke
Danish	*Type:* client-based; institution-based; group; one-to-one; bespoke
Dutch	*Type:* client-based; institution-based; group; one-to-one; bespoke (specialism: building)
	Method: intensive; non-intensive; open or flexible
French	*Type:* client-based; institution-based; group; one-to-one; bespoke
	Method: intensive; non-intensive; open or flexible
German	*Type:* client-based; institution-based; group; one-to-one; bespoke
	Method: intensive; non-intensive; open or flexible
Greek	*Type:* institution-based; one-to-one; bespoke
	Method: intensive; non-intensive; open or flexible
Italian	*Type:* institution-based; group; one-to-one; bespoke
	Method: intensive; non-intensive; open or flexible
Japanese	*Type:* institution-based; one-to-one; bespoke
	Method: intensive; non-intensive; open or flexible
Portuguese	*Type:* institution-based; one-to-one; bespoke
	Method: intensive; non-intensive; open or flexible
Russian	*Type:* institution-based; one-to-one; bespoke
	Method: intensive; non-intensive; open or flexible
Spanish	*Type:* client-based; institution-based; group; one-to-one; bespoke
	Method: intensive; non-intensive; open or flexible

SERVICES

Translating

Chinese	into English
Danish	into English
Dutch	into and out of English
French	into and out of English
German	into and out of English
Greek	into and out of English
Italian	into English
Japanese	into English
Norwegian	into English

Portuguese	into English
Russian	into English
Spanish	into and out of English

FACILITIES

| Language labs: | 10–25 places - 1 fixed, 1 portable |
| Equipment and materials: | computer-assisted language learning; portable video play-back machines |

NOTES

• has experience of undertaking language training needs analyses for employers

374   Stockton-Billingham Technical College

The Causeway
Billingham   Telephone   (0642) 552101
TS23 2DB   Fax   (0642) 360273

Contact   Mr B. Quinn, Head of Modern Languages

TRAINING
French   *Type:* client-based; institution-based; group; one-to-one; bespoke
               Method: intensive; non-intensive; open or flexible
German   *Type:* client-based; institution-based; group; one-to-one; bespoke
               Method: intensive; non-intensive; open or flexible
Italian   *Type:* client-based; institution-based; group; one-to-one; bespoke
               Method: intensive; non-intensive; open or flexible
Japanese   *Type:* client-based; institution-based; group; one-to-one; bespoke
               Method: intensive; non-intensive; open or flexible
Spanish   *Type:* client-based; institution-based; group; one-to-one; bespoke
               Method: intensive; non-intensive; open or flexible
Specialisms   business; commercial
Other   Greek can be offered, with notice

SERVICES
Translating
French   into and out of English
German   into and out of English
Italian   into and out of English
Spanish   into and out of English
Specialisms   business; commercial
Interpreting
French   simultaneous; consecutive
German   simultaneous; consecutive
Italian   simultaneous; consecutive
Spanish   simultaneous; consecutive
Specialisms   business; commercial

FACILITIES
Language labs: 10–25 places - 1 fixed
Interpreting
  facilities: under 10 places - 1 fixed
Equipment and
  materials: audio and videocassettes

NOTES
• has experience of undertaking language training needs analyses for employers

375　Stoke-on-Trent College

Stoke Road
Stoke-on-Trent　　　　Telephone　　　(0782) 208208
ST4 2DG　　　　　　　Fax　　　　　　(0782) 203504

Contact　　　　　Mrs B. Cullen, Head of Business Languages

TRAINING

Dutch	*Type:* institution-based
French	*Type:* client-based; institution-based; group; one-to-one; bespoke
	Method: intensive; non-intensive; open or flexible
German	*Type:* client-based; institution-based
	Method: intensive; non-intensive
Greek	*Type:* institution-based
Italian	*Type:* institution-based
	Method: non-intensive
Japanese	*Type:* institution-based
	Method: non-intensive
Portuguese	*Type:* institution-based
Russian	*Type:* institution-based
	Method: non-intensive
Spanish	*Type:* client-based; institution-based
	Method: intensive; non-intensive
Turkish	*Type:* institution-based
Urdu	*Type:* institution-based
Other	Additional languages can be offered, with notice

SERVICES
Interpreting

French	consecutive
German	consecutive
Spanish	consecutive

FACILITIES
Language labs:　　under 10 places - 1 fixed, 3 portable; 10–25 places - 1 fixed

NOTES
• has experience of undertaking language training needs analyses for employers

376   Stradbroke College

Spinkhill Drive
Sheffield
S13 8FD

Telephone   (0742) 392621
Fax   (0742) 649584

Contact   Mrs D. Talford, Manager, Sheffield Languages Centre

TRAINING

French   *Type:* client-based; institution-based; group; one-to-one; bespoke
             (specialisms: tourism; telephone skills)
             Method: intensive; non-intensive; open or flexible
German   *Type:* client-based; institution-based; group; one-to-one; bespoke
             (specialism: engineering)
             Method: intensive; non-intensive; open or flexible
Italian   *Type:* institution-based; group; one-to-one
             Method: intensive; non-intensive
Japanese   *Type:* institution-based; group
Russian   *Type:* institution-based; group
             Method: intensive; non-intensive
Spanish   *Type:* client-based; institution-based; group; one-to-one
             Method: intensive; non-intensive; open or flexible
Urdu   *Type:* client-based; group (specialism: medical)

SERVICES
Translating
French   into and out of English
German   into and out of English
Italian   into and out of English
Spanish   into and out of English
Specialism   engineering
Interpreting
French   simultaneous

FACILITIES
Language labs: 10–25 places - 1 fixed; over 25 places - 2 fixed
Equipment and
 materials: computer-assisted language learning

NOTES
• has experience of undertaking language training needs analyses for employers

377   Stratford-upon-Avon College

The Willows North
Alcester Road
Stratford-upon-Avon   Telephone   (0789) 266245
CV37 9QR   Fax   (0789) 267524

Contact   Mrs S. Little, Head of German

TRAINING
French   *Type:* client-based; institution-based; group; one-to-one; bespoke
                     Method: intensive; non-intensive; open or flexible
German   *Type:* client-based; institution-based; group; one-to-one; bespoke
                     Method: intensive; non-intensive; open or flexible
Spanish   *Type:* client-based; institution-based; group; one-to-one; bespoke
                     Method: intensive; non-intensive; open or flexible
Other   Italian, Russian and Dutch can be offered, with notice

SERVICES
Translating
Dutch   into and out of English
French   into and out of English
German   into and out of English
Italian   into and out of English
Russian   into and out of English
Spanish   into and out of English

FACILITIES
Language labs: 10–25 places - 1 fixed
Interpreting
  facilities: 10–25 places - 1 fixed
Equipment and
  materials: computer-assisted language learning; audio and videocassettes;
                     satellite television

NOTES
• has experience of undertaking language training needs analyses for employers

378 University of Strathclyde

Livingstone Tower
Richmond Street
Glasgow   Telephone   041-552 4400
G1 1XA   Fax   041-553 4161

Contact   Mr M. Anderson, Business Development Executive, Enterprise
Office

TRAINING

French   *Type:* client-based; institution-based; group; one-to-one
                  Method: intensive; non-intensive; open or flexible
German   *Type:* client-based; institution-based; group; one-to-one
                  Method: intensive; open or flexible
Spanish   *Type:* client-based; institution-based; group; one-to-one
                  Method: intensive; open or flexible
Other   Italian and Russian can be offered, with notice

SERVICES

Translating
French   into and out of English
German   into and out of English
Italian   into and out of English
Russian   into and out of English
Spanish   into and out of English
Interpreting
French   consecutive
German   consecutive
Italian   consecutive
Russian   consecutive
Spanish   consecutive

FACILITIES

Language labs: over 25 places - 1 fixed

NOTES

• has experience of undertaking language training needs analyses for employers
• has devised an open learning package, 'Languages for Business', in French, German
and Spanish

379   Stroud College of Further Education

Stratford Road
Stroud   Telephone   (0453) 761162
GL5 4AH   Fax   (0453) 753786

Contact   Mr V. Williams, Unit Manager

TRAINING
French   *Type:* client-based; institution-based; group; one-to-one; bespoke
                Method: intensive; non-intensive; open or flexible
German   *Type:* client-based; institution-based; group; one-to-one; bespoke
                Method: intensive; non-intensive; open or flexible
Italian   *Type:* client-based; institution-based; group; one-to-one; bespoke
                Method: intensive; non-intensive; open or flexible
Russian   *Type:* client-based; institution-based; group; one-to-one; bespoke
                Method: intensive; non-intensive; open or flexible
Spanish   *Type:* client-based; institution-based; group; one-to-one; bespoke
                Method: intensive; non-intensive; open or flexible
Specialism   business
Other   Japanese and Polish can be offered, with notice

FACILITIES
Language labs: under 10 places - 1 fixed; 10–25 places - 1 fixed
Equipment and
   materials: computer-assisted language learning; satellite television; audio and
                videocassettes

NOTES
• has experience of undertaking language training needs analyses for employers

380   Suffolk College

Rope Walk
Ipswich   Telephone   (0473) 255885
IP4 1LT   Fax   (0473) 230054

Contact   Ms S. Johnson, Language Access Centre Co-ordinator

TRAINING

Danish
: *Type:* one-to-one; bespoke (specialism: business)
  Method: open or flexible

Dutch
: *Type:* group; one-to-one; bespoke (specialism: business)
  Method: non-intensive; open or flexible

Finnish
: *Type:* one-to-one; bespoke (specialism: business)
  Method: open or flexible

French
: *Type:* client-based; institution-based; group; one-to-one; bespoke (specialisms: legal; business)
  Method: intensive; non-intensive; open or flexible

German
: *Type:* client-based; institution-based; group; one-to-one; bespoke (specialism: business)
  Method: intensive; non-intensive; open or flexible

Greek
: *Type:* one-to-one; bespoke (specialism: business)
  Method: open or flexible

Hungarian
: *Type:* one-to-one; bespoke (specialism: business)
  Method: open or flexible

Italian
: *Type:* client-based; institution-based; group; one-to-one; bespoke (specialism: business)
  Method: non-intensive; open or flexible

Japanese
: *Type:* client-based; institution-based; group; one-to-one; bespoke (specialism: business)
  Method: intensive

Polish
: *Type:* client-based; institution-based; group; one-to-one; bespoke (specialism: business)

Portuguese
: *Type:* one-to-one; bespoke (specialism: business)
  Method: non-intensive

Russian
: *Type:* client-based; institution-based; group; one-to-one; bespoke (specialism: business)
  Method: non-intensive

Spanish
: *Type:* client-based; institution-based; group; one-to-one; bespoke (specialism: business)
  Method: non-intensive; open or flexible

Swedish
: *Type:* client-based; institution-based; group; one-to-one; bespoke (specialism: business)
  Method: intensive; non-intensive

Other
: Arabic and Chinese can be offered, with notice

SERVICES
Translating

Danish	into and out of English
Dutch	into and out of English
Finnish	into and out of English
French	into and out of English
German	into and out of English
Hungarian	into and out of English
Italian	into and out of English
Japanese	into and out of English
Norwegian	into and out of English
Polish	into and out of English
Russian	into and out of English
Spanish	into and out of English
Specialism	business

Interpreting

Dutch	consecutive
French	simultaneous; consecutive
German	simultaneous; consecutive
Italian	consecutive
Spanish	consecutive
Specialism	business

FACILITIES

Language labs:	10–25 places - 1 fixed, 1 portable
Equipment and materials:	satellite television; audio and videocassettes; computer print-out facilities from European Teletext; computer-assisted language learning; interactive video

NOTES
• has experience of undertaking language training needs analyses for employers

381 University of Sunderland

Langham Tower
Ryhope Road
Sunderland   Telephone   091-515 2202
SR2 7EG   Fax   091-515 2229

Contact   Ms H. Gritzan, Senior Lecturer

TRAINING

French	*Type:* client-based; institution-based; group; one-to-one; bespoke *Method:* intensive; non-intensive
German	*Type:* client-based; institution-based; group; one-to-one; bespoke *Method:* intensive; non-intensive
Japanese	*Type:* client-based; institution-based; group; one-to-one; bespoke *Method:* intensive; non-intensive
Russian	*Type:* client-based; institution-based; group; one-to-one; bespoke
Spanish	*Type:* client-based; institution-based; group; one-to-one; bespoke *Method:* intensive; non-intensive
Other	Additional languages can be offered, with notice

SERVICES

Translating

French	into and out of English
German	into and out of English
Italian	into and out of English
Japanese	into English
Russian	into and out of English
Spanish	into and out of English

Interpreting

French	simultaneous; consecutive
German	simultaneous; consecutive
Italian	simultaneous; consecutive
Russian	simultaneous; consecutive
Spanish	simultaneous; consecutive

FACILITIES
Language labs: 10–25 places - 1 fixed; over 25 places - 1 fixed

NOTES
• has experience of undertaking language training needs analyses for employers

382   University of Surrey

Department of Linguistic and International Studies
Guildford   Telephone   (0483) 300800
GU2 5XH   Fax   (0483) 300803

Contact   Professor J. Riordan, Head of Department

TRAINING
French   *Type:* institution-based; group; one-to-one; bespoke (specialisms: legal; economics)
                  Method: intensive; non-intensive; open or flexible
German   *Type:* institution-based; group; one-to-one; bespoke
                  Method: intensive; non-intensive; open or flexible
Russian   *Type:* institution-based; group; one-to-one; bespoke
                  Method: intensive; non-intensive; open or flexible
Spanish   *Type:* institution-based; group; one-to-one; bespoke
                  Method: non-intensive; open or flexible
Swedish   *Type:* institution-based; group; one-to-one; bespoke
                  Method: intensive; non-intensive; open or flexible

SERVICES
Translating
French   into and out of English (specialisms: legal; economics)
German   into and out of English
Russian   into and out of English
Spanish   into English
Swedish   into and out of English
Interpreting
French   simultaneous; consecutive (specialisms: economics; politics; social services)
German   simultaneous; consecutive
Russian   simultaneous; consecutive
Swedish   simultaneous; consecutive

FACILITIES
Language labs: under 10 places - 1 fixed; 10–25 places - 5 fixed; over 25 places - 1 fixed
Interpreting
  facilities: under 10 places - 1 fixed; 10–25 places - 1 fixed
Equipment and
  materials: computer-assisted language learning; audio and videocassettes

NOTES
• has experience of undertaking language training needs analyses for employers
• Mr Michael Thacker, Director of the European Language Teaching Centre, is a further languages for business contact at the university

383   Sussex and Kent Language-Export Centre

University of Brighton
Falmer
Brighton   Telephone   (0273) 643339
BN1 9PH   Fax   (0273) 690710

Contact   Ms R. Damian, Business Language Courses

TRAINING
French	*Type:* client-based; institution-based; group; bespoke
	Method: intensive; non-intensive; open or flexible
German	*Type:* client-based; institution-based; group; bespoke
	Method: intensive; non-intensive; open or flexible
Greek	*Type:* client-based; institution-based; group; one-to-one; bespoke
Hungarian	*Type:* client-based; institution-based; group; one-to-one; bespoke
Italian	*Type:* client-based; institution-based; group
	Method: intensive; non-intensive
Portuguese	*Type:* client-based; institution-based; group; one-to-one; bespoke
Serbo-Croat	*Type:* bespoke
Spanish	*Type:* client-based; institution-based; group; one-to-one
	Method: intensive; non-intensive
Specialisms	legal; scientific; telephone skills; marketing; management
Other	Japanese, Arabic and Chinese can be offered, with notice

FACILITIES
Language labs: over 25 places - 1 fixed, 1 portable
Equipment and
   materials: computer-assisted language learning; satellite television; videocassettes

NOTES
• has experience of undertaking language training needs analyses for employers
• offers business briefings, especially on the German business environment

384　Sutton Coldfield College of Further Education

Lichfield Road
Sutton Coldfield
B74 2NW

Telephone
Fax

021-355 5671
021-355 0799

Contact　　　Mr R. Lambert, Senior Lecturer in Modern Languages

TRAINING

Arabic	*Type:* client-based; institution-based; group; one-to-one; bespoke
	Method: non-intensive; open or flexible
Dutch	*Type:* client-based; institution-based; group; one-to-one; bespoke
	Method: non-intensive; open or flexible
French	*Type:* client-based; institution-based; group; one-to-one; bespoke
	Method: intensive; non-intensive; open or flexible
German	*Type:* client-based; institution-based; group; one-to-one; bespoke
	Method: intensive; non-intensive; open or flexible
Italian	*Type:* client-based; institution-based; group; one-to-one; bespoke
	Method: intensive; non-intensive; open or flexible
Japanese	*Type:* client-based; institution-based; group; one-to-one; bespoke
	Method: non-intensive; open or flexible
Portuguese	*Type:* client-based; institution-based; group; one-to-one; bespoke
	Method: non-intensive; open or flexible
Russian	*Type:* client-based; institution-based; group; one-to-one; bespoke
	Method: non-intensive; open or flexible
Spanish	*Type:* client-based; institution-based; group; one-to-one; bespoke
	Method: intensive; non-intensive; open or flexible
Specialisms	catering; commercial
Other	Catalan and Ukrainian can be offered, with notice

SERVICES

Translating

Arabic	into and out of English
Dutch	into and out of English
French	into and out of English
German	into and out of English
Italian	into and out of English
Japanese	into and out of English
Portuguese	into and out of English
Russian	into and out of English
Spanish	into and out of English

Interpreting

Dutch	simultaneous; consecutive
French	simultaneous; consecutive
German	simultaneous; consecutive
Italian	simultaneous; consecutive
Spanish	simultaneous; consecutive

FACILITIES

Language labs:	10–25 places - 1 portable
Interpreting facilities:	10–25 places - 1 portable
Equipment and materials:	audio and videocassettes; satellite television; short-wave radio

NOTES
• has experience of undertaking language training needs analyses for employers

385 Sutton College of Liberal Arts

St Nicholas Way
Sutton   Telephone   081-770 6901
SM1 1EA   Fax   081-770 6933

Contact   Mrs S. Compton, Head of Area East

TRAINING

Chinese   *Type:* institution-based; group
                 Method: non-intensive
Dutch   *Type:* institution-based; group
                 Method: non-intensive
French   *Type:* institution-based; group; one-to-one
                 Method: intensive; non-intensive
German   *Type:* institution-based; group; one-to-one
                 Method: intensive; non-intensive
Greek   *Type:* institution-based; group
                 Method: non-intensive
Italian   *Type:* institution-based; group; one-to-one
                 Method: intensive; non-intensive
Japanese   *Type:* institution-based; group; one-to-one
                 Method: non-intensive
Portuguese   *Type:* institution-based; group
                 Method: non-intensive
Russian   *Type:* institution-based; group
                 Method: non-intensive
Spanish   *Type:* institution-based; group; one-to-one
                 Method: non-intensive

SERVICES

Translating
French   into and out of English
German   into and out of English
Italian   into and out of English
Japanese   into and out of English
Russian   into English
Spanish   into and out of English
Interpreting
French   consecutive
German   consecutive

NOTES
- has experience of undertaking language training needs analyses for employers
- most of the college's translating and interpreting work arises from the local authority, in connection with twin town visits or organising events for visitors from abroad

519

386   University College of Swansea

Singleton Park
Swansea
SA2 8PP

Telephone	(0792) 295621
Fax	(0792) 295718

Contact   Mrs S. Jones, Assistant Manager

NOTES
• see entry for South Wales Language-Export Centre

387 Swansea College

Tycoch Road
Tycoch
Swansea   Telephone   (0792) 206871
SA2 9EB   Fax   (0792) 208137

Contact   Mrs M. Griffiths, Head of Languages

TRAINING
French	*Type:* client-based; institution-based; group; one-to-one
	Method: intensive; non-intensive
German	*Type:* client-based; institution-based; group; one-to-one
	Method: intensive; non-intensive
Italian	*Type:* client-based; institution-based; group; one-to-one
Japanese	*Type:* client-based; institution-based; group; one-to-one
Russian	*Type:* client-based; institution-based; group; one-to-one
Spanish	*Type:* client-based; institution-based; group; one-to-one
	Method: intensive; non-intensive
Welsh	*Type:* client-based; institution-based; group; one-to-one
Other	Arabic, Greek and Portuguese can be offered, with notice

SERVICES
Translating
French	into and out of English
German	into and out of English
Italian	into and out of English
Japanese	into and out of English
Russian	into and out of English
Spanish	into and out of English

Interpreting
French	simultaneous; consecutive
German	simultaneous; consecutive
Spanish	simultaneous; consecutive

FACILITIES
Language labs: 10–25 places - 1 portable

388 Swansea Institute of Higher Education

Mount Pleasant
Swansea
SA1 6ED

Telephone (0792) 469004
Fax (0792) 475037

Contact Ms J. Davies, Senior Lecturer in Modern Languages

TRAINING

French
Type: client-based; institution-based; group
Method: intensive; non-intensive

German
Type: client-based; institution-based; group
Method: intensive; non-intensive

Italian
Type: client-based; institution-based; group
Method: intensive; non-intensive

Spanish
Type: client-based; institution-based; group
Method: intensive; non-intensive

Welsh
Type: client-based; institution-based; group
Method: intensive; non-intensive

Specialisms business; tourism
Other Japanese can be offered, with notice

SERVICES

Translating
French into English
German into English
Spanish into English
Welsh into English
Specialisms business; tourism

Interpreting
French consecutive
German consecutive
Spanish consecutive
Welsh consecutive
Specialisms business; tourism

FACILITIES
Language labs: 10–25 places - 2 fixed

NOTES
• has experience of undertaking language training needs analyses for employers
• has a language course specifically designed for front of house staff in the hotel industry and for tourist information office personnel

389   Swindon College

Regent Circus
Swindon
SN1 1PT

Telephone	(0793) 491591
Fax	(0793) 641794

Contact   Mrs D. Walker, Lecturer in French

TRAINING

French
Type: client-based; institution-based; group; one-to-one
Method: intensive; non-intensive; open or flexible

German
Type: client-based; institution-based; group; one-to-one
Method: intensive; non-intensive; open or flexible

Italian
Type: client-based; institution-based; group; one-to-one
Method: intensive; non-intensive; open or flexible

Russian
Type: client-based; institution-based; group; one-to-one
Method: intensive; non-intensive; open or flexible

Spanish
Type: client-based; institution-based; group; one-to-one
Method: intensive; non-intensive; open or flexible

Other   Dutch can be offered, with notice

SERVICES

Translating

Dutch	into and out of English
French	into and out of English
German	into and out of English
Italian	into and out of English
Russian	into and out of English
Spanish	into and out of English

FACILITIES

Language labs: 10–25 places - 1 fixed

Equipment and
materials: audio and videocassettes; interactive video; computer-assisted language learning

NOTES

• has experience of undertaking language training needs analyses for employers

390 Tameside College of Technology

Beaufort Road
Ashton-under-Lyne   Telephone   061-330 6911
OL6 6NX   Fax   061-343 2738

Contact   Mrs V. Clements, Lecturer in Business Languages

TRAINING
French   *Type:* client-based; institution-based; group; one-to-one; bespoke
                Method: intensive; non-intensive; open or flexible
German   *Type:* client-based; institution-based; group; one-to-one; bespoke
                Method: non-intensive; open or flexible
Spanish   *Type:* client-based; institution-based; group; one-to-one
                Method: non-intensive; open or flexible
Other   Italian can be offered, with notice

SERVICES
Translating
French   into and out of English
German   into and out of English
Italian   into English
Spanish   into English

NOTES
• can offer specialised work in French and German for users of information technology

391 Tamworth College

Croft Street
Tamworth
B79 8AE

Telephone	(0827) 310202
Fax	(0827) 59437

Contact   Mr D. Robinson, Industrial Languages Unit Manager

TRAINING

French	*Type:* client-based; institution-based; group; one-to-one; bespoke *Method:* intensive; non-intensive; open or flexible
German	*Type:* client-based; institution-based; group; one-to-one; bespoke *Method:* intensive; non-intensive; open or flexible
Italian	*Type:* client-based; institution-based; group; one-to-one; bespoke *Method:* intensive; non-intensive; open or flexible
Japanese	*Type:* client-based; institution-based; group; one-to-one; bespoke *Method:* intensive; non-intensive; open or flexible
Russian	*Type:* client-based; institution-based; group; one-to-one; bespoke *Method:* intensive; non-intensive; open or flexible
Spanish	*Type:* client-based; institution-based; group; one-to-one; bespoke *Method:* intensive; non-intensive; open or flexible
Other	Additional languages can be offered, with notice

SERVICES

Translating

French	into and out of English
German	into and out of English
Italian	into and out of English
Japanese	into and out of English
Russian	into and out of English
Spanish	into and out of English

Interpreting

French	simultaneous; consecutive
German	simultaneous; consecutive
Italian	simultaneous; consecutive
Japanese	simultaneous; consecutive
Russian	simultaneous; consecutive
Spanish	simultaneous; consecutive

FACILITIES

Language labs: under 10 places - 8 portable; over 25 places - 1 fixed

Equipment and
  materials: computer-assisted language learning; satellite television; audio and videocassettes

NOTES

• has experience of undertaking language training needs analysis for employers

392   University of Teesside

Borough Road
Middlesborough   Telephone   (0642) 342307
TS1 3BA   Fax   (0642) 342067

Contact   Mrs L. Luck, Language Centre Administrator

TRAINING

French
Type: client-based; institution-based (specialisms: biochemistry; business; information technology)
Method: intensive; non-intensive; open or flexible

German
Type: client-based; institution-based (specialisms: biochemistry; business; information technology)
Method: intensive; non-intensive; open or flexible

Italian
Type: client-based; institution-based
Method: intensive; non-intensive; open or flexible

Japanese
Type: client-based; institution-based
Method: intensive; non-intensive; open or flexible

Russian
Type: client-based; institution-based
Method: intensive; non-intensive; open or flexible

Spanish
Type: client-based; institution-based
Method: intensive; non-intensive; open or flexible

Other
Dutch, Greek and Swedish can be offered, with notice

SERVICES

Translating

Dutch   into English
French   into and out of English
German   into and out of English
Italian   into and out of English
Japanese   into and out of English
Russian   into and out of English
Spanish   into and out of English

Interpreting

French   simultaneous; consecutive
German   simultaneous; consecutive
Italian   simultaneous; consecutive
Russian   simultaneous; consecutive
Spanish   simultaneous; consecutive

FACILITIES

Language labs: 10–25 places - 1 fixed

Equipment and
materials: self-tuition laboratory, including six audio work-stations, three television and video stations, various audio-visual packages, and computer-assisted language learning equipment; satellite television

NOTES
• has experience of undertaking language training needs analyses for employers

393 Telford College

Crewe Toll
Edinburgh
EH4 2NZ

Telephone	031-332 2491
Fax	031-343 1218

Contact   Mrs C. Redpath, Senior Lecturer in Languages

TRAINING

Danish
Type: client-based; institution-based; group; one-to-one
Method: non-intensive; open or flexible

French
Type: client-based; institution-based; group (specialisms: tourism; engineering; scientific)
Method: intensive; non-intensive; open or flexible

German
Type: client-based; institution-based; group (specialisms: engineering; tourism)
Method: intensive; non-intensive; open or flexible

Italian
Type: client-based; institution-based; group
Method: intensive; non-intensive

Japanese
Type: client-based; institution-based; group; one-to-one (specialism: tourism)
Method: intensive; non-intensive

Portuguese
Type: client-based; institution-based; group; one-to-one
Method: intensive; non-intensive

Russian
Type: client-based; group; one-to-one
Method: intensive; non-intensive

Spanish
Type: client-based; institution-based; group (specialisms: tourism; scientific)
Method: intensive; non-intensive; open or flexible

Other
Additional languages can be offered, with notice

SERVICES
Translating

Danish	into and out of English
French	into English
German	into and out of English
Italian	into English
Japanese	into and out of English
Portuguese	into and out of English
Russian	into English
Spanish	into and out of English

Interpreting

German	consecutive

FACILITIES
Language labs: under 10 places - 1 fixed

Equipment and
  materials: audio and videocassettes

NOTES
• has experience of undertaking language training needs analyses for employers

394   Telford College of Arts and Technology

Haybridge Road
Wellington
Telford   Telephone   (0952) 641122
TF1 2NP   Fax   (0952) 243657

Contact   Mrs J. Hazleton, Lecturer

TRAINING

French   *Type:* client-based; institution-based; group; one-to-one; bespoke
                   Method: intensive; non-intensive; open or flexible
German   *Type:* client-based; institution-based; group; one-to-one; bespoke
                   Method: intensive; non-intensive; open or flexible
Italian   *Type:* client-based; institution-based; group; one-to-one; bespoke
Spanish   *Type:* client-based; institution-based; group; one-to-one; bespoke
                   Method: intensive; non-intensive; open or flexible
Other   Danish and Welsh can be offered, with notice

FACILITIES

Language labs: 10–25 places - 1 portable
Equipment and
   materials: audio and videocassettes; computer-assisted language learning

395 Thames Valley University Language-Export Centre

St Mary's Road
Ealing
London   Telephone   081-231 2416
W5 5DX   Fax   081-566 1353

Contact   Mrs A. Barton, Languages for Business Unit

TRAINING

French   *Type:* client-based; institution-based; group; one-to-one; bespoke
                 (specialisms: transport; business)
                 Method: intensive; non-intensive
German   *Type:* client-based; institution-based; group; one-to-one; bespoke
                 (specialisms: legal; business)
                 Method: intensive; non-intensive
Italian   *Type:* client-based; institution-based; group; one-to-one
                 Method: intensive; non-intensive
Japanese   *Type:* client-based; institution-based; group; one-to-one; bespoke
                 (specialism: business)
                 Method: intensive; non-intensive
Russian   *Type:* client-based; institution-based; group; one-to-one; bespoke
                 (specialisms: oil industry; business)
                 Method: intensive; non-intensive
Spanish   *Type:* client-based; institution-based; group; one-to-one
                 Method: intensive; non-intensive
Other   Additional European and Indian languages can be offered, with
                 notice

FACILITIES

Language labs: 10–25 places - 3 fixed
Equipment and
   materials: computer-assisted language learning

NOTES
• has experience of undertaking language training needs analyses for employers
• is developing materials for teaching French, German and Spanish over the telephone

Stukeley Street
off Drury Lane
London   Telephone   071-242 9872
WC2B 5LJ   Fax   071-405 3347

Contact   Mrs E. Gorb, Deputy Head of Languages

TRAINING

Arabic	*Type:* client-based; institution-based; group; one-to-one; bespoke
	Method: non-intensive
Chinese	*Type:* institution-based; group
	Method: non-intensive
Czech	*Type:* institution-based; group
	Method: non-intensive
Dutch	*Type:* institution-based; group
	Method: non-intensive
Farsi	*Type:* institution-based; group
	Method: non-intensive
French	*Type:* client-based; institution-based; group; one-to-one; bespoke
	Method: non-intensive
Gaelic (Scottish)	*Type:* institution-based; group
	Method: non-intensive
German	*Type:* client-based; institution-based; group; one-to-one; bespoke
	Method: non-intensive
Greek	*Type:* institution-based; group
	Method: non-intensive
Hebrew	*Type:* institution-based; group
	Method: non-intensive
Hungarian	*Type:* institution-based; group
	Method: non-intensive
Italian	*Type:* client-based; institution-based; group; one-to-one; bespoke
	Method: non-intensive
Japanese	*Type:* client-based; institution-based; group; one-to-one; bespoke
	Method: non-intensive
Latin	*Type:* institution-based; group
	Method: non-intensive
Polish	*Type:* institution-based; group
	Method: non-intensive
Portuguese	*Type:* institution-based; group
	Method: non-intensive
Russian	*Type:* client-based; institution-based; group; one-to-one; bespoke
	Method: non-intensive
Spanish	*Type:* client-based; institution-based; group; one-to-one; bespoke
	Method: non-intensive

Welsh	*Type:* institution-based; group
	Method: non-intensive
Other	Additional languages can be offered, with notice

FACILITIES

Language labs: under 10 places - 1 fixed

397   Thomas Danby College

Roundhay Road
Sheepscar

| Leeds | Telephone | (0532) 494912 |
| LS7 3BG | Fax | (0532) 401967 |

Contact   Mrs C. Woodrow, Workshop Manager

TRAINING

French	*Type:* institution-based; group; one-to-one; bespoke (specialism: catering)
	Method: intensive; non-intensive; open or flexible
German	*Type:* institution-based; group; one-to-one (specialism: tourism)
	Method: intensive; non-intensive
Italian	*Type:* institution-based; group; one-to-one
	Method: intensive; non-intensive
Spanish	*Type:* institution-based; group; one-to-one
	Method: intensive; non-intensive
Other	Urdu and Gujarati can be offered, with notice

SERVICES

Translating

French	into and out of English
German	into and out of English
Spanish	into and out of English

FACILITIES

| Language labs: | 10–25 places - 1 fixed, 1 portable |
| Equipment and materials: | computer-assisted language learning; audio and videocassettes |

398   Thurrock Technical College

Thurrock Management Centre
Love Lane
South Ockendon	Telephone	(0708) 863011
RM15 4HT	Fax	(0708) 861871

Contact   Dr M. G. Thomas, Head of School, Tourism and Languages

TRAINING

French
: *Type:* client-based; institution-based; group; one-to-one; bespoke (specialisms: legal; exporting)
Method: intensive; non-intensive; open or flexible

German
: *Type:* client-based; institution-based; group; one-to-one; bespoke (specialism: exporting)
Method: intensive; non-intensive; open or flexible

Hungarian
: *Type:* one-to-one; bespoke
Method: non-intensive; open or flexible

Italian
: *Type:* client-based; institution-based; one-to-one
Method: non-intensive; open or flexible

Polish
: *Type:* one-to-one
Method: non-intensive; open or flexible

Portuguese
: *Type:* institution-based; group; one-to-one; bespoke
Method: non-intensive; open or flexible

Russian
: *Type:* client-based; institution-based; one-to-one; bespoke
Method: non-intensive; open or flexible

Spanish
: *Type:* client-based; institution-based; group; one-to-one; bespoke (specialism: exporting)
Method: intensive; non-intensive; open or flexible

Swedish
: *Type:* client-based; institution-based
Method: non-intensive; open or flexible

Other
: Punjabi, Japanese, Arabic and Chinese can be offered, with notice

SERVICES

Translating

French	into and out of English
German	into and out of English
Hungarian	into and out of English
Italian	into and out of English
Polish	into and out of English
Portuguese	into and out of English
Russian	into and out of English
Spanish	into and out of English
Swedish	into and out of English

FACILITIES

Language labs: 10–25 places - 1 fixed, 1 portable

NOTES

• has experience of undertaking language training needs analyses for employers

399   Thurso Technical College

Ormlie Road
Thurso   Telephone   (0847) 66161
KW14 7EE   Fax   (0847) 63872

Contact   Mr N. Robertson, Commercial Unit Manager

TRAINING
French   *Type:* institution-based; group
                 Method: non-intensive; open or flexible
German   *Type:* institution-based; group
                 Method: non-intensive; open or flexible
Italian   *Type:* institution-based; group
                 Method: non-intensive
Spanish   *Type:* institution-based; group
                 Method: non-intensive; open or flexible
Specialism   business

SERVICES
Translating
German   into and out of English (specialism: politics)
Interpreting
French   consecutive
German   consecutive
Spanish   consecutive

FACILITIES
Equipment and
  materials: audiocassettes

NOTES
• has experience of undertaking language training needs analyses for employers

400 Tresham Institute of Further and Higher Education

St Mary's Road
Kettering   Telephone   (0536) 410252
NN15 7BS   Fax   (0536) 522500

Contact   Mr A. J. Carter, Co-ordinator for Languages

TRAINING

Czech
Type: client-based; institution-based; group; one-to-one; bespoke (specialisms: business; industrial)

Dutch
Type: client-based; institution-based; group; one-to-one; bespoke (specialisms: business; industrial)

French
Type: client-based; institution-based; group; one-to-one; bespoke (specialisms: business; scientific; industrial)
Method: intensive; non-intensive; open or flexible

German
Type: client-based; institution-based; group; one-to-one; bespoke (specialisms: business; industrial)
Method: intensive; non-intensive; open or flexible

Greek
Type: client-based; institution-based; group; one-to-one; bespoke (specialisms: business; industrial)

Italian
Type: client-based; institution-based; group; one-to-one; bespoke (specialisms: business; industrial)
Method: intensive; non-intensive; open or flexible

Japanese
Type: client-based; institution-based; group; one-to-one; bespoke (specialisms: business; industrial)

Russian
Type: client-based; institution-based; group; one-to-one; bespoke
Method: intensive; non-intensive

Spanish
Type: client-based; institution-based; group; one-to-one; bespoke (specialisms: business; industrial)
Method: intensive; non-intensive; open or flexible

Other
Danish can be offered, with notice

SERVICES

Translating

Czech	into and out of English
Danish	into and out of English
Dutch	into and out of English
French	into and out of English
German	into and out of English
Greek	into and out of English
Italian	into and out of English
Japanese	into and out of English
Portuguese	into and out of English

Russian	into and out of English
Spanish	into and out of English
Interpreting	
Czech	simultaneous; consecutive
Danish	simultaneous; consecutive
Dutch	simultaneous; consecutive
French	simultaneous; consecutive
German	simultaneous; consecutive
Greek	simultaneous; consecutive
Italian	simultaneous; consecutive
Japanese	simultaneous; consecutive
Portuguese	simultaneous; consecutive
Russian	simultaneous; consecutive
Spanish	simultaneous; consecutive

FACILITIES

Language labs: over 25 places - 2 fixed

NOTES

- has experience of undertaking language training needs analyses for employers
- Mr William John Gaye, Business Development Manager, is another languages for business contact at the institution

401 Trinity and All Saints College

Brownberrie Lane
Horsforth
Leeds   Telephone   (0532) 584341
LS18 5HD   Fax   (0532) 581148

Contact   Mrs J. Foale, PICKUP Officer

TRAINING

French   *Type:* client-based; institution-based; group; one-to-one; bespoke
                     Method: intensive; open or flexible
German   *Type:* client-based; institution-based; group; one-to-one; bespoke
                     Method: intensive; open or flexible
Spanish   *Type:* client-based; institution-based; group; one-to-one; bespoke
                     Method: intensive; open or flexible
Specialisms   financial; packaging industry
Other   Additional languages can be offered, with notice

SERVICES
Translating
French   into and out of English
German   into and out of English
Spanish   into and out of English
Interpreting
Spanish   consecutive

FACILITIES
Language labs: under 10 places - 1 fixed; 10–25 places - 1 fixed

NOTES
- has experience of undertaking language training needs analyses for employers
- virtually all the institution's business language tuition is 'bespoke'

402   Trinity College

College Road
Carmarthen   Telephone   (0267) 237971
SA31 3EP   Fax   (0267) 230933

Contact   Dr A. Hiscock, Lecturer

TRAINING
French   *Type:* client-based; institution-based; group; one-to-one; bespoke
                    Method: intensive; non-intensive; open or flexible
German   *Type:* client-based; institution-based; group; one-to-one; bespoke
                    Method: intensive; non-intensive; open or flexible
Russian   *Type:* client-based; institution-based; group; one-to-one; bespoke
                    Method: intensive; non-intensive; open or flexible
Welsh   *Type:* client-based; institution-based; group; one-to-one
                    Method: intensive; non-intensive; open or flexible
Specialisms   cultural; education
Other   Spanish can be offered, with notice

SERVICES
Translating
French   into and out of English
German   into and out of English
Russian   into and out of English
Welsh   into and out of English
Interpreting
French   simultaneous; consecutive
German   simultaneous; consecutive
Russian   simultaneous; consecutive
Welsh   simultaneous; consecutive

FACILITIES
Language labs: 10–25 places - 1 portable
Interpreting
  facilities: 10–25 places - 1 portable

403   Trowbridge College

College Road
Trowbridge
BA14 0ES

Telephone (0225) 766241
Fax   (0225) 777148

Contact   Mrs M. Anderson, Language Co-ordinator

TRAINING

French
Type: client-based; institution-based; group; one-to-one; bespoke (specialisms: police; food)
Method: intensive; non-intensive; open or flexible

German
Type: client-based; institution-based; group; one-to-one; bespoke (specialisms: waste systems; rubber industry)
Method: intensive; non-intensive; open or flexible

Italian
Type: client-based; institution-based; group; one-to-one; bespoke
Method: intensive; non-intensive; open or flexible

Spanish
Type: client-based; institution-based; group; one-to-one; bespoke
Method: intensive; non-intensive; open or flexible

SERVICES

Translating
French   into and out of English
German   into and out of English
Italian   into and out of English
Spanish   into and out of English

Interpreting
French   simultaneous; consecutive
German   simultaneous; consecutive
Italian   simultaneous; consecutive
Spanish   simultaneous; consecutive

FACILITIES

Equipment and
 materials: computer-assisted language learning

NOTES

• has experience of undertaking language training needs analyses for employers

404 University of Ulster at Jordanstown

Newtownabbey	Telephone	(0232) 365131
BT37 0QB	Fax	(0232) 362824

Contact   Mrs M. McCurdy, Director of Foreign Languages for Export

TRAINING

Arabic	*Type:* institution-based; group; one-to-one *Method:* non-intensive
Dutch	*Type:* client-based; institution-based; group; one-to-one; bespoke *Method:* non-intensive
French	*Type:* client-based; institution-based; group; one-to-one; bespoke *Method:* intensive; non-intensive; open or flexible
German	*Type:* client-based; institution-based; group; one-to-one; bespoke *Method:* intensive; non-intensive; open or flexible
Hungarian	*Type:* institution-based; group; one-to-one *Method:* non-intensive
Indonesian	*Type:* client-based; institution-based; group; one-to-one; bespoke
Italian	*Type:* client-based; institution-based; group; one-to-one; bespoke *Method:* non-intensive
Japanese	*Type:* client-based; institution-based; group; one-to-one; bespoke *Method:* intensive; non-intensive
Polish	*Type:* client-based; institution-based; group; bespoke *Method:* intensive; non-intensive
Portuguese	*Type:* client-based; institution-based; group; one-to-one
Russian	*Type:* institution-based; group; one-to-one *Method:* non-intensive
Spanish	*Type:* client-based; institution-based; group; one-to-one; bespoke *Method:* intensive; non-intensive; open or flexible
Other	Additional languages can be offered, with notice

SERVICES

Translating

Arabic	into and out of English
Chinese	into and out of English
Danish	into English
Dutch	into and out of English
French	into and out of English
German	into and out of English
Hungarian	into and out of English
Italian	into and out of English
Japanese	into and out of English
Polish	into and out of English
Portuguese	out of English
Russian	into English

Spanish	into and out of English
Swedish	into and out of English
Turkish	into and out of English

Interpreting

Arabic	consecutive
Dutch	simultaneous; consecutive
French	simultaneous; consecutive
German	simultaneous; consecutive
Hungarian	consecutive
Italian	consecutive
Japanese	consecutive
Polish	simultaneous; consecutive
Portuguese	consecutive
Spanish	simultaneous; consecutive
Swedish	simultaneous; consecutive

FACILITIES

Language labs:	under 10 places - 1 fixed; 10–25 places - 6 fixed
Equipment and materials:	audiocassettes

405   Uxbridge College

Enterprise Development Service
Central Avenue

Hayes	Telephone	081-569 3448
UB3 2DD	Fax	081-569 3063

Contact   Dr S. Jordan, Training and Development Officer (Commercial Languages)

TRAINING

French   *Type:* client-based; institution-based; group; one-to-one
                    Method: intensive; non-intensive; open or flexible

German   *Type:* client-based; institution-based; group; one-to-one
                    Method: intensive; non-intensive; open or flexible

Italian   *Type:* client-based; institution-based; group; one-to-one
                    Method: intensive; non-intensive; open or flexible

Russian   *Type:* client-based; institution-based; group; one-to-one

Spanish   *Type:* client-based; institution-based; group; one-to-one
                    Method: intensive; non-intensive; open or flexible

Other   Additional languages can be offered, with notice

SERVICES

Translating

French	into and out of English
German	into and out of English
Italian	into and out of English
Spanish	into and out of English

Interpreting

French	consecutive
German	consecutive
Italian	consecutive
Spanish	consecutive

FACILITIES

Language labs:	10–25 places - 1 fixed
Equipment and materials:	satellite television; audiocassettes

NOTES

- has experience of undertaking language training needs analyses for employers
- provides support and consultation for companies wishing to set up language resource centres
- offers family training schemes
- provides courses such as business language competence, telephone communication skills and Saturday intensives

406   Wakefield College

Margaret Street
Wakefield   Telephone   (0924) 370501
WF1 2DH   Fax   (0924) 201998

Contact   Mr N. Moult, Language Training Consultant

TRAINING

French   *Type:* client-based; institution-based; group; one-to-one
                 Method: intensive; non-intensive; open or flexible

German   *Type:* client-based; institution-based; group; one-to-one
                 Method: intensive; non-intensive; open or flexible

Italian   *Type:* client-based; institution-based; group; one-to-one
                 Method: intensive

Japanese   *Type:* client-based; institution-based; group; one-to-one
                 Method: intensive; non-intensive; open or flexible

Russian   *Type:* client-based; institution-based; group; one-to-one; bespoke
                 Method: intensive

Spanish   *Type:* client-based; institution-based; group; one-to-one
                 Method: intensive

Other   Any other languages can be offered, with notice

FACILITIES

Language labs: under 10 places - 1 fixed, 1 portable; 10–25 places - 1 fixed; over 25 places - 1 fixed

Equipment and
  materials: computer-assisted language learning; interactive video

NOTES

• has experience of undertaking language training needs analyses for employers
• interpreting available on request, for existing clients

407 Walford College of Agriculture

Walford
Baschurch
Shrewsbury   Telephone   (0939) 260461
SY4 2HL   Fax   (0939) 261112

Contact   Mr P. Attard, Lecturer

SERVICES
Translating
French   into English
German   into English
Spanish   into and out of English
Specialism   agriculture
Interpreting
French   consecutive
Specialism   agriculture

FACILITIES
Language labs: under 10 places - 1 portable

408 Walsall College of Technology

St Paul's Street
Walsall   Telephone   (0922) 720824
WS1 1XN   Fax   (0922) 29967

Contact   Mr B. Bartram, Senior Lecturer

TRAINING
Dutch   *Type:* client-based; institution-based; group; one-to-one; bespoke
French   *Type:* client-based; institution-based; group; one-to-one; bespoke
             Method: intensive; non-intensive; open or flexible
German   *Type:* client-based; institution-based; group; one-to-one; bespoke
             Method: intensive; non-intensive; open or flexible
Italian   *Type:* client-based; institution-based; group; one-to-one; bespoke
             Method: non-intensive
Japanese   *Type:* institution-based; one-to-one; bespoke
Russian   *Type:* client-based; institution-based; group; one-to-one; bespoke
Spanish   *Type:* client-based; institution-based; group; one-to-one; bespoke
             Method: non-intensive; open or flexible
Other   Danish and Greek can be offered, with notice

SERVICES
Translating
Dutch   into and out of English
French   into and out of English
German   into and out of English
Italian   into and out of English
Russian   into and out of English
Spanish   into and out of English
Interpreting
Dutch   simultaneous; consecutive
French   simultaneous; consecutive
German   simultaneous; consecutive
Italian   simultaneous; consecutive
Japanese   consecutive
Russian   simultaneous; consecutive
Spanish   simultaneous; consecutive

FACILITIES
Language labs: under 10 places - 1 portable; 10–25 places - 1 fixed
Interpreting
  facilities: over 100 places - 1 fixed
Equipment and
  materials: computer-assisted language learning

NOTES
• has experience of undertaking language training needs analyses for employers

409   Waltham Forest College

Forest Road
London   Telephone   081-527 2311
E17 4JB   Fax   081-523 2376

Contact   Mrs K. Maynard, European Language Unit Co-ordinator

TRAINING
French   *Type:* client-based; institution-based; group; one-to-one
                      (specialisms: insurance; business)
                      Method: intensive; non-intensive; open or flexible
German   *Type:* client-based; institution-based; group; one-to-one
                      Method: intensive; non-intensive; open or flexible
Italian   *Type:* client-based; institution-based; group; one-to-one
                      Method: intensive; non-intensive
Spanish   *Type:* client-based; institution-based; group; one-to-one
                      Method: intensive; non-intensive; open or flexible
Other   Additional languages can be offered, with notice

FACILITIES
Language labs: over 25 places - 1 fixed

NOTES
• has experience of undertaking language training needs analyses for employers

410   University of Warwick

Language Centre
Coventry
CV4 7AL

	Telephone	(0203) 523462
	Fax	(0203) 461606

Contact   Mr P. Parker, Language Centre Manager

TRAINING

Chinese
Type: institution-based; group; bespoke (specialism: business)
Method: intensive; non-intensive

Dutch
Type: institution-based; bespoke (specialism: business)
Method: intensive; non-intensive

French
Type: client-based; institution-based; group; one-to-one; bespoke (specialisms: engineering; legal; business)
Method: intensive; non-intensive; open or flexible

German
Type: client-based; institution-based; group; one-to-one; bespoke (specialism: business)
Method: intensive; non-intensive; open or flexible

Greek
Type: institution-based; group
Method: non-intensive; open or flexible

Italian
Type: institution-based; group; one-to-one
Method: non-intensive; open or flexible

Japanese
Type: institution-based; group; one-to-one
Method: intensive; non-intensive; open or flexible

Portuguese
Type: institution-based; group
Method: intensive; non-intensive; open or flexible

Russian
Type: client-based; institution-based; group; one-to-one
Method: non-intensive; open or flexible

Spanish
Type: institution-based; group; one-to-one
Method: intensive; non-intensive; open or flexible

Turkish
Type: institution-based; group

Other
Arabic, Welsh, Swedish, Danish and Norwegian can be offered, with notice

SERVICES

Translating

Arabic	into and out of English
Chinese	into and out of English
Czech	into and out of English
Danish	into and out of English
Dutch	into and out of English
French	into and out of English (specialisms: legal; scientific; engineering)
German	into and out of English (specialism: scientific)
Greek	into and out of English
Italian	into and out of English

Japanese	into and out of English
Norwegian	into and out of English
Polish	into and out of English
Portuguese	into and out of English
Punjabi	into and out of English
Russian	into and out of English (specialisms: petro-chemical; engineering)
Spanish	into and out of English (specialism: legal)
Swedish	into and out of English
Welsh	into and out of English
Interpreting	
Chinese	consecutive
Czech	consecutive
French	consecutive
German	consecutive
Italian	consecutive
Japanese	consecutive
Polish	consecutive
Russian	consecutive
Spanish	consecutive
Turkish	consecutive

FACILITIES

Language labs:	under 10 places - 4 portable; 10–25 places - 4 fixed
Interpreting facilities:	26–100 places - 6 portable; over 100 places - 2 portable
Equipment and materials:	audio and videocassettes; satellite television; professional voice-over studio for corporate promotion or training videotapes; sound recording and editing facilities

NOTES

- has experience of undertaking language training needs analyses for employers
- can call on postgraduate students from many countries, and so can provide language training in many specialist areas
- simultaneous interpreting available on a sub-contract basis, with equipment
- proof-reading service available

411 Warwickshire College for Agriculture, Horticulture and Equine Studies

Moreton Morrell
Warwick
CV35 9BA

Telephone   (0926) 651367
Fax   (0926) 651190

Contact   Mr P. Rabbich, Curriculum Manager

TRAINING
French

Type: institution-based; group
Method: intensive

SERVICES
Translating
French   into English
Interpreting
French   consecutive (specialisms: agriculture; horticulture; scientific)

FACILITIES
Language labs: 10–25 places - 1 portable

412 Wearside College

Bede Centre
Durham Road
Sunderland   Telephone   091-511 0515
SR3 4AH   Fax   091-511 0266

Contact   Ms P. Finn, Head of School

TRAINING

French	*Type:* client-based; institution-based; group; one-to-one; bespoke (specialism: commercial)
	Method: intensive; non-intensive; open or flexible
German	*Type:* client-based; institution-based; group; one-to-one; bespoke (specialism: commercial)
	Method: intensive; non-intensive; open or flexible
Italian	*Type:* client-based; institution-based; group; one-to-one; bespoke (specialism: commercial)
	Method: intensive; non-intensive; open or flexible
Russian	*Type:* client-based; institution-based; group; one-to-one; bespoke
	Method: intensive; non-intensive; open or flexible
Spanish	*Type:* client-bascd; institution-based; group; one-to-one; bespoke (specialism: commercial)
	Method: intensive; non-intensive; open or flexible
Other	Norwegian and Dutch can be offered, with notice

SERVICES

Translating

French	into and out of English
German	into and out of English
Russian	into and out of English
Spanish	into and out of English

Interpreting

French	consecutive
German	consecutive
Italian	consecutive
Spanish	consecutive
Specialism	business

FACILITIES

Language labs:	10–25 places - 5 portable; over 25 places - 6 fixed
Equipment and materials:	audio and videocassettes; telephone training equipment

NOTES

• has experience of undertaking language training needs analyses for employers

413   West Cheshire College

The Arts Centre
Blacon Avenue
Chester   Telephone   (0244) 377595
CH1 5BD   Fax   (0244) 373463

Contact   Dr R. P. Jones, Single European Market and Modern Languages Co-
              ordinator

TRAINING
French   *Type:* client-based; institution-based; group; one-to-one
              Method: intensive; non-intensive
German   *Type:* client-based; institution-based; group; one-to-one (specialism:
              computers)
              Method: intensive; non-intensive
Italian   *Type:* client-based; institution-based; group; one-to-one
Japanese   *Type:* client-based; institution-based; group; one-to-one
Russian   *Type:* client-based; institution-based; group; one-to-one
Spanish   *Type:* client-based; institution-based; group; one-to-one
              (specialisms: hairdressing; tourism)
              Method: intensive; non-intensive

SERVICES
Translating
French   into and out of English
German   into and out of English
Spanish   into and out of English

FACILITIES
Language labs: 10–25 places - 1 fixed, 1 portable
Equipment and
   materials: audiocassettes; computer-assisted language learning

NOTES
• has experience of undertaking language training needs analyses for employers
• can offer training in other languages, through Cheshire Interchange and Merseyside
  Language-Export Centre

414   West Cumbria College

Park Lane
Workington
CA14 2RW

Telephone	(0900) 64331
Fax	(0900) 65017

Contact   Mr R. Jefferson, Senior Lecturer

TRAINING

French   *Type:* client-based; institution-based; group; one-to-one; bespoke
                Method: non-intensive; open or flexible
German   *Type:* client-based; institution-based; group; one-to-one
                Method: non-intensive; open or flexible
Russian   *Type:* institution-based; one-to-one
                Method: non-intensive
Spanish   *Type:* institution-based; group
                Method: non-intensive; open or flexible

SERVICES

Translating
French   into and out of English (specialisms: commercial; technical)
German   into and out of English (specialisms: commercial; engineering)
Spanish   into English (specialism: commercial)
Interpreting
French   simultaneous; consecutive (specialisms: commercial; technical)
German   simultaneous; consecutive (specialisms: commercial; engineering)

FACILITIES

Equipment and
  materials: portable audiocassette recorders and software; computer-assisted
                language learning

NOTES

• has experience of undertaking language training needs analyses for employers

415   West Hertfordshire College

Leggatts Campus
Leggatts Way
Watford   Telephone   (0923) 893909
WD2 6BJ   Fax   (0923) 894017

Contact   Mrs I. M. Stronach, Head of Business Languages

TRAINING

Dutch	*Type:* client-based; institution-based *Method:* non-intensive
French	*Type:* client-based; institution-based; group; one-to-one (specialism: building) *Method:* intensive; non-intensive; open or flexible
German	*Type:* client-based; institution-based; group; one-to-one (specialism: scientific) *Method:* intensive; non-intensive; open or flexible
Greek	*Type:* client-based; institution-based *Method:* non-intensive
Italian	*Type:* client-based; institution-based; group; one-to-one *Method:* non-intensive
Japanese	*Type:* client-based; institution-based; group; one-to-one *Method:* non-intensive
Polish	*Type:* client-based; institution-based; group; one-to-one
Portuguese	*Type:* client-based; institution-based *Method:* non-intensive
Russian	*Type:* client-based; group; one-to-one
Spanish	*Type:* client-based; institution-based; group; one-to-one *Method:* intensive; non-intensive; open or flexible
Swedish	*Type:* client-based; institution-based; one-to-one *Method:* non-intensive
Turkish	*Type:* client-based; institution-based; group; one-to-one

SERVICES

Translating

French	into and out of English
German	into and out of English
Italian	into and out of English
Japanese	into and out of English
Russian	into and out of English
Spanish	into and out of English

Interpreting

French	simultaneous; consecutive
German	simultaneous; consecutive

Italian	simultaneous; consecutive
Japanese	simultaneous; consecutive
Spanish	simultaneous; consecutive

FACILITIES

Equipment and
materials: audio and videocassettes; computer-assisted language learning

NOTES

• has experience of undertaking language training needs analyses for employers

416   West Kent College

Brook Street
Tonbridge
TN9 2PW

Telephone   (0732) 358101
Fax   (0732) 771415

Contact   Mrs C. Tomlinson, Language Services Manager

TRAINING
Dutch   *Type:* client-based; institution-based; group; one-to-one; bespoke
French   *Type:* client-based; institution-based; group; bespoke (specialisms:
            architecture; pharmaceutical; tourism)
            Method: intensive; non-intensive; open or flexible
German   *Type:* client-based; group; one-to-one; bespoke (specialism: finan-
            cial)
            Method: intensive; non-intensive; open or flexible
Italian   *Type:* client-based; institution-based; group; one-to-one; bespoke
            Method: intensive; non-intensive; open or flexible
Japanese   *Type:* client-based; institution-based; group; one-to-one; bespoke
            Method: intensive; non-intensive; open or flexible
Russian   *Type:* client-based; institution-based; group; one-to-one; bespoke
            Method: intensive; non-intensive; open or flexible
Spanish   *Type:* client-based; institution-based; group; one-to-one; bespoke
            Method: intensive; non-intensive; open or flexible
Other   Bulgarian, Arabic, Czech and Greek can be offered, with notice

SERVICES
Translating
Dutch   into and out of English (specialism: tourism)
French   into and out of English (specialisms: tourism; financial; technical)
German   into and out of English (specialisms: tourism; financial; medical;
            technical; commercial; legal; engineering)
Italian   into and out of English (specialism: tourism)
Japanese   into and out of English
Russian   into and out of English
Spanish   into and out of English (specialism: banking)
Interpreting
French   simultaneous; consecutive
German   simultaneous; consecutive

FACILITIES
Language labs: 10–25 places - 1 portable
Equipment and
   materials: computer-assisted language learning; interactive video; audio-visual
                 materials; satellite television; Teletext

NOTES

- has experience of undertaking language training needs analyses for employers
- offers voice-over translation, for promotional videos, in French, German, Spanish, Dutch, Italian and Japanese

417 University of the West of England

Frenchay Campus
Coldharbour Lane
Bristol   Telephone   (0272) 656261
BS16 1QY   Fax   (0272) 763843

Contact   Ms S. Evans, Language Services Co-ordinator

TRAINING
Arabic	*Type:* institution-based; one-to-one; bespoke
Dutch	*Type:* client-based; institution-based; group; one-to-one; bespoke
French	*Type:* client-based; institution-based; group; one-to-one; bespoke (specialisms: legal; business) *Method:* intensive; non-intensive; open or flexible
German	*Type:* client-based; institution-based; group; one-to-one bespoke (specialisms: legal; business) *Method:* intensive; non-intensive; open or flexible
Italian	*Type:* client-based; institution-based; group; one-to-one; bespoke (specialism: business) *Method:* intensive; non-intensive; open or flexible
Japanese	*Type:* client-based; institution-based; group; one-to-one; bespoke *Method:* intensive; non-intensive; open or flexible
Polish	*Type:* client-based; institution-based; group; one-to-one; bespoke
Portuguese	*Type:* institution-based; one-to-one; bespoke
Russian	*Type:* client-based; institution-based; group; one-to-one; bespoke (specialism: business) *Method:* intensive; non-intensive; open or flexible
Spanish	*Type:* client-based; institution-based; group; one-to-one; bespoke (specialisms: legal; business) *Method:* intensive; non-intensive; open or flexible
Swedish	*Type:* client-based; institution-based; group; one-to-one; bespoke
Other	Additional languages can be offered, with notice

SERVICES
Translating
French	into and out of English (specialisms: commercial; legal; medical)
German	into and out of English (specialisms: commercial; legal; medical)
Italian	into and out of English (specialisms: commercial; legal; medical)
Japanese	into and out of English
Russian	into and out of English (specialism: computers)
Spanish	into and out of English (specialisms: commercial; legal; medical)

Interpreting
French	consecutive (specialisms: commercial; legal)
German	consecutive (specialisms: commercial; legal)
Italian	consecutive

Japanese	consecutive
Russian	consecutive
Spanish	consecutive (specialisms: commercial; legal)

FACILITIES

Language labs:	under 10 places - 1 portable; over 25 places - 1 fixed
Interpreting facilities:	under 10 places - 1 fixed
Equipment and materials:	satellite television; audio and videocassettes

NOTES

- has experience of undertaking language training needs analyses for employers
- offers translating and interpreting facilities in a wide range of languages
- offers French and German learning packages for lawyers

418   West Suffolk College

Out Risbygate Street
Bury St Edmunds   Telephone   (0284) 701301
IP33 3RL   Fax   (0284) 750561

Contact   Mr P. Dudley, Unit Head

TRAINING

French   *Type:* client-based; institution-based; group; one-to-one; bespoke
            Method: intensive; non-intensive; open or flexible
German   *Type:* client-based; institution-based; group; one-to-one; bespoke
            Method: intensive; non-intensive; open or flexible
Italian   *Type:* client-based; institution-based; group; one-to-one; bespoke
            Method: intensive; non-intensive; open or flexible
Japanese   *Type:* client-based; institution-based; group; one-to-one; bespoke
            Method: intensive; non-intensive
Russian   *Type:* client-based; institution-based; group; one-to-one; bespoke
            Method: intensive; non-intensive
Spanish   *Type:* client-based; institution-based; group; one-to-one; bespoke
            Method: intensive; non-intensive; open or flexible
Other   Additional languages can be offered, with notice

SERVICES

Translating
French   into and out of English
German   into and out of English
Italian   into and out of English
Japanese   into and out of English
Russian   into and out of English
Spanish   into and out of English
Interpreting
French   simultaneous; consecutive
German   simultaneous; consecutive
Italian   simultaneous; consecutive
Japanese   simultaneous; consecutive
Russian   simultaneous; consecutive
Spanish   simultaneous; consecutive

FACILITIES

Equipment and
  materials: audio and videocassettes

NOTES

• has experience of undertaking language training needs analyses for employers

419 West Sussex Institute of Higher Education

The Dome
Upper Bognor Road
Bognor Regis   Telephone   (0243) 865581
PO21 1HR   Fax   (0243) 841458

Contact   Mr J. Naysmith, Senior Lecturer

TRAINING
Portuguese   *Type:* institution-based; group; bespoke
                 Method: intensive

FACILITIES
Language labs: 10–25 places - 1 fixed

NOTES
• training in Portuguese can be undertaken in Portugal, in association with the ESE de
Faro, Universidade de Algarve

420   City of Westminster College

25 Paddington Green
London   Telephone   071-723 8826
W2 1NB   Fax   071-724 4827

Contact   Ms J. Beeson, Principal Lecturer and Deputy Head of Business
Studies

TRAINING

French   *Type:* client-based; institution-based (specialisms: business; design;
architecture)
Method: intensive; non-intensive

Italian   *Type:* client-based; institution-based

Other   German can be offered, with notice

421 University of Westminster

School of Languages
18 Euston Centre

London	Telephone	071-911 5009
NW1 3ET	Fax	071-911 5007

Contact   Mr J. Lonergan, Director, Short Courses

TRAINING

Arabic
Type: institution-based; group; one-to-one; bespoke (specialisms: diplomatic; military)
Method: intensive; non-intensive; open or flexible

Bengali
Type: institution-based; group; one-to-one; bespoke (specialism: business)
Method: intensive; non-intensive; open or flexible

Bulgarian
Type: institution-based; group; one-to-one; bespoke (specialism: diplomatic)
Method: intensive; non-intensive; open or flexible

Chinese
Type: institution-based; group; one-to-one; bespoke (specialism: business)
Method: intensive; non-intensive; open or flexible

Czech
Type: institution-based; group; one-to-one; bespoke (specialism: business)
Method: intensive; non-intensive; open or flexible

Danish
Type: institution-based; group; one-to-one; bespoke (specialism: business)
Method: intensive; non-intensive; open or flexible

Finnish
Type: institution-based; group; one-to-one; bespoke (specialism: business)
Method: intensive; non-intensive; open or flexible

French
Type: client-based; institution-based; group; one-to-one; bespoke
Method: intensive; non-intensive; open or flexible

German
Type: client-based; institution-based; group; one-to-one; bespoke
Method: intensive; non-intensive; open or flexible

Greek
Type: institution-based; group; one-to-one; bespoke (specialisms: business; military)
Method: intensive; non-intensive; open or flexible

Gujarati
Type: institution-based; group; one-to-one; bespoke (specialism: business)
Method: intensive; non-intensive; open or flexible

Hebrew
Type: institution-based; group; one-to-one; bespoke (specialism: business)
Method: intensive; non-intensive; open or flexible

Hungarian	*Type:* institution-based; group; one-to-one; bespoke (specialisms: business; diplomatic)
	Method: intensive; non-intensive; open or flexible
Indonesian	*Type:* institution-based; group; one-to-one; bespoke (specialism: business)
	Method: intensive; non-intensive; open or flexible
Italian	*Type:* client-based; institution-based; group; one-to-one; bespoke
	Method: intensive; non-intensive; open or flexible
Japanese	*Type:* institution-based; group; one-to-one; bespoke
	Method: intensive; non-intensive; open or flexible
Malay	*Type:* institution-based; group; one-to-one; bespoke (specialism: business)
	Method: intensive; non-intensive; open or flexible
Norwegian	*Type:* institution-based; group; one-to-one; bespoke (specialisms: business; secretarial)
	Method: intensive; non-intensive; open or flexible
Polish	*Type:* institution-based; group; one-to-one; bespoke
	Method: intensive; non-intensive; open or flexible
Portuguese	*Type:* institution-based; group; one-to-one; bespoke
	Method: intensive; non-intensive; open or flexible
Punjabi	*Type:* institution-based; group; one-to-one; bespoke
	Method: intensive; non-intensive; open or flexible
Romanian	*Type:* institution-based; group; one-to-one; bespoke
	Method: intensive; non-intensive; open or flexible
Russian	*Type:* client-based; institution-based; group; one-to-one; bespoke
	Method: intensive; non-intensive; open or flexible
Serbo-Croat	*Type:* institution-based; group; one-to-one; bespoke (specialisms: military; business)
	Method: intensive; non-intensive; open or flexible
Slovene	*Type:* institution-based; group; one-to-one; bespoke
	Method: intensive; non-intensive; open or flexible
Spanish	*Type:* client-based; institution-based; group; one-to-one; bespoke
	Method: intensive; non-intensive; open or flexible
Swahili	*Type:* institution-based; group; one-to-one; bespoke
	Method: intensive; non-intensive; open or flexible
Swedish	*Type:* institution-based; group; one-to-one; bespoke
	Method: intensive; non-intensive; open or flexible
Thai	*Type:* institution-based; group; one-to-one; bespoke
	Method: intensive; non-intensive; open or flexible
Turkish	*Type:* institution-based; group; one-to-one; bespoke (specialism: legal)
	Method: intensive; non-intensive; open or flexible
Urdu	*Type:* institution-based; group; one-to-one; bespoke
	Method: intensive; non-intensive; open or flexible
Other	Additional languages can be offered, with notice

SERVICES
Translating
Arabic	into and out of English
Chinese	into and out of English
Danish	into and out of English
Dutch	into and out of English
French	into and out of English
German	into and out of English
Greek	into and out of English
Italian	into and out of English
Japanese	into and out of English
Korean	into and out of English
Portuguese	into and out of English
Russian	into and out of English
Spanish	into and out of English

Interpreting
Arabic	simultaneous; consecutive
Chinese	simultaneous; consecutive
Danish	simultaneous; consecutive
Dutch	simultaneous; consecutive
French	simultaneous; consecutive
German	simultaneous; consecutive
Greek	simultaneous; consecutive
Italian	simultaneous; consecutive
Japanese	simultaneous; consecutive
Korean	simultaneous; consecutive
Portuguese	simultaneous; consecutive
Russian	simultaneous; consecutive
Spanish	simultaneous; consecutive

FACILITIES
Language labs:	under 10 places - 1 portable; over 25 places - 1 fixed
Interpreting facilities:	under 10 places - 1 portable; 26–100 places - 1 fixed
Equipment and materials:	satellite television; audio and videocassettes; computer-assisted language learning

NOTES
• has experience of undertaking language training needs analyses for employers
• offers translating and interpreting facilities in many languages

422 Westminster College

Battersea Park Road
London
SW11 4JR

Telephone	071-720 2121
Fax	071-498 1907

Contact   Ms V. Foote, PICKUP Co-ordinator

TRAINING

French   *Type:* client-based; one-to-one; bespoke
                Method: intensive; non-intensive
German   *Type:* client-based; institution-based
                Method: intensive; non-intensive
Italian   *Type:* institution-based; one-to-one
Japanese   *Type:* institution-based
Russian   *Type:* institution-based
Spanish   *Type:* client-based; institution-based
                Method: intensive; non-intensive
Specialisms   hotel trade; catering; tourism; business; broadcasting

SERVICES
Translating
French   into English
German   into English
Specialism   technical

FACILITIES
Language labs: under 10 places - 1 portable; 10–25 places - 1 fixed

NOTES
• has experience of undertaking language training needs analyses for employers

423   Weymouth College

Cranford Avenue
Weymouth   Telephone   (0305) 208888
DT4 7LQ   Fax   (0305) 208885

Contact   Mr R. Harrison, Flexible Learning Centre Co-Director

TRAINING
French   *Type:* client-based; institution-based; group; one-to-one; bespoke
                    Method: intensive; non-intensive; open or flexible
German   *Type:* client-based; institution-based; group; one-to-one; bespoke
                    Method: intensive; non-intensive; open or flexible
Italian   *Type:* client-based; institution-based; group; one-to-one; bespoke
Russian   *Type:* client-based; institution-based; group; one-to-one; bespoke
Spanish   *Type:* client-based; institution-based; group; one-to-one; bespoke
                    Method: intensive; non-intensive
Other   Japanese can be offered, with notice

FACILITIES
Language labs: under 10 places - 1 fixed
Equipment and
  materials: computer-assisted language learning; audiocassettes

NOTES
• has experience of undertaking language training needs analyses for employers

424 Wigan College of Technology

PO Box 53
Parsons' Walk
Wigan   Telephone   (0942) 494911
WN1 1RS   Fax   (0942) 820257

Contact   Mr R. Faugier, Industrial Language Co-ordinator

TRAINING

French   *Type:* client-based; institution-based; group; one-to-one; bespoke
            Method: intensive; non-intensive; open or flexible

German   *Type:* client-based; institution-based; group; one-to-one; bespoke
            Method: intensive; non-intensive; open or flexible

Italian   *Type:* client-based; institution-based; group; one-to-one; bespoke
            Method: intensive; non-intensive; open or flexible

Russian   *Type:* client-based; institution-based; group; one-to-one; bespoke
            Method: intensive; non-intensive; open or flexible

Spanish   *Type:* client-based; institution-based; group; one-to-one; bespoke
            Method: intensive; non-intensive; open or flexible

Other   Portuguese can be offered, with notice

SERVICES

Translating
French   into and out of English
German   into and out of English
Italian   into and out of English
Russian   into and out of English
Spanish   into and out of English

Interpreting
French   simultaneous; consecutive
German   simultaneous; consecutive
Italian   simultaneous; consecutive
Spanish   simultaneous; consecutive

FACILITIES

Language labs: 10–25 places - 1 portable
Equipment and
   materials: audio and videocassettes; computer-assisted language learning;
                 satellite television

NOTES

- has experience of undertaking language training needs analyses for employers
- is producing a booklet and audiocassette which will provide a survival guide for
  holiday coach drivers who regularly travel abroad

425 Wigston College of Further Education

Station Road
Wigston Magna
Leicester   Telephone   (0533) 885051
LE8 2DW   Fax   (0533) 880823

Contact   Mr D. Harris, Language Centre Manager

TRAINING

Dutch   *Type:* client-based; institution-based; group; one-to-one
French   *Type:* client-based; institution-based; group; one-to-one
               Method: intensive; non-intensive; open or flexible
German   *Type:* client-based; institution-based; group; one-to-one
               Method: intensive; non-intensive; open or flexible
Italian   *Type:* client-based; institution-based; group; one-to-one
               Method: intensive; non-intensive; open or flexible
Portuguese   *Type:* client-based; institution-based; group; one-to-one
Russian   *Type:* client-based; institution-based; group; one-to-one
Spanish   *Type:* client-based; institution-based; group; one-to-one
               Method: intensive; non-intensive; open or flexible
Other   Additional languages can be offered, with notice

FACILITIES

Language labs: 10–25 places - 1 fixed
Equipment and
  materials: audio and videocassettes; computer-assisted language learning;
                  satellite television

NOTES

• has experience of undertaking language training needs analyses for employers

426 University of Wolverhampton Language-Export Centre

Stafford Street
Wolverhampton
WV1 1SB

Telephone	(0902) 322450
Fax	(0902) 322739

Contact   Mr S. Williams, Head of Languages for Business Centre

TRAINING

French   *Type:* client-based; institution-based; group; one-to-one; bespoke
          Method: intensive; non-intensive

German   *Type:* client-based; institution-based; group; one-to-one; bespoke
          Method: intensive; non-intensive

Italian   *Type:* client-based; institution-based; group; one-to-one; bespoke
          Method: intensive; non-intensive

Japanese   *Type:* client-based; institution-based; group; one-to-one; bespoke
          Method: intensive; non-intensive

Russian   *Type:* client-based; institution-based; group; one-to-one; bespoke
          Method: intensive; non-intensive

Spanish   *Type:* client-based; institution-based; group; one-to-one; bespoke
          Method: intensive; non-intensive

Other   All other languages can be offered, with notice

SERVICES

Translating

Dutch	into and out of English
French	into and out of English
German	into and out of English
Italian	into English
Japanese	out of English
Russian	into and out of English
Spanish	into and out of English

Interpreting

Dutch	consecutive
French	consecutive
German	consecutive
Italian	consecutive
Japanese	consecutive
Russian	consecutive
Spanish	consecutive

FACILITIES

Language labs: under 10 places - 1 portable; 10–25 places - 5 fixed

Equipment and
materials: computer-assisted language learning; interactive video; satellite television; audiocassettes

NOTES
- has experience of undertaking language training needs analyses for employers
- arranges language courses abroad, through partner institutions

427   Woolwich College

Villas Road
Plumstead
London   Telephone   081-855 1216
SE18 7PN   Fax   081-854 2194

Contact   Mrs D. Everatt, Short Course Co-ordinator

TRAINING

Bengali   *Type:* client-based; institution-based; group; one-to-one; bespoke
Chinese   *Type:* client-based; institution-based; group; one-to-one; bespoke
French   *Type:* client-based; institution-based; group; one-to-one; bespoke
             (specialism: business)
             Method: intensive; non-intensive
German   *Type:* client-based; institution-based; group; one-to-one; bespoke
             (specialism: business)
Gujarati   *Type:* client-based; institution-based; group; one-to-one; bespoke
Hindi   *Type:* client-based; institution-based; group; one-to-one; bespoke
Italian   *Type:* client-based; institution-based; group; one-to-one; bespoke
             (specialisms: business; scientific; computers)
Japanese   *Type:* client-based; institution-based; group; one-to-one; bespoke
Punjabi   *Type:* client-based; institution-based; group; one-to-one; bespoke
Russian   *Type:* client-based; institution-based; group; one-to-one; bespoke
Spanish   *Type:* client-based; institution-based; group; one-to-one; bespoke
             (specialism: business)
Urdu   *Type:* client-based; institution-based; group; one-to-one; bespoke

NOTES
• has experience of undertaking language training needs analyses for employers

428 Worcester College of Technology

Deansway
Worcester
WR1 2JF

Telephone	(0905) 723383
Fax	(0905) 28906

Contact   Mr S. Allison, Head of Languages

TRAINING

French
> *Type:* client-based; institution-based; group; one-to-one; bespoke (specialisms: business; police)
> *Method:* intensive; non-intensive; open or flexible

German
> *Type:* client-based; institution-based; group; one-to-one; bespoke (specialisms: business; police)
> *Method:* intensive; non-intensive; open or flexible

Japanese
> *Type:* client-based; institution-based; group; one-to-one; bespoke
> *Method:* non-intensive; open or flexible

Spanish
> *Type:* client-based; institution-based; group; one-to-one; bespoke
> *Method:* intensive; non-intensive; open or flexible

FACILITIES

Language labs: under 10 places - 1 portable; 10–25 places - 2 fixed

Equipment and
  materials: interactive video; computer-assisted language learning

NOTES

- has experience of undertaking language training needs analyses for employers
- is a video preview centre for the BBC and maintains comprehensive stocks of BBC language learning material

429   Worcestershire College of Agriculture

Hindlip
Worcester   Telephone   (0905) 51310
WR3 8SS   Fax   (0905) 754760

Contact   Mr W. H. Lamin, Senior Lecturer

TRAINING
French   *Type:* institution-based; group; one-to-one; bespoke
                   Method: non-intensive; open or flexible
Spanish   *Type:* institution-based; group; one-to-one; bespoke
                   Method: non-intensive; open or flexible
Specialism   land-based industries
Other   Italian and German can be offered, with notice

SERVICES
Translating
French   into and out of English
Spanish   into and out of English
Specialism   land-based industries

FACILITIES
Equipment and
   materials: audio and videocassettes; computer-assisted language learning

430   Worth Consulting

10 Nicholson Road
Loughborough   Telephone   (0509) 263285
LE11 3SD   Fax   (0509) 219868

Contact   Mr M. Charlesworth, Managing Director

TRAINING
French   *Type:* client-based; group; one-to-one; bespoke
              Method: intensive; non-intensive; open or flexible
German   *Type:* client-based; group; one-to-one; bespoke
              Method: intensive; non-intensive; open or flexible
Italian   *Type:* client-based; group; one-to-one
Portuguese   *Type:* client-based; group; bespoke
Spanish   *Type:* client-based; group; one-to-one; bespoke
              Method: intensive; non-intensive; open or flexible
Specialism   business

SERVICES
Translating
French   into and out of English
German   into and out of English
Italian   into and out of English
Spanish   into and out of English
Specialism   business
Interpreting
French   simultaneous
German   simultancous
Italian   simultaneous
Spanish   simultaneous
Specialism   business

NOTES
• has experience of undertaking language training needs analyses for employers

431   Wulfrun College

Paget Road
Wolverhampton   Telephone   (0902) 312062
WV6 0DU   Fax   (0902) 23070

Contact   Ms C. Edwards, Lecturer in Charge of Modern Languages

TRAINING

French   *Type:* client-based; institution-based; group; one-to-one
              Method: intensive; non-intensive; open or flexible
German   *Type:* client-based; institution-based; group; one-to-one
              Method: intensive; non-intensive; open or flexible
Italian   *Type:* client-based; institution-based; group; one-to-one
              Method: intensive; non-intensive; open or flexible
Norwegian   *Type:* institution-based; group
              Method: non-intensive
Polish   *Type:* client-based; institution-based; group; one-to-one; bespoke
              (specialism: scientific)
              Method: intensive; non-intensive
Punjabi   *Type:* client-based; institution-based; group; one-to-one
              Method: intensive; non-intensive
Russian   *Type:* client-based; institution-based; group; one-to-one
              Method: intensive; non-intensive
Spanish   *Type:* client-based; institution-based; group; one-to-one
              Method: intensive; non-intensive; open or flexible

FACILITIES
Language labs: 10–25 places - 1 fixed, 1 portable

NOTES
• has experience of undertaking language training needs analyses for employers

432　Yeovil College

Ilchester Road
Yeovil
BA21 3BA

Telephone　　(0935) 23921
Fax　　　　　(0935) 410108

Contact　　Mrs B. Foster, Associate Lecturer in Spanish and Business Languages Adviser

TRAINING

Dutch　　*Type:* institution-based; group
　　　　Method: intensive; non-intensive; open or flexible
French　　*Type:* client-based; group
　　　　Method: intensive; non-intensive; open or flexible
German　　*Type:* client-based; group
　　　　Method: intensive; non-intensive; open or flexible
Italian　　*Type:* client-based; institution-based; group; one-to-one
　　　　Method: intensive; non-intensive; open or flexible
Russian　　*Type:* client-based; institution-based; group; one-to-one
　　　　Method: intensive; non-intensive; open or flexible
Spanish　　*Type:* client-based; group
　　　　Method: intensive; non-intensive; open or flexible

SERVICES
Translating
Dutch　　into and out of English
French　　into and out of English
German　　into and out of English
Italian　　into and out of English
Spanish　　into and out of English

FACILITIES
Language labs:　　10–25 places - 1 fixed
Equipment and
　materials:　　audiocassettes; computer-assisted language learning

NOTES
• has experience of undertaking language training needs analyses for employers
• is part of a four college consortium, called Somerset Language Training, the other members of which are Strode College, Bridgwater College and Somerset College of Arts and Technology

433 University of York

Fluentalk Language Services
The King's Manor

York	Telephone	(0904) 433901
YO1 2ED	Fax	(0904) 433906

Contact   Mrs F. Vassie, Short Course Development Officer

TRAINING

Arabic	*Type:* client-based; institution-based; group; one-to-one; bespoke
French	*Type:* client-based; institution-based; group; one-to-one; bespoke *Method:* intensive; non-intensive
German	*Type:* client-based; institution-based; group; one-to-one; bespoke *Method:* intensive; non-intensive
Italian	*Type:* client-based; institution-based; group; one-to-one; bespoke *Method:* intensive; non-intensive
Japanese	*Type:* client-based; institution-based; group; one-to-one; bespoke *Method:* intensive
Polish	*Type:* client-based; institution-based; group; one-to-one; bespoke *Method:* non-intensive
Portuguese	*Type:* client-based; institution-based; group; one-to-one; bespoke *Method:* intensive
Russian	*Type:* client-based; institution-based; group; one-to-one; bespoke *Method:* intensive; non-intensive
Spanish	*Type:* client-based; institution-based; group; one-to-one; bespoke *Method:* intensive; non-intensive
Swedish	*Type:* institution-based; one-to-one; bespoke *Method:* non-intensive
Turkish	*Type:* client-based; institution-based; group; one-to-one; bespoke
Other	Norwegian, Danish, Greek and Thai can be offered, with notice

SERVICES

Translating

Danish	into and out of English
Dutch	into and out of English
French	into and out of English
German	into and out of English
Italian	into and out of English
Japanese	into and out of English
Polish	into and out of English
Russian	into and out of English
Spanish	into and out of English
Turkish	into and out of English

Interpreting

French	simultaneous; consecutive (specialisms: legal; commercial; scientific; technical)

German	simultaneous; consecutive (specialisms: legal; commercial; technical)
Japanese	simultaneous; consecutive
Russian	simultaneous; consecutive

FACILITIES

Language labs: under 10 places - 1 portable; 10–25 places - 1 fixed

NOTES

- has experience of undertaking language training needs analyses for employers
- Fluentalk has its own French and German training programme for receptionists and telephonists

434 York College of Further and Higher Education

Tadcaster Road
Dringhouses
York   Telephone   (0904) 704141
YO2 1UA   Fax   (0904) 702091

Contact   Mrs E. C. Jury, Head of Business Language Centre

TRAINING
Dutch   *Type:* institution-based; group; one-to-one
French   *Type:* client-based; institution-based; group; one-to-one; bespoke
                Method: intensive; non-intensive; open or flexible
German   *Type:* client-based; institution-based; group; one-to-one; bespoke
                Method: intensive; non-intensive
Italian   *Type:* client-based; institution-based; group; one-to-one; bespoke
                Method: intensive; non-intensive
Japanese   *Type:* client-based; institution-based; group; one-to-one
Spanish   *Type:* client-based; institution-based; group; one-to-one; bespoke
                Method: intensive; non-intensive

Specialisms   business; telephone skills
Other   Portuguese, Hungarian and Danish can be offered, with notice

SERVICES
Translating
Dutch   into and out of English
French   into and out of English
German   into and out of English
Italian   into and out of English
Japanese   into and out of English
Portuguese   into and out of English
Russian   into and out of English
Spanish   into and out of English
Swedish   into and out of English
Interpreting
Dutch   simultaneous; consecutive
French   simultaneous; consecutive
German   simultaneous; consecutive
Italian   simultaneous; consecutive
Japanese   simultaneous; consecutive
Spanish   simultaneous; consecutive

FACILITIES
Language labs: 10–25 places - 1 fixed
Equipment and
  materials: computer-assisted language learning; audio and videocassettes

583

NOTES

- has experience of undertaking language training needs analyses for employers
- can organise courses for librarians and telephonists
- offers exhibition and trade-fair language support and language help with court proceedings
- provides a wide range of language services under Fluentalk, with York University

435 Yorkshire Coast College of Further and Higher Education (Scarborough)

Lady Edith's Drive
Scarborough
YO12 5RN

Telephone   (0723) 372105
Fax   (0723) 354102

Contact   Mr R. Heath, Lecturer

TRAINING

Arabic	*Type:* client-based; institution-based; group; one-to-one; bespoke
Dutch	*Type:* client-based; institution-based; group; one-to-one; bespoke
French	*Type:* client-based; institution-based; group; one-to-one; bespoke
German	*Type:* client-based; institution-based; group; one-to-one; bespoke
Greek	*Type:* client-based; institution-based; group; one-to-one; bespoke
Italian	*Type:* client-based; institution-based; group; one-to-one; bespoke
Portuguese	*Type:* client-based; institution-based; group; one-to-one; bespoke
Russian	*Type:* client-based; institution-based; group; one-to-one; bespoke
Spanish	*Type:* client-based; institution-based; group; one-to-one; bespoke

FACILITIES

Language labs: 10–25 places - 1 fixed

INDEX OF INSTITUTIONS
BY COUNTY

The index of institutions by county allows users to identify clusters of institutions by region. Those in England are grouped alphabetically by administrative county, including the former metropolitan counties. These are followed by entries for Scotland, Wales and Northern Ireland. The bracketed number refers to the institution reference number given at the head of each entry.

Avon	City of Bath College *[25]*
	Bath College of Higher Education *[26]*
	University of Bristol *[53]*
	Brunel College of Technology *[59]*
	Filton College *[137]*
	Nailsea and Clevedon Adult Education *[259]*
	Soundwell College *[348]*
	South Bristol College *[350]*
	University of the West of England *[417]*
Bedfordshire	Barnfield College *[20]*
	Bedford College of Higher Education *[27]*
	Cranfield Institute of Technology *[93]*
	Dunstable College *[113]*
Berkshire	Bracknell College *[44]*
	Langley College *[208]*
	Newbury College *[266]*
	University of Reading *[317]*
	Reading Adult College *[318]*
Buckinghamshire	Amersham and Wycombe College *[7]*
	University of Buckingham *[61]*
	Buckinghamshire College of Higher Education *[62]*
	Milton Keynes College *[254]*
	Milton Keynes Language Centre *[255]*
Cambridgeshire	Anglia Polytechnic University *[8]*
	Cambridge Regional College *[66]*
	Huntingdonshire College *[182]*
	Isle College *[187]*
Cheshire	Chester College *[81]*
	Halton College of Further Education *[158]*
	Macclesfield College *[238]*
	Manchester Language-Export Centre *[245]*
	Mid-Cheshire College of Further Education *[249]*
	North Cheshire College *[274]*
	South Cheshire College Language-Export Centre *[351]*
	West Cheshire College *[413]*

Cleveland	Hartlepool College of Further Education [164]
	Kirby College [200]
	Longlands College of Further Education [230]
	Stockton-Billingham Technical College [374]
	University of Teesside [392]

Cleveland

Hartlepool College of Further Education [164]
Kirby College [200]
Longlands College of Further Education [230]
Stockton-Billingham Technical College [374]
University of Teesside [392]

Cornwall

Mid-Cornwall College [250]

Cumbria

Carlisle College [73]
Furness College [140]
Kendal College [192]
West Cumbria College [414]

Derbyshire

Derby Tertiary College (Mackworth) [102]
Derby Tertiary College (Wilmorton) [103]
High Peak College [175]
South East Derbyshire College [354]

Devon

Bicton College [31]
East Devon College [117]
University of Exeter [132]
Exeter College [133]
North Devon College [275]
College of Further Education (Plymouth) [308]
University of Plymouth [309]
South Devon College [352]
College of St Mark and St John [367]

Dorset

Bournemouth University [42]
Dorset Business School [107]
Norton Radstock College [292]
Weymouth College [423]

Durham

Darlington College of Technology [99]
Derwentside College [104]
University of Durham [114]
New College (Durham) [264]

East Sussex	University of Brighton *[50]* Brighton College of Technology *[51]* Sussex and Kent Language-Export Centre *[383]*
Essex	Basildon College *[23]* Chelmsford College of Further Education *[79]* Colchester Institute *[88]* University of Essex *[130]* Harlow College *[161]* South East Essex College of Arts and Technology *[355]* Thurrock Technical College *[398]*
Gloucestershire	Cheltenham and Gloucester College of HE *[80]* Gloucestershire College of Arts and Technology *[148]* Royal Agricultural College *[328]* Royal Forest of Dean College *[329]* Stroud College of Further Education *[379]*
Greater London	Barking College of Technology *[18]* Barnet College *[19]* Birkbeck College *[33]* Bromley College of Technology *[55]* Brunel University *[60]* City and East London College *[83]* City University *[85]* Croydon College *[97]* University of East London *[118]* Enfield College *[128]* Erith College *[129]* French Institute *[138]* Greenhill College *[151]* University of Greenwich *[152]* Hackney College *[156]* Hammersmith and West London College *[159]* Havering College of Further and Higher Education *[166]* Hendon College of Further Education *[167]* Hounslow Borough College *[177]* International House *[185]* King's College (London) *[196]* Kingston College of Further Education *[197]* London Guildhall University *[225]*

University College London *[226]*
University of London *[227]*
University of London *[228]*
London Language-Export Centre (LEXCEL) *[229]*
Middlesex University *[253]*
University of North London *[281]*
College of North West London *[286]*
Redbridge College of Further Education *[319]*
Richmond Adult and Community College *[322]*
Richmond upon Thames College *[323]*
Royal Holloway *[330]*
School of Oriental and African Studies *[340]*
South Bank University *[349]*
South Thames College *[357]*
Southgate College *[364]*
Southwark College *[365]*
Sutton College of Liberal Arts *[385]*
Thames Valley University Language-Export Centre *[395]*
The City Lit *[396]*
Uxbridge College *[405]*
Waltham Forest College *[409]*
City of Westminster College *[420]*
University of Westminster *[421]*
Westminster College *[422]*
Woolwich College *[427]*

Greater Manchester

Bolton Institute of Higher Education *[38]*
Bolton Metropolitan College *[39]*
Bury Metropolitan College *[63]*
Hopwood Hall College *[176]*
Leigh College *[214]*
University of Manchester *[241]*
Manchester Business School *[242]*
Manchester College of Arts and Technology *[243]*
UMIST *[244]*
North Trafford College *[282]*
Oldham College *[297]*
University College Salford *[335]*
University of Salford *[336]*
Salford College of Further Education *[337]*
South Trafford College of Further Education *[358]*
Stockport College of Further and Higher Education *[373]*

Tameside College of Technology *[390]*
Wigan College of Technology *[424]*

Hampshire — Basingstoke College of Technology *[24]*
Cricklade College *[95]*
Eastleigh College *[123]*
Farnborough College of Technology *[135]*
International Business and Export Services (IBEX) *[184]*
King Alfred's College *[195]*
LSU College of Higher Education *[235]*
University of Portsmouth *[313]*
South Downs College *[353]*
University of Southampton *[361]*
Southampton Institute of Higher Education *[362]*
Southampton Technical College *[363]*

Hereford
and Worcester — Herefordshire College of Technology *[170]*
North East Worcestershire College *[277]*
Worcester College of Technology *[428]*
Worcestershire College of Agriculture *[429]*

Hertfordshire — Hertford Regional College (Broxbourne Centre) *[172]*
Hertford Regional College (Ware Centre) *[173]*
University of Hertfordshire *[174]*
North Hertfordshire College *[279]*
Oaklands College (Oaklands Campus) *[295]*
Oaklands College (St Albans City Campus) *[296]*
West Hertfordshire College *[415]*

Humberside — Beverley College *[30]*
Bishop Burton College *[35]*
East Yorkshire College *[122]*
Grimsby College of Technology and Arts *[153]*
University of Hull *[180]*
Hull College of Further Education *[181]*
North Lindsey College *[280]*

Kent — C4 Language Services *[64]*
Canterbury Christ Church College of Higher Education *[69]*
University of Kent at Canterbury *[193]*

Mid-Kent College of Higher and Further Education *[251]*
North West Kent College of Technology *[285]*
South Kent College *[356]*
West Kent College *[416]*

Lancashire

Accrington and Rossendale College *[4]*
Blackburn College *[36]*
Blackpool and the Fylde College *[37]*
University of Central Lancashire *[77]*
Edge Hill College of Higher Education *[125]*
Euro-Com Languages for Business *[131]*
Lancashire and Cumbria Language-Export Centre *[204]*
Lancashire College *[205]*
Adult College (Lancaster) *[206]*
Lancaster and Morecambe College *[207]*
Nelson and Colne College *[262]*
Preston College *[314]*
Runshaw College *[331]*
S. Martin's College *[334]*

Leicestershire

Brooksby College *[57]*
Charles Keene College *[78]*
De Montfort University at Leicester *[101]*
East Midlands Language-Export Centre *[119]*
Leicester South Fields College *[213]*
Loughborough College *[231]*
Loughborough University of Technology *[232]*
Wigston College of Further Education *[425]*
Worth Consulting *[430]*

Lincolnshire

Boston College *[41]*
Lincolnshire College of Agriculture and Horticulture *[217]*
Lincolnshire College of Art and Design *[218]*

Merseyside

Knowsley Community College *[202]*
University of Liverpool *[219]*
City of Liverpool Community College *[220]*
Liverpool Institute of Higher Education *[221]*
Liverpool John Moores University *[222]*
Merseyside Language-Export Centre *[247]*

Norfolk	City College (Norwich) *[84]* University of East Anglia Language-Export Centre *[115]* Easton College *[124]* Great Yarmouth College of Further Education *[150]* Norfolk College of Arts and Technology *[272]*
North Yorkshire	Harrogate College of Arts and Technology *[163]* University College of Ripon and York St John *[324]* University of York *[433]* York College of Further and Higher Education *[434]* Yorkshire Coast College of FHE *[435]*
Northamptonshire	Daventry Tertiary College *[100]* Knuston Hall Adult Residential College *[203]* Northampton College of Further Education *[287]* Tresham Institute of Further and Higher Education *[400]*
Northumberland	Northumberland College of Arts and Technology *[289]*
Nottinghamshire	Arnold and Carlton College of Further Education *[12]* Broxtowe College *[58]* Clarendon College *[86]* Newark and Sherwood College *[265]* University of Nottingham *[293]* Nottingham Trent University *[294]* People's College of Tertiary Education *[306]*
Oxfordshire	Abingdon College *[3]* Collingham, Brown & Brown Tutorial College *[91]* Henley College *[168]* Managed Learning *[240]* University of Oxford *[298]* Oxford Brookes University *[299]* Oxford College of Further Education *[300]* Ruskin College *[332]* Rycotewood College *[333]*

Shropshire	Harper Adams Agricultural College *[162]* Lydbury English Centre *[237]* Shrewsbury College of Arts and Technology *[345]* Telford College of Arts and Technology *[394]* Walford College of Agriculture *[407]*
Somerset	Bridgwater College *[49]* Frome Community College *[139]* Somerset College of Arts and Technology *[347]* Yeovil College *[432]*
South Yorkshire	Barnsley College *[21]* Doncaster College *[106]* Loxley College *[234]* Norton College *[291]* Parkwood College *[303]* Parson Cross College *[304]* Rockingham College *[326]* Rotherham College of Arts and Technology *[327]* University of Sheffield *[342]* Sheffield Hallam University *[343]* Stradbroke College *[376]*
Staffordshire	Cannock Chase Technical College *[68]* University of Keele *[190]* Leek College of Further Education *[212]* Newcastle-under-Lyme College *[270]* Stafford College *[368]* Staffordshire Language-Export Centre *[369]* Staffordshire University *[370]* Stoke-on-Trent College *[375]*
Suffolk	Lowestoft College *[233]* Suffolk College *[380]* West Suffolk College *[418]*
Surrey	East Surrey College *[120]* Guildford College of Technology *[154]* International Business and Export Services (IBEX) *[183]* Kingston Language-Export Centre *[198]*

Kingston University *[199]*
University of Surrey *[382]*

Sussex   Hastings College of Arts and Technology *[165]*

Tyne and Wear   Gateshead College *[141]*
                        Monkwearmouth College *[256]*
                        Newcastle College *[267]*
                        University of Newcastle upon Tyne *[269]*
                        North East Export Associates *[276]*
                        North Tyneside College *[283]*
                        University of Northumbria at Newcastle *[290]*
                        South Tyneside College *[359]*
                        University of Sunderland *[381]*
                        Wearside College for Agriculture *[412]*

Warwickshire   East Warwickshire College *[121]*
                        Mid-Warwickshire College of Further Education *[252]*
                        North Warwickshire College of Technology and Art *[284]*
                        Stratford-upon-Avon College *[377]*
                        Warwickshire College *[411]*

West Midlands   Aston University *[13]*
                        Bilston Community College *[32]*
                        University of Birmingham *[34]*
                        Bournville College of Further Education *[43]*
                        Brasshouse Centre *[47]*
                        Brooklyn College *[56]*
                        University of Central England in Birmingham *[76]*
                        Coventry University *[92]*
                        Dudley College of Technology *[108]*
                        East Birmingham College *[116]*
                        Hall Green College *[157]*
                        Handsworth College *[160]*
                        Henley College (Coventry) *[169]*
                        Matthew Boulton College *[246]*
                        Sandwell College of Further and Higher Education *[339]*
                        Solihull College of Technology *[346]*
                        Sutton Coldfield College of Further Education *[384]*
                        Tamworth College *[391]*

Walsall College of Technology *[408]*
University of Warwick *[410]*
University of Wolverhampton LX Centre *[426]*
Wulfrun College *[431]*

West Sussex

Brinsbury College *[52]*
Crawley College of Technology *[94]*
West Sussex Institute of Higher Education *[419]*

West Yorkshire

Airedale and Wharfedale College *[6]*
University of Bradford *[45]*
Bradford and Ilkley Community College *[46]*
Calderdale College *[65]*
Dewsbury College *[105]*
University of Huddersfield *[178]*
Huddersfield Technical College *[179]*
Keighley College *[191]*
Kitson College *[201]*
University of Leeds *[210]*
Leeds Metropolitan University *[211]*
Park Lane College *[302]*
Shipley College *[344]*
Thomas Danby College *[397]*
Trinity and All Saints College *[401]*
Wakefield College *[406]*

Wiltshire

Chippenham Technical College *[82]*
New College *[263]*
Salisbury College *[338]*
Swindon College *[389]*
Trowbridge College *[403]*

Other

British Institute in Paris *[54]*
Isle of Man College of Further Education *[188]*

Scotland

University of Aberdeen *[1]*
Aberdeen College of Further Education *[2]*
Angus College of Further Education *[9]*
Anniesland College *[10]*
Ayr College *[14]*
Banff and Buchan College of Further Education *[16]*
Bell College of Technology *[29]*
Borders College *[40]*
Cambuslang College *[67]*
Cardonald College *[72]*
Central College of Commerce *[75]*
Clydebank College *[87]*
Cumbernauld College *[98]*
University of Dundee *[109]*
Dundee College of Further Education *[110]*
Dundee Institute of Technology *[111]*
University of Edinburgh *[126]*
Elmwood Business Training *[127]*
Falkirk College of Technology *[134]*
Fife College of Technology *[136]*
University of Glasgow *[143]*
Glasgow College of Food Technology *[144]*
Glasgow College of Nautical Studies *[145]*
Glasgow Caledonian University *[146]*
Glenrothes College Language-Export Centre *[147]*
Heriot-Watt University *[171]*
Inverness College of Further and Higher Education *[186]*
James Watt College *[189]*
Kilmarnock College *[194]*
Lauder College *[209]*
Lews Castle College *[215]*
Moray College of Further Education *[257]*
Motherwell College *[258]*
Napier University *[260]*
North Glasgow College *[278]*
University of Paisley *[301]*
Perth College of Further Education *[307]*
Queen's College (Glasgow) *[315]*
Reid Kerr College *[320]*
Robert Gordon University *[325]*
Scottish College of Textiles *[341]*
University of St Andrews *[366]*
Stevenson College of Further Education *[371]*
University of Stirling *[372]*

University of Strathclyde *[378]*
Telford College *[393]*
Thurso Technical College *[399]*

Wales

Afan College *[5]*
University College of Wales, Bangor *[17]*
Barry College *[22]*
Bridgend College of Technology *[48]*
Cardiff Institute of Higher Education *[70]*
Cardiff Tertiary College *[71]*
Coleg Pencraig *[89]*
Crosskeys College *[96]*
University of Glamorgan *[142]*
Gorseinon College *[149]*
Gwynedd Technical College *[155]*
Llandrillo Technical College *[223]*
Llysfasi College *[224]*
Merthyr Tydfil Technical College *[248]*
Neath College *[261]*
Newport College *[271]*
Pembrokeshire College *[305]*
Pontypool and Usk College *[310]*
Pontypridd Technical College *[311]*
Rhondda College *[321]*
South Wales Language-Export Centre *[360]*
University College of Swansea *[386]*
Swansea College *[387]*
Swansea Institute of Higher Education *[388]*
Trinity College *[402]*

Northern Ireland

Armagh College of Further Education *[11]*
Ballymena College *[15]*
Belfast Institute of Further and Higher Education *[28]*
Castlereagh College of Further Education *[74]*
Coleraine Technical College *[90]*
Dungannon College of Further Education *[112]*
Limavady College of Further Education *[216]*
Lurgan College of Further Education *[236]*